The SUBMARINE

A Cultural History from the Great War to Nuclear Combat

DUNCAN REDFORD

New paperback edition published in 2015 by I.B.Tauris & Co. Ltd
London • New York
www.ibtauris.com

First published in hardback in 2010 by Tauris Academic Studies,
an imprint of I.B.Tauris & Co. Ltd

Copyright © 2010, 2015 Duncan Redford

The right of Duncan Redford to be identified as the author of this work has been asserted by
the author in accordance with the Copyright, Designs and Patent Act 1988

All rights reserved. Except for brief quotations in a review, this book, or any part thereof,
may not be reproduced, stored in or introduced into a retrieval system, or transmitted, in any
form or by any means, electronic, mechanical, photocopying, recording or otherwise, without
the prior written permission of the publisher

ISBN 978 1 78453 089 1
eISBN 978 0 85773 831 8

A full CIP record for this book is available from the British Library
A full CIP record for this book is available from the Library of Congress

Library of Congress catalog card: available

Duncan Redford is head of research at the National Museum of the Royal Navy (NMRN). Between 2008 and 2011 he was the Leverhulme Early Career Research Fellow at the Centre for Maritime Historical Studies, University of Exeter. He was awarded the Laughton Naval History Scholarship in 2002 and completed his PhD at the Department of War Studies, King's College London in 2006. He has written about the Royal Navy in the twentieth century in *The Royal Navy since 1900: A History* and *A History of the Royal Navy: World War II* (both I.B.Tauris) and is currently writing a history of the Royal Navy's submarine service for the I.B.Tauris & National Museum of the Royal Navy 'History of the Royal Navy' series, of which he is also the series editor. He was an officer and submariner in the Royal Navy for ten years, during which time he served aboard HMS *Torbay*, then HMS *Tireless* and *Turbulent* as the navigating officer.

'Carefully researched and passionately written.' – *Ausmarine*

'This is an excellent book which will spark much interest. It makes an important contribution, not only to naval history, but also to our understanding of the cultural development of British national identity.' – *Joseph Maiolo, Professor of International History, King's College London*

'This is an ambitious and original book which deserves to attract wide interest.' – *Paul Readman, Senior Lecturer in Modern British History, King's College London*

For my parents

CONTENTS

List of Figures	ix
Abbreviations	xi
Acknowledgements	xiii
Preface	xv
Introduction	1
1 The Submarine in Six Naval Reviews	19
2 The Submarine 1900–1914	56
3 The Effect of Unrestricted Submarine Warfare 1915–1935	91
4 The Submarine 1935–1965	128
5 The Age of the British Nuclear Submarine	165
6 The British Submarine in Film and Fiction	202
Conclusion	244
Notes	253
Bibliography	289
Index	319

FIGURES

1.1 Position of the submarines at the 1911 Coronation Review 30

1.2 Ship types as a percentage of the total number of vessels at each review 49

1.3 Ship types present at each review as a percentage of the totals in service 50

1.4 Map of Spithead, Portsmouth and Ryde, showing the approximate positions of the review lines 55

2.1. *Punch*, 23 January 1901 65

2.2 Postcard, 'One Hundred Years Apart' 66

2.3 Postcard, 'What would have Nelson said' 68

3.1 St Cyriac Church Swaffham Prior War Memorial Windows, naval images 92

3.2 St Cyriac Church Swaffham Prior War Memorial Windows, *Lusitania* sinking 93

3.3 *Punch*, 7 April 1915 105

4.1 Peace Pledge Union Pamphlets 137 & 138

5.1	Royal Navy recruiting advert	177
5.2	Royal Navy Submarine Service branch badge - the 'Dolphins' badge	179
6.1	The number of editions or print runs of cited novels	234
6.2	The numbers of cited novels published by year	236

ABBREVIATIONS

1SL	First Sea Lord
AGNA	Anglo–German Naval Agreement
BL	British Library, London
CCRO	Cambridgeshire County Records Office
DNI	Director of Naval Intelligence
IHR	The Institute of Historical Research, London
IWM	Imperial War Museum, London
LSE	London School of Economics
MoD	Ministry of Defence
MoI	Ministry of Information
NHB	The Naval Historical Branch, Portsmouth Dockyard
NNM	The National Maritime Museum, Greenwich
PmthRO	Portsmouth Record Office
PRO	The National Archives, Kew, formerly the Public Record Office
RAN	Royal Australian Navy
RN	Royal Navy
RNM	The Royal Naval Museum, Portsmouth
RNML	The Royal Naval Museum Library, Portsmouth
RNSubM	The Royal Navy Submarine Museum, Gosport, Hampshire
RUSI	The Journal of the Royal United Services Institution, latterly, the RUSI Journal
SSBN	A nuclear powered submarine armed with intercontinental ballistic missiles
SSK	A diesel-electric powered submarine that has an anti-submarine as well as an anti-ship capability

SSN	A nuclear powered but conventionally armed attack submarine capable of engaging both surface and submarine targets
VCAS	Vice Chief of the Air Staff
VCNS	Vice Chief of the Naval Staff

ACKNOWLEDGEMENTS

I have been writing this book for a number of years; it has felt at times to be much longer. I have spent a great deal of time in libraries and archives and the staff at the Portsmouth Record Office, Cambridgeshire County Records Office, Gosport Library, National Archives, King's College Library, University of London Library, London School of Economics Library, Royal Naval Museum Library deserve thanks for the time and assistance they gave. Particular thanks must go to Mr George Malcolmson who as archivist at the Royal Navy Submarine Museum was of considerable assistance and permitted me to view his own collection of submarine ephemera; Mr Bill Hetherington, Honorary Archivist of the Peace Pledge Union who was extremely helpful; Ms Jenny Wraight and the staff at the Naval Historical Branch for whom nothing was too much trouble. Mention must also be made of the advice freely given by the late Vice Admirals Sir Arthur Hezlet and Sir Ian McGeoch who were kind enough to answer my unsolicited letters.

I should also like to thank the copyright holders who have given me permission to use images of artefacts that are in their care; in a cultural history such as this their images are vital. Every effort has been taken to contact all the copyright holders, but should I have been inadvertently missed anyone out, I will be delighted to acknowledge them if they make themselves known.

During my research I have come across a great many people who have encouraged, supported, even criticized me (for the good of my soul of course). I owe a particular debt to my PhD supervisors, Dr Joe Maiolo and Dr Paul Readman whose unflagging help, support and encouragement – during and after my PhD – has been without equal. I have a huge debt of gratitude to Elizabeth Loving who copy-edited this book for me. I also should like to thank Dr Andrew Redford, who despite being an archaeologist, took the time to proof read his big brother's PhD and also Britt Zerbe who carried out the final check of this book before publication; thanks are also due to Kate Polden; Lieutenant Leigh Kenworthy, Royal Navy; Laura Rowe; Melanie Gobbitt; Krister Mason; Reuben Cooper; Doug Blackwood; Al McClusky; Al Brooks; Kevin and Michelle Harris, all of whose friendship, encouragement and support has been invaluable. Thanks must also go to the Department of War Studies, King's College London, for the financial support during my doctoral research provided through the Laughton Naval History Scholarship. I should also like to thank the Centre for Maritime Historical Studies, University of Exeter and the Leverhulme Trust for the financial and professional support and development that has been provided in the shape of an Early Career Research Fellowship. Finally, and above all, thank you to my parents for their unstinting support and encouragement since I left the Royal Navy.

PREFACE

This is a book about how the British understood submarines – their own, as well as those used against them; it is not an operational history. It is about the construction of meaning, through practice, ritual, invented tradition and cultural preconceptions and how such things can be observed through the study of an object. Through the examination of the British relationship with submarines since 1900 it is possible to see changing patterns in acceptance and tensions between different sub cultures, civil and maritime. This book will look at several themes: the submarine in naval pageantry, the fleet submarine, unrestricted submarine warfare, the impact of technology, the fictional portrayal of the submarine and the symbolism associated with the individual names given to submarines. Since 1900 the meaning constructed around submarines has changed as the submarine has progressed along a road from perdition as the weapon of the weaker power (and morally weaker power too) to a form of redemption as a major capital unit.

An examination of the meaning of the submarine to the British throws light on attitudes to maritime war as a part of the British perceptions of self in both civil and naval sub cultures. By applying a cultural methodology to the submarine, this book adds to operational histories of naval warfare by illustrating the impact meaning has on the use of an object or weapon system. In this way, the efforts by the Royal Navy to develop a fleet submarine ceases to be an operational or technological matter and instead becomes one of how the Royal Navy imagined the conduct of maritime warfare and attempted to shape the submarine to fit this ideal. Furthermore, the failure to comprehend the role the submarine would play in unrestricted warfare against non-combatants will be shown to have been shaped by existing ideals of maritime warfare that safeguarded civilians and neutral shipping.

INTRODUCTION

A Tale of two Naval Reviews

It was, everyone agreed, an awe-inspiring sight. No clearer example of sea power could be conceived. Britons were justly proud of their fleet – the most powerful collection of warships ever seen – drawn up for a royal review by the Prince of Wales to celebrate Queen Victoria's Diamond Jubilee.[1] The press gushed appreciation, believing that if the British taxpayer 'does not feel more than a thrill of satisfaction at a sight so splendid and so inspiring, he is no patriot and no true citizen.'[2] Even the French press was impressed, commenting that 'what is contemplated is far less a review than a great Naval manifestation, or, to put it in plain word, the solemn affirmation of the sea power of England….No wonder the English are proud in the consciousness of their strength.'[3]

On the day of the royal review, 26 June 1897, thousands travelled to Portsmouth on specially provided trains to witness the spectacle of 165 of the Royal Navy's ships, together with invited representative vessels from fourteen other navies drawn up in five long lines at Spithead.[4] The beaches and piers along the waterfront were crammed with day-trippers. The anchorage was a teeming mass of craft; each jammed with spectators sweating in the June sun, jostling around the black painted hulls, white superstructures and buff painted funnels of the anchored British warships. Only the presence of the royal yacht, the *Victoria And Albert*, restored some sort of order, but once the royal party had passed the pleasure craft returned and bobbed in its wake. An unofficial display of speed was provided by the experimental steam turbine powered launch *Turbinia*, which Sir Charles Parsons, the developer of the marine steam turbine, hoped would persuade the Royal Navy to take up his invention. Such was the *Turbinia*'s impact that 'from a technical point of view, there would have been no important step forward to chronicle if the Turbinia had not made her brilliant appearance.'[5]

After sunset, at 8.45 pm, the entire fleet, British and foreign ships alike, were illuminated in outline, masts, tops, turrets all picked out, by the most modern and novel of methods – electric light bulbs. Some felt that 'at night the illumination of the fleet was a spectacle which surpassed all anticipation.'[6] The *Illustrated London News* called it 'one more beautiful of its kind than human eye had previously looked upon' and thought that the illumination was the most popular feature of the day.[7] Even the normally sober and conservative *Naval Annual* enthused that 'Nothing could have been more beautiful than the effect of the fleet illuminated on the night of June 26th',[8] while the *Saturday Review* called it 'enchanting and enthralling.'[9] Even after the illumination ceased on the stroke of midnight, those who remained watching from the shore could still see the anchor lights of the great fleet gleaming in the darkness.

The review had been eagerly anticipated by observers of the naval scene; it was considered that it would 'transcend all these past [naval] reviews.'[10] Much was made of the fact that no Royal Navy vessels had been recalled from either the Mediterranean or any overseas squadron and that the fleet was almost completely made up of modern vessels.[11] After the event it was felt that:

> The most important Naval event of the last twelve months was the great Review at Spithead, which on the one hand gave the whole world a very clear idea of the maritime power of Great Britain, and was, on the other an admirable object lesson of the progress of construction achieved not only in the Navy but in the mercantile marine and the yachting world.'[12]

Furthermore, 'the fleet gathered for the Review had far surpassed any recent exhibition of Naval Power' and the *Naval Annual* noted rather tartly that 'there is nothing remarkable to record in the history of foreign Navies during the year [1897].'[13]

Yet some commentators were already wondering what the future would bring, asking whether 'posterity will ear-mark this review as the funeral ceremony of the giant ironclad…already submarine navigation has entered on the stage of practicability, whilst aerial navigation is in the stage of possibility.'[14] Rumours were circulating about French experiments that might make submarine navigation a reality, experiments that had one purpose, namely to ensure that a close blockade by a battlefleet would be impossible in the future. France had seen naval might used many times in the past and had only too clear an idea of what Britain's naval power could do. At the same time in the United States, a 'submarine wrecking boat', the *Argonaut*, a clear advance on diving bells, had been demonstrated for cargo recovery from sunken vessels, thanks to the efforts of Simon Lake.[15] While Lake's invention had a peaceful purpose, and he would continue to champion the civil uses of submarines,[16] another American, John Holland, would within a few months demonstrate a submarine vessel designed to sink a ship. The French went one step further when, in the 1898 exercises, the submarine *Gustave Zede* succeeded in hitting with a practice torpedo a battleship at anchor in an open roadstead and later when the battleship was underway.

Eighty years later, almost to the day, on 28 June 1977, Spithead again saw a fleet drawn up for a royal review. A different queen, Elizabeth II, was celebrating her silver jubilee. Again, sightseers came to Portsmouth to see the long lines of ships, although not as many as expected due to the twin handicaps of bad weather and exhaustive television coverage of the event. A hundred and one ships of the Royal Navy including hovercraft, together with vessels from seventeen other nations as well as representatives from the merchant marine and marine organisations formed long lines, over seven miles in length. Unlike the 1897 review, this jubilee inspection was hampered by poor weather, forcing a curtailment of a flypast of naval aircraft, and bad visibility also spoilt the illumination of the fleet and fireworks display. Despite the disappointing weather, one spectator felt that

> those long lines of ships, their crowded decks and superstructures, their hulls grey and white and black, their flags and ensigns, the billowing clouds of white smoke as they fired a royal salute, all made up of the most breathtaking, moving, romantic sights I have ever seen in my life.[17]

This time the ships, the capital ships, cruisers and escorts, were in grey overall, with only the hydrographic survey vessels harking back to the previous century with white and buff colours. Black, however, was the colour of a new type of vessel not seen at the 1897 review, the submarine. The battleship – formerly the arbiter of naval power had gone – killed off by expense and obsolescence in the age of aircraft, missiles and the submarines' torpedoes. The fleet aircraft carrier, too, had passed its zenith and was in its Indian summer with the Royal Navy. The most powerful ships in the world were now submarines nuclear-powered and nuclear-armed ballistic missile submarines. The Royal Navy had four, the *R* class, each armed with sixteen submarine-launched Polaris inter-continental ballistic missiles, which since the 1960s had formed the sole repository of the United Kingdom's strategic nuclear deterrent. One of these submarines was permanently on patrol, ready to shower the USSR with thermonuclear warheads if the Cold War became hot. It was felt, however, that the deterrent would be compromised if one of the *R* class ballistic missile submarines attended the review.[18]

These two events of naval pageantry neatly encompass the time period for consideration. In 1897, no British submarines existed; in 1977 there was a multitude. Not only are submarines numerous today, but they are better armed and represent the cutting edge of naval technology through construction, propulsion methods, sensor arrays and weapons. The naming of submarines has also changed; insignificant pennant numbers have given way to some of the proudest names in the Royal Navy's history, indicating a transformation in the way that people think about submarines and the part they have played in the construction of meaning.

The Submarine, Technological Determinism and the Need for a Cultural Approach

'A sense of technology as a crucial agent of change has a prominent place in the culture of modernity',[19] so goes one of the tenets of technological determinism. The impact that new technologies have had on humanity has resulted in the suggestion that technology itself has 'agency' or the power to effect change – referred to as 'hard' technological determinism.[20] On the other hand, soft determinism relies on the idea that the history of technology is the history of human actions and therefore relies on cultural, political and socio-economic factors forming a complex matrix.[21] The study of the British experience of the submarine suggests it is culture, not technological determinism or political and socio-economic considerations, which has had the greatest impact in the way a newly practicable technology is assimilated. The way in which individuals and groups within a society relate the new technology to their existing framework for understanding their society, value or belief structures and other groups is the dominant factor.[22] This book will show how British culture and identity shaped, and was in turn shaped, by the experience of the submarine.

Rather than tracing the incremental technological changes of the submarine or indeed its operational or strategic value through the twentieth century, this study will focus on the changes in understanding. Such changes show what effects the way an object is understood has on the uses to which it is put. These changes can only be investigated properly by trying to get inside the minds of the participants in ways that are difficult using traditional sources based on government records and the opinions of officials and politicians. By using a cultural approach it will be possible to strip away any confusion caused by the passage of time and explore the meaning of submarines. As Hugh

Kearney has argued, '"Culture" is an amorphous concept but it has the advantage of enabling the historian to raise questions about the life-style, customs, religion and attitudes to the past in a more fluid way than if confined to a one-dimensional framework.'[23] In this way a cultural analysis of the submarine will throw more light on the perceptions of maritime combat, identity, and the relationship with the sea than an operational history could.

A cultural approach to the subject is also necessary to explore the broader context of submarines, away from the confines of narrative, operational and policy histories. Changes in the perceptions of the purpose and value of submarines cannot be fully understood through accounts that do not address the way participants gave their world meaning through imagination. A cultural history can explore the workings of imagination and imagery on decisions that are supposed to be based on logic and reason. Furthermore, by highlighting the unspoken assumptions of a past era there can be a greater understanding of events and decisions that cannot be explained by documentary evidence. By looking at this broader context of the meaning of submarines, it will be possible to see the assumptions regarding images of power, non-combatant status, attitudes to property and warfare that act upon a weapon system and the society that deploys it. Such an approach will provide a fuller picture of the effect of submarines on Britain, as seen from contemporary perspective, thus avoiding the distortion of perceptions of the past or lapsing into anachronism.

The British experience of submarine warfare has not been subjected to a cultural approach. Indeed, cultural histories of weapon systems are few and far between. To date there are four of note: *Count Not the Dead* by Michael Hadley,[24] which looks at the cultural history of the German U-Boat arm; *Tank* by Patrick Wright,[25] which gives an excellent examination of the impact of the tank on society; E. Russell's *War and Nature*,[26] which examines the cultural relationship between chemical weapons and the chemical industry in the United States of America; and J. Ellis' *The Social History of the Machine Gun*[27] which despite the title takes a very cultural look at the machine gun. In terms of historical accuracy Ellis' work seems to perpetuate the 'machine gun myth' of the First World War, a myth that has been rigorously attacked by revisionist historians.[28] Ellis shows, however, very clearly the power of mythology and the need to understand the causes of such myths. Michael Hadley's *Count Not The Dead* also deals with myth-making and examines the relationship between political reality and cultural myth for the German submarine arm and how the Germans have interpreted and presented this aspect of their past.[29] Furthermore, all four works demonstrate very clearly that weapon systems are more than technological or policy details – they are cultural constructions,[30] the importance of which cannot be overlooked if the impact of an object such as the submarine is to be appreciated.

There are also a number of works which use a cultural approach covering areas not traditionally associated with either military or naval history, such as gender issues, feminism, literary studies, memory and remembrance.[31] Particularly noteworthy is the work by Michael Paris on literature, war and culture. He has produced an illuminating general survey of the subject, as well as books on aerial warfare and the First World War.[32] Others, such as John Keegan with his *Face of Battle*, have taken the view that there is a need to let the participants in battle speak for themselves to illustrate the changes in the way warfare was understood, rather than concentrating on the high command.[33] John Lynn's *Battle: A History of Combat and Culture* highlights the differences between the discourse and reality of warfare, between an idealised theory and the practice of warfare.[34] The most obvious thing about all these books is their emphasis on land warfare; not one uses the sea as its backdrop for understanding warfare or those who practised it. Keegan alludes to a possible reason why, that of the degree of centralised command in twentieth-century sea warfare. Quite literally, sailors are all in the same boat and cannot make the same level of individual choices about when and whom to fight, or when to run away, that a soldier can.[35] The personal experience of sailors and their lack of freedom might, however, limit the scope of potential social histories, but such lack of individual freedom of action and opinion does not limit the cultural impact of the perceived purpose. The distinction between social and cultural histories is therefore an important one, especially when the scope of individual action is so limited.

The cultural history of weapons, and naval history in particular, has been overlooked by many historians, who have tended to concentrate on the 'pure' military history and technological aspects of warfare.[36] Through the greater use of cultural approaches to warfare, a better understanding of armed force and weapon systems both in peace and war can be gained. After all, weapons have effects on individuals and, through them, culture. This change in individuals and culture can perhaps in turn change the nature of the weapon and force acceptance of new ideas and technology.

This cultural history of the British experience of submarine warfare will build on the existing work that has been done on the use of submarines by and against the British. However, there are far too many books that are either dedicated to the study of submarines, or discuss them as part of a wider examination of sections of naval history, to mention every author, article, paper or book that has been produced. Authors including R. Compton-Hall, a prolific writer on the subject of submarines, and the journalist, D. Van Der Vat, have helped bring the history of submarines to the attention of the lay person, but these have concentrated on operational history and descriptions of contemporary submarines and life aboard them.[37] The British use of submarines has attracted interest from PhD scholars but these theses tend to concentrate on the operational and technological aspects of the submarine.[38] Academic authors, such as A. J. Marder, S. W. Roskill and N. N, have addressed the history of submarines as part of wider naval policy and strategy.[39] Finally, the 2001 centenary of the submarine in British service also brought a small crop of books, mostly histories of each class of British submarine since 1901, often lavishly illustrated.[40] Perhaps the only academically rigorous book on submarines published in support of the centenary was the Navy Records

Society's volume of selected and edited primary documents on *The Submarine Service 1900–1918* which was further improved by Nicholas Lambert's introduction.[41] None of these works, however, use a cultural approach.

This book will enhance operational and technological aspects of British submarines by showing how the submarine impacted on different parts of British society and their respective cultures and ethos: the submariners, the 'general service' Royal Navy, the politicians and civil observers. It will highlight gaps or discrepancies between thought and action that were the result of cultural preconceptions. It will also show how the unspoken assumptions, which formed British culture or identity, forced submarine developments down certain routes in preference to others. This book will also examine the people behind the object, not as an oral history or a selection of memoirs, but show how, through symbolism and ritual, groups can produce a political or corporate identity. As David Kertzer has noted, through ritual 'incumbent power holders seek to bolster their authority, and revolutionaries try to carve out a new basis of political allegiance.'[42] Although Kertzer is referring to what might classified as mainstream political activities, it is certainly only a short step to take the ideas of political symbolism and ritual into a corporate environment such as the armed forces. The submarine service shows how a corporate identity can be formed within a wider grouping and the tensions this can create, without the added complication of inter-service rivalries. These corporate rituals and symbolism can take many forms, with the use of pageantry, in the form of naval reviews and launching ceremonies playing an important part in the cultural constructions that surround the submarine; differences between how this is used by the submarine service and the wider navy, known as 'general service', shows the ebb and flow of corporate politics. The ritual and symbolism will also be reflected through how British submariners set themselves apart from those in 'general service' (the surface fleet), and how their identity was maintained and enhanced.

The Sea and National Identity

Although this book is primarily a cultural history of the submarine in Britain, the submarine's impact on a very specific aspect of culture – national identity – will also be examined to illustrate how identity and culture shaped the response to, and use of, the submarine. 'Underhand, unfair and un-English'[43] was, according to Admiral Sir Reginald Bacon, the general view of submarines before the First World War. Whether the sentiments he attributes to the British are correct is not actually important; the fact that it raises the issue of the impact that the submarine had on identity is. Bacon's choice of words is interesting, choosing as he did to use the term English rather than British. Was this deliberate? Did Bacon, an officer in the British Royal Navy, consider the submarine to be a purely English affair with no impact on the Scots, Welsh or Irish? Probably not, it is more likely that this is just one example of the English (unlike their Celtic counterparts) accidentally or deliberately confusing English with British identities, and vice versa.[44] Indeed, it has been pointed out that English identities constituted the dominant identity in the nineteenth century, claiming for itself the characteristics of Britishness[45] and it is therefore necessary to consider protestations of English identity as possibly British, after all the Navy League in 1895 referred to England's not Britain's naval power.[46]

Four nations history has encouraged scholars to think more geographically, 'to see London as a world metropolis and Cardiff as a coal one; to map the British diaspora; and to log the two-way traffic in peoples and ideas across the Atlantic, to recover the North Sea and Baltic connection.'[47] However, Britain, or rather the political state is the classic example of the 'state-nation', the state identified not by ethnicity but by state institutions such as Parliament and the monarchy[48] and that 'Britishness sat lightly on top of the constituent nationals'.[49] The Royal Navy is clearly one of these state-nation institutions, being above the construction of Welsh, English, Irish or Scottish identity in a way impossible for the British Army given its reliance on regiments with local county based affiliations;[50] the Navy was a unifying feature for all four nations.[51] Unfortunately, interest in identity issues has concentrated on religion, state formation and conflict, and more pertinently, the interest in the institutions and associated symbolism has not included the Royal Navy,[52] despite Jan Rüger's plea for more interest to be shown in the maritime aspects of identity.[53] Yet by its very nature, this 'four nations history' is surrounded by a maritime domain over (or under) which these exchanges had to take place, helping to provide an 'other'.[54] Importantly for such exchanges within a four nations framework the Royal Navy as an institution 'ignored the sub-nationalisms of the islands it defended.'[55] The possibility of difficulties in reconciling the overarching role of the Navy with four nations history perhaps explains why, given the interest in identity issues, the Royal Navy and the maritime aspect of national identity have remained so neglected. As Linda Colley had pointed out 'We badly need, I think, a kind of Braudelian exploration of when and to what extent the sea came to be viewed by the British as a decisive "natural" frontier',[56] but perhaps what is really needed is a Braudelian exploration of the relationship with the sea as a means by which exchanges of identity took place rather than just as a frontier between an 'us' and a 'them.' Just as it is '…only by adopting a 'Britannia' approach that historians can make sense of the particular segment [of national or regional identities] in which they may be primarily interested, whether it be "England", "Ireland", "Scotland", "Wales", Cornwall, or the Isle of Man',[57] it is also true that by considering the maritime dimension the identities of the constituent islands and their populations will also 'emphasize how much these cultures have experienced in common.'[58]

Yet a narrow focus on the maritime aspects of national identity, badly needed though it is, could obscure an important concept. The neglect of contrasting subnationalisms in preference to the analysis of a wider British/English identity could mask an interplay between cultures that do not sit well within the framework of four nations history. In particular, the divergence of corporate and civil culture when considering maritime affairs is an important one, and one that will not be reflected in four nations or British identity frameworks. Why is such a divergence important? It is important because the Royal Navy as an institution 'ignored the subnationalisms of the islands it defended.'[59] Therefore, what the Royal Navy knew or felt as a corporate entity or culture, could be, and sometimes was, very different from that felt by the civil populace irrespective of their own loyalties. At the same time, mariners, be they merchant or Royal Navy, had a very different understanding of the sea: it was a familiar, if dangerous, workplace. To a landsman the sea could be a source of danger, hostility, the unknown, wealth or opportunity – a whole host of 'others' dependant on the individual viewpoint, all of which could be at variance with that perception of 'others' by mariners who were more likely to view the sea in relation to its position as their workplace. Even the way sailors dressed and the language they used set them apart from their landsman counterparts.[60] Nor has the passage of time improved matters, a twentieth-century submarine or destroyer and its crew would be just as superficially familiar[61] to a member of the public as their eighteenth-century counterparts, drawn from and moulded by society but, at the same time, separate from it. Thus the Navy was an 'other' to the civil population.

At the same time, the sea could be seen as an 'other' – something that caused society to unite against.[62] With regard to the sea this view is illustrated by the efforts from the eighteenth century onwards to tame the ocean, to make it safe, to civilise it though advances in navigation – Harrison's chronometer, charts, hydrography, the provision of recognisable bouyage and lighthouses by Trinity House, as well as the rescue role of coastguards or the establishment of a volunteer lifeboat system. Yet the sea could also be an 'other' as a medium by which 'others' were brought into conflict, either as invaders, as Linda Colley has suggested,[63] or as the means by which the Britons moved into the spheres of 'others' who were not believed to be natural seamen unlike the British, or as an industrial sphere of business and trade.

When in this book national identity is considered, it is the part played by the Royal Navy, and specifically the submarine, that is of importance, rather than the maritime industries such as the British Mercantile Marine and the fishing fleet. As Kenneth Moll has argued, the British needed little urging to show an interest in their navy during the Edwardian period when both main political parties supported in one form or another naval supremacy;[64] the idea that Britain might lose control of the sea was unthinkable too all except the 'most eccentric Radicals...'[65] Even for low paid factory workers, despite the compact between the Radical Liberals and the Labour movement, the Navy was 'one of the fixed points of the universe, admitting of no question or discussion.'[66]

There was not, however, a simple interaction between perceptions of the Navy and seapower and national identity. Instead, the maritime domain could influence identity in two very broad ways. First, the sea and the Navy could act as a means of security from hostile powers, a manifestation of the belief that island-hood imposed a geographical security in contrast to British perceptions of continental powers.[67] This security of island-hood could be seen in a belief that invasion was difficult, or in times of naval challenges, a possibility – the sea could at times 'seem less a symbol and guardian of national identity, than the means by which invasion from without might come.'[68] As a result, as Admiral Bacon pointed out in an article for the *Nineteenth Century and After* 'The people of Great Britain have had ingrained in them, both by heredity and tradition, an instinctive faith in the Royal Navy as their main safeguard in times of peril.'[69] As well as providing security, island-hood could be seen as exposing vital imports of food and raw materials to interdiction by hostile powers should the Navy be defeated or drawn away – a more frightening variant of the 'bolt from the blue' invasion fear. The island-hood security idea could present itself as a perceived superiority of the British as seamen due to their island status, or a moral superiority due to a special relationship with the sea. Churchill, describing his views of unrestricted submarine warfare in his memoirs, commented that 'to sink her [a merchant ship] without providing for the safety of the crew, to leave that crew to perish in open boats or drown amid the waves was in the eyes of all seafaring peoples a grisly act'.[70]

Second, the Navy in particular could influence ideas of global power and position within the construction of identity. This second area could encompass a narrow belief in the supremacy of the Royal Navy – 'For England "there is nothing between sea supremacy and ruin"'[71] – or a more sophisticated analysis centred on the role of seapower and Empire – 'Every one knows that if the Navy should not be decidedly superior to any other Navy the empire must come to an end, and Great Britain cease to be a Great Power.'[72]

Furthermore, often both areas of interaction were considered in an interlinked manner. Admiral Sir Doveton Sturdee told the readers of *Brassey's Naval and Shipping Annual* in 1923 that:

> It was generally recognised that a strong and efficient Navy was essential for the safety of the Empire, due to its far-flung Dominions 'on which the sun never sets'; this conclusion was strengthened by the realisation that the home-country now depends on the import of four-sixths of the necessities of life.[73]

Sturdee has clearly conflated ideas of global position and power through the Empire with that of the command of the sea needed to ensure the safety of imports to the home islands, demonstrating the interrelated nature of ideas regarding the sea and the Navy.

Into this flux of conceptions regarding the sea, Navy, local, national and British identities, surfaced the submarine in 1901. How the submarine interacted either in reality or perception with these existing ideas determined whether the submarine was seen by the British as a threat or a support to their security and identity. In British eyes, the submarine faced a long journey from perdition to redemption.

Book Structure

This book consists of six chapters. Chapters One and Six deal with the submarine at the Coronation and Jubilee reviews, and the submarine as depicted in imaginative literature and film from 1900 through to the 1980s, respectively. These two chapters flank four chronological ones that examine the submarine and its impact on British culture. The four chronological chapters will examine themes that run throughout the period 1900 to 1977 such as attitudes to non-combatants, reconciling the submarine with traditional expressions of seapower, the fleet submarine and naming policy.

Chapter One (The Submarine in Six Naval Reviews) will examine the royal reviews at Spithead in 1902, 1911, 1935, 1937, 1953 and 1977 as a vehicle for following the fortunes of the submarine service at public events. The chapter argues that the reviews were an invented tradition and that contradictions in the messages sent by the reviews can be resolved by understanding the different audiences for each of the reviews. By reading the reviews as cultural artefacts in conjunction with government documents, together with sources such as postcards and souvenirs, corporate attitudes to submarines can be assessed. In addition, the image of the submarine that the Royal Navy wished to project to various audiences will be examined.

Chapter Two (The Submarine 1900–1914) will examine the ideas that drove British submarine development in the period from 1900 to 1914, and will draw on the approaches of 'beyond the cultural turn' to look at the submarine as both a symbol and practice. The chapter will consider the militarisation of the submarine concept, the impact of the submarine on the British view of themselves as well as how cultural attitudes affected the assimilation of new technology into the Navy's corporate culture. The chapter will also introduce the fleet submarine, arguing that cultural attitudes ensured the submarine was conceptualised in a certain manner, even though the technology available would not support such ideas.

Chapter Three (The Effect of Unrestricted Submarine Warfare 1915–1935) will consider the shock of unrestricted warfare, propaganda and the impact on Britain of a weapon that was widely considered to be that of the morally as well as physically weaker power, up to the outbreak of the Second World War. The attempts to ban the use of submarines, in particular in the light of the experience of the Great War, as well as the effects of hostile submarines in the Spanish Civil War will be examined. As with Chapter Two, this chapter will look at the symbolism surrounding submarines and the practice of submarine warfare. It will also examine the contradictions in British attitudes to submarines in the interwar period and argue that such contradictions were due to the difficulties of assimilating the shock of war experience into the existing mindset regarding submarines, in both corporate and civil cultures.

Chapter Four (The Submarine 1935–1965) will look at three areas: the Anglo–German Naval Treaty of 1935, the British unrestricted submarine warfare campaign in the Second World War and the submarine in the early stages of the Cold War. By examining the reaction to the Anglo–German Naval Treaty and contrasting the response with the predictions about strategic bombing in the 1930s it will be possible to see the influence that non-combatant status had on the way the British conceived war and weapons systems as well as a growing acceptance of submarine warfare. The chapter will then look at how cultural constructions regarding making war on non-combatants survived contact with Britain's fight for survival during the Second World War and the response by the British to the Royal Navy's use of unrestricted submarine warfare against the Axis powers. Finally, the chapter will examine the submarine in the period 1945 to 1965 and how the submarine was used to demonstrate national progress and modernity, as well as being effectively reinvented as a tool that helped achieve command of the sea rather than one that destroyed it, thus supporting certain aspects of national identity, rather than, as previously, attacking them.

Chapter Five (The Age of the British Nuclear Submarine) will take the study into the cold war. It will look at the age of nuclear weapons and nuclear propulsion by returning to the two major themes of this study; the fear caused by submarines, and the efforts to create a fleet submarine. The development of the intercontinental ballistic missile armed and nuclear powered submarine (SSBN) will also demonstrate that the submarine came full circle from being the 'weapon of the weaker power' to being the most powerful weapon system ever developed. It will assess the impact of nuclear weapons and propulsion on existing cultural attitudes to submarines. The section on the fleet submarine will also look at how the adage that the answer to a submarine is not another submarine was finally turned on its head, with the idea that the submarine is the prime anti submarine weapon system. The chapter will also look at how these changes in the corporate and civil perception of submarines were developed and were manifested through launching ceremonies and naming policy.

Chapter Six (The British Submarine in Film and Fiction) will examine the lay experience of submarines and how submarines have been portrayed through fiction and film. The chapter will look in detail at how the submarine was portrayed through its fictional engagements with enemy vessels as well as examining displays of chivalry by submariners, the depiction of submariners as either heroes or villains and the popularity of the genre. Through an examination of these themes the chapter will argue that film and fiction provided the British public with the chance of experiencing submarine warfare from the safety of their homes, cinemas and lending libraries. The chapter will also show that the problems faced by the British in reconciling their use of the submarine with their value system were replicated in their efforts to assimilate the fictional submarine.

Although at first glance, this book appears to cover a very large area, it is a cultural history, with the emphasis on ideas and how they changed, so it will be possible to avoid detailed narrative treatment of the period 1900–1977. Instead, this book will concentrate on how the idea of a submarine was transformed in terms of both symbolism and practice from a small, very limited auxiliary, to the most powerful weapon system in the world. In this way this book will highlight British cultural preconceptions that were either challenged or re-enforced by the introduction and development of the submarine. To start this process it is now necessary to return to where this chapter started; the Royal reviews at Spithead.

1

THE SUBMARINE IN SIX NAVAL REVIEWS

There are few sights that can be compared to a fleet drawn up for review. A submarine passing close by on the surface may look darkly sinister and impressive, but the experience pales by comparison to the might of a battlefleet at anchor swinging in unison to the demands of wind and tide. An observer could easily be forgiven for reaching through history and comparing such a display of modern naval might with mental images conjured up by A. T. Mahan's description of the Royal Navy's Napoleonic era battlefleet, 'those storm tossed ships upon which the Grand Army never gazed',[1] particularly if an obliging squall crosses the anchorage. The symbolism of the ritual relies on preconceptions within each of us, which we use to generate the ritual's meaning.

Pageantry and the armed forces go hand in hand. Much of the corporate identity of the armed forces is based on pageantry to such an extent that it is considered normal and part of the job. Involvement in pageantry can signify acceptance, as well as colouring how outsiders perceive the armed forces through messages hidden within the symbolism of the event, but this pageantry is in reality just a ritual, passed down, often without question, over time and its original meaning can be lost or changed.

Clifford Geertz has used Ryle's image of two boys rapidly contracting the eyelid of their right eye to explain these hidden messages. For one boy it is an involuntary action; a twitch. In the other boy it is a deliberate act; a wink. As Geertz then points out, there is a world of difference between a twitch and a wink:

> The winker is communicating, and indeed communicating in a quite precise and special way: (1) deliberately, (2) to someone in particular, (3) to impart a particular message, (4) according to a socially established code, and (5) without the cognisance of the rest of the company.[2]

Applying Ryle's and Geertz's metaphor to the Spithead reviews, who is the Royal Navy winking at during a royal fleet review? What on the surface might be a relatively straightforward question is made harder to address by Geertz's point that answers are based on interpretations and second or third order interpretations at that, as 'only a "native" makes first order ones: it's his culture.'[3] In the case of naval reviews, we might consider that only those who were involved in the review – whether planners, participants on the ships, or spectators – are the 'natives' making first order interpretations. Our subsequent interpretations rely on the information these 'natives' have left behind in pictures, maps, and descriptions.

Invented Traditions, National Identity and the Coronation and Jubilee Reviews

Since the adoption of the submarine into service by the Royal Navy there have been no less than four Coronation naval reviews of the fleet – those of Edward VII (1902), George V (1911), George VI (1937) and Elizabeth II (1953). There have also been two Silver Jubilee fleet reviews in 1935 and 1977. These six reviews may be described as 'invented traditions'; 'a set of practices, normally governed by overtly or tacitly accepted rules and of a ritual or symbolic nature, which seek to inculcate certain values and norms of behaviour by repetition, which automatically implies continuity with the past.'[4] In the case of a fleet review as part of royal celebration, pageantry and ritual it is the implied longevity of the review – its claimed links to previous, but different reviews – that causes it to be an invented tradition.⁵ Although both John Leyland and the *Army and Navy Gazette* in 1911 pointed out that coronation reviews only dated from 1902,⁶ other commentators have not been as discriminating, associating the Jubilee and Coronation reviews with other 'private' royal visits to a fleet.⁷

The Coronation and Jubilee reviews were very much public spectacles, as mass transport made travel for wide sections of the community possible and mass media made public participation in such events widespread, with souvenir programmes to explain the spectacle.⁸ Rail companies ran special trains not only from London, but from around the country.⁹ The spectators were not confined to land as tour companies offered cruises, day trips and longer cruises, round the fleet on various steamers and liners.¹⁰ As motoring became widespread the Royal Automobile Club produced leaflets for motorists.¹¹ Even the souvenir programmes offered travel advice including local radio frequencies to aid the motorist as well as railway information and advice on the best viewing areas.¹² With such mass transport opportunities the public were able to attend the reviews in their thousands, with only the 1977 Silver Jubilee suffering from low attendance figures which was explained by extensive television coverage of the event, as well as bad weather.¹³

Indeed, the very fact that the 1977 review was televised indicates both an expectation of interest and a desire by the organisers to encourage interest from those unable or unwilling to travel to the Solent, an attitude that can be compared with the coverage of the 2005 'Trafalgar 200' celebrations. The preparations for exploiting mass media indicates that these reviews were national events, reported across the country by both national and local media. Journalists were given places on special trains to transport them to the review, chartered vessels to take them round the fleet, as well as radio, newsreel, and later television facilities, together with places on the warships themselves.¹⁴

The reviews also had a role in the political process. The increase in the electoral franchise due to the 1867, 1884 and 1918 Reform Acts made mass participation in politics a reality: 'Whole classes or strata of society were, in some degree tasting power for the first time…'[15] Indeed, the Jubilee Review for George V in 1935 was at the instigation of his ministers who not only hoped that the image of a proud and united people would help dissuade foreign aggression, but also that it would encourage support for the government at the rapidly approaching general election.[16] It is therefore hard to dismiss Michael Lewis' suggestion that the reviews were a means of displaying the Royal Navy's value for money to the taxpaying public.[17] Furthermore, the Coronation and Jubilee reviews were seen by contemporaries in a similar light to Lewis' assessment of the importance of the taxpayer in this new form of pageantry. The *Daily Telegraph* called the 1911 Coronation Review 'the people's review' and noted that 'The people were inspecting the fleet' and '…people have long since taken the Navy under their care, realising that if they, as taxpayers, are willing to meet the bill, the Government must perforce play the tune.'[18]

The tax issue is important as it has remained at the centre of British politics, due to a larger electorate and increasing demands for government spending during the twentieth century. The subject of taxation was especially contentious in the period after the end of the Second Boer War and immediately prior to the First World War as taxation and spending were closely linked to the desire to reduce government debt following the massive expenditure of the Boer War.[19] In the period of the Liberal Government between 1906 and 1914, there was increasing pressure for naval expenditure not only because of real and imagined naval deficiencies and rivalries with Germany, but also because of the Liberal government's commitment to costly welfare reforms.[20] The new taxes levied to fund such social and welfare spending and to meet other financial outlays, were not popular with every section of society.[21]

In addition, the idea that a naval review 'was first a very good way of showing other countries the might of Great Britain and how rash it would be to challenge that might',[22] takes on a second meaning. Not only is the review a material display of strength from what the *Army and Navy Gazette* in 1902 called 'our national weapon',[23] but it is also part of a wider display of national strength, identity and unity that depends for its success on the active participation of the public in what was the cult of the Royal Navy.[24] The presence of the media en masse at the Coronation and Jubilee reviews nationalised these events, bringing them to those unwilling or unable to travel in person to witness the spectacle. As such, the reviews at Spithead played a part in the reinforcement of national identity.

In the period prior to the end of the Second World War, the Royal Navy – through the medium of the Coronation and Jubilee reviews – contributed to ideas of national identity in a number of ways. The British had a particular attitude to the sea, believing that they possessed natural superiority as seamen due to their island status, a view that was reinforced by the need to trade via the sea and maintain a far-reaching Empire accessible only by sea.[25] As a result of these views, a strong navy seemed indivisible from ideas of British national identity, especially in the period of public enthusiasm for naval matters between 1889 and 1914.

Although the Navy was perceived as a 'national weapon' – being a British institution rather than one that was dependent on regional affiliations as was the Army with its regimental system – it was not seen as a weapon of oppression. Instead, the Navy was viewed as a means of ensuring the freedom of all seafarers of whatever nationality.[26] The *Book of Common Prayer* promoted the Navy as 'a security for such as pass on the seas upon their lawful occasions' as well as safeguarding the peace of the British Isles.[27] In the Navy League's guide to the 1897 Diamond Jubilee Review it was noted that:

> We do not build our war fleets…for the purpose of attacking anyone…or for subjecting any free and happy people to our rule. What we are building them for is to maintain the freedom of the seas…[28]

Furthermore, the preamble to the Naval Discipline Act emphasized the pre-eminent position of the Royal Navy stating that 'The Navy, whereupon, under the good providence of God, the wealth, safety and strength of the Kingdom chiefly depend.'[29] The sense of divine purpose for Britain and her Navy (and the length of time it has been generally held) can be seen in the 1740 panegyric *Rule Britannia* which declared 'When Britain first, at heaven's command', and that:

> This was the charter, the charter of the land,
> And guardian angels sang this strain.
> 'Rule Britannia' Britannia rules the waves.
> Britons never, never, never shall be slaves. [30]

As Behrman notes in *Victorian Myths of the Sea*, nations need visual symbols of nationhood: for Britain, this was the Navy and Empire, to the point where in many minds the two were interchangeable.[31] Even in the post-imperial period the association of Navy and nation persisted, in 2005 a Royal Navy public relations programme ended with a shot of the white ensign fluttering in the breeze and the narrator reminding the viewer that 'the Navy and the nation are one.'[32]

The submarine's symbolic position within the Coronation and Jubilee reviews as part of Britain's national identity is important as the submarine's inclusion in the reviews sent signals to both civil and corporate audiences. In particular, the submarine's appearance in the Navy's order of battle provoked problems for British concepts of national identity as the submarine threatened the supremacy of the battleship. This made the submarine unpopular as any threat to the Royal Navy undermined important ideas regarding the freedom to use the sea, Britain's global position and the Empire. Yet the submarine in British hands was to play a part in protecting the British Isles and securing Britain from one of the main fears associated with the 'island race' components of national identity – that of invasion.[33] Indeed, until the advent of the nuclear powered fleet or 'hunter – killer' submarine (SSN) and the nuclear powered and nuclear armed strategic missile submarine (SSBN), the submarine was not regarded as a very 'English' weapon system, in that it was an unfair method of attack. In the light of such views the inclusion of the submarine in the Coronation and Jubilee reviews between 1911 and 1977 is highly significant given the public and patriotic nature of the events: the inclusion of submarines bestowed a degree of respectability on an otherwise poorly regarded weapon system.

Thus the simple gathering of ships that forms a naval review becomes a very different event – a reflection of certain aspects of national identity, but an event pulled in different directions and, to return to Geertz and Ryle's metaphor, giving off different winks to different groups. Groups, who do not share the same language, however, might dismiss these winks as twitches. It only remains to interpret the winks and twitches that make up our understanding of the six reviews of interest: the Coronation Review for King Edward VII in 1902, the Coronation Review for George V in 1911, George V's Silver Jubilee Review in 1935, George VI's Coronation Review, the Coronation Review in 1953 for Elizabeth II and Elizabeth II's Silver Jubilee Review in 1977.

The 1902 Coronation Review

The 1902 Coronation review was the first of the 'public' naval reviews after Lord Selborne's 1901 admission to Parliament that in 1900, the Royal Navy had actually ordered five *Holland* type submarines to be built under licence at the Vickers' yard at Barrow-in-Furness.[34] Given the amount of interest generated by submarines in general and those of the Royal Navy in particular, it is reasonable to suppose that the public spectacle of the naval review would be used to show off the latest investment in new technology. Unlike improvements in machinery, armour or guns, this new technology would stand out as new and very different from the rest of the Fleet.

Yet the Royal Navy did not display its new submarines at the review, and unfortunately, there seems to be no surviving account as to why, although their absence was noted.[35] That submarines were available is beyond dispute. Captain Bacon, the first Inspecting Captain of Submarines, cabled the Admiralty informing them of the changes required to his depot ship's programme and proposing various ports and harbours along the

South coast where the two *Holland* type submarines (HM Submarines *No 2* and *3*) in company with HMS *Hazard* could be left until after the review.[36] The fact that the Senior Naval Lord had approved the proposed course of action, allowing the submarines to be dropped off at Devonport, might be considered significant.[37] If the most important officer in the Royal Navy felt it necessary to approve the decision, the presence, or not, of submarines must have been significant. Furthermore, the fact that the Senior Naval Lord should approve of a decision not to display what was without doubt the Navy's most significant technological acquisition could be taken to mean that the Admiralty was predisposed to sideline submarines.

Unfortunately, the hypothesis that the Navy's leadership was ill-disposed to submarines, neglects key information. First, it must be remembered that the Admiralty *approved* the acquisition of submarines only 24 months previously and had not had time to form an opinion on the new technology's worth.[38] Second, it also overlooks an important factor in the Royal Navy's working practices in the Edwardian period: there was no central Naval Staff before 1912 to whom routine decisions could be delegated, especially on the subject of operations and public relations, such as for a naval review.

If bias at the highest levels is unlikely, security considerations might have kept the submarines away. As late as the 1977 Silver Jubilee Review, the Royal Navy cited security reasons and compromising the nuclear deterrent if members of the *Resolution* class SSBN submarines were displayed at Spithead.[39] In 1902 the Royal Navy had proclaimed that their submarines were for experimental purposes,[40] and there might have been an unwillingness to show off the submarines to close inspection in fear that their limitations and capabilities would be divined by visiting foreign naval officers. Nor is this supposition an implausible one; after all, the only Admiralty department in existence in 1902 that could be considered as a precursor to a Naval Staff was the Directorate of Naval Intelligence. If the Royal Navy felt that other navies were worth collecting information about,[41] why should they suppose that Britain's maritime rivals would not regard the Royal Navy as a legitimate target for intelligence gathering? The security of the early submarines was taken very seriously. In a 1909 letter from the Commander-in-Chief Portsmouth to the Admiralty, the submarine depot at Haslar was listed as one of the places or objects that were not to be shown to foreign naval officers.[42] Despite this prohibition it does seem that there were concerted efforts to show off the Royal Navy's submarines, although in a manner that would make meaningful intelligence gathering difficult.[43] In light of such security considerations, the absence of the submarines only a matter of weeks after entering service might seem reasonable.

There were other reasons as to why there were no submarines on display. The *Holland* type submarines that had only just entered service were extremely unreliable. The new submarine depot ship HMS *Hazard* escorted HM Submarines *No 2* and *No 3* during their voyage from Barrow-in-Furness to their ultimate destination at Portsmouth; as soon as they were clear of the entrance to Barrow harbour both submarines broke down and *Hazard* 'had to tow the boats practically all the way to Portsmouth.'[44] However, Bacon does not mention that he left the new submarines at Devonport while proceeding in HMS *Hazard* to Spithead to participate in the review![45] It is therefore not unreasonable to assume that mechanical unreliability prevented the submarines from participating. Even if they had been at Portsmouth the submarines probably would not have been able to make their likely review positions to the south and west of Gilkicker Point without breaking down, an event that the Royal Navy would certainly have wished to avoid on such a public occasion.

There is a far more unusual reason for the two new *Holland* submarines not to participate in the review, that of unsuitable equipment. The *Holland* class had extremely primitive anchoring arrangements: a rather light anchor and cable were stowed under the casing[46] which were, it seems, simply thrown over the side. This somewhat primitive approach to anchors would not have prevented the submarines from being at the review, but the depth of water and the length of anchor chain would have done. The *Hollands* had a relatively short and light anchor chain of only fifteen fathoms (90 feet or about one shackle).[47] The chart of the area to the south of Gilkicker point (figure 1.1) shows that the water is between five and ten fathoms deep until within two hundred yards of the shore, where it shoals rapidly, preventing the *Hollands* with their short cable from anchoring safely. It therefore seems likely that the two submarines of debatable serviceability were not excluded from the review due to corporate hostility, but due to a combination of mechanical unreliability, lack of suitable equipment and security concerns.

It might be possible to infer something from the presence of HMS *Hazard* and Captain Bacon at the 1902 Review. HMS *Hazard* was an obsolete ship designated as the submarine's depot ship and, given her low fighting value, it might be expected that she would be placed in rows A and B, closest to the Gosport shore and away from the path of the Royal Yacht. Yet HMS *Hazard* was berthed towards the middle of row C, along which the Royal Yacht would pass first. Thus, she had a more prestigious position than might be expected for an obsolescent ship. There are two possible reasons for this. First, the seniority of Captain Bacon, as the new Inspecting Captain of Submarines might have warranted *Hazard*'s position in line C. However, Bacon was number 167 out of 207 captains on the Navy List making him relatively junior.[48] Second and more plausibly, the *Hazard* was the new (and only) submarine depot ship and the object was to draw the Edward VII's (and corporate) attention to the new submarines, despite their absence from the review.

Given the wide variety of possible reasons for the absence of the Royal Navy's first submarines from the 1902 Coronation Review it is difficult to draw any meaningful conclusions about the impact of the submarine through the production, reception or signification of submarines and associated support vessels at the review. The Coronation Review was produced for the public's benefit as well as the Royal Navy's, but with no submarines on display the reception of this new technology would have been negligible. It seems more than likely that submarines were too new and too unreliable to be included in the review, either because there was insufficient time for them to reach the review, which had already been postponed due to Edward VII's illness in June, or because of the uncertainty that they could reach and remain in position close inshore to Gilkicker Point.

The 1911 Coronation Review

The picture presented by the next Coronation Review only nine years later in 1911 for King George V is different. The dreadnought revolution was well underway, with the new dreadnought-type battleships and battle cruisers being used as the benchmark of naval competition as part of the earlier 1889 'two-power standard' with the result that it was 'very difficult to make people think in anything but terms of Dreadnoughts.'[49] Only two years prior to the 1911 Coronation Review the most recent naval scare had forced the Liberal government to increase the naval estimates and build more dreadnoughts[50] although the Canadians – when asked to assist with the cost – had said that they were 'more interested in boxcars [i.e. railways] than in battleships'.[51] The fact that the 1909 naval scare led to an acceleration in the dreadnought-building programme clearly supports the idea that these vessels were the accepted measure of naval power. Admiral Fisher's other playthings, the submarines, had improved rapidly since 1902, with new designs in production. The *Holland* class of submarines, already obsolete, was being taken out of service and the first British-designed submarine, the *A* class, was very close to obsolescence. Meanwhile, the nation was being rocked by a constitutional crisis and the attempts by the Liberal Party to introduce a level of social security, raising the spectre of increased taxation and pressure to cut naval expenditure.[52]

Given the numbers of submarines in service in 1911, it might be considered unusual for there to be only eight on display, two of each of the *A*, *B*, *C* and *D* classes. The 1911 edition of *Fighting Ships* gave the total strength of the submarine service as 79 submarines: twelve surviving *A* class, eleven *B* class, 38 *C* class, and nineteen *D* class.[53] This meant that just ten per cent of the service was represented, which suggests that the submarine service was relatively unimportant. The idea of relative unimportance is strengthened by the fact that 67 per cent of battleships, 34 per cent of cruisers, 52 percent of destroyers and 22 per cent of miscellaneous types in service were at the review. Furthermore, the position of the submarines close inshore off Gilkicker point (figure 1.1), away from the path of the Royal Yacht would also indicate that the Royal Navy did not place much corporate weight behind the submarine. Conversely, positioning the submarines close inshore also put them in the best position to be viewed by the watching public. Thus, the submarine might be more highly regarded as it was in a position to be best shown off to the public, unlike the larger vessels further out in the anchorage.

Figure 1.1: Excerpt from the 1911 Coronation Review chart showing the positions of the eight submarines at the review close inshore to the south of Gilkicker Point and Stokes Bay Pier. (The National Archives, ADM 179/60)

The obvious is not necessarily the correct assumption. The *Illustrated London News* produced a three-part panoramic photograph of the review as part of its coverage of the event, showing the mass of warships crowding the anchorage and commenting, a little smugly, that 'one of the finest comprehensive views of the Fleet from shore was to be had at Gilkicker Point, where our photograph was taken.'[54] The photograph clearly showed the expanse of the anchorage with even the distant ships relatively visible. Unfortunately, the closest vessels, the submarines, are barely recognisable. Indeed, the *Illustrated London News* felt obliged to inform its readers that 'the nearest vessels are submarines. These are lying very low in the water, and are almost invisible.'[55] So despite being very close to one of the best shore viewing points, submarines due to their design were very difficult to see. The statement by the *Illustrated London News* can also be taken to mean that there was also widespread public ignorance of submarines, necessitating an explanation as to what the small low objects were.

Therefore, there is a conundrum regarding the reading of the Review as a cultural artefact. Submarines had to be placed close inshore if they were to be visible because of their size; if they were placed further out in the anchorage they would be even harder for an ignorant public to see and would be obscured by other larger ships. This suggests that the submarines were stage-managed in their exposure to the public in order to raise their profile. From official correspondence it is clear that for the 1911 Coronation Review, questions were raised about the positioning of the submarines. On 25 April, the Commander-in-Chief Portsmouth felt obliged to justify the berths for submarines at the review:

> ...that the position off Gilkicker was selected for Submarines, not only because it was suitable to their requirements, but because it was not suitable to any other class of vessel and would otherwise have been left vacant.[56]

Therefore, the position was not necessarily selected to give the submarines extra publicity, but because the submarines were the only vessels that could make use of it. The most obvious reason as to why submarines were the most suitable vessels is that they had a shallow draft and hence could anchor close to the shore, providing more room for larger vessels. Unfortunately, the Admiralty's opinion as to where the submarines should have been positioned and what prompted the enquiry does not seem to have survived.

Nor can the low percentage of submarines on display be taken as an indication of the corporate culture regarding them as unimportant. Although there were only eight submarines at the 1911 Coronation Review, the reviews before the Coronation tell a different story. In 1909 at a 'private' event for Edward VII off Cowes 42 out of the 150 ships assembled for the King's inspection were submarines.[57] For such a number submarines to be present at the review can be taken to mean that these vessels formed a strong and flourishing branch of the Royal Navy. The emphasis on the submarine at a private inspection provides an interesting contrast with the idea that the Royal Navy thought of the submarine as not only the weapon of the weaker power, but also the morally weaker power, for the 1909 review was a massive display of submarine strength. The portrayal of the submarine in the 1909 review as a weapon to be proud of, as a weapon of virtue or 'of the strong',[58] can be explained by Fisher's plan for the submarine to form an important part of his strategy of 'Flotilla Defence.'[59] Thus by emphasising the numbers of submarines at the 1909 reviews for Parliament and the King, Fisher and the Royal Navy were demonstrating a new strategy to those who were in a position to influence matters.

So why was the large number of submarines at the 1909 'private' review not repeated for the 1911 'public' event? There had been one massive change in the Royal Navy between the review of 1909 and the Coronation Review for George V. Fisher, the proposer of the all big-gun battleship, the battle cruiser and a fervent supporter of the submarine, had retired just fifteen months earlier following a long, bruising and very public clash with Lord Charles Beresford – a clash that had also split the Royal Navy.⁶⁰ Nicholas Lambert suggests that the underlying reason for the Fisher-Beresford feud was a disagreement over naval policy, most likely that of flotilla defence.⁶¹ It might therefore be possible to see attempts to reunify the Navy's officer corps in the 1911 Review.

In order to reunify the officer corps it would be necessary to play down role of the dreadnought-type battleship, that had been causing controversy within and without the navy since its inception, a controversy that was considered 'too familiar a topic, especially among Naval men'⁶² as well as reducing the emphasis on submarines from the level of the King's 1909 Review. Unfortunately, to play down the presence of the dreadnoughts would have been extremely difficult with the current level of Anglo–German naval rivalry. Moreover, HMS *Dreadnought* and her successors seemed to have grabbed the public interest, thus making the presence of the dreadnought-type necessary for good public relations.⁶³ If the Navy was unable to play down the dreadnought to heal intra-service wounds due to the way the all big-gun battleship had seized the popular imagination, the only other aspects of the Fisher years that could be played down for the sake of harmony within the officer corps, were flotilla defence and the submarine. Therefore, the strength of the submarine service was played down at the 1911 review to avoid opening up relatively fresh corporate wounds.

At this point, it is again important to consider the nature of the review; the Coronation and Jubilee reviews can be considered unique public spectacles. The widespread public interest can be seen not just in the numbers of spectators on shore, but also those on the water. In the case of the 1911 Coronation Review, space was at a premium and simply accommodating all the ships and organisations wishing to participate was difficult. In preliminary discussions, it was suggested that an estimated 60 submarines were, or could be, available for the review.⁶⁴ However, the Admiralty's instruction to the Commander-in-Chief (C-in-C) Portsmouth was very clear:

> ... if there is a difficulty in finding space the Third and Fifth Destroyer Flotillas and all the Submarines (except those stationed at Portsmouth) will also be removed from the list [of vessels attending].[65]

The destroyers and submarines were of course the cornerstones of Fisher's now abandoned scheme of flotilla defence and these changes would have helped produce a review that would have pleased the public and avoided corporate divisions.

In the end, only eight submarines attended and the fact that they were all from Portsmouth was noted by the *Army and Navy Gazette*.[66] It cannot be said that this was discrimination against the submarine service, as the Third and Fifth Destroyer Flotillas were also omitted from the Admiralty's final list of vessels attending the review,[67] possibly indicating that the policy of flotilla defence was the object of corporate disfavour. It also reinforces the C-in-C Portsmouth's comments to the Admiralty about the position of the submarines in the review; the numbers of submarines and the position of them was a function of space available in the anchorage. This is in itself revealing, however, as it was submarines that had to be cut in order to get the necessary numbers of surface ships into the anchorage to present a suitably impressive public spectacle, where it could be best been seen from the shore. Pleasing the public was the aim of the review, healing corporate wounds was a subsidiary consideration.

The last aspect of the 1911 Coronation Review that has to be considered is the portrayal of submarines in the programmes and guides produced by various bodies to commemorate the event, all of whom seem to have followed the Admiralty's lead. In the official guide for the review produced by the Admiralty for its guests on board various vessels following the Royal Yacht round the fleet, submarines were placed on the very last page after the torpedo boats.[68] The fact that the submarine was the last vessel to be described in the guidebooks for the 1911 Review as well as the reduction in the numbers of submarine present at the review when compared to the 1909 Reviews is significant. It shows the insignificance of the submarine and suggests that tensions had been set up by the submarine and its part in flotilla defence at both the corporate and civil levels. If the Fisher-Beresford dispute had been about personalities and thwarted ambition, as has been suggested,[69] then why was the Navy split between the two camps? Lambert's suggestion that naval policy and flotilla defence was the root of the bitter dispute seems very plausible and would have certainly exacerbated the personality clash between the two admirals.[70] If the Royal Navy had difficulties accepting the submarine as a saviour, then it is easy to believe that the public would have had an even harder job accepting the submarine and flotilla defence over the battleship and traditional battlefleet.

When the number and percentages of each type of vessel at the review are considered (and indeed the types not present at the review), it certainly seems that flotilla defence was being downplayed in favour of ships that were part of the more traditional battlefleet. Of 79 submarines in service only eight (ten per cent) were at the review anchored off Fort Gilkicker, while of 108 torpedo boats only sixteen were present, exiled at the northwestern corner of the review.[71] Yet the traditional sectors of the fleet – the battleships and cruisers – mustered 67 and 34 per cent respectively. The idea of the battlefleet being emphasized in public rather than the concept of flotilla defence is also supported by the 52 per cent of destroyers at the review. The high percentage of destroyers is important as although they had been previously a component of flotilla defence, they were, by 1911, a component of the battlefleet.[72] Thus, the playing down of the submarine and flotilla defence at the public spectacle of the 1911 Coronation Review promoted a traditional view of the battlefleet and battleship supremacy, thus reinforcing cultural preconceptions of seapower and thus national identity through the strength of the Royal Navy.

On the whole, the Review was very favourably received by both public and professionals alike with press coverage remaining favourable both during and after the event. Perhaps the Review provided a welcome break from the constitutional crisis posed by the passage of the Parliament Act and the budget. Such favourable coverage was not repeated in the 1935 Silver Jubilee Review.

The 1935 Silver Jubilee Review
During the twenty five years leading up to the 1935 Silver Jubilee Review the submarine had become more important. Submarines had made a profound impact of the conduct of the war at sea between 1914 and 1918 but the British perception of that experience was almost totally negative. Furthermore, the submarine had also been the subject of several abolition attempts in the aftermath of the Great War, and the Royal Navy had gone through a considerable period of retrenchment.

In the 1935 Jubilee Review, despite the legacy of unrestricted submarine warfare, the submarine escaped from its previous position in these state events. Although eleven submarines were placed in line C running west–north-west from Gilkicker Point across Stokes Bay, another eleven were placed at the western end of lines D and E, between which the Royal Yacht would pass. The senior submarine officer, now a Rear Admiral, was also present at the review in line D, flying his flag in the depot ship HMS *Titania*, one of five flag officers in that line, out of a total of fourteen flag officers at the review.

Overall, there were 157 warships at the review of which 22 were submarines and three were submarine depot ships.[73] This equated to 14 per cent of the total Fleet at the review and 43 per cent of the total number of submarines in the Navy. This compares favourably to the other new branch of the Royal Navy, aviation, which had two aircraft carriers out of six at the Review or 33 per cent of those in service. For the other vessels present such as cruisers and battleships, there were eighteen out of 51 (35 per cent), and nine out of twelve (75 per cent) respectively, while just sixty nine destroyers in service out of 168 (41 per cent) were at the Review.[74] The high percentage of battleships present emphasizes its continuing importance as a symbol of naval power, yet the submarine comes out rather well with only the battleships having a higher percentage of ships at the review. The figures for the proportions of ships present are given extra significance by the Navy's belief that 'the Review gives us a great opportunity of encouraging the Press to bring the Navy vividly before not only the people of this country, but of the Empire and indeed the world.'[75] If there was any corporate culture that espoused hostility to the submarine and the submarine service, it is hard to believe that either the proportion of submarines would have been as high or that the vessels and Rear Admiral Submarines would have been positioned so prominently.

The 1935 Silver Jubilee Review also represents a watershed in the attitude of the media. The 1902 and 1911 Reviews had been warmly and positively received by the national press and professional naval commentators. In 1935, however, the Government and the Navy were widely criticised by both the professional journals and national press. The *Army and Navy Gazette* commented on what it considered to be the obsolescence of all aspects of the Fleet.[76] *The Times* reported: 'But regarding them with a professional eye, one realises that most of them are smaller vessels, like destroyers, submarines, and minesweepers, and that many more are elderly vessels.'[77] Clearly *The Times* was less than enthusiastic about the increasing presence of submarines at the review and the decrease in what the reporter would have considered the 'proper' navy – battleships and cruisers.

The 1937 Coronation Review

The third Coronation Review of the twentieth century occurred just two years after the 1935 silver Jubilee. It might therefore be supposed that little would have changed in attitudes, yet it shows contrasting views to those produced by the previous reviews when read as a cultural text.

When the Naval staff at the Admiralty were considering the composition of the review, the C-in-C Mediterranean Fleet, Admiral Sir Dudley Pound, suggested that three of his seven submarines should attend the review and that it should be the three *River* class fleet submarines.[78] Pound justified including these submarines on the basis that they would be needed for anti-submarine exercises with the ships that were being detached for the review. This provoked some debate in the Admiralty as some felt that there were sufficient submarines already available.[79] The Director of the Operations Division (DOD) went further, minuting in reply to Pound's letter that 'S/Ms [submarines] are not impressive vessels for Review purposes. It is considered all should remain in the Mediterranean.'[80] The DOD was right and others on the Naval staff agreed with him.[81] Submarines were not very impressive and did not provide spectators with a spectacle, as the *Illustrated London News* had reported 26 years previously. In the end it was decided by the First Sea Lord that the three *River* Class submarines should accompany the Mediterranean Fleet contingent.[82] Yet this decision to use the *River* Class rather than the smaller *S* class is, given the DOD's comments, full of cultural significance. By using larger submarines the Navy could be making up for the unimpressive nature of submarines at a review. If these larger submarines were placed closer to the public viewing areas near Gilkicker Point, with the smaller submarines further out, then it is highly likely that the Royal Navy was deliberately sending a message to the public. Only an examination of the positions of the submarines at the review will allow any conclusions to be drawn on this matter.

When compared to the 1935 Silver Jubilee Review, the positions of the submarines and depot ships in 1937 are broadly similar, and again the Rear Admiral Submarines flew his flag in line D down which the Royal Yacht passed before turning to pass between lines E and F. A closer examination of the position of the vessels at the review shows, however, that the three *River* class submarines (HM Submarines *Clyde*, *Severn* and *Thames*) were positioned closest to Gilkicker Point in company with the large mine-laying submarines *Grampus* and *Roroqual*, where one imagines spectators were afforded the best view of them. Conversely, the older, smaller and less impressive First World War veterans of the *H* and *L* classes were closest to the track of the Royal Yacht. In this way the older submarines would be less obvious to the public and any critical journalists who might repeat the adverse comments made about the age of the Fleet during the 1935 Jubilee Review. *The Times* picked up on this but failed to make the connection between the positions of the ships and the target audience of the review, merely commenting that:

> Among the submarines only the older classes presented themselves to the King's close inspection. The others [the newer and larger ones] were set back, less ready to the view of visitors who were later to follow the King [but closer to the shore and the mass of spectators]…[83]

It is interesting that *The Times* apparently considered the view of those in the official party as more important than that of the mass of spectators on the Gosport and Southsea foreshore. Such a statement suggests that naval reviews were not necessarily seen by some as a showcase for how wisely the government was spending money on the Royal Navy, but were instead for the benefit of the monarch not the voters. Yet the deliberate positioning of modern vessels where they could best be seen from the shore (allowing for the depth of water required for the vessels) demonstrates most clearly that the government believed that the reviews were for the electorate, not the monarch.

In terms of the numbers of ships present, the 1937 review was similar to that of 1935: 145 ships attending in 1937 compared to 157 in 1935. Like 1935 there were 22 submarines at the review, with three submarine depot ships also attending. As with the 1935 review, 75 per cent of the battleship strength attended. Importantly, the percentage of submarine command present remained the same (at 43 per cent), while as a percentage of the ships at the review the submarine rose slightly to fifteen per cent. It is the number of aircraft carriers at the Review that is most different. In 1935 there were two out of six present; in 1937 there were four out of five, surpassing the percentage of battleships and battlecruisers at the review This can be interpreted as fallout from the Royal Navy finally regaining control of the Fleet Air Arm and wishing to emphasize naval aviation. The use of a coronation review to demonstrate recent changes in government policy shows that the coronation and jubilee reviews were an effective way of communicating with people in a manner that combined change and modernity within an existing structure that comforted the viewer. Given the declining power of the monarchy from the late Victorian period onwards, the only group that could be worth such efforts by the government was the electorate, whose franchise increased dramatically over the same period. At subsequent reviews the main subject for communication would not be the continued rise of the aircraft carrier, but instead the importance of the submarine to British seapower.

The 1953 Coronation Review

The accession of Queen Elizabeth II to the throne brought another Coronation Review and the Royal Navy in 1953 has to be placed in context if the review is to be understood. In 1953, the Navy had just fought a war as part of a United Nations force in Korea, and the post-Second World War peace was not proving very peaceful due to a growing tide of cold war conflict and de-colonisation. More importantly, the Navy was struggling with the strategic impact of nuclear weapons on conventional war fighting and the resulting shape of any future world superpower conflict. If there was any single image that the public could grasp that showed the change in the Navy, it was the presence of just one battleship at the review: HMS *Vanguard*.

Analysis of the figures for total strength by type at the review reinforces this picture of change; 28 submarines and four submarine depot ships were present. This represented over 50 per cent of the submarine force and nineteen per cent of the Royal Navy ships at the review. Furthermore, the 1953 review reflected the battleship's decline as the symbol of naval power. In 1953 there were five battleships in service; of these four were in the reserve fleet and only one, HMS *Vanguard*, was at the review. This contrasts with the aircraft carrier of which nine out of eighteen (50 per cent) were present at Spithead. Such figures suggest that even at the most superficial level, submarines and aircraft carriers were of roughly equal importance in the corporate culture. Changes in the relative importance of both the aircraft carrier and the submarine at the expense of the battleship were well known in naval circles thanks to the experience of the Second World War. It is the change in the relationship between the numbers of submarines and anti-submarine vessels that is of greater importance and the one that had to be communicated to a public aware of the dangers posed by submarines. In 1953, nearly 50 per cent of the submarine force was at the Review, with less than 30 per cent of the total number of destroyers and frigates that made up the bulk of the Navy's anti-submarine forces. The review was trying to show that the submarine was more important to the Royal Navy than traditional anti-submarine forces as a result of the reinvention of the submarine as an anti-submarine weapon. Numbers, however, are only part of the way that the change in the status of the submarine was communicated; significantly, it was also evident in the positions of the submarines at the review where it is possible to read the greatest changes.

Unlike the previous reviews of 1935 and 1937, the submarine force at the review was of new construction with no pre-war vessels present. It is therefore not possible to explain the positioning of submarines as being dictated by their age, with the newest vessels closest to the public with the older vessels hidden in the centre of the review. Nor, given the locations of the submarines in 1953, does the argument that the submarines did not review well as put forward by the DOD in 1937 remain possible. In 1953 the submarines nearest to the public were much further out into Spithead than in 1937. Furthermore, as the lines of ships extended further to the west than at previous reviews, space constraints could not be a significant factor in the numbers or positioning of the submarines.

It is therefore possible that the determining factor in the positions of the submarines and associated support vessels at the 1953 review was no longer governed by the practicalities of organising a review. Instead, the relative importance of the submarine command was starting to assert itself as the dominant factor in the positions of its components at the review. This is borne out not just by a lack of evidence to support other motives for the positions of the ships, but also by the numbers of submarines and their positions. In the 1953 review, submarines and Flag Officer Submarines, are present for the first time in line F, which might traditionally be considered the line in which the most prestigious and important vessels are moored, as well as being the first line passed by the Royal Yacht. The importance of this change is reinforced by the numbers of submarine command vessels in line F: out of 37 ships, eighteen are either submarines (fourteen), submarine depot ships (three) or submarine target ships (one). The rest of the line is composed of the only battleship, all nine aircraft carriers, a seabed operations vessel and seven frigates. Importantly, the submarines in line F are placed after the aircraft carriers but before the frigates. This suggests that the corporate and civil signification of the submarine had changed, with the submarine assuming a position of greater importance than frigates and other 'flotilla' craft.

These inferences can be seen as the start of a change in the importance of submarines due to perceptions of what submarines meant to the British. The reason for such a change not being technology led is the state of submarine technology in 1953. Although experimental work was taking place with the new propulsion method of High Test Peroxide (HTP), the two experimental submarines using this propulsion method were not yet in service.[84] In fact, the submarines in service were still technologically very similar to the pre-Second World War types. Indeed, the *S*, *T*, and *U* classes were pre-war designs, although they were being updated with the addition of snorkel masts (itself a pre-war concept) and the possibility of increased battery capacity and streamlining.[85] Therefore, without any real technological breakthrough the only real explanation left is that of a change in the Navy's mindset. Such a change was caused by the experience of the Second World War, the reaction to the perceived Soviet submarine threat in the late 1940s and early 1950s and the way the submarine was being depicted in film and fiction.

The reception of the review is very interesting as despite the prominence of the submarine both in numbers and positions in the review lines, commentators failed to notice the increased importance of the submarine (although *The Times* did devote three sentences to the submarine service which included the statement that 'Among several types of warship equipped to hunt the submarine is the submarine itself.'[86]) Instead, commentators noted the high numbers of both aircraft carriers and anti-submarine frigates and destroyers[87] with the submarine and mine being regarded as the greatest threats facing the Navy[88] noting that the 'Service has changed to meet modern requirements.'[89] There was one comment that emphasized the submarine; the *Manchester Guardian* thought that 'it was the submarine rather than the big ships which from a distance were most impressive in the review itself, for only they altered shape when fully manned on deck',[90] an interesting observation given the DOD's opinion in 1937 that 'S/Ms are not impressive vessels for Review purposes.'

What appears to have worried observers the most was the state of the Navy itself and what this said about Britain. Concern was voiced that it was the Royal Navy and not others 'that ought to be making the running and establishing the modern trend.'[91] It was noted that the Royal Navy was no longer the largest navy in the world, being numerically inferior to those of the United States and Soviet Russia.[92] These concerns, as conveyed to the public, obviously are a reflection of the still important part played by the Royal Navy in the construction of national identity. The fact that the Navy was no longer the greatest naval force in the world meant that not only was Britain's ability to believe in itself as a global power weakening, but also that the belief in the Navy to provide security was in doubt, hence the emphasis in the reports of the review on anti-submarine warfare and mine-sweeping forces.

Twenty-four years were to elapse until the next review. In that time the Royal Navy underwent a series of changes in doctrine, technology and operational areas, all of which had to be communicated in a manner that would unify rather than divide opinion about the Royal Navy against a background of economic failure, de-colonisation and growing links with the European Economic Community.

The 1977 Silver Jubilee Review

By 1977 the United Kingdom had withdrawn from east of Suez, de-colonisation was complete and the Navy was orientated towards a NATO role. Fixed-wing aircraft carriers that had been so prominent in the 1937 and 1953 Coronation Reviews were in their last gasp as the 1966 Defence Review had cancelled the next generation of strike carriers and the remaining modernised fleet carriers were to be scrapped by the end of the 1970s.

An analysis of the composition of the Review is revealing. There were fourteen Royal Navy submarines present out of 101 Royal Navy warships, auxiliaries and hovercraft equating to thirteen per cent of the fleet at Spithead; a reduction from the 1953 Coronation Review figure. However, analysis of the different types of submarine is useful as it shows that although no Polaris SSBN submarines were present, four out of nine hunter-killers (SSNs) were (44 per cent of those in service) while 52 per cent of the diesel electric-powered patrol submarines (SSKs) were also present. Overall, 44 per cent of all submarines in the Royal Navy were at the review. This compares to 52 per cent of frigates and a hundred per cent of aircraft carriers and helicopter cruisers. Given the small numbers of traditional capital units in service, it seems that every effort must have been made to ensure that they were present to give the Review impact.

The most interesting aspect of the 1977 Review is the position of the submarines. The SSKs were berthed alongside the track of the Royal Yacht and were closer to the head or eastern end of the lines than ever before. It is in the SSN, however, that we see a very discernible change. All four SSNs were moored at the head of their line, opposite the remaining heavy units of the Royal Navy. Thus it can be very strongly argued that this positioning signifies that the submarine, and the nuclear powered SSN in particular, was one of the most important units in the

Fleet and at the review, and that the meaning of submarines within a naval review environment had changed by 1977.

That the profile had undergone a transformation by the time of the 1977 Silver Jubilee is supported by the emphasis placed on submarines by the official souvenir brochure. Unlike earlier years when submarines were frequently the last vessels to be mentioned, and often in a cursory fashion, the 1977 official souvenir programme was startlingly different. In a clear attempt to educate the reader as to the importance of the submarine over existing forms of seapower such as the aircraft carrier, the section entitled 'Warships of the Royal Navy' discussed the Polaris SSBNs first, despite the fact that none were actually at the review, then came the hunter-killer SSNs and finally the SSK diesel electric patrol submarines.[93] The programme drew attention to the fact that ten out of the eighteen SSKs were at the review.[94] Only once the submarines had been discussed, did the programme's author describe aircraft carriers, helicopter cruisers (themselves a new type of vessel, being rather hideous conversions of the post-war cruisers *Blake* and *Tiger*), and the rest of the surface fleet. If this was not enough publicity for the submarines, the programme continued its education of the reader with three pages, well illustrated, solely on the submarine service.[95] Furthermore, by leading discussion about the ships of the Royal Navy with an section about the Polaris SSBNs, it seems that the nuclear missile submarines were either a non-issue thanks to the collapse of the Campaign for Nuclear Disarmament as a national movement in the mid 1960s, or that it was part of an attempt by the Royal Navy to rehabilitate the SSBN in the eyes of the public.

Before too much is read into this, the background of the souvenir booklet's author must be considered. John Winton was a retired submarine officer who had made a very creditable career as a naval journalist and writer. It could be considered that, as a former submariner, a degree of partisanship had entered Winton's writing. This argument might be more plausible were it not for the fact that this was the official programme whose contents would have been approved by the Royal Navy, unlike the privately produced programmes, such as that written by M. Critchley, which does not place the submarine quite as highly.[96] Critchley discussed the submarines after he detailed the aircraft carriers and cruisers at the review.[97] Moreover, other articles written by Winton about the review, such as those for the *Illustrated London News* did not show any degree of partisanship.[98] Therefore, it is necessary to conclude that Winton was doing what the Navy wanted and it suited the Navy to push submarines as the arbiters of naval power; after all they could hardly push fixed-wing carrier aviation after the 1966 decision to end fast-jet aviation in the Royal Navy.

The reception of the 1977 Review is perhaps the most problematic. Spectators were few in numbers and nowhere near the million plus that were expected,[99] suggesting a degree of disinterest and the fact that it could be watched on television. Portsmouth's *The News* thought that rumours about likely traffic difficulties and overcrowding had deterred spectators.[100] Yet the media displayed some interesting contradictions in their coverage of the submarine. Some newspapers followed a traditional approach to the submarine by playing down its importance. *The News – Fleet Review Souvenir* placed its description of the submarine service on page 14, after the description of foreign warships present; only the description of civil vessels at the review came after it.[101] The *Daily Mail* contented itself with declaring that the submarine 'best symbolised the remote and unheroic nature of modern sea warfare' and observed facetiously that, 'As the trend to submarines continues, there seems no reason why the next Royal review shouldn't take place completely under water'; while *The Times* remarked that 'Most sinister were the long black submarines'.[102] Other newspapers joined with the Royal Navy in talking up the SSN as the capital ship of the modern navy.[103]

It is, however, the comments that touched on national identity issues that are the most interesting, for although there were grumbles in the press about the size of the navy,[104] there were also allusions to both the symbolism of the position of the submarines in the review and the role of the Royal Navy in the construction of national identity. In a remarkably perceptive article, the *Guardian* noted that the SSNs had 'moved to the head of the anchorage to mark their emergence as the ships of the future'[105] commenting that,

> ... the intriguing question is how far sheer sentiment of a kind which infects some sailors as well as the crowds ashore on occasions like this has been subtly responsible for the limited scale of our submarine programme since Dreadnought put to sea in 1963...[106]

The *Guardian* also thought that 'the tradition that is being nostalgically celebrated at Spithead today is that of Britain's Imperial past...'[107] while the *Daily Express* thought that 'No other Service is so interwoven with the almost every aspect of our national life.'[108] The *Guardian*'s choice of language is interesting, suggesting that the Review was a celebration of a now dismembered empire, and that the paper not only disapproved of Britain's imperial past but also anything that reminded the public of it, such as the Royal Navy. Yet when taken with the other comments that the imperial 'sentiment...has been subtly responsible for the limited scale of our submarine programme...'[109] it suggests that the *Guardian* is blaming the echoes of Britain's imperial past for its failure to embrace the nuclear submarine and a NATO role. Both newspapers clearly thought that the Royal Navy was synonymous with certain aspects of Britain's past and present. In an allusion to the importance of Britain's global importance in the construction of national identity it was noted that 'the Royal Navy clings to the edge of the big league with its NATO role and the strategic capabilities of its polaris submarines.'[110] Submarines were now seen in public as being an essential part of maintaining Britain's global position and national identity, falling into line with the corporate culture that since 1967 had thought that nuclear submarines were the 'hallmark of a first-class navy.'[111] In this way, by shoring up pretensions to great power status that could by 1977 no longer be justified by economic, imperial or other forms of naval power, the submarine had now an important role in supporting British national identity thorough the status the SSN and SSBN conferred.

The mixed reception of the submarine in the Review also indicates that although the submarine had been of increased corporate importance since the 1950s and had assumed the mantle of the Royal Navy's main offensive weapon from 1966 onwards, public perceptions of the submarine lagged behind. It seems that the 1977 review represents for the submarine the cusp of general acceptance, supported in no small way by the statistical trends provided by the analysis of the numbers of ships present at the reviews between 1902 and 1977.

Statistical Trends 1902–1977

The increase in the submarine's relative importance over the period from 1902 to 1977 has been clearly demonstrated by the larger numbers of submarines at the reviews, either as a percentage of the fleet at the review (figure 1.2) or as a percentage of the total numbers in service (figure 1.3). As figure 1.2 shows, as far as the pre-Great War reviews were concerned, the submarine was absent from the 1902 review, for reasons already discussed, yet in 1911 it made up just 4.8 per cent of the ships on display. A rise from zero to nearly five per cent during such an experimental period of the submarine's history could be considered as very creditable and indicative of an organisation that was embracing new technology. Such a view would be reinforced by the Coronation and Jubilee reviews during the inter-war period. In the 1935 Silver Jubilee Review the figure was fourteen percent with a barely appreciable rise to fifteen per cent two years later at the Coronation Review for George VI. Thus the interwar period while showing a considerable increase on the pre-Great War period also shows a level of consistency, although this could well be a distortion caused by the close proximity of the two Reviews. Post-Second World War, the percentages show a further rise to nineteen per cent in 1953, but then drop back in 1977 to below that of the previous Silver Jubilee Review with submarines accounting for thirteen per cent of the fleet. What is

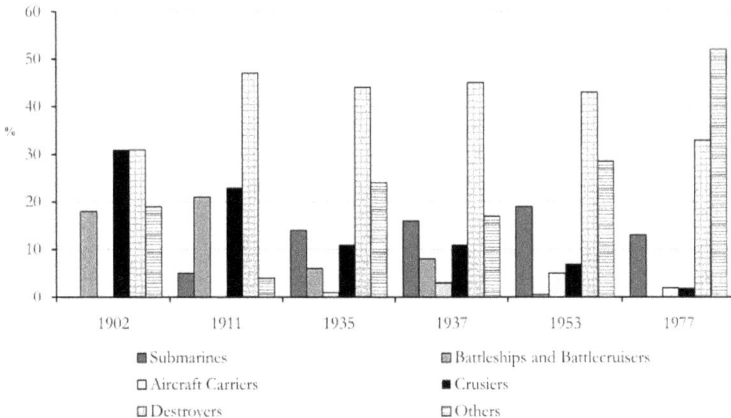

Figure 1.2: Ship types as a percentage of the total number of vessels at each review.

interesting is the steady increase in the numbers of submarines as a percentage of the total number of vessels at each review from 1902 to 1953. Such an increase from zero to nineteen per cent indicates a growing desire to display the submarine in a public sphere and to demonstrate that money was being well spent. Thus not only might it be argued that these figures show an increasing acceptability of the submarine but that they also show a belief at the corporate level that the public will expect submarines to be displayed as part of the fleet.

Increases in submarines as a percentage of the total number of ships at each review between 1900 and 1953 mirror those for the proportion of the submarine force as a percentage of the number of ships on review; in 1977 that too saw a fall (see figure 1.3). Figure 1.3 shows clearly the increasing importance of the submarine through their numbers as a percentage of the total numbers of vessels in service that were present at each review. In 1911 only eight submarines (ten per cent of those in service) were at the review. Just before the outbreak of the Second World War this had risen to 22 or 43 per cent of all submarines in Royal Navy service. This reached a peak of nearly 50 per cent of the submarine command with the 1953 Coronation Review,

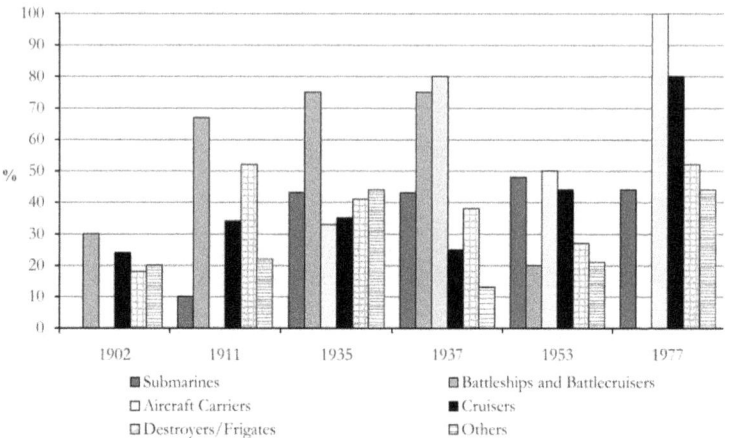

Figure 1.3: Ship types present at each review as a percentage of the total in service.

before falling back to 44 per cent at the 1977 Silver Jubilee Review. Overall since 1935, over 40 per cent of all submarines in service at the time of a review were on display to the public, a relatively constant figure when compared to the variations seen in other ship types. This suggests that, despite the long-term decline in the Royal Navy's strength after 1918, from the late interwar period onwards the submarine has achieved a plateau of acceptance in first the corporate and then the civil spheres as the reviews reflected the expectations of both groups. Furthermore, given the decline of traditional capital units, first the battleship, then the aircraft carrier and cruiser, as the Navy has contracted, the static nature of the percentages of submarines present at the reviews actually displays their increasing importance.

Conclusions

A naval review is one of the most complex pieces of pageantry in use. It is visually impressive and, due to its size and the media attention it attracts, capable of engaging even with disinterested sections of the public because it is so unusual and is laden with symbolism. The understanding of the reviews is further complicated by the fact that what today is generally accepted as a naval review, the Coronation and Jubilee review, is an invented tradition dating from no later than 1887. Yet, because of the civil and corporate interest, taking a snapshot view of each of the six Coronation or Jubilee reviews from 1902 onwards can be very misleading due to the numbers of different interpretations that can be placed on the composition of the fleet and the positions of the vessels in the anchorage. It is therefore necessary to step back and consider the trend of these reviews. In this way it is possible to see how the review has changed and how, as a result of this change, meaning has changed and perceptions about the submarine have altered.

The production of the naval reviews between 1902 and 1977 and the submarine as a part of such reviews has to be considered in both the contemporary and historical contexts as well as the 'authorship' of the Coronation and Jubilee naval reviews. The authorship of the reviews as state occasions has remained stable throughout the twentieth century, with the Royal Navy playing its part in the establishment and continuation of an invented tradition that forms part of a greater royal ritual. The use of reviews as part of the wider royal ritual coincides with the most significant changes in the standards of education, the great increased electoral franchise, transport and media which have allowed much greater mass participation in the ritual of the review. This transformed the ownership of the Coronation and Jubilee reviews from one that was the preserve of the monarch and the Navy, to a public ownership. However, the 'private' reviews of the fleet by Royalty or politicians, such as those in 1909, 1938, or 1965, were also a part of naval pageantry, but importantly the review as a public spectacle was coupled to a very rapid acceptance that these Coronation and Jubilee reviews were a necessary part of the wider royal ritual.

As an invented tradition, the Coronation and Jubilee reviews have superficially hijacked the conventions of the older non-public review. Thus, in terms of significance, it is possible to read the review as a cultural text, but the usual language is incorrect. For the Coronation and Jubilee reviews, the audience is the public not the monarch. Thus reading the review in terms of the old conventions of importance in naval pageantry such as proximity to the path of the Royal party will only give a fragmented image and specifically does not appear to work for submarines in the 1902, 1911, 1935 or 1937 reviews.

With the changes to the Fleet between 1937 and 1953 through developments such as technology and strategy, the way in which a naval review should be read with regard to submarines changed, but not necessarily because of any radical technological development in submarines. By 1977, however, the reading of submarines as part of the review process was now technology led, even if the 'language' needed to read the review is one that would have been familiar to a navy enthusiast of an earlier age: namely position relative to the head of the line.

Those aspects of the review that would only be understood by the Navy, such as the positioning of Flag officers commanding sections of the Navy, did remain constant throughout the period, presumably because it is a matter of professional importance rather than one of lay interest. Throughout the period under consideration the positioning of the senior officer of the submarine branch has moved closer to that most prestigious area of the review, the head of line F. At the same time, the position of the submarines at each successive review have moved further south and east towards the most prestigious positions at the head of the lines.

These six reviews called on images of earlier reviews which were very different in nature when compared with the public displays of naval power for the masses from 1887 onwards. The target of the Coronation and Jubilee reviews between 1902 and 1977 was the public, either as direct observers of the event, or distant participants using the nationalising power of the media to involve them in the process. The reception of the reviews at the time and since has been generally favourable, and the general reduction in naval power has attracted adverse professional comment, both at the time and since. However, the submarine has avoided any approbation at most reviews, but then in 1977 it was singled out for special notice either in the press or more significantly in the souvenir programmes. Yet the presence of the submarine at events which held so much visual symbolism for the construction of national identity around myths of the sea, empire, island status and the Navy is highly significant. Although never articulated explicitly, it seems clear that there was a deliberate attempt to associate the submarine with the positive aspects of the fleet, culture and national identity through its inclusion in the reviews, at both the civil and corporate levels, when the natural reaction to the submarine was to disparage it as representing an 'unfair', un-English mode of warfare. If there had not been the positive reinforcement of the submarine provided by its inclusion in the patriotic festivals that were the Coronation and Jubilee reviews, the only way of giving the submarine meaning would have been through its use by hostile powers in ways that threatened components of British culture, either the Fleet directly or the Fleet's ability to protect the empire and the British Isles.

With the 1953 review, the submarine starts to become associated with traditional capital units as the submarine's positions within the 1953 and 1977 reviews reflect the perceived importance of the branch, which in turn is supported by the numbers present at the review. Yet this was not a technologically driven process as the development of the submarine in the pre-nuclear propulsion age had been incremental and evolutionary rather than revolutionary. The effect of a technological revolution due to the use of nuclear propulsion can be clearly seen in the 1977 Silver Jubilee Review. Significantly as a part of a cultural text, the nuclear powered SSNs at the 1977 review were in the positions of greatest importance while the other conventionally powered submarines, while still well placed under the traditional reading of a review, were in positions of lesser importance but the importance of the SSN only seemed to be on the edge of civil consciousness.

These six reviews have shown the growth of the importance of the submarine and the striking effect that new technology can have on a reading of such an event as a cultural text. However, these reviews only go part of the way to placing the submarine in its proper cultural context. It is therefore necessary to consider the way that the submarine was understood by both the corporate and civil cultures and its interaction with cultural preconceptions during the period that saw the submarine introduced into British service, a time when it was characterised as being 'underhand, unfair and un-English.'

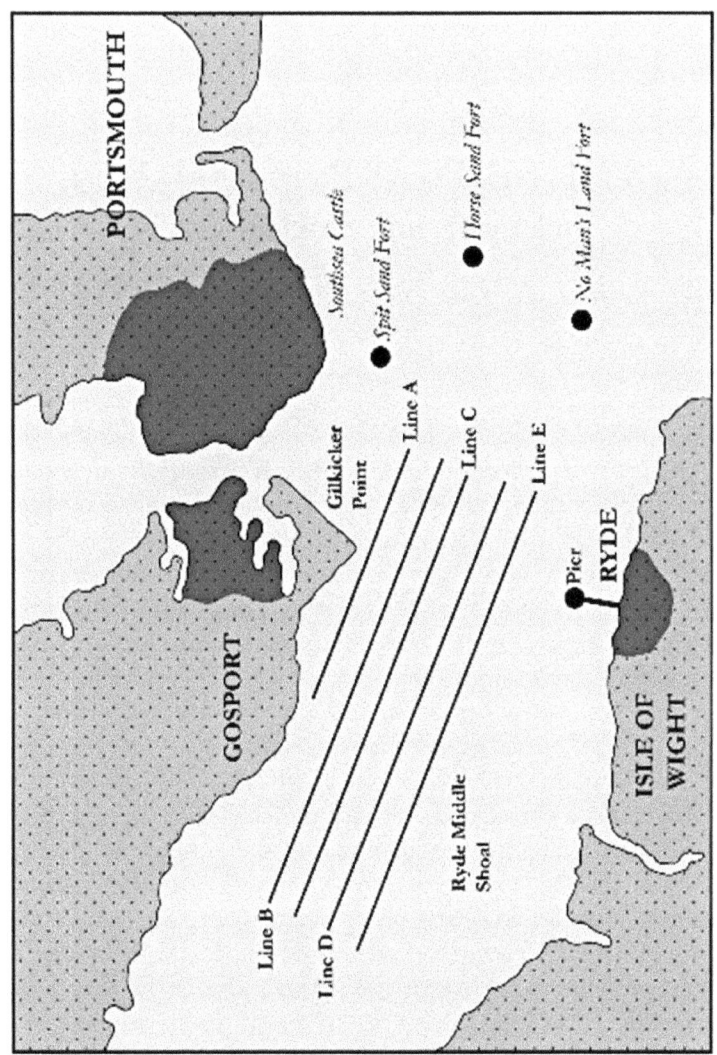

Figure 1.4: Map of Spithead, Portsmouth and Ryde, showing the approximate positions of the review lines.

2

THE SUBMARINE 1900–1914
'Underhand, unfair and un-English'[1]

The submarine did not leap into existence in a cultural void. Rather, it was understood by the British through its interaction with their existing concerns, preconceptions and indeed prejudices although it cannot be assumed that acceptance of the submarine indicated approval of it. Early reactions to the submarine in both the corporate and civil spheres fall into three broad categories, each of which played a part in the production, signification and reception of the submarine as a cultural artefact. Although these categories are linked, they will be discussed separately. First, the militarisation of the submarine – the manner in which submarine technology was assimilated and given meaning – needs to be considered. Second, the challenges the submarine posed to British national identity and the conduct of maritime warfare will be examined. Finally, having identified the way submarine technology was given meaning and challenged ideas about British identity, the reaction of the Royal Navy and the way in which the submarine was integrated into the fleet will be analysed.

This chapter will examine these broad areas and how the submarine interacted with British culture between 1900 and 1914. It will demonstrate that cultural preconceptions played a major part in the assimilation of the submarine concept in Britain through images of seapower, chivalry and the cult of the battlefleet. Before these three areas can be discussed the cultural preconceptions that existed before the advent of the submarine and into which it was assimilated need to be understood. As Cynthia Behrman has demonstrated, a belief in the romance of the sea, myths about island-hood and national character combined to produce a distinct late-Victorian mindset, which coloured British culture in the period up to 1914.[2] Yet as Behrman also notes, these myths are not completely absent today, although they are 'virtually dead' as part of the construction of national identity.[3] The submarine played its part in shaking the foundations of the mythology surrounding the British relationship with the sea that was used to construct national identity in the run-up to the First World War.

It is also necessary to situate the perceptions of the Royal Navy and its principal weapon system – the battleship – in British culture, which was the context for the introduction of the submarine by the Navy. The masses of tables comparing the relative fighting value of each type of ship every year in Brassey's *Naval Annual* demonstrates the extent which the battleship was in the forefront of public interest when considering naval power.[4] Furthermore, in the *Naval Annual*, and the later *Fighting Ships* edited by F. T. Jane, the battleship was always the first type of vessel to be considered in each national section.[5] The articulation of the two-power standard as an easy method of measuring British naval power following the 1888 naval scare, the 1889 Naval Defence Act and the 1897 Diamond Jubilee review, where national safety was counted in battleships, imprinted the type on British culture.[6] Nor was this view of the Royal Navy's supremacy held by just the British themselves; the French thought that the British equated supremacy at sea with numbers of battleships and that they were fixated with the concept of the decisive battle and traditional squadronal warfare rather than exploring the potential of new technologies such as the submarine.[7]

The emotional value of the battleship and the Royal Navy as part of British culture and national identity was enhanced by its association with the acquisition of the Empire, a fact that would have been almost universally regarded as working to the global common good.[8] Even the Liberal Party who was determined to reduce naval estimates, as well as journalistic supporters such as A. S. Hurd, recognised the role the battleship had played: 'We have carved out the [British] Empire with the line-of-battle ship.'[9] The Conservative *National Review* agreed with the Liberals that the fleet (and thus battleships) and the creation of Empire were inextricably linked. [10] Furthermore, in the 25 years prior to 1914 '…the British Empire and the Royal Navy became twin symbols in the popular mind: the Empire vital to Britain's greatness and her world role, and the navy as the key link in imperial defence.'[11] In many respects the battleship was synonymous with the Royal Navy, Imperialism and perceptions of national identity.

The dreadnought 'revolution' from 1906 onwards further boosted the battleship mindset.[12] Although there was a great deal of professional debate over the utility of the all big gun battleship and new battlecruisers, the civil observer of the naval scene was presented with a new type of vessel that was visually superior to previous ships. When Germany passed a new naval law, expanding their dreadnought building programme and provoking a naval crisis in Britain in 1909, public opinion demanded more dreadnoughts not submarines to meet this new threat. Even cigarette card sets were printed displaying images of the Royal Navy's dreadnoughts in the aftermath of the 1909 scare. The strength of this preference can be demonstrated by the despairing remarks of Colonel Repington, correspondent to *The Times* and in favour of the use of submarines, who in 1910 thought that 'It is very difficult to make people think in anything but terms of Dreadnoughts.'[13] As late as 1976, the military historian John Keegan could use the phrase 'Super-Dreadnought' to describe a tank, confident that, even in the missile age, readers of what was a popular rather than academic military history book would understand the metaphor.[14]

The battleship ethos and Mahanite strategic principles affected even the civil view of naval warfare by ritualising battle. Whereas in the Napoleonic period British warships often succeeded in overwhelming and capturing larger men of war, either individually of as part of an inferior force,[15] the Edwardian Navy had become stratified in combat. A fleet's reconnaissance screen would clash with its enemy counterpart and the destroyers with enemy torpedo craft, while the battleship would fight battleships. The threat of torpedo attack from surface ships hastened such stratification.[16] Before 1910 most admirals considered that engagements would occur between battleships,[17] and civilian observers translated this into a medieval joust between an armoured elite; a 'tournament of super-Dreadnoughts, tilting at each other mid sea.'[18] Such ideas of a medieval armoured elite had very strong links to the revival of the chivalric code in the nineteenth century and its association with the idea of the Victorian and Edwardian gentleman.[19] There are also parallels between the divisions within the Royal Navy and the rapid stratification of late Victorian and Edwardian society into much more clearly defined class groupings than had hitherto existed.[20] The battleship could be regarded as a member of the upper class or aristocracy of warships; in terms of personnel, the superiority of the executive officers over the engineer coincides with civil attitudes regarding activities fit for gentlemen and the low opinion of those working in industry.[21]

Such a cultural context was bound to influence the way in which the submarine was assimilated by both civil culture and the Royal Navy's corporate culture. The Royal Navy was a key component of national identity and within this structure the battleship dominated British maritime thinking – strategically, operationally, tactically and socially. The actual and implied power conferred by the battleship was the cornerstone of Britain and its maritime Empire. British concepts of national identity, as well as domestic and imperial security, were all bound up within images of the strength and security of the battlefleet and its constituent battleships, and any technology that challenged this security was viewed with deep suspicion and indeed fear. This then was the psychological background that would influence the meaning given to the submarine by the British, when the adoption of submarine technology took place and the concept was militarised.

The Militarisation of the Submarine

Submarine technology was, and remains, by default neutral, in that it can be used with equal ease (or indeed difficulty) for both civil and naval applications; it allows humans to travel underwater and there is no requirement for it to be used for warlike ends. The militarisation[22] of the concept is a key indicator of how the British understood the world around them at the time the submarine was developed, and how they responded to the potential opportunities and threats of the new technology. Submarines, even when demonstrated as a practical proposition, were not generally seen as peaceful inventions. From the mid-nineteenth century onwards, the pioneers of civil applications for submarine technology almost all gave up developing submarines for peaceful use and concentrated instead on sinking hostile warships.

With the exception of Señor Monturiol's experiments in Spain during the 1850s, the Reverend Garrett's research[23] and Simon Lake's work with his *Argonaut*, almost every submarine pioneer – Bourne, Drebbel, Bushnell, Fulton, and others – had been interested solely in using submarines to sink warships. Even Monturiol, Garratt and Lake eventually applied their inventions to warlike rather than peaceful ends in order to try to attract financial support.[24] As a result of this emphasis on naval applications, the submarine was perceived already in 1901 as a weapon; the military aspects of submarines dominated, and not the civil uses.

Even before the Royal Navy adopted the submarine, the concept had been militarised for the British. Jules Verne, author of probably the most famous submarine story first published in 1870, made use of the submarine to show off the potential for undersea exploration with his descriptions of finding Atlantis or sailing beneath the ice cap and visiting the South Pole.[25] However, Verne's creation, the *Nautilus*, also sank ships belonging to the 'accursed nation'[26] (alleged to be Russia[27]). Despite all of the adventures of exploration that are encountered during *Twenty Thousand Leagues Under the Sea*,[28] it is *Nautilus* sinking the ships of the 'accursed nation' that provided the most resonate images. Verne's obituary in the *Spectator* noted that:

> Forty years ago it may have seemed most absurd for a 'steel cigar' like the 'Nautilus' to pierce her way under the Pacific, ramming and sinking the mercantile marine and warships of the "accursed nation" of which Captain Nemo was the implacable enemy; but today it is certain, not merely possible that the naval policy of all the Great Powers of the West and East will be largely influenced and directed by the knowledge acquired in the last few years of the powers of the submarine. Jules Verne built better than he knew when he imagined out the hideous fear of the unknown and unseen which must always influence the moral [sic] of a war fleet expecting an attack from under the water.[29]

Nowhere does the obituary mention civil uses for the submarine or Verne's use of the *Nautilus* as a vehicle for exploration as well as vengeance.

The relative immaturity of submarine technology was not the reason for the militarisation of the submarine. John Holland, the designer of the Royal Navy's first submarines in 1901, did not concentrate only on warlike applications, but also advocated the use of the submarine for commercial purposes as both a passenger and cargo vessel, noting that the submarine would avoid the perils of fog with the risks of collision as well as the great evil of seasickness.[30] Thanks to reports in *Review of Reviews*, Holland's thoughts quickly became known in Britain.[31]

Holland was not alone in looking for peaceful applications of submarine technology. Simon Lake had developed a 'submarine wrecking boat' or an undersea exploration submarine, but not all submarine enthusiasts were quite so optimistic about the civil uses of submarine technology. Colonel Field, a regular commentator on Edwardian submarine technology, shrewdly observed in 1908 that 'The third class of submarines, those intended for passenger transport, will probably never exist, save in the imaginations of their ingenious and sanguine designers.'[32] Even before Field disparaged passenger submarines, the *Review of Reviews* called Holland's article 'very interesting, if a little too optimistic'.[33] Certainly the propulsion technology available at the time would have made submarine passenger transport far slower surface ships, while the design characteristics of a submarine would have limited its usefulness as a freight vessel. As to the evils of seasickness, Field thought that 'they, in most people's opinions, would be endurable when compared with the alternative of a prolonged confinement in a subaquatic iron dungeon'.[34] The nature of Field's language, likening the submarine to a cruel form of imprisonment, helps illustrate the depth of fear that had to be overcome. This, perhaps, is the nub of the issue: submarines were too frightening for passenger use.

This interest in 'subaquatic dungeons' manifested itself through the British public's morbid fascination with submarine accidents and their aftermath such as the loss of the crew of submarine *A1* in 1904.[35] The funeral of the victims was the subject of a postcard, indicating there was sufficient public interest to produce commercial memorabilia. Such images also indicate an appetite for sensationalist stories as well as a specific interest in submarines. Of the 26 postcards with submarines as their subject held at the Portsmouth Record Office, 13 refer to four submarine accidents between 1904 and 1912 (including one French accident) and there is no reason to believe that the proportions are unrepresentative of the degree of public interest in submarine accidents.[36]

There is, however, the possibility that the interest in submarine accidents reflected a general fascination with being trapped, whether underground, as in mining disasters, or underwater. Reports in the *Spectator*, for example, following fatal submarine accidents such as the explosion on *A5* or the loss of *A8*, do not suggest such a morbid fascination. Instead, they expressed concern that the thoughtless reaction by the public might lead to the cessation of submarine activity by the Navy.[37] It cannot be assumed that the *Spectator*'s opinion was universally held by the public, as conflicting attitudes could coexist within British culture. The fear of being trapped underwater, however, no matter how it manifested itself, no doubt contributed to the feeling that despite the claims of pioneers like Holland, passenger carrying submarines were unrealistic, leaving Lake's *Argonaut* as the only realistic civil application.

Lake's *Argonaut* and the extensive trials he carried out, are a testament to the fact that although deep-ocean exploration in the wake of Nemo and the *Nautilus* was impossible, civil applications for seabed exploration, salvage and construction in coastal waters were viable. Indeed, Lake's first successful trial in 1897, earned the praise of the *Naval Annual*.[38] More importantly, the successful trial of the *Argonaut* in 1897 predated the demonstration of Holland's torpedo-armed design, as well as the 1898 success of the French submarine *Gustave Zede* in torpedoing a battleship during exercises.[39]

The relative technological success of Lake's *Argonaut* combined with his lack of commercial success prompts the conclusion that other considerations must have led to the militarisation of the submarine. It could be argued that the militarisation of the submarine was down to pure economics: without government financial assistance, any submarine experiment would founder. Lake's *Argonaut* was very much a one-off; the submarines that were produced – such as John Holland's early experiments in the USA – demonstrated the technological possibilities and were designed to attract government money or possibly private funding for military uses. The expense of submarine development can also be seen as a reason for the contrasting approaches to exploration at sea and on land. Although an expedition to explore regions of Africa or even the poles, could be realistically sponsored by the public or the fledgling non-governmental bodies of the pre-nuclear age,[40] this was not possible for an exploration of the deep ocean either financially or technically. Furthermore, the Royal Navy had lost interest in 'exploration' after the 1850s – although its interest had really centred on surveying and the production of charts – as the now unexplored tracts of land were distant from the seas and navigable rivers.[41]

The argument that financial considerations forced the militarisation of the submarine is rather unsatisfying as Lake did not have government backing for his *Argonaut* and it was a proven success, maximising the capabilities of the contemporary technology.[42] Therefore the militarisation of the submarine concept was due to cultural preconceptions rather than the more tangible arguments of finance and technology, coupled to a lack of any perceived need to explore the deep ocean once the safety of surface navigation was assured. On the other hand, unexplored land masses provided ample opportunity for trade, missionary work, national pride and reinforcing a sense of racial superiority over the 'inferior' peoples discovered.[43]

Even when images of Lake's submarine were used in cartoons, such as that shown in figure 2.1, they did not suggest a peaceful use of the sea, but illustrated the threat submarines posed to British seapower. It might be considered strange that an unarmed submarine like Lake's *Argonaut* was used, rather than a representation of one of the Holland-type torpedo-armed submarines, particularly as the wheels on which the *Argonaut* trundled around the sea bed can be clearly seen in the cartoon. This suggests that *all* submarines were viewed as a threat to seapower. Moreover, the cartoon demonstrates the often obsessive secrecy that surrounded submarines when used as weapon platforms – Lake's exploration submarine was simply better known to the public and therefore was recognisable as a symbol of the submarine. At the same time photographs and postcards frequently framed the submarine (or, in figure 2.3, its periscope) in a war-like setting reinforcing the idea that the submarine was only conceived as a weapon, and a particularly sinister one at that. In particular, figure 2.2 alludes to the Nelson centenary of 1905 thereby strengthening the concept that submarines had only a war-like function by associating them with Britain's premier naval hero. The postcard also suggests continuity with the Navy's (and national) history, despite the obvious clash of modernity, by the juxtaposition of the submarine with tradition, symbolised by the 'Old Wooden Wall', thus placing the revolutionary submarine and all that it threatened within a comfortable conceptualisation of national identity as seen through a common past.

"ROUSSEAU'S DREAM."

Neptune. "LOOK OUT, MY DEAR, YOU'RE MISTRESS ON THE SEA; BUT THERE'S A NEIGHBOUR OF YOURS THAT'S TRYING TO BE MISTRESS UNDER IT."
Britannia. "ALL RIGHT, FATHER NEP.—I'M NOT ASLEEP."

["M. ROUSSEAU, the inventor of the submarine warship, says, that the advantage of the submersible system would be incontestable, but that certain problems have arisen of which the solution has not been altogether realised"... "The belief of M. ROUSSEAU, however, is that the type of the submersible is perfectible, and that the difficulties will be overcome."—"*Moniteur de la Flotte*," quoted in "*Times*," January 16.]

Figure 2.1: Punch, 23 January 1901. (Punch)

Despite being almost universally conceived as a weapon by the British, when submarines appeared in a civil context they were lampooned. In March 1901 *Punch* reflecting the interest in Britain's new submarines produced a cartoon entitled 'Oxford and Cambridge (sub) river boat race 1950' illustrating a complete sub-aquatic version of the varsity boat race with submarines instead of boats. The fact that the civil uses of submarines could be used as an object of fun, indicates that the concept had been heavily militarised in British culture. The journalistic interest in submarines was likewise almost completely consumed by the thought of the submarine as a weapon system.[44] This is in itself a telling indication of the thinking surrounding submarines, as it appears from the outset that the British were unable to view the submarine as anything other than a weapon.

The combination of the literary heritage in the shape of *Twenty Thousand Leagues Under the Sea*, poor financial rewards for civil applications and the attitude of the British to exploration at sea all encouraged the militarisation of the submarine. This militarisation had a profound impact on the public's perceptions of combat and their national identity.

Figure 2.2: 'One Hundred Years Apart', 1905 Postcard. (Portsmouth Record Office)

The Submarine and British Perceptions of Maritime Combat

British perceptions of maritime combat ensured that it was not possible to rationalise the submarine or give it meaning as anything but a potential danger. When considering the impact of the submarine on national identity and the attitudes towards naval combat, there are a number of factors that need to be discussed, including growing feelings of insecurity, views on freedom and how ideals of fair play and chivalry influenced British attitudes to the submarine.

The torpedo craft and the submarine in particular undermined Britain's sense of security by enabling attacks on Britain's first and last line of defence – the battlefleet. The French success in 1898 when a battleship was hit with a practice torpedo fired from a submarine during exercises demonstrated the danger that was posed to the British fleet.[45] Previously, the battleship had been almost immune to attack except by its own kind and with the security of the battleship came the perceived security of Britain. The submarine destroyed such ideas.

The *Punch* cartoon (figure 2.1) and the postcard photograph (figure 2.3) both allude to this attack on British security. In the cartoon, Neptune warns Britannia that there was a submarine threat to her naval mastery of the sea. There is also a suggestion here of a relationship between Neptune (the sea) on one hand, and Britannia (Britain) on the other; a relationship that is special to them and excludes all others,[46] since Neptune does not warn Britannia of the dangers posed by the submarine to all seafarers. Rather, Neptune's warning refers to Britannia's ownership of the sea, an idea of ownership that had resonance within society at the time. The words 'It is on the Navy under the Providence of God that the safety, honour and welfare of this realm do chiefly attend' which are carved around the main building of Fisher's Britannia Royal Naval College Dartmouth indicate that the cartoon's dialogue reflected deeply held values for both the military and civil spheres. It can be inferred from this and the deliberately friendly tone of the cartoon's dialogue that that there was a popular perception of a special relationship with the sea and that ownership of it,[47] of Britannia being its 'mistress,' was important to the British sense of national identity and that the submarine placed this relationship in jeopardy.

Figure 2.3: 'What would have Nelson said?', Postcard 1914. The writing to the left of the gun muzzle reads 'submarine periscope...' (Unknown)

Figure 2.3 on the other hand suggests that security is being undermined through impotence in the face of an attack. In the photograph the periscope of the submarine can be seen moving in a harbour while the gun crew in the foreground stands impotent, unable to strike at the submerged weapon. The photograph emphasizes the fact that now there was a weapon other than the battleship that could take on the present arbiters of seapower and, moreover, could win.[48] Thus, any feeling of security generated by Britain's superiority in battleships would have been undermined by reported successes in submarine navigation. Just as importantly, the immature concepts of deterrence in Edwardian Britain were based on seapower and the dominance of the battleship. Submarines attacked, literally, the basis of pre-nuclear deterrence and with it a British concept of freedom. The postcard with its caption 'What would Nelson have said? 1805–1914 HMS Victory – Airship Parsival – submarine submerged' also suggests unhappiness with modernity; the ancient three-deck battleship reflecting the past glories of the Royal Navy while the new innovations threaten naval supremacy. This is significant given that by 1914 the Navy had won its dreadnought construction race with Imperial Germany, had a strong submarine arm that was increasingly operated as part of the battlefleet and was embarking on experiments with both airships and aeroplanes, and one which could lend support to a widely held impression that the Admiralty was still too conservative for Britain's good, as had been alleged in the period running up to the naval scares of the 1880s and the 1889 Naval Defence Act.

The British clearly associated their navy with freedom – a vital component of national identity. Edwardian historian John Leyland thought that the freedom of an Englishman was guaranteed by seapower,[49] and the words on the façade of Britannia Royal Naval College echoed this sentiment. The appearance of photographs such as figure 2.3 emphasized the threat posed by submarines to national identity by conjuring images of the hostile boats slipping past harbour defences to attack the Royal Navy and, thus, Britain's freedom. There was a widespread belief that

British seapower also bestowed freedom throughout the world.[50] Furthermore, seapower was not perceived as a threat to British parliamentary liberties, unlike the centuries-old dislike of a standing army in peacetime. The benevolence of seapower was even recognised in prayer. The Naval Prayer asks God for the Royal Navy to 'be a security for such as pass on the seas upon their lawful occasions…'[51] with no hint as to the nationality of those to be defended, just that they were using the sea lawfully. In this environment, even before the advent of unrestricted submarine warfare, the submarine could be viewed as a threat not just to the traditional freedoms of the British and their conceptions of national identity, but also the world because of its ability to attack the basis of seapower and through this, the lawful use of the sea and the commerce of all nations.

It is therefore no accident that the Royal Navy took to dismissing the submarine in the years before 1901 as the 'weapon of the weaker power' to the point where the phrase was in wide circulation and continued in use after the Royal Navy had publicly admitted experimenting with submarines.[52] Quite simply, only nations who were physically and morally weak would bother with the submarine, when thanks to Mahan and his supporters, everyone else knew that the battleship was the true source of sea and national power.[53] At the same time, the phrase would also bolster domestic opinion by reassuring the public that anyone who bothered with submarines was, by definition, impotent and had no chance of challenging Britain's naval supremacy. The *Hampshire Telegraph and Naval Chronicle* commented in 1911 that:

> It is unnecessary to discuss the question as to which of the great Powers is responsible for this horrible form of modern warfare – for it is horrible. A submarine is an unseen foe, which with so many advantages in its favour, creeps along under the water and delivers a blow which destroys a fine warship and sends perhaps 800 men into eternity, while affording them little chance of defence.[54]

In 1914, *Blackwood's Magazine* was of the opinion that 'Some of us find it hard to believe that any "man-of-war" which dare not overtly confront an enemy and conquer in an exchange of blows, can ever dominate the sea.'[55] The fact that opinions such as those above could be expressed between ten and thirteen years after the British submarine programme became public, demonstrates the strength of feeling about submarines. In particular, the language in the *Hampshire Telegraph and Naval Chronicle*'s Coronation supplement is particularly loaded; the submarine 'creeps', it has 'so many advantages' suggesting perhaps an unfair advantage, the submarine's target is a not an enemy warship but a 'fine warship' and there is 'little chance of defence.'

The use of the phrase 'weapon of the weak' suggests also that the submarine was seen in certain quarters as being morally weak. It was felt that the battleship encapsulated the British character. Thus, 'Encounters with great ships constitute an honest, dogged, above-board form of warfare that suits the Anglo-Saxon temperament' while the submarine 'was not an honest weapon.'[56] Attitudes to the submarine reveal how the British thought about themselves and naval warfare in the years leading to the First World War: the submarine was not just the weapon of the materially weaker power, but also the morally weaker power. The reaction to the prospect of submarine warfare clearly shows the deeply cherished belief in fair play and courage that combined physical with moral weakness: 'Victory has never so far gone to those who fight by evasion, by concealment, by striking in the dark, by waiting for the unguarded moment, – points they may score, but they have never won in the end.'[57] Such sentiments are important; they imply that sea warfare will be a conflict between warships rather than a war against commerce. It does not mean that the use of submarines in a war on commerce had not been discussed,[58] but as Churchill stated in 1913, echoing the majority view, the idea was 'frankly unthinkable' and 'I do not believe this would ever be done by a *civilised* [author's emphasis] power.'[59] Yet there was no technical, tactical or indeed strategic reason to assume that submarines would not be used as an economic weapon. Indeed, submarines were used to great effect in this role in both World Wars; only cultural attitudes can explain such a deep- seated belief in what was morally right and the need for fair play.

It is hard not to see a link with these ideals of courage and fair play and the aversion to submarine warfare with the growth of the public school system[60] in the late Victorian period, especially when considering *Vitaï Lampada*, Henry Newbolt's famous ode to the public school sportsman ethos, with its emphasis on duty, bravery and the need to 'play the game'.[61] One headmaster in the 1880s was noted for his emphasis on personal bravery: 'During match days at cricket or football he was often to be heard censuring any boy who funked a fast ball or the scrimmage at football.'[62] As Professor Dixon notes, 'the private [public] school's ethic of honour and fair play, so admirable in itself, leads to disastrous results when mistakenly imputed to those… who play the game by a different set of rules.'[63] The submarine could play to a very different set of rules from those observed by the rest of the Royal Navy.

The cult of athleticism that was the public (and preparatory) school system's greatest contribution to British culture would have had a lasting effect on notions of fair play and perceptions of the submarine. Team sports such as football was encouraged, as 'it puts a courage into their hearts to meet any enemy in the face.'[64] While the advent of long-range gunnery and the armoured ship made looking the enemy in the face a difficult proposition in naval warfare, it was impossible to even see a submarine as it crept towards its victim. By choosing to hide underwater from an 'honest' sea fight and attack while the enemy was looking the other way, the submarine was not conforming to the 'fair' way of waging naval warfare as inculcated by the public schools as well as more generally by middle and the upper class values.

The preparatory and public school's drive to produce gentlemen would have affected views of the submarine thorough the cult of chivalry that transformed views of gentlemanly virtues in the Victorian period.[65] This code of chivalry or 'manliness' can be likened to an almost fundamentalist approach to the concepts of fair play as personified by Thomas Hughes' creation, Tom Brown, which presented 'manliness' in a very attractive light.[66] Hughes, Dr Arnold, Tom Brown and the public school system portrayed a 'world of decency, independence, informality, self sacrifice and authentic inward religious faith, of games hard fought and honestly won.'[67] The chivalrous gentleman had to excel at sports, but be motivated by the pleasure of playing rather than a desire to win; he had to be brave, straight-forward, honourable, a leader – in short the typical gentleman amateur.[68] In this world the submarine would have been viewed rather dimly as it sneaked unseen below the waves waiting for a chance to torpedo the symbol of naval power without warning or opportunity for defence or retaliation. The technical requirements of submarines also made an amateur ethos a liability, an approach that would not have been equated with gentlemanly values.[69]

The public school system may also have played a part in producing a cultural predisposition against the submarine in the middle and upper classes not only through its ethos, but also through the subjects taught especially the emphasis on the classics which did not prepare students for careers involving science and technology.[70] The object of such schools, it has been argued, was 'to turn out gentlemen…who, without the necessity for soiling their hands, did not require special skills or technical ability', and there was 'an almost total neglect of science and technology.'[71] Thus, the products of this system did not necessarily see science and technology as part of their lives; engineer officers had been considered as tradesmen and had been excluded from the wardroom for many years during the transition from sail to steam propulsion. The one thing that submarines require is an interest in technical matters and an ignorance of, or distaste for, such subjects would not have helped the assimilation of either new technology or ideas. It might, however, go some way to explaining the derogatory term for the submarine service that was in use by the start of the First World War – 'the trade'. The term 'the trade' even turned up as the title and last line of each verse for Kipling's 1916 poem about British submarines – *The Trade (Sea Warfare)*:[72]

> They bear, in place of classic names,
> Letters and numbers on their skin.
> They play their grisly blindfold games
> In little boxes made of tin.
> Sometimes they stalk the Zeppelin,
> Sometimes they learn where mines are laid,
> Or where the Baltic ice is thin.
> That is the custom of 'The Trade.'

The use of phrases like 'little boxes made of tin' and grisly blindfold games' might suggest a mixture of contempt and disgust. However, the rest of the poem shows that any such contempt and disgust is mistaken as 'no flag is shown, no fuss is made' about them and:

> Their feats, their fortunes and their fames
> Are hidden from their nearest kin;
> No eager public backs or blames,
> No journal prints the yarn they spin
> (The censor would not let it in!)
> When they return from run or raid.
> Unheard they work, unseen they win.
> That is the custom of 'The Trade'.

Instead, Kipling's verse highlights the public ignorance of British submarine activities and indeed the effectiveness of what Kipling calls the 'the one-eyed death' in taking the war to the enemy.

It is also possible to see British national identity affecting the acceptance of the submarine through fiction. Aside from Jules Verne, there were numerous works of fact and fiction involving the submarine between 1894 and 1914. Some of the fiction was what can be best described as pulp fiction, such as G. Thorne's *Sweetheart Submarine* (1911), E. Turner's *The Submarine Girl* (1909),

H. Strang's *Lord of the Seas* (1909), G. Griffith's *The Stolen Submarine* (1904) and P. F. Westerman's *The Flying Submarine* (1912) and *The Rival Submarines* (1913). Others were aimed at the children's market of which H. Collingwood's *The Log of the Flying Fish* (1894) and *With Airship and Submarine* (1908) are examples. It is worth noting that with two exceptions, all the above titles were published between 1908 and 1913, by which time the submarine had passed beyond the experimental stage and was being slowly integrated into the battlefleet.

While this cluster of titles indicates that knowledge of submarines was sufficiently well distributed within a literate society for submarines to be used as a setting for fiction, it does not reveal how the British thought of themselves. Although these novels have little literary worth, nevertheless the characterisation speaks volumes to the historian. Without exception, the British lead males are examples of a clichéd public-school type of muscular Christian and even non-British heroes are motivated by duty and honour.[73] In *Sweetheart Submarine*, Lieutenant Joyce has 'remarkable scientific attainments and proven courage' and is 'obviously a leader of enterprises'; he comes from a 'good family' and is prepared to sacrifice his fiancée in the name of duty and honour rather than betray his country.[74] *The Flying Submarine*'s lead character is described as 'a fine active specimen of the British naval officer' with 'a powerful looking face that betokened courage and sagacity' who was 'devoted to his profession and a hard worker'[75] while the man who commands a hostile submarine is 'an unprincipled scoundrel and a scourge to humanity.'[76] Verne's Nemo, however, is a very different proposition, isolated from the rest of the world, but not depicted in the black and white terms that Collingwood, Thorne and Westerman present their heroes and villains.

Although Verne's creation is demonstrably far superior, a cultural explanation for the apparent literary failures of the British genre emerges. The portrayal of British submariners as clean-cut gentlemen was in stark contrast to the perceptions of submarines as essentially ungentlemanly. How could British officers be portrayed as submarine heroes when the submarine itself contradicted the concepts of chivalry and fair play that were intrinsic to the ethos of the gentleman? A gentleman could not associate with a weapon that hid from its opponents. Hiding from a fight could not be considered heroic as it contradicted the ideas of chivalry and manliness; it wasn't something Tom Brown would have done. This might account for the obscurity of these titles in comparison to *Twenty Thousand Leagues Under the Sea*. At the same time, the success of Nemo as a character could well be due to the fact that he was *not* a gentleman from the British point of view; Nemo had a deep interest in science and technology, he was an engineer.[77] Thus Nemo did not contradict popular perceptions of the sort of person that would use submarines.

These factors of insecurity, freedom and fair play combined to produce a less than enthusiastic attitude to the submarine: 'British opinion has always been sceptical' of submarines, Hurd commented in 1902.[78] A year earlier, Burgoyne, another enthusiast, commented that 'Englishmen have shown so great an abhorrence for all things connected with submarine navigation' that it would affect the sales of books on the history of submarines.[79] Even Captain Bacon, the officer tasked with introducing the submarine into British service, pointed out in his memoirs that in 1900 the submarine was regarded as a low class of weapon, underhand, unfair and un-English echoing Admiral Wilson's misquoted belief that submarine crews should be hanged as pirates,[80] a view that gained wide currency. Furthermore, describing submariners as 'pirates' would have struck a chord with the British views of fair play and firmly associated the submarine as an object of evil.

By adopting the submarine, given the strength of belief in its 'unfair' nature, the British were faced with a technology that challenged their national identity. Therefore, if the submarine was to be assimilated into the Royal Navy, it had to be absorbed in a manner that could be explained as reinforcing the British values of freedom and fair play as well as minimising any perceptions of an attack on national security. However, the militarisation of the submarine and British culture left little room for manoeuvre. The only way that the cultural threats posed by the submarine could be neutralized was to ensure its *physical* integration in the surface orientated fleet.

The Submarine and the Surface Fleet.
The submarine's relationship with the surface fleet was tightly bound up in the Royal Navy's corporate culture, and one that had relied heavily on Mahanite principles with the elevation of the battlefleet to cult status. By looking at the relationship between the submarine and the surface fleet it is possible to see the how the navy viewed the submarine both symbolically and in practice, as well as to examine how the corporate culture forced the submarine down certain developmental paths.

The Royal Navy's view of the submarine in practice is demonstrated through the submarine's participation in battlefleet exercises. These exercises can be read as a test of inclusion or acceptance. Those units exercising with the fleet gain a measure of inclusiveness or acceptance with the Royal Navy, while those that cannot, or will not, participate lose out. In many respects the exercises can be seen as a dance and the components of the fleet as the dancers, performing the ritualised acts of 'fleetwork'. The ritual of 'fleetwork', that of ships manoeuvring together in tightly controlled formations, can be described as an 'invented tradition' not only because it is a product of the late nineteenth century, but also because the purpose of fleetwork, like an invented tradition, is to 'inculcate certain values and norms of behaviour by repetition'.[81] Furthermore, it is easy to make the mental leap that as fleets have existed for centuries, there have always been precise fleet manoeuvring exercises or 'fleetwork'. However, the sailing navy that Nelson knew was incapable of achieving the precision demanded by first steam tactics and later fleetwork. Quite simply, the sailing navy – dependant as it was on the force of the wind – could not guarantee equal motive force for the ships in what might be charitably described as a formation, let alone have comparable handling characteristics, when the rate and diameter of a turn for a given angle of rudder are the basis of fleetwork.[82] Furthermore, at this date inter-ship communications had not been formalized sufficiently to allow the gyrations associated with late Victorian and Edwardian fleetwork.[83]

Yet, as Andrew Gordon has convincingly argued, fleetwork together with smartness and paint, became one of the mainstays of the new steam-powered Royal Navy, to the point where it displaced its true role as part of a naval officer's ship handling education.[84] Even today, fleetwork, or Officer of the Watch manoeuvres as it is now called, are still practised in simulators and at sea to hone confidence and ship handling skills when in close company with other vessels. The movements of these drills are similar to those of a formal dance.[85] Indeed, Rudyard Kipling in 1899 likened the steam tactics of the battleships to a 'stately quadrille' while the cruisers had a 'barn-dance',[86] with these nautical dancers first moving closer, then apart, turning, crossing and reversing their order. The formal dance also acts as a courtship ritual; those that cannot perform the steps remain outsiders and do not get to benefit from participation.[87] In this way, the submarines, by being unable to join in the dance were both outside the fleet and unable to court it. The dance also forces a degree of central control over the participants by demanding conformity in order to allow the dance to progress.

As a dance, from the perspective of the submariners, the exercises left much to be desired. The overriding aspect of the 1904, 1906, 1910, 1912 and 1913 exercises with the battlefleet was the lack of realism. Instead of exploring the capabilities of the submarines in service at the time, the exercises were organised in a manner almost guaranteed to produce results that favoured the surface fleet and the battleship.[88] The submariners were forced to dance to the tune of the surface fleet rather than having the opportunity to work out a dance of their own that suited the strengths and weaknesses of their vessels. Even the official reports thought that 'the artificial conditions of peace manoeuvres sensibly modify any conclusion that could be drawn from the recorded facts.'[89]

It would be easy to think that such restrictive exercises reveal nothing about the corporate culture and submarines. In fact, restrictions on the use of the submarines tell much about the attitudes within the Royal Navy and what was perceived as important. The restrictive nature of the exercises illustrated the importance of the surface fleet and a Mahanite strategy to the Royal Navy. By hamstringing submarines, the Navy showed that they wished to protect the battleship ethos believing in the superiority of the gun over the torpedo. In a 1910 article for *Blackwood's Magazine*, Colonel Repington declared that 'It is also certain that it must be a perfectly hated idea to senior officers of the Navy that a wretched little submarine should dominate waters in which a Dreadnought proudly sails.'[90] Repington's choice of language is important: as a supporter of submarines, he sought to highlight the lack of rationality that coloured many people's views of the submarine. The timing of his statement is equally important. Writing in 1910, he cannot be describing a knee-jerk aversion to a strange technology and a challenge to an existing mindset as was seen between 1898 and 1902. Instead, Repington is illustrating the hold over corporate culture that the surface navy had during a period of intense naval and technological competition with Imperial Germany. Submarines are the 'wretched' usurpers while dreadnoughts are the proud heirs of seapower. The easiest way for the surface navy to neutralise these usurpers was to force the submarines into joining their dance rather than developing one of their own. In this way the Navy echoed the civil prejudices about modes of fighting at sea.[91]

This does not mean that the submarines were effectively ostracized (the Royal Navy was building submarines as fast as it could), rather that the submarine was discriminated against by a highly stratified (almost class riven) surface fleet that used fleet manoeuvres to bolster its own position and importance. In this climate of restrictive exercise conditions and internal conflict, there was a remarkably realistic set of manoeuvres carried out by the submarine service without any surface fleet involvement.[92] In 1910 the submarine service embarked on a series of trials to test the ability of *C* class submarines to operate at extended ranges. The exercise demonstrated that navigational accuracy was sufficient to allow operations at distances of 250–300 nautical miles from a base.⁹³ The ability to operate up to 300 miles from a base meant that the submarines had the endurance to operate with the fleet if required and these exercises must be seen as a method of demonstrating the ability of the submarine to work with the battlefleet. The exercises involved several submarines and throughout the manoeuvres they were treated as a single tactical unit and manoeuvred as such on the surface in the manner of a division of destroyers or capital ships. Through the emphasis on working as a single tactical unit on the surface, the exercise is clear evidence that rather than approaching the subject of submarine warfare with a blank sheet of paper, the Royal Navy and its battlefleet ethos was forcing the submarine – and the submarine service – down a route that supported the surface fleet ideals.

By using submarines primarily as a surface weapon and by deploying them as a single tactical unit, the submarine service was making an obvious attempt to join the fleetwork dance. Only by being able to use and manoeuvre numerous submarines as a single tactical unit in the same way as the surface fleet of battleships, cruisers and destroyers, would the submarines be accepted. The concentration on using the submarines as a single tactical unit would, as far as the surface fleet ideal was concerned, help turn the aggressive thinking behind these exercises into something acceptable to the battlefleet ethos by subordinating submarine offensive action to the battlefleet and its dance. This shows the ingrained nature of the battlefleet/battleship ideals by making the submarines behave as much as possible like their surface counterparts. It can therefore be regarded as a big step towards an extremely close physical integration of the submarine service with the surface fleet at a tactical level, rather than a looser integration at the operational or strategic levels that would play to the submarine's strengths.

Yet efforts were made to integrate the submarine in a loose operational and strategic framework. Fisher's use of the submarine as part of his flotilla defence concept (1904–10), casting them as weapons of virtue or 'of the strong',⁹⁴ was the high point of the submarine's involvement in naval strategy rather than direct assimilation by the battlefleet at the tactical level. Flotilla defence was a sea denial strategy that would prevent invasion of the United Kingdom by establishing a close blockade of an enemy coast with torpedo craft, while at the same time allowing the projection of power into far-flung corners of the globe by the battlefleet.[95] As discussed in Chapter one, flotilla defence was probably the basis of the Fisher/Beresford dispute and the polarization of the officer corps during this period.[96] So it is unsurprising that after Fisher's resignation as First Sea Lord in January 1910 the exercises that were held that year reinforced the ideal of integration with the surface fleet. Integration with the surface fleet would have had the effect of helping to smooth over the cracks that had appeared in the officer corps as a result of the Fisher/Beresford feud.

The 1913 manoeuvres, the last before the outbreak of war, represented a sea change in the mindset of the some of the seagoing, non-submarine navy – the battleship navy. These manoeuvres, the battleship navy felt, demonstrated a new aspect of submarine warfare. There was an increased radius of action thanks to the new D and proposed E class submarines, which was seen as introducing an entirely new element in naval warfare.[97] Yet an increase in radius of action had been practically demonstrated three years earlier with the trials involving C class submarines, and been discussed as far back as 1905 with the sketch requirements for the D class.[98] Furthermore, the submarine service had been considering the offensive employment of submarines from the start of the 1904 exercises in the Solent.[99] The only explanation for a change of this magnitude is that there had been a massive cultural shift within the Royal Navy due to an increased fear of the torpedo as a result of improved technology.[100]

The 1913 post-exercise report considered that the modern D and E classes were able to impose a close blockade 'in the old sense of the word' and that there was a pressing need for increased radio communication facilities in the submarines.[101] At the same time, all the D and E class submarines were allocated to the 'hostile' fleet[102] so that they would have 'a better opportunity of doing offensive work.'[103] This shows a maturity of thought that had, it seems, arrived almost overnight. Instead of the Royal Navy trying to find a way to impose a close blockade with surface ships despite interference from hostile submarines, the report's writers had finally stumbled upon the idea that submarines used offensively and in sufficient numbers would be able to impose the cherished ideals of a close blockade in what was regarded as the Nelsonian tradition. It is particularly noteworthy that this transformation in the way submarines were conceived by the battlefleet was not due to advances in submarine technology; the *D* and *E* class submarines were incremental developments of the earlier *A*, *B* and *C* classes.

The use of submarines in a close blockade or for flotilla defence would, however, dangerously unbalance the fleetwork dance by allowing submarines the ability to operate away from their dance partners in the fleet in an independent manner. Admiral Custance was probably referring to such a suggestion when he stated that submarines were 'too untried in war to place exclusive reliance on them' and that 'the war efficiency of these vessels is apt to be over rated.'[104] Yet it is interesting that the attempt to give the submarines an independent role after the demise of flotilla defence was conceptualised through a traditional close blockade strategy in keeping with the Mahanite view of Napoleonic naval strategy: 'those far distant, storm beaten ships, upon which the Grand Army never looked...'[105] At the same time, integration would have been attractive to the submariners as it would have hinted, through involvement with the fleetwork dance, greater acceptability and status for the submarine service.

It was also noted that a submarine on the surface at night would be harder to see and hit than a conventional torpedo boat and that a higher surface speed would increase its potential.[106] Yet the emphasis on submarines operating on the surface hints at efforts to physically or tactically integrate the submarine rather than at the operational or intellectual level. More importantly, the potential underwater performance of contemporary submarines was relatively high; the 1918 *R* class had a submerged speed of 15 knots, compared with 9 knots for the *D* and *E* classes. Such an increase in submerged performance was not due to a technological breakthrough, but instead resulted from the shape of the submarine's hull being optimised for underwater rather than surface capabilities.[107] The emphasis on surface performance rather than submerged capabilities was deliberate. Jellicoe's allusion to the night-fighting attributes of the submarine in his report[108] was quite correct, as the Germans demonstrated in the Second World War, but it is the comparison to the torpedo boat that is of interest. The torpedo boat, just like the destroyer – the other mainstay of the 'flotilla' craft – operated en masse with a number of ships delivering a co-ordinated attack as a single tactical unit, whether by divisions, sub-divisions, or flotillas. By 1914 it was being publicly reported that the 'manoeuvring powers and general above water invisibility, has enabled them [submarines] to take over the duty of the surface torpedo-boat – that of delivering night attacks on the surface.'[109] Furthermore, the report's comments on the need for a high surface speed reinforce the idea of a battlefleet conceptualisation of integration and the delivery of a closely integrated night time surface attack.

If, however, the emphasis had been placed on submerged attack by submarines at night two consequences would have been apparent. First, the submarine would be slowed, as submerged speeds were lower than surface speeds, thanks to the existing designs of submarines optimising their surfaced performance. Second, there was the problem of communicating between the submerged submarines and the tactical commander. Despite the development of the fleet submarine concept from 1910 onwards and the demands for high surface speed that that non-specialists such as the Director of Naval Construction insisted upon,[110] it was not until 1913 that an effective method of communicating between dived submarines was adopted. The Fessenden apparatus that was enthusiastically taken up by the Royal Navy's torpedo school relied on a pulse of sound using Morse Code as its language to pass messages.[111] Yet, Morse Code in a naval environment suffers from one major disadvantage; it is not secure, requiring the encoding and subsequent decryption of all messages to prevent them being intercepted, which adds time to the process of passing information. Indeed the time that the enciphering process imposed on communications was such that Morse Code (as used in wireless telegraphy) was too slow for tactical rather than operational and strategic uses at sea.[112] Submarines using an underwater communication system had the added disadvantage of the sea itself which could bend and distort sound.[113] Importantly, there is no record of any exercise being held to assess the use of the Fessenden Apparatus in co-ordinating submerged attacks. Such a lack of attention to a rather fundamental problem, coupled with the emphasis on surface-handling characteristics demonstrates that surface-orientated mentality predominated.

The 1913 exercise report's comparison between submarines and torpedo boats therefore encourages the idea that the submarine was part of the fleet in the same way the flotilla craft were. From 1913 onwards, even if the submarine was being twisted into conforming to a battlefleet-dominated role, it was at least gaining greater acceptance in the corporate and public arenas. This acceptance came, however, almost completely as a consequence of the submarine being understood through its relationship with the battlefleet at a tactical level and its ability to participate in the fleetwork dance.

The conclusions reached as a result of the 1913 manoeuvres on the use and usefulness of submarines provoked reaction by some of the senior participants (the opinion of more junior officers was not sought). Admiral Sturdee gave credit to what he called the 'excellent management' of the submarine force by 'its officer' but still believed that the threat posed by these very submarines was not as serious as the manoeuvres indicated.[114] Even the use of the term 'its officer' implies a single leader wielding control over all the submarines, rather than a number of individual submarine commanding officers operating together to achieve a common aim. The *Naval Review* took the opposite view; it thought that 'In peace time exercises submarines have not had time to properly assert themselves, and there have not been enough of them.'[115] As the *Naval Review* went on to point out, just in case the message was not sinking in, 'the struggle now lays [sic] between surface ships and submarines' and that 'every year the radius of effectiveness of the [submarines] is being extended' while 'they remain as potent for evil in their own sphere as the day they were first commissioned...'[116]

The pressures of the culturally conditioned battlefleet ethos and the desire for a physical integration of the submarine into the fleet led directly to the development of the fleet submarine concept. This new type of submarine was clearly designed to work as an integral part of the fleet at sea in the same way as the destroyer flotillas and light cruiser squadrons. This twin ideal of battleships and fleetwork (which as the types of ships in the fleet increased was extended to cover all those 'in' the fleet) might also explain the desire to integrate the submarine service physically in a fleet. The ability to join in the fleet's – and therefore the battleships' – dance signified acceptance in the same way that first the torpedo boat from around 1885 onwards and then the destroyer from about 1892 onwards, had joined the dance and become physical components of the fleet. [117] The attempts to develop a 'Fleet' submarine from 1910 onwards, despite the immature nature of the available propulsion technology as well as command and control technology, has to be seen as a reflection of these ideals. Indeed, the need for physical integration with the fleet dance produced a class of submarine during the First World War that became a byword for maritime misfortune – the *K* class Fleet submarine. These submarines were characterised by many undesirable traits such as unintentional diving whilst on the surface, a tendency to dive hopelessly out of control and a great many openings in the pressure hull thanks to the need to use steam propulsion on the surface.[118] The fact that these vessels remained in service until 1931, despite their very obvious shortcomings as submarines, demonstrates very clearly the desire for physical integration with the surface fleet.

In order to integrate with the surface fleet, the submarines also required similar command and control facilities as the minor vessels of the fleet (such as the destroyers), so that the 'steps' of the required dance could be passed to them. Due to limited communications technology, this could only be achieved while the submarine was on the surface; any attempt to take part in the fleet evolutions while the submarine was dived would be prevented not just by the submarine's low submerged speed but also by the lack of communications with the surface. Yet immature technology did not prevent the development of fleet submarines. The *K* class were described as having the bridge control facilitates of a picket boat,[119] but this was still an improvement on the existing types of submarines. Given these eventually insuperable difficulties, the decision to pursue a tactical integration with the battlefleet and its dance, rather than an operational integration that played to the submarine's strengths, was due to cultural perceptions of the importance of the fleet and its components. The immature technology, although contributing to the initial failure of the fleet submarine concept, did not determine the decision to proceed with fleet submarines in the years before the start of the First World War. Instead it was the way in which the British imagined submarines and the method by which they were integrated within an existing cultural construction centred on the veneration of the battleship and the battlefleet that set the Royal Navy on the path to find a successful fleet submarine. These factors also put a different slant on the decision to appoint an outsider, Captain Roger Keyes, as Inspecting Captain of Submarines in 1910, who, in his own words, 'could be relied upon to bring the submarine service into close touch and co-operation with the fleet.'[120]

It is particularly interesting, considering the mindset within the Royal Navy, that the greatest calls for a fleet submarine came not from submarine specialists tired of being looked down on physically and morally from those on the quarterdecks of the great battleships,[121] but from non-specialists. These individuals did not understand what was technologically possible or even tactically desirable but they did want the submarine to be a physical part of the fleet. In this context, the appointment of an outsider (Keyes was the first Inspecting Captain who was not recommended for the post by his predecessor)[122] to break the submarine service's closed shop is significant. The two previous Inspecting Captains of the submarine branch had both served under Bacon during his tenure as the first Inspecting Captain,[123] Keyes on the other hand was an outsider who had no submarine experience as well as limited technical knowledge and he proved unable to stand up to vested interests within the Directors of Naval Construction's department.[124]

It was these non-submarine specialists such as the Director of Naval Construction and the Controller that demanded high surface speed above all other design characteristics.[125] By demanding high surface speed over underwater performance, technology was pushed in a particular direction to conform with existing attitudes and prejudices regarding the submarine – attitudes that were to a significant extent determined by cultural conceptions. Very significantly these non-specialists used the terminology of 'fast submarine destroyer' to describe the idea (not to be confused with an anti-submarine vessel such as the later R class anti-submarine warfare submarine) of a submersible destroyer that was capable of close co-operation with the line of battle. This conceptualisation of the submarine as a tactical or physical part rather than an operational or intellectually integrated part of the fleet was continued with the suggestion of submarine cruisers.[126] Yet the description of this imagined submarine cruiser was that it should watch for hostile squadrons, have good habitability and radius of action as well as a high surface speed to overhaul hostile vessels before diving for a submerged attack, thus taking the place of light cruisers. With the exception of a high surface speed, this is almost a perfect description of the capabilities of the patrol or overseas submarine such as the D and E classes; however, by describing it as a submarine cruiser, a whole new emphasis is made. Cruisers were important commands, with prestige and a vital role; above all, light cruisers were an integral part of the battlefleet.[127] In this light it is by no means odd that F. T. Jane, the founder of *Fighting Ships* thought in 1912 that 'The submarine battleship may appear and render obsolete the "Dreadnought" of today!'[128] Again, this indicates both the pervasive nature of the battleship ethos and the idea that the submarine could be used as a physical part of the battlefleet, although in this extreme case, physically supplanting the battleships. Jane's statement conjures up images of submarines deployed in line of battle, manoeuvring as one unit.

When the fleet submarine was deployed in the shape of the steam and battery-powered *K* class submarines in the middle of the First World War, their integration as part of the battlefleet was beyond doubt. The Twelfth and Thirteenth Submarine Flotillas, consisting of the *K* class fleet submarines were allocated positions in the cruising disposition of the Grand Fleet as well as given detailed instructions as to how and when they were to engage an enemy force as an integral part of the fleet.[129] By integrating with the fleet, the submarine became part of the traditional understanding of seapower rather than a threat to it.

Conclusion

The way in which the British understood the submarine in the period 1900–1914 was determined largely by cultural attitudes. Indeed, the only way to make sense of British involvement with the submarine at this time is through the analysis of the ideas that were in circulation prior to the launch of *Holland 1* in 1901. British culture and national identity was bound up in the attitude to seapower, with the battleship having iconic status in naval and civil perceptions of the fleet. The fleet itself was integral to British views of freedom, while British views of fair play meant that stealthy and secretive weapons like the submarine were treated with deep suspicion.

In many ways the submarine challenged too many British norms and values to gain ready acceptance and approval, and although acceptance was eventually achieved it was not wholehearted – it formed an 'other'. Approval, however, was a different matter, and it is clear that British beliefs of chivalry and fairness and the way they conferred meaning on what it was to be British and a gentleman meant that disapproval of the submarine concept was present even before the outbreak of the First World War and the use of unrestricted submarine warfare by the Germans. Indeed, the use of unrestricted warfare by a naval power such as Germany that had failed to defeat the British Navy in a surface battle, would have rammed home to the British the idea that submarines were the weapon of both the physically and morally weaker nation.

It is also clear that in terms of the production of the submarine concept as a cultural artefact, the militarisation of submarine technology played a very significant role in how it was brought before the public. This and the failure to produce viable civilian usage naturally affected the reception and signification of the submarine. However, the signification of the submarine, how it related to the formal conventions of the time, has to be considered not just in terms of how the submarine affected British views of combat or themselves, or indeed integration with the fleet, but also the cultural hinterland. The submarine did not relate well to normative constructions of British national identity; it challenged the British view of formal conventions of combat, freedom and themselves. As a result of this clash with the cultural predisposition of the British, the reception of the submarine was relatively poor and the British by and large could only relate to the submarine by conceptualising it in terms of a surface vessel.

Therefore, it can be considered that the production, signification and reception of the submarine concept together with the three areas that have been discussed in this chapter as separate considerations were in fact interdependent in many ways. The militarisation of the submarine was not inevitable, but the process had started in fact and fiction well before 1900 and the British helped hasten it with their attempts to integrate the submarine into their concept of seapower. Feelings of national and naval insecurity pushed the British to consider the submarine in naval rather than civil terms, but the images that reinforced the idea of the submarine as a weapon in turn increased British feelings of insecurity. The British view that they were the pre-eminent naval power ensured that they could only view submarines as a threat to their concepts of freedom and fair play. The need to comprehend the submarine in relation to existing ideals of naval power generated the desire to physically integrate the submarine with the battlefleet, as this would reduce the cultural threat it posed.

The fleet submarine concept was the natural result of the intertwined nature of the militarisation of the submarine, British preconceptions of seapower and the importance of the battlefleet. Once the idea of the submarine was militarised, it was a threat to British conceptions of seapower which centred on the supremacy of the battleship and battlefleet. A threat to seapower was in turn perceived as a threat to British freedom. A close tactical or physical integration into the fleet, rather than a looser operational one, reduced the threat posed by the adoption of the submarine by making it physically subservient to the imagined guarantor of British freedoms, the battlefleet.

Once physically integrated into the battlefleet, the adoption of surface fleet norms, as demonstrated by inclusion in the fleetwork dance, the submarine also became less 'unfair' and 'underhand' because the capabilities of stealth and secrecy that helped make it unwelcome to the British were not utilised in full. Instead, the adoption of surface fleet mentalities to the submarine ensured that surface fighting capabilities were emphasized rather than sub-surface ones, a phenomenon which reached its apogee in the K class fleet submarine.

The British reinvention of the submarine as a component of the battlefleet left them highly exposed, culturally, tactically and strategically, to opponents who conceived the submarine in different ways. By investing the submarine with their own cultural preconceptions and prejudices, the British found that when the submarine was used against them in a manner that contradicted such perceptions they could only understand it as the weapon of the morally as well as the physically inferior power. As a result of investing the submarine with their own cultural preconceptions, the British had great difficulty in adjusting their understanding of the submarine to the reality of unrestricted submarine warfare.

3

THE EFFECT OF UNRESTRICTED SUBMARINE WARFARE 1915–1935

'Piracy unashamed'[1]

The A14 and A11 are dual carriageways now, designed to speed motorists across the Cambridgeshire fens as quickly as possible. If, on the other hand, there is time to spare a motorist might take the local roads through villages such as Burwell and Fordham, but even then the chances are that Swaffham Prior would not be seen except as a sign as the car passed along on the B road that now bypasses the village to the south. Swaffham Prior is a small, peaceful village in the Fens distinguished by having two churches set within one churchyard, one of which – St Cyriac's – possesses a remarkable set of three stained glass windows which form the village's war memorial.

Two of the windows depict scenes from the Great War – including trenches, tanks, aircraft, zeppelins and field hospitals – while the last window represents peace, and the opportunity for man to enjoy the fruits of his labours. The experience of modern total war, even for an isolated village like Swaffham Prior, was shocking, as shown by the images in these windows. In amongst the eighteen images of war and the nine images of peace that make up the memorial, it is the treatment of naval warfare that is of particular interest. Not one of the three images of the Great War at sea relates to the clash of dreadnoughts at Jutland, an omission that is all the more striking considering the pre-war

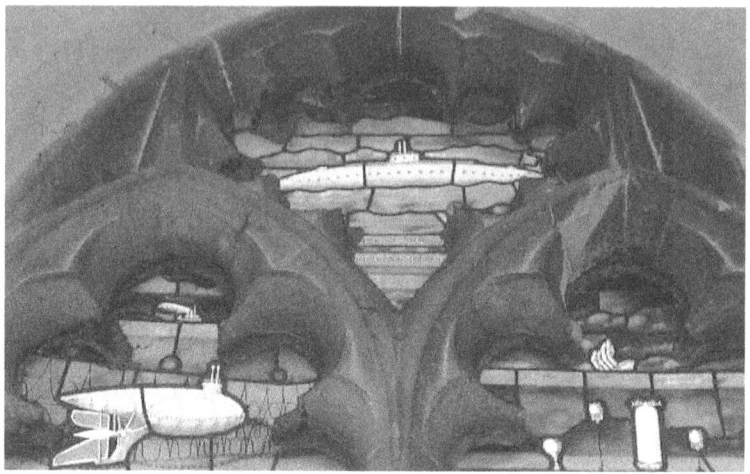

Figure 3.1. Swaffham Prior War Memorial Window, St Cyriac Church, naval images. (Author's photograph)

emphasis on the battleship and battlefleet that so consumed the British. The absence of any images of dreadnoughts either in battleship or battlecruiser form may reflect a deep disappointment with the way the surface war at sea had failed to present the public with a second Trafalgar.[2] The fact that the only maritime images in the memorial consist of submarines and an image of the sinking of the *Lusitania*, one of the most notorious episodes of the unrestricted submarine warfare campaign, must be considered to be of great significance. In addition, the driving force behind the memorial, the local squire, was an enthusiastic advocate of new technology[3] so he might well have chosen to portray the contemporary pinnacle of naval technology, the dreadnought, in one of the scenes.

As the close-up in figure 3.1 shows, all three images of naval warfare are centred on the submarine. At the very top of the window is an image that the church guide professes to be a representation of a British *E* class submarine,[4] while the image below left is an image of a German mine laying submarine caught in anti-submarine nets.[5] The last image is that of mines

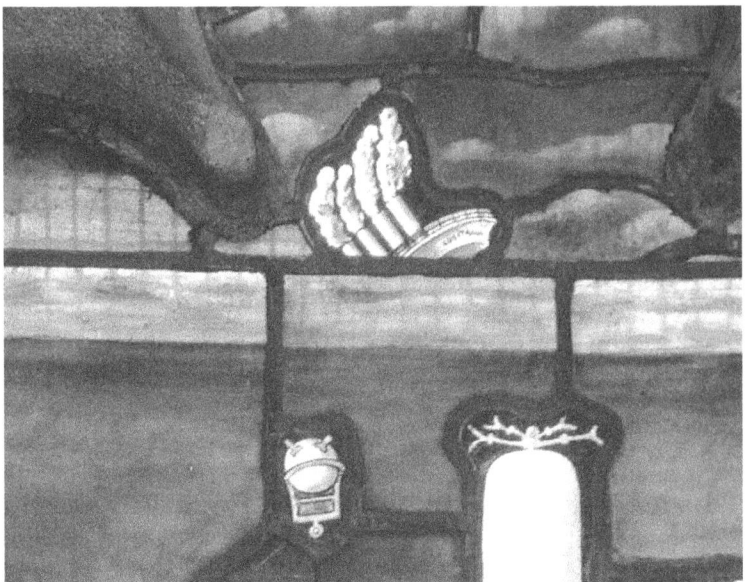

Figure 3.2. Swaffham Prior War Memorial Window, St Cyriac Church, Lusitania sinking. (Author's photograph)

with a sinking ship (figure 3.2) representing the Cunard liner *Lusitania*, which was sunk with heavy loss of life without warning by a German submarine in 1915.[6] The depiction of the *Lusitania* shows a close resemblance to a German medal struck in 1915 to commemorate the sinking, an event exploited by British propaganda and familiar to many in the immediate aftermath of the war.[7] As the subject matter on the Swaffham Prior memorial indicates, submarines and especially unrestricted submarine warfare, was a new and horrifying development, even for the inhabitants of a remote inland village.

This chapter will focus on unrestricted submarine warfare as a cultural construction and the reaction to it between 1915 and 1935. In addition, there will be an examination of the early warnings that submarines might be used in a way deemed to be most offensive to the British showing that although some of the warnings were remarkably accurate regarding the likely form of submarine warfare, they were disregarded, often because the idea of sinking non-combatant vessels without warning was unthinkable. This chapter will argue that the reason for this was British cultural attitudes to maritime conflict and non-combatants. The abhorrence caused by unrestricted submarine warfare will be discussed with particular reference to the use of the term 'piracy', and a cultural explanation for public hostility to the submarine will be put forward by demonstrating that the attitude to submarine warfare was tied up with the general civil culture regarding non-combatants and private property. Finally, the chapter will discuss the Royal Navy's reaction to the stigmatization of the submarine in British culture, as demonstrated by the types of submarine that it chose either to develop or consider for construction.

Early Warnings about Unrestricted Submarine Warfare

Perhaps the biggest question about the use of the submarine prior to the advent of unrestricted submarine warfare in February 1915 is why did the idea of attacks on merchant vessels receive so little credibility? The sense of bafflement in some historians of the period is evident from their assessments of the Royal Navy and, by default, Britain, in the run up to the First World War. On the first page of the first chapter of *Find and Destroy: Antisubmarine Warfare in World War I*, Dwight Messimer states that 'At the beginning of World War I neither side fully understood the power of the submarine as an offensive weapon.'[8] John Terraine in his well-regarded foray into the subject of submarine warfare states that, 'In the case of submarines and anti submarine warfare, it is a simple fact that, until 1915, everything about it was new; there was no previous experience for guidance, and everything was changing all the time.'[9] On the other hand, Angus Ross suggests that it was bureaucratic and parochial resistance by Britain's naval elites which was the problem.[10]

The charge that the failure to foresee the use of the submarine in a commerce-raiding role was down to the newness of the technology is misleading. First, it implies a misunderstanding of what a submarine was. The submarine was a weapons platform, just like any other warship and its purpose was to get to a position where it could use its weapons against a target. The fact that the targets were assumed to be warships does not mean that no other vessel could be targeted if desired. Second, by the time of Germany's first unrestricted submarine warfare campaign in 1915, the submarine had been part of the Royal Navy's world for 15 years, including six months of that vital trigger for the naval thought process – actual war experience. Furthermore, in 1901, the submarine had been brought into service specifically to find out what it was capable of achieving and just as importantly what could form a defence against it. Indeed, the Secretary to the Admiralty was quite explicit about this in his 1901 statement to Parliament.[11] Thus the charge of being too new and having too little experience might stand up if considering the situation in 1901, but not in 1914, or even 1915, when the British were operating the *D* and *E* classes of 'Overseas' submarines. By 1914 both British and German submarine technology had advanced sufficiently to produce submarines which were clearly capable of operating against merchant ships. Furthermore, Fisher's Admiralty was deeply committed to economic pressure as a decisive weapon[12] so why did the use of the submarine as a means of applying economic pressure come as such a surprise?

The failure to see the submarine as a commerce raider cannot be reasonably ascribed to a failure in either the Navy's personnel or training. Those officers in positions of responsibility were the best of their profession with years of practical experience in their fields of specialisation. Furthermore, by 1914, the Royal Navy had a healthy respect for the submarine – one born out of the knowledge of what it was actually capable of thanks to the 1913 fleet manoeuvres.[13] Yet only a few people appear to have considered the use of the submarine as a commerce raider prior to 1914; notably Admiral Fisher and the novelist Sir Arthur Conan Doyle. Fisher, in one of his famously florid memos, written in 1913 after his removal from office, suggested that the submarine would be used as a commerce raider and that the method of attack would not be in accordance with the prize regulations.[14] Fisher had sent his memo to, amongst others, a leading Conservative politician, Arthur Balfour. Conan Doyle seems to have independently developed the idea of unrestricted warfare and used it in the plot of a 1914 short story for *The Strand Magazine* where the Royal Navy is rendered impotent by the hostile submarines of a small navy who successfully force the surrender of Britain by sinking merchant ships without warning, thus paralysing trade and the supply of food to the United Kingdom.[15] The ideas of both Fisher and Conan Doyle were dismissed by expert opinion.[16]

Yet the fear of a war on trade had exercised the Royal Navy for years, since before Philip Colomb had argued that the United Kingdom's greatest fear was not invasion but an enemy blockade, making him in Azar Gat's view the foremost theoretician of the 'blue water school'.[17] Since 1877, considerable efforts had gone into devising methods of preventing commerce raiders from operating against trade.[18] The importance of trade had been realised by strategists with Julian Corbett noting in 1911 that:

> Anything, therefore, which we are able to achieve towards crippling our enemy's finance is a direct step to his overthrow, and the most effective means we can employ to this end against a maritime State is to deny him the resources of sea-borne trade.[19]

That Britain was a major maritime state, and therefore vulnerable to such a form of attack was not lost on Corbett who described at length historical examples of attacks on British trade and the methods employed to counter them.[20]

Therefore, the historian is faced with a paradox: the Royal Navy made considerable advances in almost every aspect of submarines and submarine warfare in support of, or as a physical component of a battlefleet, yet it ignored the one possibility that was to prove to be the most taxing use of the submarine that a maritime trading nation could face – commerce raiding. It is impossible to understand such an omission in the Royal Navy's investigations into submarine warfare from the viewpoint of operational histories. The technology was there; the submarines were there, and were more than able to take on slow steaming merchantmen after practising against fast manoeuvring warships; the fear of commerce raiders was there. The personnel were capable of assessing and appreciating the dangers posed by hostile submarines. Unfortunately, these various concepts were not brought together, a failing that Professor Dixon has called 'cognitive dissonance'.[21]

The military psychologists' label of 'cognitive dissonance' is only the name, the symptoms and the type of disease are known, but as to why the ailment took one particular form over another is not known: the 'why' is missing. This 'why', the bridge between the cognitive dissonance and the operational history of the submarine, can be found in a cultural reading of the period. In fact, what the historian is confronted with is what Robert Darnton has called the joke you do not understand, or the image that defies comprehension.[22] Unrestricted submarine warfare was not a joke for the British but it was an image that defied comprehension. In John Lynn's view, 'Technology did not dictate a single best use, but rather it presented alternatives and the choices soldiers [or, it might be argued in this case, sailors] made within that range reflected their cultural values.'[23]

Thus, it was not a failure of intellect or technology, but rather the inability to think outside cultural constructs that led to unrestricted submarine warfare being such a shock to the British. The attitudes towards the submarine during the period 1900–1914 and the revulsion in all its forms that followed the advent of unrestricted submarine warfare is symptomatic of John Lynn's difference between the reality of war and a culture's perceptions of war.[24] Just as importantly, the use of training exercises in the period before the First World War had the feel of a medieval tournament, a highly ritualised and idealistic view of battle. Such a heavily controlled representation of warfare allows the participants to play out their understanding of warfare without having to reconcile it to an unsavoury and very dangerous reality (in the case of medieval warfare) or a culturally unimaginable future (in the case of submarine warfare).

Of the warnings that the reality of submarine warfare might not conform to the British pre-war attitudes, perhaps the most important one is a work of fiction – Arthur Conan Doyle's short story for *The Strand Magazine* 'Danger! Being the Log of Captain John Sirius.'[25] The story is important for a number of reasons, not least of which was the reaction to it. Importantly, it was a work of fiction, unlike Fisher and Hall's memorandum or C. W. Domville-Fife's 'Submarines of the World' or W. E. Cairnes factual piece for the *National Review* some 14 years earlier.[26] As a work of fiction, in a popular magazine, the story would have had a far wider cultural impact than Fisher's memorandum, a piece of private correspondence or Domville-Fife's specialist work on submarines.

Conan Doyle depicts Britain as the victim of submarines, rather than their conqueror where the British fleet initially defeats the 'navy of one of the smallest powers in Europe' – a state called Norland – and establishes a traditional blockade having burnt their main port of Blankenberg.[27] Yet the British Fleet is overcome by just eight enemy submarines that had deliberately avoided an action with the Royal Navy and instead carried out a commerce war that starved Britain into submission.[28] One of Conan Doyle's final images is of the triumphant submarines passing through the British Fleet following the United Kingdom's surrender:

> The crews clustered thick along the sides of the vessels to watch us. I can see now their sullen, angry faces. Many shock their fists and cursed us as we went by. It was not that we had damaged them – I will do them the justice to say that the English, as the old Boer War has proved, bear no resentment against a brave enemy – but that they thought us cowardly to attack merchant ships and avoid the warships….War is not a big game, my English friends. It is a desperate business to gain the upper hand, and one must use one's brain in order to find the weak spot of one's enemy. It is not fair to blame me if I have found yours. It was my duty.[29]

As Colonel Repington had pointed out in 1910, four years before Conan Doyle's short story, over ten million people in London and the surrounding areas relied on food transported by sea to the Thames.[30] The capital was dependent almost completely on sea-borne transport for its fuel and raw materials; an interruption to such transport, Repington thought, might lead to great suffering and perhaps rioting.[31] By 1914 almost 60 per cent of the calorific value of all food consumed in Britain, about 40 per cent in crude weight and around 50 per cent in value was from overseas, with the working classes consuming proportionally more in food imports than other social groups.[32]

Nor was fear of famine or starvation in wartime limited to the years immediately before the First World War. In 1897 a group of landowners tried to pressure the Conservative government into forming national granaries and holding a Royal Commission on food supply.[33] The concerns over food supply in war continued and did finally result in a Royal Commission in 1903,[34] but as the notes included at the end of 'Danger!' show, in 1914 there was still a body of opinion that desired action on food supply in the shape of national granaries.[35]

Most importantly, the submarine was being used against merchant shipping, and while Domville-Fife and Colonel Repington suggested that this might happen,[36] the manner of attack suggested by Conan Doyle would have been new and shocking as it was contrary to the prize rules. The very first attack of the story involves the torpedoing of a steamer without any warning, a clear breach of the prize rules. Conan Doyle softens the blow by emphasising the large number of survivors: 'We saw boat after boat slip down crowded with people as swiftly and quietly as if it were part of their daily drill.'[37] In the second attack, again without warning, there is no such cushion for the reader with Captain Sirius announcing that 'more than two hundred, including seventy Lascars and forty passengers, were drowned.'[38] In 'Danger!' all merchant shipping trading with Britain was a target, including neutrals and Conan Doyle spells out this issue by the use of one of the few pieces of dialogue:

'Are you the Captain?' I asked.

'What the _____' I won't attempt to reproduce his language.

'You have food stuffs on board?' I said.

'It's an American ship, you blind beetle!' he cried. 'Can't you see the flag? It's the *Vermondia* of Boston.'

'Sorry Captain,' I answered. 'I have really no time for words. Those shots of mine will bring the torpedo-boats, and I dare say at the moment your wireless is making trouble for me. Get your people into the boats.'[39]

It is most significant that this attack on the American steamer is the first that was carried out under the prize rules. Possibly even Conan Doyle's vivid image of future submarine warfare could not conceive that neutral vessels, even those in a war zone or likely to be carrying contraband, would be sunk on sight, which is itself is a telling example of how existing attitudes to property would help condition the discourse on war.

Throughout the story, Captain Sirius recounts the affects of the sinkings with rising insurance rates, rapidly increasing food prices, higher infant mortality, culminating with the most frightening image for the British establishment – revolution.[40] Conan Doyle conjured up for his readers a picture of riot and murder as starving workers rampaged through the cities. He reported that 'There was serious rioting in the Lanarkshire coal-fields and in the Midlands, together with a socialistic upheaval in the East of London, which had assumed the proportions of a civil war'.[41] Furthermore, 'In the great towns starving crowds clamoured for bread before the municipal offices and public officials everywhere were attacked and often murdered by frantic mobs, composed largely of desperate women who had seen their infants perish before their eyes.'[42]

The *Strand Magazine* even contacted well-known Admirals and naval experts to solicit their views, to which Conan Doyle thoughtfully added notes.[43] All of the responses to Conan Doyle's story failed to give any real credence to the prospect of unrestricted submarine warfare. Admiral Domvile thought that submarines 'are not yet capable of the... performances described'; Admiral Penrose observed that no 'civilised nation will torpedo unarmed and defenceless merchant ship.'[44] Admiral Henderson concurred as he felt that 'No nation would permit it, and the officer who did it would be shot.'[45] Instead, the majority of respondents suggested to Conan Doyle that his story demonstrated the need for granaries.[46]

Admiral Beresford's contribution pointed out that 'We have done something to meet the dangers to our food supplies by arming some of our merchantmen, but we shall never be really secure until we have installed granaries in the country.'[47] Admiral De Horsey pointed out that he had *never wavered* in his belief that securing food supplies was an absolute necessity and that he had *repeatedly suggested* that the solution to food supply in war was the establishment of granaries with three months supply of food.[48] Admirals Penrose and Kennedy, together with the naval commentator F. T. Jane agreed, all thought that granaries were the solution to a food shortage in war, whatever the cause.[49] On first consideration, the calls for granaries imply that the respondents thought that submarines might affect the food supply in some way, but on closer reading the responses were merely a function of existing concerns over food supply, concerns that had been in circulation for much of the Edwardian period.

It might be expected that Fisher, as a former First Sea Lord, would be taken more seriously than a popular fiction writer such as Conan Doyle. This was not the case. Fisher suggested in his 1913 paper that unrestricted submarine warfare, the sinking of merchant vessels without warning was to be expected, as submarines were physically incapable of operating in accordance with the prize rules.[50] Thus the only option a submarine would have in a campaign against commerce was to sink her target, either having first stopped and searched it for contraband, or on sight. Naturally, such a suggestion had very serious implications for a maritime trading nation, particularly when involved in a period of major naval competition with a naval rival. Yet Churchill in his memoirs *The World Crisis* states that:

Neither the First Sea Lord [Battenberg] nor I shared Lord Fisher's belief that the Germans would use submarines for sinking unarmed merchantmen without challenge or any means of rescuing crews. It was abhorrent to the immemorial law and practice of the sea. Prince Louis [Battenberg] wrote to me that Lord Fisher's brilliant paper 'was marred by this suggestion.'[51]

Privately Churchill wrote to Fisher saying that:

> There are a few points on which I am not convinced. Of these is the greatest is the question of the use of submarines to sink merchant vessels. I do not believe this would ever be done by a civilised power.[52]

So ended the consideration at the highest naval policy level of a very accurate forecast of the conduct of the rapidly approaching submarine campaign.

Colonel Repington in his 1910 series of articles 'New Wars For Old' realised that British trade was vulnerable to submarine attacks: '…trade by way of sea will probably be almost suspended until the submarine menace is disposed of.'[53] Repington did not, however, discuss the methods by which submarines would disrupt trade so it is impossible to say whether he had any views on unrestricted submarine warfare. Despite the warning in his article on the submarine menace, the admittedly small section devoted to submarine attacks on trade seems to have aroused no interest.

Nor was the idea of unrestricted submarine warfare the first intimation for the British that commerce would be attacked without warning. The teachings of the Jeune École in the late 1880s had demonstrated clearly the intention to use surface torpedo boats to attack merchant vessels without warning in order to produce massive financial panic rather than starvation.[54] Indeed, the Jeune École was later singled out by the Member of Parliament, Commander Bellairs, in 1924 as being to blame for unrestricted submarine warfare.[55] The real issue, however, was the British attitude to commerce warfare. In the 1901 manoeuvres Admiral Wilson, playing the hostile or 'French' side, used his surface torpedo-boat destroyers as commerce raiders, much to the disgust of *The Times*.[56] Yet Fisher's and Repington's warnings about the likely outcome of submarines being used in support of economic or commercial warfare, brief though they were, were played down, while Conan Doyle's story was interpreted as demonstrating the need for national granaries[57] – quite mistakenly as Conan Doyle was a long-standing advocate of a Channel tunnel to solve any wartime food supply problems.[58] In the absence of any evidence of wilful neglect or culpable stupidity, the reason for failing to recognise the latent threat to commerce posed by the submarine was one of how the British constructed meaning regarding non-combatants and private property.

The Shock of Unrestricted Submarine Warfare and the Stigmatisation of the Submarine

The shock of unrestricted submarine warfare is evident not only from an isolated and unusual war memorial, but also through the language used by the British to describe their reaction to such a mode of warfare as well as their post-war responses to it. Taken as a whole, the language associated with unrestricted submarine warfare was highly emotive and heavily charged with very negative imagery. As the epigraph at the start of the chapter suggests, the majority of the language about unrestricted warfare concentrates on images of piracy. As early as April 1915, even before the sinking of the *Lusitania*, the *Illustrated London News* was using headlines such as 'Germany's Worst Piracy. The Torpedoing Of The Liner "Falaba."'[59] In his 1918 tribute to the British Navy, the journalist Archibald Hurd made much use of the piracy metaphor in the sections dealing with the menace of the submarine, mentioning it seven times in as many pages, together with references to 'inhumanity', 'barbarity', 'barbarism', 'callous indifference', and 'disregarded the laws of nations.'[60] Churchill described the events of the unrestricted submarine campaign in his memoirs as: 'To sink her [a merchant ship] incontinently was odious; to sink her without providing for the safety of the crew, to leave that crew to perish in open boats or drown amid the waves was in the eyes of all seafaring peoples a grisly act, which hitherto had never been practised deliberately except by pirates.'[61] Churchill clearly seems to have regarded the Germans as landlubbers rather than seafarers, possibly explaining their piratical behaviour. He continued that: 'The brutal features inseparable from the submarine attack on merchant vessels, and the miserable fate which so often overtook the passengers and civilian crew, inspired this [anti-submarine] warfare with exceptional fierceness.'[62]

Nor were cartoonists immune to the stigmatization of the submarine, as the savage imagery of the *Punch* cartoon (figure 3.3) demonstrates. It clearly shows representations of women drowning, with a German submarine officer looking on with a look of evil pleasure on his face. The U-boat itself is called U666, a clear reference to the antichrist and to the idea that unrestricted submarine warfare was the work of the devil. Just in case the reader of the cartoon was in any doubt that non-combatants were being murdered, the artist has thoughtfully included a representation of a merchant vessel sinking in the background.

The cartoon is highly stylised and meant to convey the horror of sinking merchant ships without warning and, as such, the likelihood of a submarine hanging around to gloat over its handiwork is unlikely. Yet despite its lack of realism, the cartoon does show how abhorrent the British found German actions not just at sea, but, as the caption suggests, also on land, particularly with regard to attacks on Belgian civilians who may or may not have been involved with guerrilla warfare. The comparison to land warfare is more important than may be realised at first, as it clearly shows how, for Britain, the meaning of warfare was produced in a very definite manner that venerated 'civilised' and 'fair' behaviour, which helps explain the stigmatization of the submarine.

A GREAT NAVAL TRIUMPH.

GERMAN SUBMARINE OFFICER "THIS OUGHT TO MAKE THEM JEALOUS IN THE SISTER SERVICE. BELGIUM SAW NOTHING BETTER THAN THIS."

Figure 3.3: *Punch*, 7 April 1915. (*Punch*)

One of the 'atrocities' carried out on land by the Germans was, of course, chemical warfare.[63] The combination of the almost simultaneous sinking of the *Lusitania* with the first German gas attack, together with the 'rape of Belgium' made Germany seem utterly uncivilised to the British.[64] The use first of chlorine gas and later other chemical weapons, produced a great deal of public hatred for the Germans and the image of gas-blinded soldiers shuffling to the rear, their eyes covered in bandages each with a hand on the shoulder of the man in front, had a profound impact on domestic perceptions of the land war.[65] The British rapidly developed counter-measures and retaliated with gas attacks of their own on German forces.[66] Indeed, the British quickly became the world leader in chemical warfare and although during the First World War they never committed themselves to the first use of a new chemical agent, they had anticipated the development of each agent used by the Germans. This allowed the British to develop counter-measures and build up stocks to allow for almost immediate retaliation. The British willingness to use methods of warfare formerly considered ungentlemanly or uncivilised, and their refusal to retaliate with an unrestricted submarine campaign of their own can only be rationalised by considering attitudes in Britain to private property and non-combatants. Chemical warfare was practised by both sides against the soldiers of the enemy while unrestricted submarine warfare fell on private property and non-combatants, hence the ready association with piracy.

The piracy metaphor was very long lived. Searches through the newspapers of the late First World War and inter-war period continually throw up references to submarine warfare as piracy. As late as 1976, an account of the Royal Navy in the inter-war period referred to Italian submarine activity in support of the Nationalist cause during the Spanish Civil War as piracy.[67] The use of the phrase is given even more importance in this particular case as the author, Stephen Roskill, was a middle-ranking Royal Navy officer at the time of the Spanish Civil War. Roskill is therefore just as likely to be revealing his own views of submarine warfare through a slip of the pen as he is to be presenting an objective view of the submarine.

Even the official history of the war on seaborne trade used highly emotive language to describe the German use of unrestricted submarine warfare, calling it 'repugnant alike to the spirit of humanity and to international law...' together with references to 'inhumanity' and 'odium' and 'indifference alike to law and humanity...'[68] Archibald Hurd, perhaps unsurprisingly, produced a book immediately after the armistice, entitled *Ordeal by Sea*, which was a highly emotive account of the war against trade as conducted by the Germans. Hurd used the epigraph of 'Piracy Unashamed' to head his third chapter in which he detailed, in quite lurid language, the revulsion of the civilised world against unrestricted submarine warfare.[69] *The Times* on various occasions between 1916 and 1937 made references to piracy in the context of submarine warfare.[70] The references to 'piracy' when describing submarine warfare was not only reserved for German actions but was employed to express general disapproval about all submarines.

However, the use of the term was not welcomed by the Royal Navy. In particular, its inclusion as part of the Root resolutions at the Washington Conference in 1921[71] which laid down the principle that submarines were under the same obligations as surface warships when dealing with merchant vessels, was opposed by the Royal Navy on the grounds that:

> Great Britain is compelled to keep submarines and a resolution of this nature will imperil our submarine personnel. Officers will not remain in a service where they have always a distinct liability of being publicly branded as pirates and in time of war have a distinct chance that in consequence of some slight error of judgement involving the destruction of a merchant ship they may be called before a foreign court and condemned offhand as pirates.[72]

The passage is interesting as it confirms that using the term 'piracy' to describe submarine warfare had indeed stigmatized the submarine. Furthermore, it also confirms the unstated assumption by the Admiralty that although unrestricted submarine warfare would not be used in future as an instrument of policy, accidents could and would happen in wartime. Indeed, the disadvantages of the submarine in identifying hostile vessels while submerged in the early 1920s, due to reliance on the visual acuity of the officer at the periscope and the limited vision that was possible through it, made misidentification a distinct possibility:

> It has to be borne in mind that it is very easy for a submarine officer to destroy a merchant ship in error. The difference may only be one of determining whether an oiler [oil tanker], for example, is a private merchant ship, or whether she is a fleet auxiliary. Submarines...have all the rights and privileges of other warships...they have the right to sink public [sic] armed vessels of the enemy, including their fleet auxiliaries, but of course excluding hospital ships.[73]

Fortunately for the Royal Navy's submarine service the Root resolutions were never adopted, although discussions in the fleet about the implications of the Washington Treaty with regard to submarine 'piracy' rumbled on for a few years.[74] The failure to adopt the Root resolutions was doubly fortunate in that although the British had not used unrestricted submarine warfare during the First World War, and had taken pains to point this out in the official histories and internal documents,[75] they did carry out unrestricted submarine warfare after 1939.

Yet unrestricted submarine warfare was not piracy. Piracy is robbery and murder on the high seas by private individuals. Unrestricted submarine warfare, even allowing for the destruction of property and life at sea is more akin to privateering, the government-sponsored act of seizure of property at sea by individuals. Privateering had, however, been made illegal by the 1856 Declaration of Paris.[76] On the other hand, piracy conjures up images of murder, ruthlessness, and uncivilised behaviour that struck a chord with the British experience of unrestricted submarine warfare. Yet the role of propaganda in the adoption of piracy as the generic term for unrestricted submarine warfare must be considered. To use piracy to describe unrestricted submarine warfare is a propagandist's tool. Although it is technically an incorrect description for unrestricted submarine warfare, it does confer illegitimacy on the user as well as providing an easily absorbed image with which to frame an understanding of the act. Using the term also played on preconceptions of proper behaviour and the treatment of non-combatants. Pirates, thanks to fictional characters such as Long John Silver are renowned for theft of private property and murder, in particular the cold blooded act of making a captive 'walk the plank.' Unrestricted warfare may not have involved theft, but it did deny the rightful owners use of their property and caused the deaths of non-combatants, a strong enough link for wartime polemists to characterise the actions as piracy. Once the image was implanted in civil consciousness it proved difficult to overturn.

The shock of unrestricted submarine warfare also manifested itself in more subtle ways such as through advertising. Players' Navy Cut cigarettes used an image of the British submarine *E9*, which had sunk a German cruiser and destroyer as part of its advertisement in the *Illustrated London News* for 20 February 1915,[77] at virtually the exact time that the first German unrestricted submarine warfare campaign commenced. Almost certainly as a result of the public outcry over sinking merchant ships without warning, Player's did not run the image again, preferring instead not to have any pictures, or to use images of aircraft – an interesting outcome for a product that proclaimed its *naval* character.[78]

The shock of unrestricted warfare also manifested itself in more general attitudes to the submarine. The first reaction of the British was to attempt to abolish the submarine. This in itself is a major contrast with the pre-First World War attitude, expressed in Parliament in 1905 by Arthur Balfour, Conservative party leader and Prime Minister, that it would not be possible to abolish the submarine.[79] Yet having failed to get submarines abolished in general at the 1919 Versailles settlement due to the intransigence of the French (although the specific case of forbidding Germany to have submarines was agreed), the British continued to promote the abolition of submarines, rather than the use of unrestricted submarine warfare. At the 1921 Washington Naval Conference, the 1930 London Naval Conference and the 1932 General Disarmament Conference at Geneva,[80] resolutions preventing the use of submarines were defeated by the French. Resolutions were, however, agreed in the 1930 London conference governing the use of unrestricted submarine warfare and the reassertion of the requirement for all warships, surface or submerged, to operate according to the principles of stop and search.[81]

The continued use of submarines and the legacy of unrestricted warfare attracted adverse comment in both the 1920s and 1930s. In mid December 1928 the *Evening Standard* published a cartoon called 'The Devil's Toyshop'. In it, the devil could be seen, surround by various types of weapons, rubbing his hands in glee at the approach of Stanley Baldwin and Austin Chamberlain. The day before the cartoon was published, the *Evening Standard*'s leading article had drawn attention to Lloyd George's comments that 'the nations of the world are heading straight for war', and the article illustrated this point by reminding readers that 'Signor Mussolini told his hearers that they read every day of the launching of cruisers, submarines and other pacific instruments.'[82] Noteworthy was the prominence given to the submarine hanging from the ceiling amongst all the Devil's 'pacific instruments', partially obscuring the cruisers or battleships, which could be alluding to the submarine's greater importance relative to other naval forces in the light of the experience of the First World War. At the same time, the cartoon concentrated on political figures rather than the admirals and generals who would have wielded the objects within the 'Devil's Toyshop.' This can be interpreted as suggesting that submarine warfare was not seen as a naval but rather a political problem that could only be solved by a general disarmament, such as that advocated at the various Geneva Armament Conferences in the inter-war period. The *Evening Standard*'s article also drew attention to the First World War as 'the war to end war' and noted the increasing tensions between France and Italy.[83] Overall, both the leading article and the cartoon allude to the circumstances that preceded the First World War which were repeating themselves: increasing international tensions and naval competition.

Despite the obvious shock felt by the British at being on the receiving end of unrestricted submarine warfare there still remains the why: why was one particular type of warfare so abhorrent to the British? In order to understand why one particular type of economic warfare could be received so negatively by a maritime power that had successfully use naval power to wage economic warfare over hundreds of years, it is necessary to examine the position of the non-combatant and private property in British maritime culture.

The Non-Combatant and Private Property in British Maritime Culture

Although it is possible to ascribe all of the pejorative language and images used about the submarine to wartime propaganda, the fact that such language and images continued through the inter-war period and beyond, suggests that more than propaganda was involved. Unrestricted submarine warfare attacked deeply held British beliefs about the conduct of maritime warfare. The severity of the shock caused in Britain by unrestricted submarine warfare provides an important insight into cultural attitudes. In the previous chapter it was argued that in the period up to the outbreak of unrestricted submarine warfare in 1915, the meaning of submarines had been constructed in a very specific way that allowed the submarine to be accepted as part of the battlefleet in order that it did not pose a threat to established ideas of seapower and national identity. With the use of unrestricted submarine warfare against Britain, a very different meaning to submarines emerged that challenged several British preconceptions about the way sea warfare was and should be carried out, and as has been intimated above, this can be understood though the British views of neutrality, non-combatants and private property.

Discourse on war presents a tension between the reality of warfare and the belief structures of a society, imposing conventions and laws on the conduct of war, and essentially trying to make reality confirm to a particular concept of conflict.[84] In the period up to 1916, there had been many attempts to modify the discourse on fighting at sea, with particular emphasis on the involvement of non-combatants and property rights – merchant shipping and commerce. Indeed, the debate in Britain over maritime property rights had, by the outbreak of unrestricted submarine warfare, been active with varying degrees of objectivity or passion since the Seven Years War over 150 years previously and can be closely linked to the efforts to civilise war at sea. As Michael Howard notes about the period up to 1914, it was, thanks to international arbitration and peace treaties, an era when 'the abolition of war, that dream of the eighteenth-century philosophers, seemed almost within reach...'[85] Just as importantly, Howard also argues that the liberal tradition of opposition to war, notably in the hundred years prior to 1914 thanks to the benefits of trade, had reached the point where it was difficult to differentiate between some sections of the pacifist and free trade camps.[86]

The culture of capture was also dependent on the historical experience of hundreds of years of experience in fighting at sea. During the battle of Trafalgar, the British managed to capture sixteen ships from the combined French and Spanish battlefleet, but only one enemy vessel was destroyed during the battle.[87] Indeed, capture had an important political purpose, providing the fleet with obviously foreign names, 'every one an advertisement for a victory.'[88] During the Revolutionary and Napoleonic Wars the proportion of the British Fleet made up of foreign prizes was never less than a quarter.[89] War experience, admittedly a century before, was that maritime weapons were not ship killers; they did not destroy ships, they incapacitated the ship's ability to fight, primarily by killing and wounding the crews until one side surrendered.[90] Indeed, with the formalisation of the prize rules as a way of gaining fortunes for the victorious ships' company, capture rather than destruction was encouraged.[91] The advent of the torpedo and modern gunnery technology transformed warships into ship killers as well as man killers, but with knowledge of sea fighting confined to an earlier age, there was no experience to overturn the culture of capture. The descriptions of the exercises held by the Royal Navy in the period 1890 to 1914 are littered with references to umpiring decisions that give the result of the battle as capture, rather than the ship in question having been sunk.[92]

Coupled with this tradition of maritime capture, both naval and mercantile, were the liberal attitudes to war and commerce that gained prominence during the long peace of 1815–1914. The repeal of the Corn Laws and Navigation Acts as part of the political pressure for free trade brought unprecedented economic liberalism to Britain. Economic liberalism was widely seen as the best way to improve relations between peoples, which entailed an openness to British goods and services, while protectionism came to be seen as an unnatural restraint.[93] As Anthony Howe has noted, 'What was most unusual in late Victorian Britain was the comparative failure by the 1890s of any alternative economic prescription to free trade.'[94] When the Conservatives campaigned for protectionism and tariff reform between 1906 and 1914, they lost every election to the Liberals with their free trade and radical agendas.[95] With free trade came the pressures for the end of privateering, achieved with the Declaration of Paris in 1856. War was seen as an activity between states, not individuals. Furthermore, the lives and property of non-combatant individuals was to be respected. Cobden thought that war should be 'brought as much as possible to a duel between Governments and their professional fighters, with as little stimulus from the hope of plunder and prize money as possible.'[96] Even Cobden's political adversary Palmerston agreed, believing that wars were won by armies and fleets, not by inflicting economic or financial losses on individuals.[97] With the abolition of privateering, even the Navy lost interest in commerce raiding, preferring to concentrate on fleet rather than frigate actions.[98]

The underlying assumption behind much of the Liberal and free trade position was that with Britain actively pursuing free trade, there was little requirement to go to war and therefore in any future conflict, the country would strive to remain neutral.[99]

With the assumption of increased neutrality came the codification of belligerent and neutral rights. As late as 1907, international efforts continued to refine these rights, in particular the various definitions and categories of contraband, allowing neutrals the prospect of continuing to trade normally, or even profit from increased trade, as belligerents sought to use the immunity conferred on neutrals to protect their goods.[100]

Although the philosophies of capture at sea and free trade were mutually exclusive, hence the extensive debate over belligerent rights, their combination in civil, political and naval consciousnesses produced the idea that the destruction of property at sea was morally wrong.[101] Furthermore, the acceptance of the view that war was between states and not individuals made the killing of non-combatants most unpalatable as 'civilised warfare strives to avoid unnecessary suffering by making a distinction between combatants and non-combatants.'[102] Thus by 1914, non-combatant status for individuals and their private property was closely related to concepts of what was fair and just in warfare.[103] These views were sufficiently strongly held by a cross-section of the country to be considered a part of British culture; it was how they understood their world.

The submarine and unrestricted warfare attacked this view in a way that was completely alien to the British, and although historically Britain had both waged and been the victim of commerce wars that targeted merchant shipping, these had involved neither the destruction of property nor the wholesale loss of life at sea. The difference in attitudes to capture under international law and the destruction of private property explains the paradox of the British favouring the use of economic pressure (Fisher's Admiralty was the latest in a long line) while being unable to reconcile it with the use of unrestricted submarine warfare. At the same time, an unrestricted submarine warfare attack on British trade was an attack not just against the British government, or one designed to create the institutional panic and social revolution that was the aim of the Jeune École.[104] Instead, by cutting food supplies it was an attack against the civil population, involving civilians in war in a way that was quite unfamiliar as well as offending their views that warfare was a matter for states rather than individuals. Such a point of view was likely to be especially entrenched in Britain due to her island status which isolated her civilians from the battlefield, unlike their continental counterparts. In such an environment the stigmatization of the submarine and the profound shock caused by unrestricted submarine warfare are easy to comprehend.

The Royal Navy's Reaction to the Stigmatisation of the Submarine

Despite the odium and the stigmatization of the submarine during and after the German use of unrestricted submarine warfare, the British continued to develop the submarine. Indeed, during the inter-war period, the submarine service saw more experimentation than in the period up to the First World War. Yet, as David Henry has noted, the service had to fight for its survival throughout the period due to political attempts to secure the abolition or limitation of submarines.[105]

The Royal Navy, however, seems to have firmly accepted the need for submarines. The title for the Royal United Services Institution prize essay competition in 1919 was 'The Influence of the Submarine in Naval Warfare' and the winning essay concluded that the submarine would remain a menace to surface warships as well as trade, and that abolition was a 'Utopian idea'.[106] As this essay indicated, the Royal Navy's reaction to unrestricted submarine warfare could not have been more different from the political and civil vilification of the submarine. Another entry in the competition pointed out that when regarding submarines as commerce raiders:

> This is the use of submarines which has chiefly caught public attention, for the reason that it has more immediate effect on them than any other, and during the war, affected the whole population of the United Kingdom. Putting all the blame for misfortunes on submarines they wish this weapon to be abolished at the Peace Conference, and yet

are quite ignorant of the causes of its success and its probable effect on future warfare.

Attacking enemy commerce is a legitimate act of war and has always been used by this country and others for attaining their object.[107]

More importantly, it was felt that 'the question of sinking enemy merchant ships is perfectly justifiable' but that there was a distinction between enemy and neutral shipping.[108] The essay competition was not the only example of professional journals considering the impact of the submarine. During the inter-war period there were more than a dozen articles in the *Journal of the Royal United Services Institution* relating to various aspects of submarine warfare, while the *Naval Review* produced ten essays on the subject.

What is missing from the articles on submarine warfare in the semi-official journals, such as the *Naval Review* and the *Journal of the Royal United Services Institution*, is the sense of outrage, anger and stigmatization of the submarine that characterised discussion outside professional circles. Nor was this dispassionate approach limited to the service journals. Admiral Jellicoe's account of the German submarine campaign, *The Crisis of the Naval War*, is remarkable for its lack of emotive language, especially when compared with that of the journalist Archibald Hurd's populist volume *Ordeal By Sea*. In *Ordeal by Sea* the reader was treated to a 58 page tirade against the German unrestricted submarine campaign as well as to chapters entitled 'Piracy Unashamed', 'The Murder of Captain Fryatt', 'The Violation of the Red Cross', and 'The Last Betrayal'.[109] In *The Crisis of the Naval War*, however, the unrestricted attacks are called 'depredations' while a two-paragraph discussion on unrestricted warfare contains no emotional language, or indeed judgements on the morality of the German action.[110]

Perhaps the dispassionate appraisal of the submarine was due, in some degree, to increased familiarity with the submarine. The Royal Navy and its submarine service entered the peace of the interwar period with five distinct types in service: monitor (the

M class), anti-submarine (the *R* class), fleet (the *K* class), minelaying (a variant of the *E* class), and patrol (everything else). The harbour and coastal defence concepts of the Edwardian era had been swallowed up by the patrol type and soon the cruiser and aircraft carrying submarines would make their brief appearances with the Royal Navy, while serious consideration was given to specialist harbour-attack midget submarines.[111] By 1924, the programme for post-war construction had solidified into plans for fleet submarines, cruiser submarines and patrol types (including those fitted for mine-laying).[112] By looking at each of these three types, as well as the proposals for the midget submarine, the manner in which the Royal Navy gave their submarines meaning in the light of the experience of unrestricted warfare can be understood.

During the interwar period the submarine service continued to tinker with the idea of a fleet submarine; indeed not only was the *K* class kept in service, but an allegedly improved version, *K26*, was completed, which remained in service until 1931. Regarding the doctrine surrounding the fleet submarine, it was argued that 'the principal duty of the Fleet submarine is to attack the enemy Capital Ships with torpedoes.'[113] By 1924 it was felt by the Naval Staff's Tactical Section that:

> Fleet submarines are not a defence against enemy Fleet submarines, nor are they an essential tactical unit of a fleet, so that possession of this type of craft by a possible enemy does not necessitate the British Fleet having them, as is the case, for example, with Light Cruisers or Destroyers.[114]

Three years later at a meeting of the Sea Lords to discuss future submarine policy, it was noted that although Fleet submarines were desired, it was felt by the Assistant Chief of the Naval Staff that 'it was not entirely clear that in these days of small fleets of quick manoeuvre the submarine could be used tactically.'[115]

The overriding impression from the minutes of the 1927 Sea Lords' meeting is one of uncertainty: Fleet submarines might be useful, and although not expressed as such, there is the sense that the submarine was regarded as a 'force multiplier' in an environment where the power of the battlefleet was constrained by treaty. Yet the Sea Lords were unsure whether what they were looking for in a Fleet submarine, notably a high surface speed to keep up with the battlefleet, was technically possible.[116] This uncertainty led to the policy regarding Fleet submarines being described in 1934 as 'a kind of see-saw policy' since the end of the First World War.[117] Despite the uncertainty over the Fleet submarine the idea that the submarine should be part of the battlefleet remained strong, so strong indeed that in the 1930s, a class of three diesel electric-powered Fleet submarines, the *Thames* (or *River*) class, was constructed, but they proved to be too slow for fleetwork with the battlefleet.[118]

The idea of the submarine as a force multiplier, even if an unspoken one, is an important and subtle change in the way the Royal Navy understood submarines. Instead of viewing submarines with regard to their ability to participate in the fleetwork dance that characterised the pre-First World War development of the submarine in Britain, and the threat or otherwise the submarine posed to the Royal Navy's command of the sea, the submarine was now seen as an opportunity to maximise the power of a smaller fleet even if it was not a physical part of the battlefleet in the way that cruiser and destroyer screens were. It is also important that this avenue of thought and tactical development precluded the use of submarines as a commerce raider. Letters to the Commander-in-Chief Mediterranean Fleet and Commander-in-Chief Atlantic Fleet pointed out that one of the submarine's roles was the 'exercise of control [of the sea]' with the rider that this did not include attacks on merchant shipping.[119]

One of the developments that caused a great deal of discussion was the perfection of a 'cruiser' submarine, with Rear Admiral Nicolson, the Rear Admiral (Submarines), describing it 'as just a great advance in submarines as the original "Dreadnought" was in her day to the previous type of battleship...'[120] This was a strong endorsement of a type of submarine at a time when the Royal Navy's solitary example of this type, *X1*, still had not completed her trials and was something of an unknown quantity. The cruiser submarine concept has been written off as a failure but this disregards the impact of culture and the tensions that war experience set up regarding the submarine. In short, *X1* can be seen as an attempt to reconcile conflicting naval and civil cultures and their concepts of the submarine.

The Royal Navy needed to justify the retention of its own submarines (rather than explain away the failure to abolish them) in a manner that would be acceptable to public opinion, which even junior officers had noted was extremely powerful.[121] The cruiser submarine can be seen as a way of reconciling these conflicting cultures. It was anticipated that action against commerce would almost certainly form part of any future conflict, just as it had in the past,[122] and war experience had demonstrated that the submarine was a good commerce raider. However, the Royal Navy was not able for political reasons – which were based on cultural preconceptions regarding non-combatants and property rights – to carry out unrestricted submarine warfare with enemy vessels being sunk on sight. Instead, submarines had to have the appearance of observing the niceties of maritime warfare and that meant stop and search.

To carry out a policy of stop and search, submarines needed a heavy gun armament to encourage merchant ships to 'heave to' in order to allow access for the boarding party, as the alternative was the unacceptable torpedoing. *X1* had an exceptionally heavy gun armament in the form of two twin 5.2 inch gun mountings, complete with advanced gunfire control systems (contemporary destroyers had four 4 inch guns in single mountings). *X1* did, however, have a relatively light torpedo armament. The heavy gun armament would have allowed her to carry out the acceptable cruiser form of commerce raiding, as the Rear Admiral (Submarines) noted in 1926:

> 6. In this consideration it should be noted that she could easily carry supernumeraries in sufficient numbers to form a crew of the first Merchant ship captured and in such ship she could accommodate the crews of successive ships

captured and sunk; such ship keeping more or less in company until completely loaded with the crews of destroyed vessels, when they could be given a course to the nearest land and the supernumeraries re-embarked in X1.[123]

Note the emphasis on safeguarding enemy or neutral mariners following the *capture* and only then the *destruction* of their vessel. In this way, *X1* could wage a campaign against merchant shipping and get round the lack of prize crews that had bedevilled previous attempts by submarines to operate within what were considered civilised rules. At the same time, it took into account that, thanks to the decisions at the Washington Conference, which were no doubt aided by the flood of pejorative language that had accompanied the German unrestricted campaign, a merchant ship's lifeboats in bad weather or out of sight of land were not a place of safety for the crew. Thus, the British were examining the employment of submarine warfare in ways that did not offend cultural sensibilities over non-combatants and private property rights, while regaining the ability to wage economic warfare.

The cruiser submarine concept ultimately foundered not on the impracticalities of prize crews for captured vessels, or necessarily on money (as it was recognised that *X1* was an experiment),[124] but on the fact that perfecting the tactical employment of a cruiser submarine concept would not benefit Britain. As the Director of the Tactical Division pointed out, a successful cruiser submarine would disadvantage Britain more than any other nation because:

> The submarine cruiser is undoubtedly the most effective type of craft that can be produced by our enemies to menace our Seaborne Trade. For this reason it is a matter of utmost importance that Great Britain should refrain from advertising the utility of such a craft to the world at large.[125]

Such a policy statement clearly has parallels with the Royal Navy's attitude to the development of the submarine prior to 1900. Of course, the Director of the Tactical Division was making an assumption that the limitation by treaty of patrol type submarines carrying out an anti-commerce campaign would actually be a deterrent. Such an assumption is not necessarily as naïve as it first seems, but not because of the British attitude to non-combatants and private property on the sea. Instead, the assumption that a lack of cruiser submarines would deter unrestricted submarine warfare might well have been based very firmly on the experience of the First World War – when the reaction to unrestricted submarine warfare was instrumental in bringing in neutral powers such as the United States on the Allies side.[126]

Although eventually the decision was made to pursue the overseas/patrol submarine concept in the inter-war period, this was not necessarily for the reasons of financial stringency that David Henry suggests.[127] In many respects, the decision to continue the incremental development of the patrol type submarine can be interpreted through the failure of other concepts that were more amenable to British culture, both naval and civil. The cruiser submarine could not be developed because once successfully introduced it was viewed as being exceptionally dangerous to British commerce. On the other hand, the fleet submarine, which complemented rather than challenged British views about maritime warfare, could not be pursued for technical reasons: it proved impossible to produce a propulsion system for the Fleet submarine that was fast enough, either above or below the surface, to keep up with the Fleet without relying on steam power. Thanks to the less than joyous experiences of operating the *K* class in war and peace, steam power for a submarine would remain unacceptable until the advent of the marine nuclear reactor. Therefore, the only type of submarine that remained practical was the patrol submarine.

The last type of submarine to be considered is the only type that was not developed during the inter-war period – the midget submarine. This was not a new concept for harbour attack but had had been suggested in 1914 by Commander Godfrey Herbet.[128] Herbet's concept was for a two-man submarine to attack the German fleet at anchor, thus negating the reluctance of the German High Seas Fleet to come out and engage the British Grand Fleet. If the idea had been developed, it would have also negated the possibility of the Grand Fleet having its long awaited opportunity for a second Trafalgar, with the German High Seas Fleet playing the part of the French and Spanish. The fact that the concept was not taken up was due in no small way to the realization that the midget submarine in Herbet's proposal was essentially a suicide craft, and Churchill as First Lord, refused to go ahead with it unless there was a reasonable chance that the submarine's crew would survive.[129]

In 1924, Max Horton, who had achieved some fame and indeed notoriety while commanding *E9*, proposed midget submarines for harbour attack roles while he was commanding a submarine squadron. Having ironed out the problems of crew survival that had sunk Herbet's proposal ten years earlier, he felt that:

> The Devastator aims at being a weapon which will deal a vital blow to a fleet inside a defended harbour or operating on the coast. Used in this way, *it is more our weapon than that of any foreign power, as such an attack would require command of the sea* [my emphasis].[130]

The fact that the midget submarine was 'more our weapon' and viewed as being subsidiary to, although part of, the command of the sea is telling. First, it shows the constraints that cultural constructs about acceptable methods of warfare placed on the tactical development of the submarine in Britain. By ruling out unrestricted warfare the British ensured that continued attempts were made to integrate the submarine into the fleet weapon system. Second, it also shows an independent offensive spirit and doctrine that were at odds with the concept of the Fleet submarine, both in its pre and post-First World War forms and owes more to the spirit of the independent operations of the overseas/patrol submarines.

Such a difference in operational concepts suggests a breakdown in the corporate culture regarding the submarine. On one hand, the official mind supported the fleet submarine concept as it continued the long-standing efforts to understand the submarine through a battlefleet perspective while the supporters of the midget submarine (and patrol submarine) were effectively challenging the battlefleet hegemony that had been attempting to subsume the submarine since before the First World War. Yet the proposals for the midget submarine were phrased in such a way so as to appeal to the battlefleet ethos; a midget submarine attack 'required command of the sea.'[131]

It is clear, therefore, that the Royal Navy put a great deal of effort into making submarines acceptable at the corporate level during the inter-war period. The corporate efforts to produce a justifiable face to submarine warfare were constrained by the need to present the submarine in a light that would be acceptable to both political and civil cultures in the light of the First World War experience of unrestricted submarine warfare. The overall impression of the corporate culture is one of increasing approval for the submarine, tempered with the desire not to upset the iconic status of the battleship. In this framework the decision to start giving submarines names rather than numbers becomes important.

In 1926 the Admiralty was faced with its first major post-war construction programme. The question arose whether the new patrol submarines should receive names or numbers while the *O* class prototype was still under construction – apparently as a result of an Australian decision to call their two new *O* class submarines *AO1* and *AO2*,[132] following on from previous practice. The First Sea Lord, Earl Beatty had gone on the record on 3 December 1925 as believing that '…the practice should now be adopted of naming our Submarines. No sentiment and no historical interest can be attached to a number. Also their size and complement appear to merit a name.'[133] As a result of this discussion the Admiralty Board decided to commence naming submarines starting with the O class as of 21 December 1925, and *O1* was renamed *Oberon* prior to her launch in September 1926.

Earl Beatty's statement is not, however, as straightforward as it might first seem. The idea that the O class size and complement appeared to merit a name is not borne out by the data. The full load displacement of *O1* was 1490 tons and the follow on members of the class displaced 1784 tons fully loaded, while the ship's company mustered 56 officers and men.[134] The *K* class, laid down over ten years previously, had a full load displacement of 2565 tons while the sole example of the batch II *K* class, the post-war *K26*, displaced 2770 tons.[135] Both batches of the *K* class also had larger complements than the O class with 58 and 65 officers and men respectively.[136] The *M* class, like *K26* laid down during the war, but completed afterwards were of similar size to the *K* class.[137] Therefore, the idea that the size and complement of the O class meant these new submarines warranted names is contradicted by the facts.

Thus, Earl Beatty's view that no sentiment and history can be attached to a number increases in importance. Given the desire for names with a history that a ship's company could venerate, it might be expected that these first names to grace submarines would have been important names from the Navy's past. Yet the actual names used did not necessarily reflect the views of the First Sea Lord.

Of the nine names selected for the O class, including the two for the Royal Australian Navy (RAN), five were new names that had never before been used for a warship: *Olympus, Oswald, Otus, Otway* (RAN) and *Oxley* (RAN), none of which gave the crews of these submarines much history to appreciate. Indeed, with the exception of *Odin,* none of the names that had been used before had been applied to what might be considered major warships. Given the previous histories of the nine O class names, it is hard to square the history of these names with the desires of the Admiralty Board. The names used were not ones whose histories might inspire crews and although they shared a classical theme, another rationale must have been at work behind the selection of the names. Indeed, they were very ordinary in terms of their previous use, their history and achievements.[138] It is therefore likely that the very ordinariness of these names was the deciding factor as they did not allow the submarines to project an important image on top of the fillip they had received in gaining names in the first place. These names give an image of a minor supporting role. The follow on classes of the *P* and *R* submarines hold up this image of a bit-part player on the naval scene: only three out of the ten names had been used for any vessel larger than a fifth rate, destroyer or sloop.[139] With such insignificant histories there were hardly grounds for the submariners to feel a special attachment to the first names used for British submarines, despite the First Sea Lord's intentions.

Conclusion

The reaction to unrestricted submarine warfare in the period up to the Anglo–German Naval Agreement of 1935 and the start of serious rearmament by Britain from the mid-1930s onwards, can be characterised by the tensions that different cultural preconceptions raised over the employment of submarines. In the hundred years prior to the use of unrestricted submarine warfare, the British had come to understand the world through the medium of free trade and capture at sea, both of which emphasized in one way or another the preservation of private property. The submarine, through unrestricted warfare, directly attacked these ideals and involved the civil population in a mode of warfare that was totally unfamiliar to them.

In terms of the production of submarine warfare, it is very important to remember that the British did not implement unrestricted submarine warfare, they experienced it. Nor did they use it as a reason to launch a retaliatory campaign in the manner of chemical weapons. This says much about the British attitudes to war – chemical warfare against enemy combatants was acceptable, but a submarine campaign that struck both directly and indirectly against non-combatants was not. Indeed, there would not be as overt a threat to the British civil population until the development of effective strategic bombing that could attack both war-making potential and the civil population as indiscriminately as unrestricted submarine warfare.

The signification of unrestricted submarine warfare is bound up with the fact that it obviously attacked the conventions, both economic and legal, of the Victorian and Edwardian period, again transforming it into an 'other'. The British, thanks to their understanding of free trade and the earlier concepts of capture at sea had a very strong view of how maritime war should be conducted regarding private property and the need to protect non-combatants, with very close parallels to the concepts of the gentleman and chivalry discussed in the previous chapter. The British understood their world in such a way that unrestricted submarine warfare could not fail to be abhorrent to them. The tensions that unrestricted submarine warfare caused in relation to these cultural constructions not only greatly affected the reception of submarine warfare, but also helped cause the somewhat schizophrenic attitude to the submarine. Civil and political sensibilities called for abolition, while the submarine service contradicted this by seeking to develop the submarine in a manner that did not offend cultural constructs regarding the proper conduct of war at sea by again assimilating the submarine through the battlefleet rather than as an economic weapon. In the inter-war period, however, unlike before the First World War, the submarine was tacitly acknowledged as potentially a force multiplier at a time of naval armament limitations rather than a threat to British command of the sea. The tensions that unrestricted submarine warfare caused in British culture can also been seen in the reception of submarine warfare both during the First World War and in the inter-war period.

The civil and political reception of unrestricted submarine warfare was almost universally highly unfavourable to the point of vilification. In particular, the constant comparison with piracy gave the submarine as well as unrestricted warfare a degree of stigmatisation that lasted for the entire interwar period. The level of shock and stigmatisation that was generated shows how deeply held were the views on non-combatants and private property in the wider culture. The Royal Navy, on the other hand, did not attempt to stigmatize the submarine as a result of their war experiences, instead they preferred to emphasize the fact that they did not wage that form of warfare, nor would they do so. The increasing levels of acceptance and approval of the submarine at the corporate level were also seen in the decision to name submarines. Yet the names given to submarines were not classic names with long and glorious histories in the Royal Navy, instead they were names that had graced minor war vessels, thus reinforcing an image of the submarine still being subservient to the battlefleet.

Overall, the British experience of unrestricted submarine warfare exceeded their worst expectations; the weapon of the morally and physically weaker power had traumatised the British. The submarine had fundamentally challenged their views on the global economic system, their views on the proper form of maritime warfare and through its attack on the whole population their sense of security that already had been under pressure since the 1900s. It would take, however, another war, another unrestricted submarine warfare campaign and new and more frightening challenges to the British conceptualisation of warfare to reduce the odium and hatred that the bulk of Britain reserved for the submarine.

4

THE SUBMARINE 1935–1965
'A momentous change in the attitude to the submarine'[1]

At around 5pm on 9 April 1940 the German merchant vessel *SS Amasis* (7,129 gross registered tons) was sailing through the Skagerrak in the vicinity of 58° 13' North, 11° 13' East, watched, with considerable interest, by a submerged British submarine. The *Amasis* was sailing out of the obscurity which had blanketed her career until then as she was about to become the first merchant ship to be sunk without warning by a British submarine – the British *S* class submarine *Sunfish*. The Captain of the *Sunfish*, the rather unfortunately named Lieutenant Commander Slaughter, had been observing the German vessel through the periscope while the signal from the Vice-Admiral Submarines authorising attacks without any warning was decoded and read out to him. Just as the signal had finished being read 'the sights came on…so I fired.'[2]

The decision on 9 April 1940 to allow British submarines to carry out some form of unrestricted submarine warfare is one of the most important events in the story of how the British understood submarines. In the space of just over seven months of combat experience during the 'Phoney War', the British overcame their long-standing opposition to unrestricted submarine warfare and embarked on a series of submarine campaigns extending from home waters through the Mediterranean to the Far East. However, the importance of the decision to embark on an unrestricted campaign does not mark the start of a period when the perceptions of the submarine as a threat to Britain were slowly revised. From 1935 onwards a shift had begun in how the submarine was viewed by the British, and increasingly it was seen as an acceptable means of exercising seapower. 1935 was also the year of the Anglo–German Naval Agreement, with the final rejection of one of the foundation stones of the British response to submarine warfare, that of abolition, and its replacement with a degree of acceptance, although in part conditional on the limitation of submarine size, numbers and weapons. Thirty years later in 1965, the British submarine service entered the nuclear age – a time when the capabilities and potential of the submarine changed forever – forcing a reinvention of how the submarine was understood at both the corporate and civil level.

These two key dates in understanding the perceptions and preconceptions about submarines and submarine warfare encompass a period that saw the almost total reversal of British attitudes to submarines. During this time, the policy to abolish the submarine was itself abolished. In the Second World War the British embarked on a successful and vigorous unrestricted campaign of their own against Axis merchant shipping. In the post-war period, they reinvented their perceptions of the submarine at the corporate level. After years following a course that only led to perdition, during this thirty-year period the submarine turned around and started towards redemption.

This chapter will investigate the impact of the Anglo–German Naval Agreement on British views of submarine warfare and will read the event from a cultural perspective so as to understand how the British gave submarines meaning at the end of the interwar period. The Anglo–German Naval Agreement, with its acceptance, indeed its encouragement of German submarine rearmament, marks a major shift in the corporate attitude to the submarine: was this shift mirrored in the wider (and possibly less well informed) civil and political cultures? The chapter will also examine the move towards a British acceptance of unrestricted submarine warfare and try to establish whether such a move was a retaliatory measure against an established German submarine campaign, or a final acceptance of the realities of modern submarine warfare. With this acceptance, was there a clear breach between the attitudes of the official mind and the mass of the public? The chapter will look at the impact of the submarine in the post-war period, but prior to the introduction of nuclear power and sea-based nuclear weapons into British service. What lessons did the Royal Navy learn from the Second World War and how did this change corporate attitudes to the submarine? By looking at these areas, the degree of reinvention of attitudes or move towards redemption, both civil and corporate, can be assessed.

The divergence between corporate and civil cultures makes the period between 1935 to 1965 so important to the cultural impact of the submarine. Until 1935, both corporate and civil cultures had viewed unrestricted submarine warfare as something abhorrent – the submarine was a threat to the battle-fleet that had to be contained. The corporate response had been to attempt to assimilate the submarine via the fleet and cruiser submarine concepts in ways that supported British conceptualisations of sea warfare, while the civil response was to roundly condemn the submarine as a weapon. From 1935 this started to change, with corporate culture embracing the submarine first as part of a means of controlling hostile rearmament, and then, rather enthusiastically, as a means of maintaining control of the sea.

The civil culture, however, remained generally opposed to the submarine, oscillating between outright hostility and ambivalence; the use of the submarine in naval diplomacy was greeted with dismay in some quarters, and the use of German unrestricted submarine warfare provoked a hostile, if muted, response. Only with the failure to sink a German liner without warning was there an upsurge of interest in, and condemnation of, the Navy's lack of action by some sections of the press. Once the British started an unrestricted campaign the civil response both during and after the war was to ignore it. In the post-war period the civil culture only really responded to the submarine as a tool for demonstrating British superiority; little notice was paid to the change in corporate perceptions of the submarine. As a result of this divergence the chapter will have to address the operational issues and concerns that prompted the corporate reappraisal of the submarine, as well as examining the oscillations in civil culture.

The Anglo–German Naval Agreement

As Joseph Maiolo points out in *The Royal Navy and Nazi Germany 1933–39*, the Anglo–German Naval Agreement (AGNA) has been described variously as a blunder, the cause of the failure of the 'Stressa Front', and the first act of appeasement.[3] Maiolo argues, very persuasively, that the criticisms of the agreement do not stand up and that the AGNA was 'consistent with an elaborate programme that aimed to adjust the international order to advance Britain's long-term prospects as the world's leading sea power.'[4] Naturally, British attempts at every naval armaments conference since the end of the First World War to abolish submarines can be seen as part of, or indeed the precursor to, this policy in the mid-1930s. By attempting to get submarines abolished as part of naval disarmament conferences in the interwar period, the British were seeking to do away with the strongest potential challenge to their traditional views of seapower, centred on the battleship and battlefleet as part of a balanced, multi-purpose fleet. Yet there is a fundamental difference between the AGNA and Britain's previous efforts to abolish the submarine: the treaty made no attempt to abolish the submarine, but instead imposed a limit on its numbers.

The most obvious conclusion that can be drawn about the treaty is that at a corporate level the submarine was seen not only as a lesser threat, but also given the terms offered to Germany, as an important part in obtaining the agreement. The First Lord of the Admiralty, Sir Bolton Eyres Monsell, said publicly that German submarine construction was not a matter for concern. In a BBC broadcast the First Lord pointed out that as other countries had submarines and refused to give up that right (a jibe aimed at the French and Italians), Germany 'must clearly have the right to build submarines...'[5]. In a move that can only have been an effort to shore up public support, Eyres Monsell was also at pains to point out that if Germany felt the need in the future to build more submarines:

> ...the whole German submarine tonnage at all times will be within the total tonnage calculated from the ratio 35 to 100; that is to say, the German Government will only exercise the right to build more than 35 per cent of our submarines at the expense of tonnage in some other category.[6]

Or, if Germany built more submarines it would reduce the numbers of ships that could be built in other categories, making their fleet unbalanced and easier for their surface units to be defeated.

The First Lord's lack of concern was not shared by others. *The Times* thought that:

> It is sure to cause considerable surprise that, in the very weapon which created by far the greatest danger to British safety during the War, Germany may, in an emergency and after discussion with us, build up to a strength which, if concentrated in home waters will exceed British submarine strength immediately available.[7]

Nor did the *Morning Post* consider German submarines a good thing as although they were ideal for the Baltic, they 'could in sufficient numbers, also dominate the North Sea and the English Channel.'[8] Others, such as the *New Statesmen and Nation*, were more concerned with the less than happy noises coming from other European countries at Britain's unilateral agreement,[9] reflecting the internationalist perspective of the British political left of the time. Indeed, the AGNA was considered as one of the main reasons why the Stressa Front broke up.[10]

The condemnation of the 1935 decision to allow Germany to build submarines was, however, reasoned and moderate in tone and without the hysteria that had been previously associated with submarines.[11] In particular, the widespread 'piracy' jibes of the First World War and its immediate aftermath were absent. Indeed, some commentators pointed out that the submarine was only one of many problems facing Britain. Admiral Sir Herbert Richmond treated himself to a rant in the *Fortnightly Review* about the deficiencies of Naval policy since the end of the First World War and noted that 'It is not, however, the submarine alone which threatens shipping in the narrow seas.'[12] Richmond's next sentence made clear that he was considering the threat to trade rather than the constraints enemy submarines placed on a battlefleet when he stated that 'flotilla craft is not only not a less, but in certain circumstances a greater, threat to commerce.'[13] The *Spectator* agreed with Eyres Monsell in blaming the attitudes of other powers for the need for Germany to have submarines:

> Here other countries have the situation in their own hands. This country desires to abolish submarines altogether. If they accept that, then Germany can have none at all – for 45 per cent [of the British submarine strength] of nil is nil.[14]

In other words, if the French and Italians hadn't opposed every attempt to abolish the submarine since 1919, the Royal Navy would not have had any submarines and Germany would not have had an argument for building her own. Hector Bywater, in an article entitled 'The German Naval Renaissance' for the Nineteenth Century, thought that the German submarines did not pose much of a threat as their small size (only about 250 tons) meant they were 'not suitable for ocean service, but they would be dangerous enough in the narrow seas.'[15] The choice of 'ocean service' by Bywater is important as it shows an association of size and endurance with the ability to threaten Britain. Small German submarines based on the far side of the North Sea would have to brave the Dover Straits or travel around the north of Scotland before they could even think about threatening British oceanic trade.

All the noise and bluster, both at the time and since, about the 1935 agreement and its role in appeasing and encouraging Nazi Germany,[16] has helped to obscure the key point recently raised by Maiolo, that the Germans were persuaded to build a fleet that the British were best prepared to defeat – a balanced if smaller version of the Royal Navy.[17] The balanced fleet has been the cornerstone of British policy regarding the Royal Navy's force structure. As the name suggests, it relies on the idea that no one section of a navy predominates, allowing it to carry out all possible maritime tasks in peace and war, ranging from naval diplomacy through mine warfare and trade protection to the clash of fleets in a Mahanian decisive engagement for command of the sea.[18] Balanced fleets, because they are made of up a mix of different capabilities, run the risk of being defeated in detail by an enemy force that is specialized in a particular mode of fighting, such as commerce raiding, which might have stretched the interwar Royal Navy to breaking point.[19] When considered from the submarine perspective, Maiolo's insights become even more profound: the British permitted and encouraged the Germans to build submarines as part of their balanced fleet, thus trapping them within their own Tirpitzian cultural constructs of how seapower should be dispensed. Although it might be considered that the British were also prisoners of their own cultural preconceptions of seapower, it must also be remembered that the Royal Navy had in some way recognized this when they decided to tease the Germans into building the sort of navy the existing British force structure was best able to defeat.[20]

This is a very significant and indeed sophisticated change in position by the British at the corporate level, as not only had they given up attempts to abolish the submarine, but also they had permitted its use, thus showing the start of a divergence between corporate and civil attitudes to the submarine. As *The Times* (and indeed many others beforehand) pointed out, 'Submarines are not the antidotes to submarines' but, more importantly, 'reciprocal equality in their numbers of tonnage bears little relation to the measures – known to have greatly improved in recent years – which can be taken to parry their activities.'[21] It is the reference to anti-submarine measures that helps flesh out the very sudden change in official attitudes to submarines: the British thought they had the means to defeat a submarine attack, particularly one that was mounted by a force tailored to meet the demands of a balanced fleet rather than a war on commerce.

The Royal Navy, as George Franklin and Willem Hackmann point out, had made significant progress in anti-submarine warfare.[22] Convoy, obviously, had played an important part in defeating past submarine threats and was expected to do so in the future.[23] Technology had also played a major part through the development of an echo-ranging device that was capable of detecting both submerged and surface targets. By the late 1920s, ASDIC (sonar) was a viable if limited detection system that continued to develop. After 1932, all new build destroyers were fitted with ASDICs and about the same time the role of trawlers in anti-submarine work was reassessed and ASDIC sets developed for them.[24] The fact that the Admiralty had put considerable effort into designing new types of escort vessels in the mid-1930s might also have played a part in reducing corporate perceptions of the submarine threat.[25] At the same time, considerable effort had gone into anti-submarine training aids, which would allow the rapid assimilation and training of an expanded wartime anti-submarine force.[26] Tactical development was not ignored either, with exercises and much development on the screening of fleets and merchant vessels by surface, air and, in some cases, subsurface assets, producing an integrated approach, as well as more traditional 'offensive' techniques.[27] By 1938 success rates in anti-submarine exercises had reached 70 per cent against British submarines who understood the limitations of ASDIC and used countermeasures to reduce the effectiveness of the searching craft.[28] The Royal Navy clearly believed that they had drawn the sting from the tail of the submarine.

It is clear, however, that there were considerable misgivings within the corporate culture about the ability of the Royal Navy to withstand air attacks, hence the development of the armoured fleet carrier, anti-aircraft cruisers and heavy (if ultimately ineffective) anti-aircraft armaments, particularly on some of the new designs of escort vessels that had a dual purpose anti-air and anti-submarine role.[29] Overall, it seems that the threat of bombing of both naval and civil targets had a profound impact on both corporate and civil cultures within Britain during the 1930s. Books on the use of the bomber were widespread,[30] and as Williamson Murray has noted, they described in frightening detail the imagined effects of such an attack, prophesying cities destroyed, riots and the collapse of government,[31] echoing Arthur Conan Doyle's 1914 description of the collapse of Britain following an unrestricted submarine campaign.[32] More importantly, the air warfare books were more widespread in comparison to those regarding submarine warfare. The concerns over strategic bombing were increased by politicians' public pronouncements, with Stanley Baldwin coining the famous phrase 'the bomber will always get through.'[33] The bomber and the threat of aerial attack had supplanted the submarine and the fear of starvation in the public imagination.

Baldwin's pessimism about the impact of bombing attacks was shared by many of his political colleagues.[34] The First Sea Lord even went as far as to describe the bombing of towns as 'a method of warfare which is <u>revolting</u> & un-English.'[35] Such fears throughout the entire populace helped to generate 'an outspoken public campaign supporting disarmament' with the bomber, not the submarine, seen as 'the most frightening weapon of the day'.[36] Disarmament campaigners such as the Peace Pledge Union (PPU) ignored the submarine, reserving their ire for the bomber (figure 4.1). Indeed, the PPU does not seem to have considered submarine warfare at all until the 1960s and then only as part of the anti-nuclear campaign.[37] Indeed, all the extant PPU pamphlets for the interwar period emphasize the fact that the target for the bomber was the civil population; nor can the context of the Spanish Civil War cannot be ignored when look-

BURN THE BABIES !

THERE ARE SOME THINGS no one would do—not even in the name of Patriotism. For instance, no one, however loyal, would put his neighbour's baby on the fire at the suggestion of the Secretary of State for War. ....

BABIES, WE FEEL, ARE NEUTRAL

BUT MODERN WARFARE means war from the air. War from the air means bombing babies.

IS IT WORSE TO PUT THE BABY ON THE FIRE — OR THE FIRE ON THE BABY? You can't "defend" your country without burning your neighbours' babies. "The only defence is in offence, which means that you have got to kill women and children more quickly than the enemy," says Mr. Baldwin.

ISN'T THERE A BETTER WAY of settling the disputes of Governments and Financiers?

Dr. "Dick" Sheppard thinks there is. Sign the Peace Pledge:—
"I renounce war and I will never support or sanction another",

and send it on a post card to:—

THE PEACE PLEDGE UNION, 96, REGENT STREET, W.I,

T W. Pegg & Sons, Ltd., Walham Green, S.W.6.

Figure 4.1a. Peace Pledge Union Pamphlet. (PPU)

Figure 4.1b. Peace Pledge Union Pamphlet. (PPU)

ing at these pamphlets. The pamphlets take an especially emotive line, referring to the burning of babies and stating that 'There are some things no one would do – not even in the name of Patriotism'.[38] This suggests that patriotism in itself is a dangerous means of making people act in ways they would normally find abhorrent, such as the indiscriminate bombing of non-combatants.

The national identity issues raised by the fear of the bomber are interesting as they echo earlier fears of the submarine and they all centre on the issue of non-combatants and indirectly ideas of being an island race. The idea that indiscriminate bombing is 'revolting and un-English' clearly parallels pre-First World War condemnation of the submarine, and particularly the use of unrestricted submarine warfare, as something that would never 'be done by a civilised power.'[39] The common thread in the revulsion over unrestricted submarine warfare and aerial bombing was, of course, its selection of non-combatants and their private property as the target. It is, however, the conceptions of island-hood within national identity that made this a powerful force in the British psyche. Britain's island status had protected it from invasion for centuries and the insularity conferred by being an island was a key concept in national identity;[40] submarines were originally used by the Royal Navy as part of harbour and coast defences in order to prevent a seaborne attack and subsequent invasion, with the navy being seen as the first and last line of defence.[41] Britain's frontier was the sea: the English Channel had allowed the country to selectively absorb European culture over the centuries without succumbing to continental despotism.[42] Moreover, since the eighteenth century, the Royal Navy had been seen as a non-despotic form of defence, which unlike the army, did not threaten Parliamentary freedoms.[43]

First the submarine and then the bomber threatened the security provided by island-hood. The submarine exposed the country to starvation and economic turmoil, real and imagined, by attacking non-combatant ships essential for food and trade while the battlefleet sailed helplessly above, although it was hoped that convoys as well as improvements in tactics and technology would reduce the submarine threat to manageable proportions. Now the bomber enabled, for the first time, a direct attack on anyone on the island, irrespective of the Royal Navy and English Channel that together had defended Britain for centuries. Island status was no longer a guarantor of security, especially for non-combatants.

In the light of widespread public fears about air warfare, both its unknown quantity compared to unrestricted submarine warfare and the apocalyptic descriptions of bombing in the late interwar period,[44] it is unsurprising that the submarine took on a less threatening meaning in civil culture. At the same time, the advances in ASDICs and matériel would have reduced the significance of the submarine as a threat at the corporate level, even before the British decided to try to use their anti-submarine countermeasures to encourage other states to abandon the submarine. As early as 1927, the British considered mounting a deception operation over their anti-submarine capabilities that at the time would support their position at the Geneva disarmament conferences. Such action was rejected for fear of the consequences if the ruse were ever discovered.[45] However, in 1929, some of the restrictions regarding ASDIC were lifted.[46] By the mid 1930s the Royal Navy had sufficient experience of operating ASDICs and were confident enough in its real capabilities to use it as part of a policy to influence potential enemies' submarine policies.[47]

In March 1935, the Parliamentary Secretary to the Admiralty informed the Commons that 'the convoy system would not be introduced at once on the outbreak of war.'[48] Roskill suggests that Lord Stanley must have been expressing the views of the Naval Staff and the Board of the Admiralty.[49] Roskill's contention that this equates to neglect of anti-submarine measures may not be correct,[50] as Lord Stanley's words can also be seen as indicating confidence, even if mistaken confidence, in the Royal Navy's ability to counter the submarine. After all, a contemporary observer could be forgiven for thinking that if, in the light of the experience of the First World War, convoy was not required to protect shipping from submarine attack, then the threat posed by submarines generally (as opposed to specifically German ones) might not be that great.

Despite the fears of air warfare displacing the submarine as the cultural bogeyman in the late interwar period, the submarine still exerted a perceived threat as evidenced by the less than warm civil response to the submarine aspects of the AGNA. The submarine continued to be regarded as a problem rather than an opportunity by British civil culture. In the first three days of September 1937, the *Daily Express* gave front page coverage to the activities of the unknown submarines that were supporting Franco in the Spanish Civil War. It was noted on 1 September 1939 that the latest attack in the Mediterranean was the sixteenth to occur since 1 August.[51] On 2 September it was reported that the British destroyer HMS *Havock* had been attacked (although the torpedo had missed its target) and that 'Ministers [were] Facing Submarine Menace.'[52] 3 September saw the reporting of destroyer reinforcements for the Mediterranean Fleet as well as another attack on a merchant ship by an unknown 'pirate submarine.'[53] These were not the only serious events – the Sino–Japanese conflict was also heavily reported, particularly the fighting around the treaty port of Shanghai.[54]

These pressures, effectively amounting to imperial strategic overstretch[55] with the submarine playing a significant part, were rather neatly summed up in a cartoon in the *Daily Express* on 4 September 1937. In the cartoon, a lion wearing a sailor's cap to represent the Royal Navy, is tethered to a rock in the Mediterranean by the policy of non-intervention in Spain. The lion's tail is being gripped by a shark-like submarine, unsurprising given the high level of unknown or hostile submarine activity since August 1937. The lion is also being bothered by insects, one a mosquito labelled Palestine, where the Royal Navy had been engaged in imperial policing,[56] and a wasp called the Labour party (Labour was opposed to any form of armaments and also had opposed non-intervention). [57] If things were not bad enough, in the background China and Japan are fighting – another potential problem for the Royal Navy. The Royal Navy, according to the cartoon, was plagued by the numerous demands being made upon it, and the submarines had rendered the surrounding seas unsafe. Only the experience of war and a reversal of a long-standing British policy about the conduct of maritime war would see the submarine becoming widely regarded as an opportunity as well as a threat.

The British Unrestricted Submarine Campaign

Perhaps the most important factor concerning the way meaning was constructed through the use of submarines in this period, was the way in which the British viewed non-combatants and thus unrestricted submarine warfare. As discussed in the previous chapter, the use of unrestricted submarine warfare during the First World War was a one-sided affair; the British suffered from it, but did not retaliate in kind against Germany. Indeed, the British were at pains to demonstrate in the interwar period that they had fought according to the Prize rules.[58]

Yet the period 1935–65 saw a complete reversal of the British corporate attitude to unrestricted warfare from one of disdain to that of enthusiastic participation. It would be wrong, however, to ascribe any direct link between the reaction to the Anglo–German Naval Treaty, its aftermath and the British decision to adopt unrestricted submarine warfare. While the Anglo–German Naval Treaty can be read as a reduction in the fear of the submarine and greater approval of it as part of a balanced fleet, at least at the corporate level, it did not mean that the British would themselves adopt unrestricted submarine warfare. The decision to use unrestricted submarine warfare is about attitudes to non-combatants and not the submarine as such. The most important factor in considering this reversal of attitudes is that it was not necessarily a wartime phenomenon. Instead, the Royal Navy's submarine service had by 1939 discussed the possibility of a British unrestricted submarine warfare campaign, or at least not operating in accordance with the Prize rules and interwar naval treaties.[59]

Unfortunately, it appears that the original document produced by the Rear Admiral Submarines in June 1939 and the resulting correspondence with the Naval Staff divisions prior to the letter of 3 August mentioned below, has been destroyed.[60] The only traces of the discussion are three tantalising paragraphs in a post-war (1953) Admiralty publication – CB3306 (1), Naval Staff History of the Second World War, Submarines, volume I – stating that:

> Though there were many individual exceptions, the ideas generally held by submarine officers at the beginning of the [Second World] war, as a result of peacetime experiences, were roughly as follows: -
> (a) That in waters covered by enemy shore-based aircraft, e.g. the North Sea, it was a hazardous operation to proceed or remain on the surface for any length of time during the daylight, and that even showing a lot of periscope incurred considerable risk.
> (b) That, even outside these waters, the stopping of merchant ships for visit and search, entailing long periods on the surface, was likely to be so hazardous for the submarines that it was not worth the risk.
> These limitations were recognised before the outbreak of war, and Rear Admiral (S) took up the question of the use of submarines against enemy overseas trade and communications, the term 'communications' being held to include enemy transports, supply ships etc. whether in convoy or sailing singly. Rear Admiral (S) pointed out that as a result of these restrictions, submarines were trained and taught that their sole function was to attack enemy surface warships, and they were not even supplied with the Manuals given to all [British] surface warships as a guide in their attack on the trade and communications of the enemy. The Naval Prize Manual was not issued to submarines until the end of 1939. [after the war had started!]
> In a further letter dated 3rd August 1939, Rear Admiral (S) withdrew his suggestions of attacks on trade, and pro-

posed that dangerous areas be declared round various British possessions, in which submarines should have freedom to attack and sink enemy convoys without warning. Their Lordships took the view that this was undesirable at the commencement of a war, observing that dangerous areas could only be defined, as such, by means of mines and that the necessity for being free to initiate reprisals, without reproach from neutrals, made the notification that an area was dangerous by any method, other than mines, to be deprecated. It would be and was, however, considered as occasions for reprisals arose.[61]

This throws up a number of issues about attitudes to submarine warfare and non-combatants. First, there is the complete neglect of anti-commerce operations even when carried out in accordance with the Prize rules. Such neglect is, however, understandable in the light of the considerable odium that had been heaped upon the heads of the submariners regarding the use of unrestricted attacks on trade and the belief held in the interwar period that lifeboats could not be considered a place of safety for a merchant vessel's crew and passengers.[62] Even in wartime, pre-war attitudes and 'proper' behaviour held out. On 3 September 1940, the *T* class submarine HMS *Truant* stopped the merchantman *Tropic Sea* that had been taken as a prize by the German armed merchant raider *Orion*. The *Tropic Sea* was carrying British and Norwegian prisoners back to Occupied France and on being stopped by the *Truant*, the German prize crew scuttled her. The *Truant* picked up the British and Norwegian prisoners and left the prize crew in the lifeboats. Hezlet when analysing this action after the war was obviously thinking of the Treaty of London strictures that lifeboats were not to be considered a place of safety, as he pointed out in a footnote the correctness of the *Truant*'s actions – the *Truant* had not sunk the *Tropic Sea*, this was done by the German prize crew, and so the British were under no obligation to pick them up.[63]

Second, the differentiation between trade and communications is significant. As the Naval Staff history states, 'communications' were taken to mean transports and supply ships, with the inference being that these ships, despite any possible ancestry as mercantile vessels, were legally naval auxiliaries. Trade, on the other hand, might be interpreted as genuine merchant vessels proceeding on their lawful business. This of course has a resonance with the discussion during and after the Washington Naval Conference over the use of the term 'pirate' to describe attacks on trade by submarines and the Naval Staff's concerns over misidentifying an auxiliary warship, transport or troop ship (a legitimate target) with a genuine merchant vessel that was protected by treaty.[64] At the same time, reference is made to attacks on trade and communications indicating at least a desire to carry out trade warfare in accordance with the naval treaties as well as against vessels engaged in the direct support of naval or military operations.

The third paragraph is even more interesting as it advocates abandoning an attack on trade while proposing the use of 'dangerous areas'. The use of such nuances in the language suggests a corporate body that was to some extent uncomfortable with the public admission of plans for unrestricted submarine warfare. By avoiding a direct comparison with an attack on trade and instead using the rather vague 'dangerous areas', greater room to manoeuvre in wartime could be gained, especially regarding that of retaliation. Indeed, the final terminology used by the naval staff history to describe what actually happened was 'sink on sight zones', far less vague in intent than 'dangerous areas', but still avoiding the phrase 'unrestricted submarine warfare'.[65]

The use of unrestricted submarine warfare as a reprisal was a new departure for the Admiralty and the submarine service; after all, it had been conspicuous by its absence in British responses to the German submarine campaigns of the First World War.[66] The fact that the Admiralty was prepared to contemplate action that only twenty years previously had been considered unacceptable, shows clearly a change in attitudes to submarine and non-combatant casualties, and is probably very closely linked to the growing fears in the 1930s over mass civilian casualties caused by bombing. What had been merely worries about the possibility of air attack in the early and mid-1930s, had, by 1939, become an expectation of heavy civilian casualties from indiscriminate bombing in the event of a major war.[67]

In the light of the Admiralty's suggestions that unrestricted submarine warfare might be used as a retaliatory measure, the actual circumstances of the decision to declare the first 'sink on sight' areas were rather different. It seems that rather than being a retaliatory measure, the decision to operate unrestricted submarine warfare or 'sink on sight zones' was a rushed decision at the highest political and corporate levels in response to almost impossible operational and tactical circumstances as the Norwegian campaign opened. The Naval Staff history noted 'the difficulty in identifying merchant ships as transports' and that 'the activity of [German] surface and air patrols precluded any attempt at interception on the surface.'[68] In practice, this meant that British submarines were impotent, as they could not differentiate between legitimate merchant vessels and those that were operating as some form of naval auxiliary, thus preventing a submerged attack. It was also impossible, due to the high risk of attack by aircraft, to surface in order to carry out stop and search of any suspicious vessels in accordance with the Prize rules, and thus resolve doubts about whether or not a vessel was a legitimate target.

If sink on sight was a retaliatory measure, the British chose an odd time to implement it, having failed to do so in the light of previous German actions against merchant vessels, such as the sinking of the liner *Athenia* without warning on 3 September 1939. This does not mean that the Germans operated unrestricted submarine warfare from the outset. The Germans themselves were expecting their submarines to operate under the Prize rules and held a secret investigation into the actions of the U-boat commander responsible for the *Athenia*'s sinking.[69] He was found to have acted in good faith, believing the *Athenia* was an armed merchant cruiser[70] (i.e. a legitimate target), which illustrates very clearly the difficulties in target identification that had so worried the Royal Navy during the Washington Treaty negotiations.[71] Nor did the British choose to retaliate in the manner suggested in the pre-war correspondence regarding attacks on enemy trade when, on 4 October 1939, the Germans cancelled the Prize regulations in waters out as far as 15° West.[72] It is hard not to agree with Roskill's analysis of the German actions in 1939 that, although the Germans avoided using the term unrestricted warfare, it was in operation against British and French shipping by mid-November 1939.[73] Certainly, sections of the British press believed this was the case, as the 'piracy' comment in the *Evening Standard*'s 20 November 1939 cartoon 'A losing game' testifies; given Germany's cancellation of the prize regulations as far out as 15° West it is impossible to see how the cartoon could be referring to any other mode of warfare. Importantly, the use of unrestricted submarine warfare, with its piracy connotations, was seen as 'a losing game' for Hitler by the press and the public, suggesting that interwar advances in anti-submarine warfare had rendered unrestricted warfare ineffective. The 'losing game' might also be highlighting an expected adverse neutral reaction that would, as in the First World War, bring America into the war on the Allies' side. Yet, despite the pre-war discussions over the Royal Navy following a 'sink on sight' policy, the British did not retaliate or implement a policy of unrestricted warfare until 9 April 1940.

Perhaps unsurprisingly, it is not possible to find in the National Archives, Naval Historical Branch papers or the Royal Navy Submarine Museum archive, any indication or reference to staff discussions on the conditions for a retaliatory strike using some form of unrestricted warfare. Instead, the decision to use a sink on sight zone came very suddenly at a War Cabinet meeting on 9 April 1940 when the First Sea Lord asked for 'the approval of the War Cabinet to draft instructions to our submarine commanders to attack without warning all shipping in the Skagerrak.'[74] The First Sea Lord went on to assure the Cabinet that 'Normal mercantile shipping had been held up' and 'that any other ships were ships of war or transports.'[75] The approach by the First Sea Lord emphasizes the impromptu nature of the discussion, as the First Sea Lord was a professional advisor to the Cabinet; a political issue like a decision to implement unrestricted submarine warfare should have been brought up by the First Lord – Churchill – the political head of the Royal Navy, and not his senior advisor. Furthermore, the First Sea Lord asked for permission to draft orders not to implement an already agreed plan. The Cabinet meeting the following day helped to emphasize the unplanned nature of the decision as the Secretary of State for Air asked permission for RAF aircraft to attack merchant shipping in the Skagerrak without warning.[76] The First Sea Lord also informed the War Cabinet that 'the Germans had announced that all traffic in the Skagerrak had been stopped' and that 'Any merchant ships must therefore be either troopships or storeships.'[77] Although the minutes do not record any discussion either on 9 or 10 April regarding the use of unrestricted warfare, the efforts to reassure the Cabinet that while the enemy vessels that were going to be attacked might have looked like merchant ships, they were in fact auxiliaries, does suggest that there might have been some dismay at the proposal. Again, this does not tally with a planned escalation in retaliation for enemy actions.

The difficulties faced by the Royal Navy during the Norwegian campaign were considerable. Both Roskill and Barnett point out the limitations imposed by German air superiority,[78] while the Naval Staff history demonstrated clearly the difficulties airpower placed on submarines trying to operate according to the Prize rules.[79] These difficulties forced a reconsideration of the submarine within the Royal Navy's culture as it was recognized that the submarine was the only tool through which the Navy could undertake sea control, rather than one that threatened their ability to exercise command of the sea. Admiral Forbes, the Commander-in-Chief Home Fleet during the Norwegian campaign, signalled to the Admiralty that he intended to leave attacks on German shipping in the southern sea areas off Norway to submarines due to the enemy's air superiority.[80] Hezlet, a rather distinguished submariner with a splendid war record from the Second World War, has seized on

Forbes' signal as 'a momentous change in the attitude to the submarine' and that the submarine was now seen as an essential part of stronger navies and not just an auxiliary or the weapon of the weaker powers.[81] Roskill, a distinguished gunnery specialist and member of the Naval Staff during the Second World War, thought that in light of Forbes' signal, submarines 'were unlikely effectively to dispute let alone deny, the short sea routes such as those across the Skagerrak and Kattegat.'[82] Given that British submarines sank or severely damaged more German heavy warships[83] than any other weapon system, it is hard to agree with Roskill, but it is also hard to agree with Hezlet – the submarine was not as acceptable as he suggested: yet.

For all the operational discussions at a corporate level regarding the use of unrestricted warfare and the submarine's ability to project command of the sea, it seems that civil culture had already swung in favour of a more aggressive posture by Britain towards inflicting non-combatant casualties on her enemies. In particular, one incident suggested that the British public might have had fewer scruples about the use of unrestricted submarine warfare than the Government and Admiralty. In December 1939, news leaked out that a British submarine had sighted the German liner *Bremen* but had not attacked as it had not been possible to act in accordance with the prize rules. According to a 1942 history of the British submarine service, Up Periscope, the 'majority of the British people gasped with anger…'[84] While the objectivity of Up Periscope is questionable as it was written at the height of the Mediterranean campaign where unrestricted submarine warfare was carried out by the British, it is also clear that some sections of the British press were incandescent with rage over the escape of the *Bremen*. The *Daily Mirror* gave a highly sarcastic report of the event and ran a large cartoon suggesting that Nelson would have disapproved strongly of the inaction of his successors.[85] The cartoon's caption of 'International Decency My Blind Eye!' sums up clearly the outrage felt by the *Daily Mirror*, while the banner across the cartoon of 'for reason's of International Decency!' suggests that already such sentiments are outmoded and inappropriate. The *Daily Express* ran the headline 'The question all Britain is asking today WHY DIDN'T WE SINK THE BREMEN?'[86] The Royal Navy was condemned as being 'too chivalrous' and the question 'shall the Navy be praised or blamed for their restraint in the matter?' was posed; it was reported that nine out of twelve people would have sunk the *Bremen*.[87] The *Daily Mail* took a more ambivalent view pointing out, somewhat prematurely, that:

> Such inhumanity will never blot British Naval records. But the strange episode of the Bremen will revive in the minds of many people the question 'Are we at war or not?'[88]

However, press opinion was divided over the *Bremen* affair with the 'quality' broadsheets taking a different, more sophisticated view from that of the tabloids. The *Manchester Guardian*, holding true to the interwar dislike of non-combatant casualties, condemned the 'thoughtless comment in London', since to torpedo the *Bremen* without warning was 'precisely the kind of conduct we condemn in the German Submarine Service'[89] and *The Times* agreed.[90]

What is interesting is that despite all the emotive language that had been attached to unrestricted submarine warfare during the First World War and the interwar period, the British were more than willing to let their submarines loose on merchant shipping. Even more astounding after the attitudes to non-combatants displayed before 1939, was the absence of piracy analogies or highly emotive language in newspapers to describe the new German submarine campaign.[91] Spring 1940 represents a break point between two different conceptualisations of submarine warfare.

The use of unrestricted submarine warfare during the Second World War by all major combatants, threw up a paradox for the British in their assimilation of the experience of submarine warfare: how to celebrate the successes of their own submarine force while castigating that of their enemies who were using essentially the same mode of warfare? It seems that this paradox was dealt with by simply ignoring it, or rather the British use of such 'ungentlemanly' methods. As a result British accusations of 'piracy' or general maritime beastliness by the Axis powers are conspicuous by their absence after Spring 1940 when Britain declared 'sink on sight' zones.

More importantly, admissions by the British in the media that they were using unrestricted submarine warfare are also missing. Instead, the victims of the British campaign were described by the press in ways that suggest the ships sunk were acting as naval auxiliaries and were therefore a legitimate target: 'Another unescorted enemy vessel; a large east-bound supply ship, was also attacked, hit by two torpedoes and sunk.'[92] Note that this is a description of an unrestricted attack, the vessel was unescorted, was attacked by torpedoes with no suggestion of being searched first and was sunk rather than taken as a prize or scuttled. Not only was unrestricted submarine warfare being played down, so too was the part played by submarines, even allowing for the Royal Navy's traditional avoidance of publicity. As the 'Weekly Home Intelligence Report' observed in August 1943 'There is some demand for more news, but the "general opinion" is that the "Silent Service" is keeping up its policy of silence.'[93] The knock-on effect of this lack of discussion about the activities of the submarine service had an impact even on the corporate sphere. The submarine service Staff Officer Personnel, Captain R. Shelford noted that he 'had so many distressing scenes with men who, already covered in war medals, begging me to help them get back into destroyers, trawlers or motor torpedo boats – anything, in fact, rather than submarines…'[94] In the end Shelford had to take up the matter with the Admiral (Submarines) who arranged for an improvement in the publicity given to British submarines and their activities.

Even when the activities of the submarines received more publicity, discussing unrestricted submarine warfare was avoided. In a Ministry of Information booklet on submarines, written after five years of war, the authorities could not bring themselves to use the phrase 'unrestricted warfare'. In fact, the pamphlet tried to play down the use of sink on sight rules by implying it was actually the Germans' fault: 'When it became clear that the Germans were using merchant ships and neutral vessels to send military supplies [author's italics] through the Kattegat and Skagerrak and up the Norwegian coast, orders were given to British submarines in certain areas to sink at sight.'[95] British portrayals of the German submarine campaign, however, were frequently brutal in their treatment of the realities of being on the receiving end of unrestricted submarine warfare as demonstrated during and after the war by the prominence of the writings of Nicolas Monsarrat. Monsarrat's first two books were published as serialised articles in the *Daily Telegraph* in 1942 and 1943 as well as in traditional book format (the third was serialised by Trident).[96] In wartime books such as *HM Corvette* (first published in 1942), Monsarrat did not hold back from describing men (and, in the post-war *Cruel Sea*, women too) drowning, dying of exposure or fuel oil poisoning, and being burnt alive as a result of submarine attacks.[97]

Despite the playing down of the British unrestricted campaign within civil culture during the Second World War (while still illustrating the horrors of being on the receiving end of such a campaign, but in less hysterical terms than previously), there had been a change, at the corporate level, in the way the British submarine was regarded. Non-combatant status of potential targets no longer hampered the British submarine and the submarine itself was seen in some quarters as a way of achieving command of the sea rather than just denying it to an enemy. These changes in the way the submarine was imagined became more widespread in the post-war period as the submarine was reinvented as the preferred means of carrying out anti-submarine warfare.

At the same time, the submarine service had enthusiastically embraced the piracy image that, in the First World War and interwar period, had been used with such great effect to stigmatize submarine warfare. Now, in the Second World War, the submarine service made use of the piracy symbol – the Jolly Roger flag[98] – to proclaim its own victories. Yet the prevalence of black and white rather than colour film and photographs ensured that the real impact of the victories recorded on each boat's Jolly Roger was lost as it is almost impossible to differentiate between the red colours used to signify a warship sunk or damaged, and the white of a merchant vessel. There is also no authoritative explanation as to why the submarines en masse adopted the piracy symbol in the Second World War; it is alleged that Max Horton used one during the First World War and it is possible that Second World War submariners were consciously aping their predecessors. Alternatively, the use of the Jolly Roger might have been part of an early manifestation of the desire to stamp a separate identity on their service, much in the way that the submarine branch badge and naming policy was used in the 1970s. Just as importantly, the piracy image seems to have been quickly accepted, it was not censored from the 1943 film *We Dive At Dawn* where the use of the Jolly Roger to signify success was made at both the start and end of the film. The lack of ready stigmatization following the use of the Jolly Roger, and indeed the lack of any condemnation for British submarines carrying out unrestricted submarine warfare, provided the submarine with not only a sense of increased naval importance as it entered the post-war world but public acceptance, if not approval.

Overall, it seems that with regard to unrestricted submarine warfare, there was a divergence between corporate and civil cultures in the period during, and immediately prior to, the Second World War. Prior to the outbreak of war, corporate culture had discussed and identified scenarios that might lead to a British unrestricted submarine campaign, but without carrying out the necessary steps to prepare the civil culture for such action. Since British unrestricted campaigns were not initiated as a retaliatory measure, but rather as a means of achieving command of the sea, indicates a significant degree of corporate acceptance of submarine warfare in all its forms. In particular, the reliance on the submarine to carry out what had previously been a battlefleet function – that of command of the sea – is significant as it shows the submarine being far more important than had been suggested in the pre-war period. The enthusiastic acceptance of the Jolly Roger symbol and the differentiation between merchant and naval vessels sunk also suggests a corporate culture at ease with the idea of unrestricted submarine warfare. Civil culture, on the other hand, continued to display disquiet at the idea of unrestricted submarine warfare and initially was condemnatory of German actions. Civil attitudes to unrestricted warfare, however, quickly became ambiguous, with the British submarine campaign from April 1940 onwards being largely ignored, despite indications in December 1939 that retaliatory action following the Bremen incident was expected. The divergence between civil and corporate culture during the Second World War, did not, however, last into the post-war period.

The Submarine 1945–65

The submarine departed the Second World War with some optimism for its future: the British had come to terms with their participation in unrestricted submarine warfare, admittedly with some reluctance to draw attention to their very successful wartime forays into the realm of 'sink on sight.' At the same time, technological advances suggested that the submarine might have a greater role to play in anti-submarine warfare, and even the disturbing image of a fast submarine that could defeat current surface based counter-measures had the possibility of being turned to Britain's advantage. More importantly, the use of primitive nuclear bombs had given strategic bombing a weapon system that could shatter a nation, in the way interwar airpower commentators had feared, making starvation by unrestricted submarine warfare a far less threatening possibility both politically and to the civil populace.

Yet the invention of such an awesome weapon as the nuclear bomb did not render the submarine obsolescent or encourage any moves for its abolition. Rather, the experience of war had cemented the role of the submarine in that critical British concept of seapower – the balanced fleet. During all the wrangling over the shape of the post-war fleet and the economic problems associated with the transformation of a civil economy and welfare state, the Navy tried hard to protect its submarine force. In February 1946, a proposal was put forward that by

December that year, there would be a reduction in the numbers of fleet aircraft carriers, battleships, cruisers, escort vessels and destroyers, but that the submarine force would remain at the same level.[99] The way in which the submarine was imagined had changed.

This change was not, as could have been expected given wartime experience, towards an acceptance of unrestricted submarine warfare requiring the maintenance of the submarine force. After all, there was no target for such a submarine force. The Soviet Union, about whom there were some concerns,[100] was a continental power against whom effective economic pressure was problematical. It seems, however, that even given the limited opportunities for striking against a continental power, British submarines would not only undertake offensives against Soviet warships, but would also carry out unrestricted submarine warfare against the Soviet merchant fleet in the event of war.[101] Such a change in attitudes to non-combatants is very important; much of the odium heaped on the submarine from 1915 onwards was due to its impact on the treatment of property and non-combatants in maritime warfare and its use by morally weaker powers, not just those that were physically weaker. Now the British had not only used unrestricted warfare in a war of national survival (as well as launching devastating attacks on civilians from the air), but were planning to do so again if national survival was threatened by Soviet aggression in Europe: the morality of such actions in a war of national survival was not questioned. In British eyes, the submarine was no longer the weapon of the morally weaker power.

Now the meaning of the submarine was again constructed around a very traditional naval issue: command of the sea. This time the submarine was not 'an auxiliary or the weapon for the weaker powers'[102] but an important method of exercising control of the sea. The submarine was seen as the only weapon system that could operate close to the increasingly sophisticated Soviet coastal defences.[103] Furthermore, from early 1948 onwards, the highest priority for the Royal Navy's submarine force was anti-submarine warfare.[104] The days of the submarine being perceived as the weapon of the morally and physically weaker power were ending. The submarine was starting its move towards becoming the new capital unit of the first-rank naval powers, a move that would be completed by the advent of the nuclear- powered fleet submarine.

This change in the way submarines were understood by the British, from that of a weapon at odds with their understanding of seapower, to one that actively supported that concept is an important one. The importance of this change is emphasized by the longevity of the view that submarines did not follow the normal 'rules' of naval technological development. These 'rules' laid down that the answer to bigger and better battleships, for example, was bigger and better battleships, and that like vessels fought like, or ran the risk of being overwhelmed by a stronger unit. From the very beginning, it was considered that the answer to a submarine was not another submarine;[105] hence the presence of submarines in a hostile fleet did not require submarines as a response. By abandoning such a posture and making submarines a major part of achieving command of the sea by destroying an enemy's submarine force, the meaning of the submarine was reinvented at the corporate level from a threat to heavy units – such as aircraft carriers – to one that gave them freedom to operate effectively.

This was not the first time the Royal Navy had tried using submarines for anti-submarine warfare. All submarines in both the First and Second World Wars had been encourage to attack surfaced enemy submarines, while in the First World War a submarine specifically for anti-submarine warfare had been developed – the 1918 R class. By the end of the Second World War sinking a hostile submarine was sufficiently important to the Royal Navy that the submarine service celebrated such successes on their Jolly Roger flags, which were flown to indicate a successful patrol. Instead of using the normal red bar on the flag to indicate an enemy warship sunk, a hostile submarine was indicated by a bar with a U superimposed on it.

In order to reinvent the submarine as an effective anti-submarine platform after the Second World War, a number of problems relating to speed, sensors, noise and weapons had to be resolved. In short, British submarines in the late 1940s, the *S*, *T* (pre-war designs) and *A* class (war design) were not up to three-dimensional anti-submarine warfare; attacks on a submerged submarine were almost impossible until better weapons and sensors were perfected from the late 1950s onwards.

The reinvention of the British submarine as an anti-submarine weapon system was given impetus by the introduction of new, streamlined 'fast battery' vessels – the *Porpoise* and later *Oberon* class submarines – with a higher submerged speed than when on the surface, coupled with considerable attention to noise-reduction techniques.[106] From the start both classes were designed to act as anti-submarine warfare platforms as well as in the traditional anti-ship role and are considered to be some of the finest conventional type submarines of their period.[107] The importance of both the anti-submarine and anti-ship aspects of the Royal Navy's plans for its own submarines are reinforced by the fact that, while the fast battery types were being designed and constructed, the British embarked on a reconstruction programme for some of the newer pre-war designed *T* class and all the surviving *A* class. The boats were streamlined, and external torpedo tubes and gun armaments were removed to increase submerged speed and reduce noise. They were given high capacity batteries and the *T* class conversions were given more powerful electric motors. Coupled with the earlier implementation of snorkel masts to allow the use of diesel motors for propulsion and battery charging while at periscope depth, together with submarine versus submarine exercises,[108] these reconstructions produced a vast improvement in the capabilities of the submarine force. Yet at the public display of submarine strength at the 1953 Coronation Review, the increased importance of the submarine as both an anti-submarine weapon and as a means of maintaining command of the sea escaped widespread notice within the civil sphere. Indeed, even the anti-submarine role of the submarine was lost in the media discussions of mine warfare and traditional anti-submarine platforms such as surface ships. Clearly, the technological advances that were apparent to the public in the post-war period, such as the highly obvious streamlining of the *A* and *T* class as well as the speed of the *Ex* class, were not driving the civil cultural perceptions of the submarine.

The partial successes and outright failures in submarine propulsion, sensor, and weapons development during this period[109] did not undermine the fact that the way in which the submarine was understood had fundamentally changed in the post-war Navy. The very breadth of innovation that was tried is testament to the new importance of anti-submarine warfare and the start of the role of the submarine as the primary anti-submarine platform. The fact that many of these innovations, such as the quest for high submerged speed, as well as the anti-submarine warfare emphasis of the Navy, reached across into the public consciousness in the years after the 1953 Coronation Review shows the importance that this new meaning for submarines had for the British.[110] Furthermore, it also demonstrates that there was still a divergence in the way the submarine was imagined between corporate and civil cultures. The corporate conceptualisation of the submarine was based on its ability to provide the Royal Navy with command of the sea.

Conversely, the civil conceptualisation of the submarine centred on what it demonstrated about British superiority at a time when both the Empire and the economy were under increasing pressure. The speed of the experimental *Ex* class submarines, *Explorer* and *Excalibur*, was emphasized in the press; the submarines were unofficially claimed to be 'so successful that these are now the fastest submarines in the world.'[111] Moreover, politicians lamented the 'lack of accepted standards [which] prevents us from trying for an underwater speed record to add to the records on the water, in the air and on land which Great Britain already holds.'[112] Nor was it just speed that was used to demonstrate the British submarine 'firsts'. Sharing the front pages of the national newspapers with the Coronation Review was the news that a British submarine had carried out the first submerged crossing of the Atlantic.[113] The *Daily Mail* even went as far as to call HMS *Andrew*'s feat 'An Everest in reverse.'[114] Even the lack of nuclear power did not prevent the superiority of British submarines being trumpeted in the press. In 1960 *The Times* commented that 'while by many submarines are thought of only as nuclear-propelled boats if they are to be fully efficient, in the latest Porpoise class submarines, six of which have been built since the war, the Navy has a silent, speedy and manoeuvrable vessel of proved ability.'[115] Clearly with the *Dreadnought* under construction it was acceptable to draw favourable comparisons between the *Porpoise* class SSKs with nuclear propulsion. This does not mean, however, that the prospect of the Royal Navy falling behind other powers was viewed as acceptable; in 1953 the *Manchester Guardian* rebuked the government as 'It is the Royal Navy not the other navy that ought to be making the running and establishing the modern trend.'[116] It seems clear that the *Manchester Guardian*'s rather caustic comments had been provoked by announcements regarding the American development of a nuclear-powered submarine. Ten days before the article in the *Manchester Guardian*, *The Times* had announced 'that the world's first atomic submarine, the Nautilus, will probably undergo its seagoing tests next year.'[117] Submarines were being transformed from being a threat to the civil populace to being part of the means of defending it from starvation in the event of a hostile cold war unrestricted submarine warfare campaign.[118] Just as importantly, advances in submarine technology were used to support the idea that Britain remained a great power.

The increased importance of the submarine to the Royal Navy was shown by the way it used images of submarines in their earliest recruiting campaigns during the 1950s and early 1960s.[119] Although most of the advertising emphasized the aircraft carrier and the Fleet Air Arm, the submarine was used as a recruiting tool. However, some advertisements depicting submarines were used to emphasize the importance of naval aviation; one example in the Sea Cadet in July 1957 showed a modernized *T* class submarine but stated that:

In many ways Britain's New Navy is ahead of the times. In the new Carrier Groups, with their secret weapons and other devices you can go all over the world among the finest company you'll ever meet.[120]

The advertisements emphasized the modernity of the Royal Navy; it was 'Britain's New Navy' clearly suggesting that the criticisms of the Royal Navy falling behind at the time of the 1953 Coronation Review[121] were incorrect or outdated. One advertisement, prepared for the *Daily Express* listed the fundamental problems of submarine development, speed and endurance, and told readers what developments the Navy was making to put them 'well ahead in all these aspects of submarine development.'[122] The submarine was touted as 'One of our most important weapons' and that submarines were 'Packed with ultra-modern and secret equipment'.[123] However, attention was not drawn to the opportunities for potential officers recruits within the submarine service, nor was the service advertised as a separate body in contrast to the Fleet Air Arm which was advertised as a separate service with career opportunities for potential officer candidates.[124]

When the recruitment campaigns featuring images of the submarine are taken together with press coverage of British submarine 'firsts', such as the speed achieved by HMS *Explorer* and *Excalibur*, or HMS *Andrew*'s submerged crossing of the Atlantic, there is a clear perception that the submarine had increasing importance coinciding with a cultural preoccupation with modernity and technology. In particular, the growing acceptability of the submarine as a part of the Royal Navy's publicity and recruiting efforts seems to be based on the ability to use the submarine to demonstrate the qualitative superiority of the Royal Navy in order to make up for its decreasing size and shrinking global role.

Although the changes in the way the British, particularly at a corporate level, understood the submarine cast it in a more favourable light, the submarine still was regarded as of lesser importance at the bureaucratic level, particularly when compared to other new arms such as naval aviation. Since the inception of the submarine, it had been under-represented at the very centre of naval policy and corporate understanding – the Admiralty and naval staff – and despite the advances and changes of the period 1935–65, this remained essentially the case. In particular, there was no single staff division responsible for the doctrinal and operational development of the submarine. Instead, naval staff divisions had responsibility for different aspects of submarine warfare, with the Directorate of Torpedo, Anti-Submarine and Mine Warfare having the most input on the subject. Additionally, as Eric Grove in *Vanguard to Trident* points out, there were frequent disagreements over policy between the submariners (led by Flag Officer Submarines and his Squadron commanders) and the 'surface oriented sailors of the Staff.'[125] This situation can be contrasted with that of naval aviation which had two naval staff divisions dedicated respectively to maritime air power and fending off the bureaucratic depredations of the Royal Air Force and Air Ministry. Additionally, unlike the submarine service, naval aviation interests were represented on the Admiralty Board by the Fifth Sea Lord. The senior submariner was not only not a member of the Admiralty board, but was also geographically separated from the Admiralty as Flag Officer Submarine's Headquarters (except when Max Horton was Vice-Admiral Submarines during the Second World War – he insisted to being relocated to London)[126] were at HMS *Dolphin* in Gosport. The Royal Navy would comprehensively re-invent the meaning of their submarines only with the loss of the carriers and the introduction of nuclear technology.

Conclusions

Although the themes discussed in this chapter cannot be regarded as linked in terms of cause and effect, when taken as a whole they do point to the period between 1935 and 1965 as one of significant change in terms of what the submarine meant to the British in both the corporate and civil cultures. Prior to 1935 the submarine had been a threat to British concepts of seapower and non-combatant status, which in turn had influenced how the British used the submarine. From 1935 onwards, the submarine was generally seen as a lesser threat, thanks to horror stories about future air warfare, certainly at the civil level, and at the corporate level as a means of trying to get potential enemies to conform to cultural attitudes in the way seapower should be delivered, to the Royal Navy's net benefit. The Anglo–German Naval Treaty in many ways signified the start of the acceptance of the submarine as an essential part of that holy grail of the British Naval Staff, a balanced fleet. It was not, however, the British Fleet that was important, but instead the German Fleet under a resurgent Nazi government. By encouraging the Germans to build the fleet that best suited the Royal Navy to fight, the British helped change the production of their own cultural perceptions of the submarine from a threat to an opportunity for naval arms control.

Perhaps the greatest change in the submarine during the period 1935 to 1965 has to be its signification in terms of cultural conventions. The Anglo–German Naval Treaty marked the acceptance of the submarine at the diplomatic level by ending attempts to abolish it outright, a massive change in posture given previous British attitudes to and experiences of the submarine. More importantly, the decision by the British to use unrestricted submarine warfare, shows that the way in which meaning was constructed regarding submarines had changed. The use of unrestricted submarine warfare had, in the eyes of the British, gone from being the act of the physically and morally naval power, to being an acceptable method of waging warfare in an era when conflict was understood in its relation to wars of national survival. Yet such an important change in the attitude to submarine warfare cannot be seen as a retaliatory measure. Instead, the fundamental change in the perception of submarine warfare was as a result of operational and tactical circumstances, rather than the political act that such retaliation would suggest. The changes also highlight revisions in the attitude to non-combatants at the most fundamental level. Yet again though, it is possible to speculate that the predicted horrors of bombing and the actual experience of the German Blitz generally desensitized British qualms about non-combatant casualties.

What it is equally important is the way that the British coped with the signification of conducting unrestricted submarine warfare whilst at the same time experiencing the depredations of a hostile campaign. The apparent disregard of the British submarine campaign and the seeming discomfort at using the phrase 'unrestricted submarine warfare' to describe the rather successful, if small-scale campaigns fought by the British, suggests that the reception of submarine warfare was still a very difficult subject. Yet by turning a blind eye to their own employment of unrestricted submarine warfare during the Second World War, as well as the plans to use unrestricted warfare in the event of a later conflict with the Soviet Union, the British were actually forcing the submarine to conform to preconceptions that reinforced certain aspects of national identity – namely the continued reverence for non-combatant status and private property at sea. In this way, the depiction of the submarine in the post-war era which emphasized a dislike for sink on sight policies, and the promotion of the submarine as the new anti-submarine weapon without drawing attention to the use of unrestricted warfare, can be reconciled.

The production of a new meaning for the submarine between 1945 and 1965 as an anti-submarine platform was very much a corporate issue. This change in meaning involved reconsidering the submarine as an aid to command of the sea, rather than a threat to it. The British noted that the submarine was the only vessel that would be able to carry out a close blockade of an enemy coast and for that reason was best suited to intercept transiting hostile submarines between their bases and targets in the Atlantic. This in turn also suggests a paradox, that although the British had reinvented their perception of their own submarines, the image of hostile submarine warfare was, not unrealistically for a maritime nation, one of unrestricted submarine warfare. The importance of this process was demonstrated by the considerable resources that were put into anti-submarine warfare, both in terms of subsurface, surface and air assets.

It is the change in signification of the submarine due to its reinvention as an anti-submarine warfare platform that is particularly striking. The development of the hunter-killer submarine impacts on two important naval traditions – that of the balanced fleet, and that of command of the sea, both longstanding and important British cultural constructs that expressed a distinct view of seapower, completing a process that started with the Anglo–German Naval Agreement and was continued through the experiences of war. Between 1935 and 1965 the submarine became part of the balanced fleet concept, at first admittedly, by being used to help mislead the Germans into building a fleet that suited the British to fight in the event of war, but also by becoming an anti-submarine warfare platform; given Naval sensitivities about the interdiction of supply routes by Soviet submarines, this is not particularly surprising. At the same time, by becoming an essential part of the concept of the balanced fleet, the submarine became part of the concept that came with a balanced fleet – that of command of the sea.

The reception of these post-war changes can be regarded as warm at a corporate level and generally disinterested at the civil level. Interest was only really expressed at the civil level when the submarine was used as a tool to demonstrate British superiority, either in the modernity of its equipment, or the performance of its vessels, but any such interest was intermittent and spasmodic. The general disinterest at the civil level with the submarine as a threatening weapon system, can be seen as a continuation of the late interwar public obsession with the bomber and attacks from the air. In the post-war period the fear of aerial attack was given a major boost by nuclear weapons, thus making the threat of slow starvation rather less worrying than the end of Britain within four minutes. It would take another technological change, that of nuclear propulsion and submarine-based nuclear missiles, to propel the submarine back into a civil perception of fear and destruction.

5

THE AGE OF THE BRITISH NUCLEAR SUBMARINE

'They've pinched a bit of fire from the sun and put it inside that submarine.'[1]

On 28 June 2005, the Royal Navy held its first fleet review at Spithead since the Silver Jubilee Review in 1977. This time, however, the occasion was not a celebration of a Royal event such as a coronation or jubilee, but the two hundredth anniversary of the Battle of Trafalgar. The review was held in June rather than on 21 October – the date of the battle – in the hope of better weather.[2] Possibly as many as 250,000 spectators attended, crowding the beaches at Southsea and the Gosport peninsular, while others took to small boats in an effort to see an international fleet of 167 ships, of which 67 were from the Royal Navy.[3]

The media approach to this review was very different from that at the 1977 Silver Jubilee Review nearly 30 years earlier. The lack of television coverage of the event was severely criticised.[4] The press coverage laid less emphasis on maps and lists of ships to convey the magnitude of the event and relied instead on a multitude of pictures to allow the reader to visualise the scene, even if without the traditional maps, the photographs presented a rather fragmented image of the event. The by-product of the shift in the press depiction of the event was a change in the importance of the ships themselves and, in particular, the submarine. Without maps to illustrate the review, the submarine was overlooked in the photographs being almost unrecognisable was clearly demonstrated in the *Daily Mail*'s front-page photograph of the review. The picture showed almost the entire fleet, and while the aircraft carriers, destroyers and auxiliaries can all be seen, the submarines, because of their small size and position low in the water, could be confused with a blemish on the photograph.[5] In many respects the press coverage of submarines was no better than at the 1911 Coronation Review when, in its coverage of events at Spithead, the *Illustrated London News* informed its readers that the small shapes in the foreground of one picture were, in fact, submarines.[6] The media coverage of submarines vindicated a comment made by an Admiralty staff officer nearly 70 years earlier that 'S/Ms [submarines] are not impressive vessels for review purposes.'[7] Indeed, none of the photographs published in *The Times*, the *Daily Telegraph*, the *Guardian* or *Daily Mail* as part of their coverage of the Trafalgar 200 Review, focused on the submarines.[8]

Despite the emphasis on the human interest side of the review at the expense of maps and statistics, the review was generally well received by the press. There was none of the criticism of the composition of the fleet that had accompanied the 1935 Silver Jubilee Review,[9] although the *Daily Mail* did note that it would be 'churlish to point out that vessels from 35 other countries had to be drafted in to deliver a display that the Royal Navy would have once put on single-handed'.[10] However, adverse comments were reserved for the perceived political correctness of the review when the organisers, in a seeming desire to avoid causing offence to the French and Spanish in the re-enactment of a Napoleonic era sea battle, used 'Red' and 'Blue' ships rather than representations of the national fleets.[11] However, only one article – in the *Guardian* – criticised both the form and purpose of the review noting that 'Everything to do with today's celebrations is either essentially trivial or essentially suspect' and 'Today is a day for sentimentality; October 21 1805 was something dedicated to something altogether sterner: the uncompromising pursuit and annihilation of the enemy.'[12]

All the British submarines present at the review were nuclear-powered fleet submarines that in terms of engineering and technological achievement could only be surpassed by space exploration. In fact, the SSNs with their dual-purpose torpedoes, as well as anti-ship and land-attack missiles, were the most formidable warships present at the review. Yet defence issues in general, and submarines in particular, had by 2005, been relegated to a marginal aspect of human-interest stories. Such ambivalence about the atomic age is a new facet of British culture – atomic warfare has been one of the most feared weapons and divisive subjects, supplanting the earlier bogeymen of unrestricted submarine warfare and the conventional bomber.

This chapter will look at how the nuclear age changed civil and corporate perceptions of the submarine through its application of nuclear power and weapons. To cover such a wide range of submarine activity, three topics will be examined. The first is the corporate reaction of the Royal Navy to both nuclear-powered submarines, and the appearance of the nuclear-armed missile submarine. The 1960s was a period of great change for the Royal Navy, not least due to the introduction of new types of submarine, and these changes in both the Royal Navy as a whole and in submarine development had an impact on how, at the corporate level, the meaning of submarines was constructed. This opening section will also discuss the reappearance of the Fleet submarine concept. The change in collective understanding of the submarine and the desire to promote it as the Royal Navy's main offensive weapon will be analysed in the next two sections, discussing the public face of submarines as seen through naval pageantry and the anti-nuclear movement. The third section will examine the symbolism of the submarine naming policy during the period.

The Royal Navy and Nuclear Submarines

The change in submarine operations brought on by nuclear power cannot be under-estimated. Even before the first British nuclear-powered Fleet submarine (HMS *Dreadnought*) had entered service, the Royal Navy had experienced a Fleet submarine, the *USS Nautilus*, working with the Home Fleet.[13] As part of Operation Rum Tub, *Nautilus* made a dived passage during which British submarines, surface units, and the Royal Air Force's Coastal Command attempted to intercept her. The Home Fleet's Operations Officer, a former submariner, noted that:

> the most remarkable part of the of the whole operation was her success as a dived escort for HMS *Bulwark*, a role which she had never before contemplated, let alone rehearsed. She had no difficulty holding her station on the screen and easily detected the only two enemy submarines which came within range of her sonar.[14]

The Royal Navy now had proof that a nuclear submarine could easily work with a fleet in a way that a conventionally powered one could not. It cannot be seen as a coincidence that the nuclear-powered submarine was termed by the Royal Navy the 'Fleet' submarine, especially when the renewed interest in submarines operating with surface groups (direct support) in the Cold War is considered.[15] Yet the emphasis on a Fleet submarine suggests a continued effort to integrate the submarine into the mainstream Navy. By emphasising that this new and revolutionary form of submarine was a Fleet asset, it helped produce a mechanism for imagining or understanding the nuclear-powered submarine in a way that would not threaten the surface Fleet. It has even been suggested that at one period, the Royal Navy viewed SSNs as independently powered variable-depth sonars,[16] indicating that these new Fleet submarines were seen by some as units dependent on the surface for command and tactical control rather than autonomous weapon systems.

Almost unlimited propulsive power and submerged endurance did not remove all of the traditional stumbling blocks for submarines operating in direct support of surface units: poor communications prevented the easy exchange of information between submarine and surface ship which in turn limited the ability to differentiate between friendly and hostile submarines.[17]

In the light of these problems a consensus developed that direct support was ineffective and dangerous, and using submarines in indirect or associated support to surface units was better and safer for NATO SSNs while allowing the surface Fleet and air assets greater freedom of action in the anti-submarine battle.[18] The direct support or escort role was not given up easily. As late as 1974, 17 years after Operation Rum Tub, there were still staff papers discussing 'linked' and 'unlinked' escort scenarios for the SSN force.[19] Indeed, the longevity of the 'linked' operational concept indicates the desire to integrate the submarine into the Fleet as a tactical unit, a desire that was in part reflected in contemporary novels.[20] In staff papers it was noted that 'linked' direct support (the use of a submarine as a mobile variable-depth sonar controlled by a surface ship) was ineffectual:

> Studies have shown that the use of a nuclear submarine in this role is not an effective employment. When close to a force using active sonar the SSN must also operate actively and, in the case of a fast force, must sprint and drift in order to retain his station and still conduct his search. It was found that an enemy SSN was usually able to work round the SSN (EL) and attack the force or even the SSN (EL) or its link ship.[21]

However, the use of the submarine as an 'unlinked' escort about 30,000 yards ahead of the force was considered more successful, paving the way for submarines to support surface forces from a distance rather than as part of the close screen.[22]

With the end of the Cold War, the submarine service again picked up on operations with surface units. Rear Admiral Perowne, the Flag Officer Submarine, told a Royal Navy public relations magazine *Broadsheet 96/7* that 'The emphasis in submarine operations was shifted towards support of the Joint Task Group and Littoral Warfare.'[23] The following year, in an article called 'The Submarine Service – A Bright Future?', *Broadsheet* stated that 'the SSN can make a significant contribution while working as an integrated member of a Task

Group'.[24] The same article pointed out that the perennial problems of tactical communications with a submarine were being resolved. The level of integration between submarine and surface force envisaged through the *K* class submarines 80 years earlier had finally been achieved.

The effort to integrate the submarine with the Fleet, if spasmodic at times during the hundred-year history of British submarines, demonstrates clearly that meanings regarding undersea warfare had been constructed around the battlefleet. The longevity of the Fleet submarine concept – finally perfected in the 1990s – in the face of technological failure and alternative methods of exploiting submarine warfare suggests that these meanings were based more on cultural attitudes than operational need. Each and every effort to produce a viable Fleet submarine concept had a battlefleet construction of seapower as its basis, which avoided making war on non-combatants. As far as the British submarine was concerned, it had to be understood through its relationship to the battlefleet and its latter day successors, an understanding that was based on a respect for private property, international law and non-combatants, as discussed in previous chapters.

Nor does the integration of the submarine into the Fleet mean that the SSN was welcomed by all sections of the Royal Navy. The faction that was under the most political and financial threat during the gestation of the SSN was the fixed-wing carrier fraternity. Between the mid-1950s and 1966 the Fleet Air Arm, supported by a considerable body of the Royal Navy, had been trying to obtain the replacement of the war built aircraft carriers that were not best suited to the larger, faster, jet-powered fighter-bombers that were entering service.[25] During the 1950s and early 1960s, the aircraft carrier had been at the centre of the Royal Navy's case for a limited war and power projection role against the missile based future envisaged by the 1957 Sandys Defence Review. The 1966 decision to cancel the aircraft carrier replacements and wind up fixed-wing aviation in the Royal Navy, primarily on cost grounds by the recently centralised Ministry of Defence,[26] was a profound shock to much of the

Navy, although certain parts of the surface warfare and submarine communities had not been fully behind the carrier programme.

Due to this long running debate about the future of the aircraft carrier, the SSN was not necessarily considered a welcome addition to the Fleet as the nuclear submarine and aircraft carrier replacement programme were to a degree in competition with each other for limited resources. After the cancellation of the CVA-01 project in 1966,[27] investigations into what a carrier-less Navy would look like argued that 'The Navy should never again be allowed to become so heavily reliant – as it had been in the era of the aircraft carriers – on a very small, very expensive class of ship…'.[28] As a result of this desire to avoid over-reliance on a few very expensive vessels, it was felt that the Royal Navy could not afford more than one major strike weapon for use against surface forces,[29] and that it 'should be the SSNs, which also have a powerful offensive capability against enemy submarines…'.[30] Some felt that the SSN was still underrated,[31] despite strong endorsement, although the idea of an all submarine Fleet, tempting though it was in easing the problems of air defence without aircraft carriers, was not feasible because it was not 'wholly applicable to our concept of operations', although, rather enigmatically, no further explanation was offered in the paper.[32] The editor of *Jane's Fighting Ships* summed up the feeling in the Royal Navy in the foreword to the 1966–67 edition by saying that 'while the Fleet Air Arm has every justification for despondency, the Submarine Service is elated for numerically in the number of ships, and probably technically too, it is the strongest arm of the Royal Navy.'[33]

To observers within the Royal Navy, it was clear that the emphasis on the SSN's war fighting potential ignored the many peacetime tasks faced by the Navy and that furthermore, 'the SSN carries no boats, so she is of little use to a vessels in distress; she has no towing facilities; she has little room for men or stores to assist in earthquake or volcano-stricken areas.'[34] This a matter of some importance: naval diplomacy, public relations and the opportunities to influence foreign governments through assistance, disaster relief and goodwill visits all contributed to the Royal Navy's value to the government in peacetime. However, it was noted that for 'showing the flag' or naval diplomacy, 'the sleek black shape of a nuclear submarine would now spell out the Royal Navy's presence and power more forcibly'.[35] For the first time, the submarine's sinister appearance played in its favour. What had caused this change in attitudes? It is obvious that nuclear submarines had been conferred with images of power which in previous years would have been ascribed to the battleship; the cultural imagining of seapower had changed. However, unlike almost any other warship, the British SSNs had no weapons that could be deployed against the land until the deployment of the Tomahawk cruise missile in the late 1990s. Therefore, any images of power conferred on the SSN were not due to a fear of what it could do to a land target, but instead to what the nuclear submarine represented in terms of seapower and national technological superiority. The nuclear submarine was by far the most complex piece of military hardware and the possession of one represented a massive national technological superiority that was only surpassed by the ability to put a man in space.

The almost simultaneous adoption of the nuclear deterrent SSBNs also caused problems. Perhaps the most trivial were the standard worries that it would unbalance the battlefleet (indeed the aircraft carrier replacement programme had caused similar fears). As a result it was alleged that the Royal Navy 'was slow in developing interest in the Polaris submarine, fearing it would divert funds from the traditional fleet.'[36] There were also concerns that the costs of operating the nuclear deterrent, both financial and in terms of manning, would so 'distort the Navy that it becomes unable to discharge its traditional mission, which remains as relevant today as it ever was in the past.'[37] Fears about unbalancing the fleet did result in a corporate move against pressurising the Labour Government to restore the cancelled fifth Polaris submarine in favour of a higher priority being accorded to naval aircraft and other types of vessels for the more traditional fleet.'³⁸

The real corporate danger posed by Polaris was not to the Royal Navy, despite what it may have thought about unbalanced fleets, but to the Royal Air Force who, with the Navy's acquisition of Polaris, stood to lose sole control of the United Kingdom's independent nuclear deterrent, and with it most of its rationale to exist as an independent air force:

> The Royal Air Force proselytised the independent deterrent because they possessed the means of delivery. They fought to retain this rôle because they felt that the 'V' bomber force provided the *raison d'être* for the continued existence of the Air Force as a separate arm of the fighting services.³⁹

The Vice-Chief of the Air Staff considered that 'The enemy of the bomber is the Polaris submarine.'⁴⁰ The Royal Navy and Polaris posed a very serious threat to the RAF and, having lost the nuclear deterrent argument in 1962, they were in no mood to allow the Royal Navy to replace the aircraft carriers in 1966 which would further weaken the RAF's reason to remain a separate entity. Indeed, there is a cultural reading of these inter-service disputes. The Royal Navy was the senior service and historically *the* British defence arm, resulting in it being a key component of national identity since the Victorian period while the RAF was the most junior of the fighting services and one that had in many respects supplanted the Royal Navy in being regarded as *the* defence arm as a result of the Second World War and the Battle of Britain in particular. Thus, these disputes can also be seen as a struggle to see how defence issues would be conceptualised within British culture. It was not, however, a battle over modernity, as both services were using the newest and most advanced technologies but was rather a battle for importance.

The submarine's direct and indirect involvement as a catalyst for intra and inter-service rivalries did, as a result of the material changes forced upon the Royal Navy in the 1960s, create a new way of understanding the submarine. The clashes of corporate cultures over who was going to be the most important arm of defence resulted in the Royal Navy trumpeting the nuclear Fleet submarine as a submarine that, for the first time, was capable of achieving that still-cherished ambition of the Royal Navy – that of command of the sea[41] – independent of airpower.[42] The emphasis by the Future Fleet Working Party and many others that the SSN was now the Royal Navy's primary strike weapon for the post-1966 Fleet can be seen as a watershed in the way that the corporate meaning of the submarine was constructed.[43] In previous years, navies had seen first the battleship and then the aircraft carrier as the culmination and embodiment of naval might; now this place had been taken by the submarine, the nuclear-powered conventionally armed SSN. The possession of nuclear SSN or 'Fleet' submarines, it was argued, was the 'hallmark of a first-class navy'.[44]

The nuclear submarine, both SSN and SSBN, had in many ways come to supplant the battleship as the symbol of naval might and national technological ability, and in this way it epitomized Harold Wilson's 'white heat of technology' and his vision of a technology-led society which he had expounded at the 1963 Labour Party Conference. Wilson's speech staggered the delegates, striking a chord with the public at a time when technological change had a high degree of visibility.[45] Wilson, it seems, also 'shared with the man in the pub an emotional attachment to that ultimate virility symbol, the national deterrent.'[46] Furthermore, the Americans agreed with this view of the British submarine based deterrent: 'The nuclear deterrent is the most important of the great power symbols still in British possession.'[47] In an era that was characterized by the desire to maintain the pretensions of a great political, military and economic power,[48] the procession of SSNs and SSBNs set Britain apart from other nations. Through the adoption of nuclear power, the submarine had reached its zenith in its role in the construction of national identity. The nuclear submarine was now seen as vital in order for Britain to be regarded as a first-class naval power. The nuclear deterrent based on the Polaris submarines supported the traditional patriotic constructions of Britain as a great power.[49]

Previously the battleship, with its requirement for the most intricate engineering and multitude of different technologies, had demonstrated national technological ability. Now the nuclear submarine required even higher standards of engineering and scientific achievement in areas such as physics, meturallugy, electronics and metal working. This change in attitude was shown at the institutional level by the depiction of an SSN on the cover of Volumes 1 and 2 of the 1967 Future Fleet Working Party report which referred to the SSN as 'the Navy's main offensive weapon', commenting that 'no other type of warship holds so much potential for the future', and that it 'has brought a new dimension to naval warfare.'[50] By placing an image of an SSN so prominently on the plan for a carrier-less navy it produced a clear demonstration of corporate support for the SSN submarine, although the SSBN was conspicuous by its absence.

By 1968, senior former submariners like Ian McGeoch were arguing in the Royal Navy's own professional journal that 'the time has passed when the submarine arm of the Royal Navy could be regarded strategically, tactically and in organisation, as professionally "not my part of ship" by the rest of the Navy.'[51] It was also hoped that the changes in the Royal Navy, and the passage of time, would eventually dispel the 'apartheid'[52] that existed between the surface navy and the submariners, although 'as with the racial problem an instant solution cannot be expected.'[53] This is a clear reference to the huge changes forced upon the Royal Navy by the decision to end fixed-wing carrier aviation and the resulting emphasis on the submarine service as the main offensive weapon of the Navy. The submarine has retained its corporate importance; in 1994 the Royal Navy listed its key capabilities as aircraft carriers (although these were smaller than the old Fleet carriers), submarines and amphibious forces within a balanced fleet.[54]

The Public Face of Nuclear Submarines

Although the corporate self-image of submarines had undergone a considerable reconstruction with the advent of nuclear propulsion, nuclear missiles, the SSN and the SSBN, the public face of the submarine as a weapon in Britain was pulled in two very different ways. First, there was the image projected by the corporate culture into the civil sphere, while second, there was the opposition to nuclear weapons and later nuclear propulsion on ethical and moral grounds.

The manner in which the Navy's corporate culture was displayed to the public took several forms. There were the individual names that the Navy chose to give its new nuclear-powered submarines, which are discussed in detail in a separate section below. There was the manner in which the Navy advertised itself to the public for recruiting purposes and the part the nuclear submarine played in such a process. Lastly, there was the naval pageantry that was used to display and reinforce images of corporate and institutional approval of the nuclear submarine such as the presentation of a Queen's colour to the submarine service and introduction of branch badges, together with launching ceremonies and visits by Royalty and other dignitaries.

One of the advertisements the Royal Navy ran during the early 1960s in order to attract potential officer recruits was entitled *Underwater Warfare*.[55] The half-page advertisement featured a banner photograph of the SSN HMS *Dreadnought* and invoked the memory of Nelson (perhaps the ultimate accolade the Royal Navy could confer) with the observation that:

> In 1799 Nelson wrote to Lord Howe 'I had the happiness to command a band of brothers'. This could be said by any commander in the submarine service today.[56]

The advertisement was rounded off by pointing out that the Fleet (and by default the submarine service) was 'the life for the pick of the young men of Britain – young men who will give – and get – the best out of life.'[57] However, such advertisements did not escape criticism. Brian Callison used their style to lampoon the Royal Navy suggesting that Merchant Navy officers were perhaps the real professional, and 'Not like those ruggedly salty young men who stare at you invitingly from the pages of the Sunday supplements, about to leap straight from the bridge of the Polaris submarine that You Too Could Command into a conveniently parked sports car below.'[58] The fact that Callison could caricature the Royal Navy's advertisements (see figure 5.1 for an example) in a novel, and make the submarine a Polaris

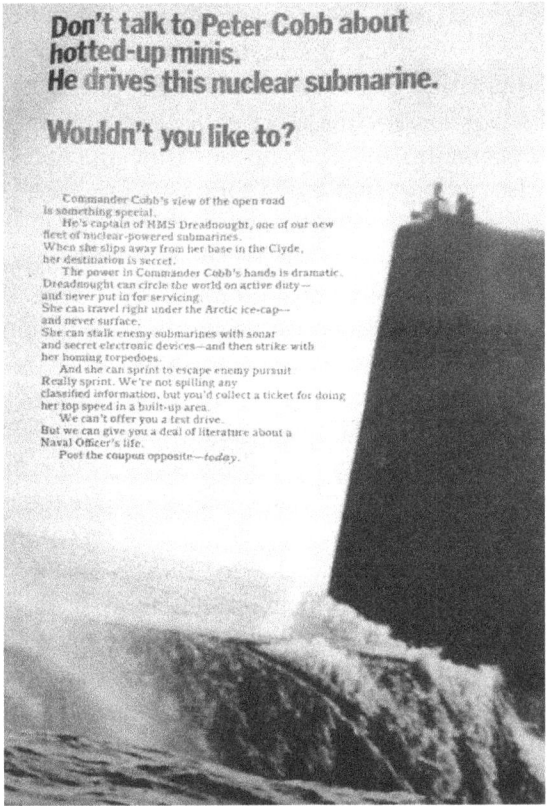

Figure 5.1: Royal Navy recruiting advert, possibly the style of advertising that inspired Brian Callison's caustic comment about submarines '...that You Too Could Command...' (The National Archives, INF 2/166)

one, shows how effective had been the recruiting campaign in projecting an image of modernity into the submarine service and that the recruiting campaign had received considerable attention. Yet the submarine service did not monopolise the Royal Navy's advertising campaign. Until the decision to end fixed-wing carrier aviation in the Royal Navy during 1966, the Fleet Air Arm received greater exposure in national recruiting campaigns run in the press.[59] After the political decision was made to cancel the CVA–01 project however, other advertisements deliberately under-emphasized the Fleet Air Arm and the fixed-wing aircraft carriers in favour of the SSN force.[60]

There were other indications that the move to a nuclear-powered submarine fleet was causing a reappraisal of the submarine. Perhaps one of the most public and important official moves to emphasize the importance of the submarine service, was the decision to give the Submarine Command its own Queen's Colour, an event that occurred just before the laying down of HMS *Dreadnought* in 1959. When the Queen presented her colour to the Submarine Command she spoke about the future of the submarine service saying that 'the striking power and versatility of submarines will increase beyond all recognition with the advent of nuclear engines and guided missiles', and that 'the nuclear submarine may well become the capital ship round which the Navy of the future will be built.'[61] Yet only the *The Times* and *Manchester Guardian* gave any attention to the ceremony; the *Daily Express*, *Daily Mail*, and *Daily Mirror* did not cover the story and the articles in *The Times* and *Manchester Guardian* did little more than strictly report the Queen's comments and avoided any commentary themselves.[62] The significance of this is straightforward: before the wider recognition of the importance of the SSN and SSBN, the submarine did not warrant attention and it is only with hindsight that the significance of the almost simultaneous keel-laying of the first SSN with the presentation of the first Submarine Service Queen's Colour is apparent. Acts such as the keel-laying and the presentation of the Queen's Colour were at the very leading edge of a corporate reinvention of the submarine and it is therefore unsurprising that their initial reception failed to draw any recognisable signification of the events.

Figure 5:2: Royal Navy Submarine Service branch badge – the 'Dolphins' badge. (Author's photograph)

The age of the nuclear submarine also saw the inauguration of a specialist badge for submariners, in the same way that Fleet Air Arm aircrew had pilot or observer, or aircrewman insignia. The new submariner's badge (figure 5.2) was announced in July 1971 in *The Times*, who stated it was 'to signify their specialist role in the service.'[63] The article went on to emphasize that the submarine badge was 'authorised by the Queen' and that 'it will be worn by officers and men either above or in the position of medal ribbons to show that they possess "special skills related to a special environment".'[64] The decision to create a special badge for submariners emphasizes the elitism conferred by 'special skills' in a 'special environment'[65] that surrounded the submarine service in the nuclear age and also the technological expertise that was required for modern submarines. This was not, however, the first attempt to have a specialisation badge for the submariners. Between 1958 and 1964 a sub-specialisation badge, to be worn on the right sleeve just above the cuff, was authorised for junior and senior ratings, but not officers.[66] It is interesting to note that officers were excluded from this earlier badge, suggesting that they were not specialists but more fully integrated into the wider Royal Navy officer class. This ratings-only badge was apparently never issued: instead, it had to be purchased by the wearer from naval stores, something that probably contributed to the low numbers actually worn as well as its unpopularity.[67]

It is hard not to see a connection between the new-found importance of the submarine to Britain in the age of the SSN and SSBN and the decision to issue a new branch badge for all Royal Navy submariners. Furthermore, the timing of the decision coincided with a period that Martin Wiener has identified with a reversal in the general British dislike of industry, change, innovation and technology.[68] Instead of dislike, Wiener argues that, under the Wilson and Heath governments between 1964 and 1974, there was a burst of enthusiasm for modernisation, to 'reshape Britain in the "white heat of a new technological revolution"...'[69] and 'break the psychological resistance, within and outside the party, to modernisation.'[70] The bubble of enthusiasm burst due to the growth of organised opposition to technological and material advances, with the new spirit of resistance embodied by John Betjeman who extended the pastoral nostalgia of his predecessors as poet laureate to suburbia as he 'disparaged the new and evoked the security of old, familiar things.'[71] Yet the Royal Navy did not have such symbols of old familiar things to provide security. The battleship was gone: the aircraft carrier and the cruiser, as well as the traditional gun and torpedo-armed destroyer were going, as was a global role.[72] For the Royal Navy there was only the submarine and the promise of prestige through modernity.

What is important to note in considering the production of these two different badges, one unpopular and one successful, is the dates of their introduction (1958–1971) and the inclusiveness of the second badge – no exemption for officers. This time frame represents the founding years of both the SSN and SSBN programmes in the Royal Navy. Thus, the public display of Admiralty approval by approving a branch badge, shows the increasing corporate acceptability of submarines. The inclusive nature of the badge also shows a desire to communicate the submarine service as a separate elite body both within the Royal Navy and to a wider public rather than play on officer/enlisted men divisions and status. Also of symbolic importance is the positioning of the badge, 'above or in the position of medal ribbons'[73] as this is the only branch or specialisation badge in the Royal Navy to be worn in that position (even aircrew have to wear their wings on the sleeve just above the cuff or rank insignia). By placing a branch badge with the position of the medals, the sense of accomplishment for the holder is enhanced while at the same time emphasising the exclusivity of the award. When, during the middle of the Second World War, the Fleet Air Arm asked for their specialisation badges to be placed on the left breast (like the RAF) rather than the sleeve cuff, it was noted that 'From time immemorial the left breast of Naval Uniform has been reserved for decorations'.[74] Only the submariners have broken this uniform taboo.

Another factor has to be considered, namely the reluctance of the Royal Navy to encourage 'private navies' within the service. Indeed, as has been argued in previous chapters, the need to assimilate the submarine within the battlefleet mentality played a large part in the construction of corporate meaning and understanding of the submarine. During the Second World War, when the Admiralty were considering requests from the Fleet Air Arm to increase the Fleet Air Arm's visibility with the service and to the public through the more prominent positioning of their 'wings', it was noted that:

> Indeed there is quite equal justification for similarly labelling our Submarine and other specialists. Had we done so in the early days of Submarines, we would undoubtedly have contributed to the establishment of a 'Submarine Service' distinct from and practically unknown to the Naval

Service generally – precisely the thing which we wish to avoid in the case of the Naval Air Service.⁷⁵

The introduction of the current badge almost 30 years later, worn by all submariners, would suggest that the Ministry of Defence and the Royal Navy were overtly admitting the creation of a separate submarine service. This has two possible implications. One is that this was an admission of the importance of the submarine to the preservation of the balanced fleet and its emergence as the most powerful conventional and nuclear weapons system in the British arsenal. Alternatively, it could reflect a final surrender to the determination of submariners to be different from the surface fleet, an idea which is given weight by the names given to the later classes of SSNs where, as discussed below, the submarine service's own history grew in importance in the selection of names for the *S* and *T* class SSNs. Whatever the reason for the 1971 decision to issue a submarine service badge, it demonstrated that there was a reconsideration of the importance of the submarine in the nuclear age, a reconsideration that can also be seen in submarine-launching ceremonies.

With the advent of nuclear-propelled and later nuclear-armed submarines there was a distinct change in the naval pageantry that surrounded the building and launching of a submarine. It is instructive to compare the launching of nuclear submarines to that of conventional submarines of the period. In 1961, a few months before the launch of HMS *Dreadnought*, the *Oberon* class submarine HMS *Otter* was sponsored by a Mrs M A Sinclair Scott,⁷⁶ who was presumably connected to the owners of Scott's Shipbuilding and Engineering (the firm that was building the *Otter.*) *The Times* article itself amounts to only just over three lines of text plus a large picture of the bows of the submarine; there is no reporting on the numbers of spectators, or of any speeches by the dignitaries at the event.⁷⁷ Furthermore, Mrs Scott is clearly not a grand VIP, which, together with the scant press reporting, emphasizes the low-key nature of the launching ceremony for HMS *Otter*.

This relatively low level of media interest, even allowing for a reproduction of a large picture of the launch at a time when pictures were still reasonably rare in newspapers, has to be contrasted with the display of corporate, establishment and media interest in the new nuclear submarines. At the laying down ceremony for HMS *Dreadnought*, the dignitary in question was the Duke of Edinburgh (clearly a VIP way above Mrs Scott), himself a former regular officer in the Royal Navy who had served in destroyers, and who observed that:

> On Monday the Queen presented her colour to the Submarine Command. Today that colour is here at Barrow with a guard of submariners to witness an event which will most certainly revolutionise the Navy as a whole and the submarine service in particular. It should be abundantly clear by now that nuclear submarines will ultimately transform the sea power of the Atlantic alliance.[78]

Such public pronouncements as to the importance of the nuclear submarine, reinforced by the presence of the Queen's consort would have sent strong signals across the public sphere that submarines were an acceptable part of British naval power. Yet, while paying tribute to the historic nature of the event, it was the novel method of keel laying that got the *Manchester Guardian*'s attention as *Dreadnought* did not have a keel in the traditional sense, so Prince Phillip operated a switch to manoeuvre the circular first section of the hull into position[79] – an interesting blend of modernity in construction methods with traditional ceremonial. Indeed, by creating a keel-laying ceremony where there was no keel to lay, the Navy was in fact expressing the modernity of everything to do with the nuclear submarine, yet doing so in a familiar, traditional manner that linked the nuclear submarine with an earlier age through the updating of existing pageantry. Change and modernity, through the context of an invented keel-laying ceremony, was being placed in a historical context suggesting continuity with the past to make the new seem familiar and less threatening.

The idea that the Royal Navy and Britain were witnessing an important change in the meaning of submarines was continued throughout the building of *Dreadnought*. Even the date of *Dreadnought*'s launch – 21 October, Trafalgar Day – had deep symbolism for Britain invoking images of Nelson: the launch of such a revolutionary submarine, implied a glorious naval future to match a glorious maritime past. The fact that the launching date would have reminded people about a more heroic past says much about the loss of national self-esteem following the Second World War, when it was painfully obvious to all that Britain was no longer the world's only maritime superpower.[80]

The launch of HMS *Dreadnought* was itself an indication of the importance that was being attached to the nuclear submarine at the corporate level. The *Dreadnought* was the first British submarine to be launched by a reigning monarch, in addition to the fact that the keel had been laid by her consort some months earlier. The presence of royalty at both the keel-laying and the launch was unusual; even during the heyday of navalism in the Edwardian period; ship launches by the monarch were rare – with the exception of King Edward VII launching the *Dreadnought* in 1906 – thanks to the nineteenth-century precedent that launches were carried out by a woman not a man.[81] Queen Elizabeth II also recalled at the launching ceremony that her great grandfather launched the previous HMS *Dreadnought* 54 years earlier and that it was considered a 'tremendous improvement in warship design',[82] with the unspoken assumption that the submarine *Dreadnought* was also a major leap in warship design, and like the battleship *Dreadnought*, marked a new era in naval technology. The name *Dreadnought* had, thanks to the revolutionary nature of Fisher's battleship, become synonymous with modernity.

The combination of Britain's first nuclear submarine with the name 'Dreadnought' was a powerful combination of modernising forces within the Royal Navy and historical continuity. In honour of the event, Vickers had a full page advertisement in the *Guardian* entitled 'freedom of the seas' that had sketches of each of the previous *Dreadnoughts*, clearly depicting both the continuity and modernity associated with the new submarine.[83] To make sure the readers got the point the Vickers advertisement went on to proclaim the 'the nuclear submarine which inherits this honoured name is the most important vessel to be built for the Royal Navy since the war.'[84] At the luncheon for the royal party and guests, the First lord of the Admiralty, now Lord Carrington, opined that 'This is a very special occasion for the Royal Navy, which I have the honour to represent, for today we have seen the birth not just of a new ship but of a new era…'[85]. The Queen's interest in *Dreadnought* continued after it was commissioned with her specifically asking for an opportunity to tour the submarine whilst it was in harbour.[86]

At the same time, it is clear that the launch was not just a corporate affair, *The Times* recorded that over 12,000 spectators turned up to witness the ceremony, including retired submariners from London who had chartered a bus to Barrow-in-Furness.[87] Even before the launch, *The Times* had been running articles in anticipation of the ceremony, accompanied by diagrams and sketches of the submarine.[88] Moreover, the Royal Navy had hammered home the nuclear submarine issue in the 1959 Royal Tournament, which, in the same month as the Duke of Edinburgh laid the keel of the submarine, staged a mock battle between nuclear submarines.[89]

Nor was the use of a high profile sponsor in the launch of the *Dreadnought* a one off. The first Polaris missile armed submarine, HMS *Resolution*, was launched by Queen Elizabeth the Queen Mother and again there were large crowds to witness the ceremony as well as special trains and coaches being laid on to cope with the demand.[90] The second Polaris submarine was launched by Mrs Denis Healey, the wife of the Secretary of State for Defence, watched by hundreds of children.[91] The second nuclear Fleet submarine, HMS *Valiant*, was launched in 1963 also by the then Secretary of State for Defence's wife, Mrs Peter Thornycroft.[92]

Yet despite all the acclamation, the launches of the SSBNs were accompanied to some extent or another by demonstrations against nuclear weapons by the Campaign for Nuclear Disarmament (CND) as well as protests during the construction of the submarines.[93] While it is easy to imagine that the Ministry of Defence and the Royal Navy would not have been unduly worried by the stories carried in a low volume weekly paper that dealt with single issue politics like *Peace News*, banner headlines in the national press would have been a different matter. Indeed, the first paragraph of the *Daily Mirror*'s coverage of the launch of *HMS Resolution* started 'Ban-the-Bomb demonstrators staged a protest...'[94] while the *Guardian* noted that 'CND demonstrators paraded almost unnoticed with protest placards near the gates of the Vicker [sic] yard.'[95] The *Daily Telegraph* on the other hand affected not to have noticed any protests.[96] In particular, the protests at the launching ceremonies would have generated a great deal of negative publicity for the Polaris project and by default the submarine. When the second Polaris submarine was launched at Camel-Lairds yard at Birkenhead *The Guardian*'s coverage was under the headline 'New Focal Points for CND' and predicted that Barrow and Birkenhead would supplant Aldermaston as the focus 'for a revitalised ban-the-bomb movement.'[97]

CND was obviously of sufficient concern to the Government so that in response to the protests, which were not just concerned with Britain's possession of the Polaris system, the Ministry of Defence in 1969 launched an advertising campaign to promote the Armed Forces.[98] Entitled 'Peace: we think it's a good idea' the advertisements stressed that the United Kingdom's Armed Forces, conventional and nuclear, were all working towards ensuring peace in Europe and that:

> Any contribution to preventing war should earn our gratitude, and the Service's contribution is incalculable. Since war would destroy all the social progress we have worked and hoped for, they themselves are performing a 'social service' as vital as any. It is a job to be proud of.[99]

While such advertisements might have had some effect on the undecided or disinterested, it is highly unlikely they would have swayed the CND activists.

The number of CND activists, however, as an indication of the degree of opposition to Polaris, is difficult to assess, not least because the movement did not start a formal membership scheme until 1966.[100] At the CND Annual Conference in 1968 it was stated that the total membership of CND was 3,959, of which 525 were more than one month overdue for renewal.[101] This figure seems very low when compared to the mass demonstrations that were a feature of the peace movement in the early 1960s, and which attracted up to 100,000 or 150,000 participants.[102] It was noted in *Peace News* that at the launching of *HMS Renown* on 26 February 1967 there were at least 1,000 protestors present, possibly more, depending on which reports were believed.[103] A total of fewer than 4,000 activists also seems low when the longevity of the anti-Polaris (and later anti-Trident campaign) and the regularity and size of some of the anti-nuclear protests is considered.[104] The total of 4,000 CND activists also seems low when the efforts required to man and support the Peace Camp established outside the Polaris base at Faslane, the protests at the Rhu narrows (where the submarines passed within shouting distance)[105] and the periodic attempts to get inside the base over a period of more than thirty years, are considered. Furthermore, the protests did not stop with the end of the Cold War, but continued as the Trident missile submarines were being constructed in the late 1980s and early 1990s.[106] What can be said from the protests at Barrow, Coulport and Faslane as well as from groups like the Scottish Campaign Against Trident, is that there was a very strong local slant to the CND activism.[107] Indeed, during the resurgence of the peace movement in the 1980s, so intense were the feelings of localism that groups frequently resisted initial attempts to bring them under the national CND banner.[108]

There are a number of factors that may be responsible for the national decline of CND which 'scarcely existed'[109] from 1963 until the 1980s. Perhaps most importantly, CND suffered from factionalism. Considering that CND was only formed in December 1958, the very public split that occurred in 1960 between those who viewed it as a conventional political pressure group and those who wanted to exploit street politics, and the resulting media attention, cannot have helped to maintain the number of activists.[110] It has also been suggested that changes in the international climate from the mid-1960s onwards contributed to the decline in CND activism. In particular, it has been argued that the Cuban Missile Crisis in 1962 not only alarmed many people but, paradoxically, it also demonstrated the ability of the superpower leaders to control nuclear weapons and avert war.[111] Furthermore, the escalation of the Vietnam War and the media coverage of that conflict demonstrated to the protest movement the violence of modern conventional war and gave the political left a new rallying cry of anti-imperialism.

An examination of the surviving conference papers at the CND archive in the London School of Economics revealed papers relating to the 1967, 1968 and 1969 conferences[112] – the very period when all the Polaris submarines were being launched and entering service. Only the 1967 conference makes any mention of Polaris, referring to an anti-Polaris demonstration that was planned for 11 November in a clear attempt to make capital out of the symbolism of Armistice Day.[113] The subject that was capturing the attention of the Annual Conferences was, however, Vietnam rather than Polaris.[114] This could suggest that, at a national level, CND was indeed focused elsewhere. On the other hand, it could mean that as the Polaris submarines were under construction and Wilson's Labour government had failed to live up to pre-election promises to cancel the entire Polaris programme,[115] CND had merely shifted its national attention to a field where policy could still be influenced. Wilson, it seems, regarded the Polaris issue as 'highly electoral'.[116] Yet it is also clear that the government thought that Polaris was sufficiently contentious so that a suggestion to name the first SSBN HMS *Churchill* was avoided in favour of the name being used on an SSN.[117]

Despite the national failure by CND to concentrate on Polaris, the division and debate over possession of nuclear weapons spilled over to effect perceptions of the submarine when the decision was made to arm submarines, first with Polaris nuclear-armed intercontinental ballistic missiles and then Trident missiles. As a result, the submarine was lumped in with nuclear weapons as a thing of horror and global destruction. Such a link seems mostly due to the efforts of locally motivated activists, particularly campaigns such as the Scottish Campaign Against Trident.[118] The tie between submarines and nuclear weapons was sufficiently strong that during the protests against the adoption of the Trident nuclear missile system that replaced Polaris, CND leaflets had images of submarines rather than of the missiles themselves or nuclear mushroom clouds.[119] Such imagery – which included a submarine sailing through a blood red sea indicate a deliberate link of submarines generally to the nuclear weapon issue. The submarine had become inseparable from the issue of nuclear weapons.

Nor was disquiet about the use of nuclear weapons confined to the civil sphere: one officer in 1965 was moved to discuss the moral aspects of the nuclear deterrent in the *Naval Review*.

> The fact that an H-bomb can produce such a vast degree of death and devastation compared with the largest conventional bomb dropped in World War II does not logically mean that it is a *lesser* matter of conscience to use the non-nuclear weapon. It makes no difference in the end whether you kill a man with a bullet or a bow and arrow; you have taken his life just the same.[120]

It was concluded, therefore, that nuclear weapons were not so much a matter of conscience, but rather one of practicalities, but 'it seems that many people outside and inside the armed Services, have acquired the wrong philosophy about the nuclear deterrent.'[121] For the *Naval Review* to have noticed opposition inside and outside the Royal Navy to nuclear weapons, the groundswell of opinion must have been quite strong, whether or not their philosophy was right or wrong.

Whatever the moral arguments regarding nuclear weapons and power, the understanding of submarines was affected at a civil and corporate level. These changes in how the submarine was perceived in Britain were very quickly translated at a corporate level by using the very names given to individual submarines to signify changes in status and use.

Nuclear Naming Policy: a Revolution in Corporate Attitudes to the Submarine?

It is clear that with the new opportunities of the nuclear age and the nuclear-powered submarine, the Royal Navy wished to emphasize the perceived importance of these vessels to both a corporate and civil audience through the medium of naming policy. Opinions were even sought from submariners as to how future submarines should be named:

> …if [nuclear] submarines are to be the important part of the Fleet that we say they are going to be, they deserve to have important names; names steeped in tradition going back to the earliest days of the Navy hitherto given to important ships of their day – in other words, big ones – and now to be handed on to the important ships of the future [submarines], that will again bear the brunt of the battle.
>
> Coupled with this, however, it is important to let new 'tradition' have air to breathe, and since submarine names are only one generation old, this means having a number of newish names as well.[122]

Perhaps the clearest example of the imagery the Royal Navy was seeking to associate with its new type of submarines was the decision to name the first nuclear-powered hunter killer submarine HMS *Dreadnought*. The name *Dreadnought* was clearly linked with Fisher's big gun battleship *Dreadnought* and in this respect its use emphasized the revolutionary nature of nuclear-powered submarines. The First Lord, the Earl of Selkirk, was keen to make a comparison between the old and new *Dreadnought*s in terms of seapower and technology when he announced the name of the first British SSN in July 1959: 'We are calling this ship *Dreadnought* because it is opening a new epoch just as was the old *Dreadnought*, built fifty years ago.'[123] The imagery used by the First Lord was not an accident, the Admiralty deliberately associated this new type of submarine with technological superiority and pass on subtle messages to both a corporate and public audience:

> After considerable discussion the Committee agreed that the most suitable choice would be DREADNOUGHT. This name had been considered by Flag Officer, Submarines, who preferred VULCAN on the grounds that DREADNOUGHT might conjure up in the minds of some people a rather ponderous type of ship. The Committee felt, however, that the name has a unique attraction in that it represents a land-mark in Naval history, associated as it is with the most revolutionary war-ship design, and it was fitting, therefore, that should be used for the first "Jet-Age" submarine.[124]

Using the name *Dreadnought* allowed the Navy to not only associate itself with cutting-edge technology for a 'jet-age' submarine and a glorious tradition of victories, but also send a message as to its own view of this new type of submarine; these were important vessels, capital ships in the same way Admiral Fisher's *Dreadnought* was. The decision to use the name *Dreadnought* for the first British nuclear powered submarine combined tradition with technology, together with the idea of a leap forward in how seapower could be delivered. Furthermore, the name *Dreadnought* would emphasize the new 'capital' ship nature of the nuclear attack submarine. The nuclear-powered submarines under construction were revolutionary: capable of high underwater speeds with an almost unlimited endurance, these submarines were true submarines, independent of the surface and only limited by the willingness of the crew to remain submerged. The nuclear submarine would truly dread nought.

Yet by the very choice of the name for such a special vessel, the Navy showed that it was in fact holding back from fully embracing the nuclear Fleet submarine. Traditionally, the first capital ship of a new sovereign's reign was named for the monarch, and these had all been battleships.[125] Therefore, if the SSN or Fleet submarine was as important to the Royal Navy as some people suggested at the time, then the name HMS *Queen Elizabeth* should have graced the first British SSN, but it did not. Indeed, the Royal Navy was intending to name the 1966 CVA–01 strike carrier design as HMS *Queen Elizabeth*.[126]

Just in case the message about the importance of these new 'fleet' submarines was insufficiently clear, the Navy sought to underline the concept with the choice of names for the subsequent vessels. Originally it was intended that the new SSN force would be given battlecruiser names starting with 'In'. This again speaks volumes about how the Navy viewed these vessels. Like the battlecruisers of the Fisher era these nuclear submarines were seen as the 'ship[s] of the future' that 'will undoubtedly control sea communications' and as a result should be given old battlecruiser names.[127] It is easy to see the parallels between the fast, high-endurance heavily armed battlecruisers that together with the dreadnoughts amounted to a revolution in naval construction and technology, and the fast, long-range SSNs with their heavy torpedo armament that, it was hoped, would revolutionise the submarine's part in naval warfare. The use of the name *Invincible*, however, was ruled out due to the explosive nature of battlecruiser *Invincible*'s sinking at the Battle of Jutland.[128] Fortunately, the decision to use *Inflexible* as the lead ship and class name for the first of the all British-SSNs (*Dreadnought*'s reactor and main machinery were supplied by the United States) was overturned as 'the epithet of inflexibility is the last one that we should wish to apply to the Navy and to these new submarines in particular'.[129] Perhaps it was felt that the image of an unyielding, unbending vessel was appropriate for the Fisher era when Britain would not surrender her position of naval superiority to Imperial Germany. However, it was not, perhaps, an appropriate image for a navy that had to play a part in alliance politics with all the compromises that a less pre-eminent status now required, nor was the suggestion of obstinacy that came with the name *Inflexible* suitable for a navy that was actively embracing new technology. It is noteworthy, however, that *Inflexible* was considered an appropriate name for a later submarine in the class as 'it would not have quite the same effect as if it were applied to the leading ship of the class.'[130] This suggests a feeling existed that much of the imagery that would surround a new class of vessel would be bound up with the name of the lead member of the class; hence SSNs being known as the *Inflexibles* might not be desirable while the *Indefatigables* would create positive mental associations. Quite simply, the literal meaning of *Inflexible* meant the wrong image would be produced, no matter how many battle honours were carried by the name. On the other hand, the name *Indefatigable* for the lead ship would convey 'very aptly the essential quality of these nuclear boats.'[131] The SSN was, indeed, tireless underwater, with an almost indefatigable power source, as well as being difficult to destroy.

A similar problem was encountered with the name of the lead vessel of the *R* class nuclear ballistic missile armed submarines. It was initially agreed that the names would be *Revenge*, *Resolution*, *Repulse* and *Renown*. However, it was soon felt, that calling the lead submarine and the resulting class of SSBNs '*Revenge* submarines' would be counterproductive, although there was no problem with having a follow-on submarine called *Revenge*:

> These strike me as most excellent names…I suppose REVENGE is about the best name for a ship which one could possibly have. Nevertheless, I am inclined to wonder whether we would be really wise to christen SSBN 01 REVENGE. The essence of the British POLARIS fleet is deterrence and the concept of REVENGE seems to me to imply that deterrence would have failed. I am a little bit inclined to feel that those who are opposed to the concept of a British deterrent would find this grist to their mill.[132]

This could seem to be over-sensitivity about what is, after all, just a name, but the Controller was right in his Minute – the concept of deterrence is an uneasy bedfellow with that of revenge. In the end *Revenge* was the last R class SSBN to enter service, while the first of the class was given the name *Resolution*, a name more in keeping with the philosophy of deterrence, something that was considered 'a good augury' by one professional observer.[133] It is also worth noting that of the four *V* class SSBNs, *Vanguard*, *Victorious*, *Vigilant* and *Vengeance* that now form the second generation of the Royal Navy's nuclear deterrent, *Vengeance*, like *Revenge*, entered service last. The choice of, and order in which the names were used, also suggests a civil rather than a corporate audience for these particular submarine names, perhaps unsurprising given the very vocal (if rather small) anti-nuclear campaign lead by CND. However, given the lack of press commentary on the names of the *R* and *V* class SSBN it seems that the Royal Navy overestimated the likely public reaction to the names.

The Admiralty's agonising over the right names in the right order for the SSBN force throws up an interesting point about the cultural history of weapons. Prior to the nuclear age weapons succeeded through use, but with the SSBN and indeed all post-Second World War nuclear weapons they succeeded through not being used. In such a scenario, the image of the weapon becomes very important, and therefore the time spent by the Admiralty as it tried to create the right impression about its SSBN force was not time wasted; in fact it was a vital part of the image of the weapon system which cumulatively would ensure its non-use and success.

One thing is striking about the names eventually chosen for the Royal Navy's first generation of SSNs and SSBNs – *Dreadnought*, *Valiant*, *Warspite*, *Conqueror*, *Courageous*, *Churchill*, *Resolution*, *Renown*, *Repulse* and *Revenge* –which is the lack of any link to the submarine service. All of the above names, with the exception of *Churchill*, had been previously used for traditional capital ships: battleships and battlecruisers, and some considered this a reflection of the increased importance attached to these submarines from a very early period, especially the SSBNs.[134] Indeed, six of the nine names that had been used before had been associated with battleships while the other three were or, in the case of *Courageous*, had started life[135] as battlecruisers. The submarine service's own past, which the Captain 1st Submarine Squadron thought would provide inspiration for good names,[136] is conspicuous by its absence. The use of names that had previous associations with the submarine service would not have generated any association with either capital ships or indeed the increased importance of the SSN and SSBN to the Royal Navy for the general public.

Three of the names, *Valiant, Warspite* and *Churchill* are especially significant for two very different reasons. *Valiant* and *Warspite* were chosen for the next two follow-on SSNs after *Dreadnought*. Both names were famous for the exploits of eponymous battleships in the Second World War.[137] The name *Valiant* was first used in 1759 and the name had accumulated no less than 16 battle honours.[138] *Warspite* had an even more impressive record having received 25 battle honours starting with the raid on Cadiz in 1596.[139] As for *Churchill*, this was a new name, but its significance was bound up with the fact that it was named after Sir Winston Churchill. The decision to name an SSN after Churchill was not an easy one. Early discussions centred on the fact that applying the name to a new frigate or destroyer would be too dissimilar to the other names already used for such vessels and that a more significant ship should receive the name *Churchill*.[140] Churchill family members proved to be less than enthusiastic with the Ministry of Defence's suggestion that the Assault Ship HMS *Fearless* should be so renamed, on the grounds that it was not 'enough of a "fighting ship" and a "capital ship" to live up to the name…'[141]. Instead, they instead asked if the first Polaris submarine could be named *Churchill*, thus making it very clear the level of importance they felt should be associated with the name.[142] This was rejected by the Secretary of State for Defence due to 'the political sensitivity of Polaris submarines'[143] who suggested as an alternative one of the new SSNs under construction, which won the support of the

Churchill family.[144] Clearly, the new SSBNs and SSNs were 'capital ships.'

One indicator of importance has eluded submarines – the naming of a vessel after the sovereign or consort. Nuclear-powered and nuclear submarines might well have been revolutionary and considered very important with names to reflect this, but they were not given the names *Queen Elizabeth* or *Duke Of Edinburgh*. It seems that with the demise of battleships and battlecruisers as part of the fleet, only aircraft carriers were suitable ships for such an honour.[145] Even when the aircraft carrier replacement design CVA–01 was cancelled in 1966, no subsequent vessel was named for the sovereign or consort, although the closest name to one reflecting royalty was the 1972 *HMS Sovereign*, an *S* class submarine.

Yet despite the conscious decision to use former capital ship names on the new SSNs and SSBNs to signal the capital ship status of this new type of submarine, there was a reaction against the policy, perhaps indicating the submarine service's increasing sense of prestige, as seen with the decision to grant a branch badge in 1971. The meaning associated with submarines names was slowly reconstructed from that of future battleship to one that reflected the history not of the Royal Navy as a whole, but that of the submarine service. The reaction against capital ship names, either former battleship or aircraft carrier, was relatively swift; in 1968 it was noted by the chairman of the Ships' Names Committee that 'there is no great support for carrier names at this stage'[146] and instead a new tradition centred on names previously associated with submarines was developed from the 1970s onwards. Of the four classes to enter service from the 1970s onwards, the *S* and *T* class SSNs, the *U* class SSKs and the *V* class SSBNs, only the *V* class names had no previous links with the submarine service, instead relying on battleship and aircraft carrier names. Naturally, such an emphasis on names associated with earlier submarines would not place as much importance on battle honours due to the very short time that some of the names had been in use. Three out of six *S* class fleet submarines, *Swiftsure*, *Superb*, and *Spartan* were given names that had been last used on cruisers.[147] Two of the three remaining class members, *Sceptre* and *Splendid*, were given names that had been last used by the previous 1930s vintage *S* class submarines.[148] Only one name, the 1972 *Sovereign* was new and was possibly a compliment to Queen Elizabeth II on the twentieth anniversary of her accession, whilst remaining true to the usage of starting submarine names of this class with an 's'.

The successor to the *S* class, the *T* class SSNs, were an even greater reversion to the submarine service's own history at the expense of capital ship imagery and deep-seated corporate memory. Of the seven vessels launched over the ten-year period between 1981 and 1991, six of the names had previously been used on the 1930s era *T* class diesel-electric patrol submarines, although of these names only two (*Tireless* and *Talent*) had been used for submarines and no other type of vessel.[149] Furthermore, of these six names, only one (*Triumph*) also had an association with capital ships, having previously graced both an aircraft carrier and a pre-Dreadnought battleship; it also happens to be the oldest of the names used for the *T* class as it dates back to 1561.[150] The other names (*Torbay, Talent, Tireless, Turbulent*, and *Trenchant*) had never been used on any vessel larger than a destroyer. One particular aspect of previous submarines' history shows through in the use of *Torbay, Turbulent* (and indeed, *Upholder*, the lead submarine of the aborted *U* class SSK conventional submarine in the 1990s) – that of gallantry. The commanding officers of each of the previous submarines to receive these names had been awarded the Victoria Cross during the Second World War.[151]

Yet these later submarine names which reflect the Submarine Service's own history were those which have received the most public criticism. In correspondence published in the *Navy News* during 1997, the decision to use the names *Astute, Ambush* and *Artful* was greeted with some disappointment as they did not have any battle honours and the names had only ever been used on the previous *A* class late second generation patrol submarines dating from 1945.[152] The correspondent, M Thompson continued:

The Royal Navy has a long, terrific history and tradition second to none and I feel that this ought to be reflected in the naming of proposed warships.

Sometimes it is a disadvantage to be the silent service [submarine service]. A long Battle Honours Board displayed is a great reflection of past glories and gives the modern navy something to live up to in today's world.[153]

Here is a very clear reaction to the use of a short-term 'submarine' history as opposed to that of a long-term general naval history that venerates a more comprehensive view of the Royal Navy's past. It is also significant that these comments are made in the *Navy News*. The *Navy News* is the Royal Navy's own paper, which, although available to the public, tends to be read by sailors and retired sailors; there is no comparable discussion of the value or symbolism of the names selected for the *A* class in national daily newspapers. This suggests that the naming policy was of far greater concern to corporate rather than civil culture, and that corporate concerns, for example those raised over the possible public reception of names such as *Revenge* and *Inflexible* during the 1960s, might have been spurious. Furthermore, the submarine service's use of names is an invented tradition in that, although they have little or no noteworthy history, they are being read against a background of historic names being used to tie today's Navy to a sense of tradition and victory through accumulated battle honours associated with old names.

Such a use of the submarine's short-term history over the broader past of the Royal Navy produces a paradox. At the very time that the submarine, in its SSN and SSBN incarnations, is being hailed as the new capital ship and offensive weapon of the Royal Navy, the submarine service starts to reject the capital ship imagery and turns to its own past for inspiration. Indeed it seems that this turning away from the Navy's own past not only coincides with the broad acceptance of the submarine into the Royal Navy's corporate culture, but also with declining civil interest in defence-related issues as a whole, and specifically in the Royal Navy.

Conclusion

The most obvious consequence of the introduction of the nuclear submarine was the revival of the Fleet submarine concept, although this time it was eventually successful as the combination of a nuclear reactor's almost unlimited power and modern communication systems overcame the previous stumbling blocks by the mid-1990s. The persistence and eventual success of the Fleet submarine idea shows how fundamental, and indeed consistent, was the Navy's understanding of the submarine – it could only be understood at a corporate level through its success as part of a battlefleet based on the concept of a balanced fleet capable of undertaking almost any task asked of it in peace or war. The production of the submarine from the corporate perspective was solely concerned with its integration within an existing framework that emphasized rather than challenged the British ideas of seapower.

The reception of the Fleet submarine or SSN was mixed and depended on the sub-cultures within the Royal Navy. Certainly, this new type of submarine was seen as threatening to some groups, such as the carrier fraternity. Yet circumstances beyond the direct control of the submariners allowed the reconstruction of the submarine as the primary offensive conventional weapon within the battlefleet, replacing both the surface ship and maritime airpower. These outside influences forced changes in the signification and reception of the submarine that have characterised the period from HMS *Dreadnought* onwards.

The production of the missile submarine and its signification owes much to inter-service rivalries and politics, but the politics of Polaris had an impact on the signification of the SSN. Polaris was a direct political threat to the RAF, who reacted very badly at the bureaucratic level to the Navy's acquisition of the independent nuclear deterrent. This very negative reaction impacted on other Royal Navy programmes such as the aircraft carrier replacement, and thus it changed the context by which the Royal

Navy understood itself. After the 1966 decision to cancel the CVA–01 aircraft carrier project following concerted and deep rooted opposition from the RAF, the Royal Navy had to reinvent its own understanding of itself in the context of a fleet without large strike carriers. Such a reinvention had an impact on the signification of the SSN programme and the fleet submarine idea, making the submarine far more important to the Royal Navy than could have been expected when the *Dreadnought* was laid down in the late 1950s.

The changes in the signification of the submarine, both SSN and SSBN, were reflected in the changes to naval pageantry and the symbolism this imparted both before and after the ructions of the CVA–01 cancellation. Submarines had become things worthy of royal association, in terms of launching ceremonies and visits. At the same time the names given to both the *R* and *V* class SSBNs as well as the *Valiant* class SSNs emphasized the capital ship status of the submarine. In particular, the battleship names given to the early SSNs take on extra significance due to the changes in context that the Royal Navy faced in the late 1960s with the end of the strike carrier in sight. Yet the later SSNs, those that made up the *Swiftsure* and *Trafalgar* classes, show a different signification process, that of the Submarine Service reclaiming the submarine for itself. This reclamation process can be seen through both the names given to the vessels, which had previously graced an early generation of submarines, at the expense of traditional names that harked back to a pre-submarine era. It seems that having been recognised as the most important part of the Fleet, the submariners were consciously using symbolism to set themselves apart, so reproducing the independence from the surface fleet that had characterised pre-nuclear submarines.

However, the reception of the ballistic missile-armed submarine was driven by public concerns over nuclear weapons rather than a desired corporate image. The protest movement made use of the submarine as a symbol and, through the means of numerous leaflets and pamphlets, tied the image of the submarine to that of nuclear weapons and the consequences of their use. The introduction of nuclear weapons onto submarines revived the submarine as a symbol of fear and hatred for some sectors of the community at the time that a publicly acceptable image of the submarine as a weapon had come about and was being reflected in the literature and films on the subject.

6

THE BRITISH SUBMARINE IN FILM AND FICTION

'People are influenced more than they would care to admit by novels…'[1]

The submarine has been part of British life in some way, shape or form for over a hundred years. In previous chapters, the submarine as a cultural artefact has been analysed from both the civil and corporate perspectives to show how meaning surrounding it was constructed. Yet, despite the odium that has been heaped on the submarine at various points since 1901, the submarine remains a relatively unknown quantity for those outside the submarine service. The lack of knowledge about submarines, British or otherwise, moved the House of Commons Defence Committee in 1991 to comment that:

> The Submarine Service is an elite and somewhat self-contained world: as a result the role of the submarine can be misunderstood, underestimated or neglected. **We consider that one priority task for Flag Officer Submarines and for MoD is to look at ways of increasing professional, parliamentary and public understanding of the Submarine Service.**[2]

The Defence Committee were not alone in sharing these views; years earlier a former submariner, W. G. Roberts, conceded in his memoirs that:

> While the Royal Navy has always been known as the Silent Service, the Submarine Service is far more silent. We hear little about the Service except when there is a disaster or tragedy.[3]

The Royal Navy's reputation for being the 'silent service' is simply explained. It was almost impossible for journalists to gain access to naval exercises or battles. On land a journalist could follow the army and rapidly make observations available to his readers via telegraph and later telephones. If a journalist was invited to join a warship, all the means of communicating with the outside world such as post or telegraph were firmly under naval control. Added to this was the fact that naval warfare from the dreadnought era onwards was a very long-range affair, making description of events difficult. These factors were taken to the extreme by the operating environment of the submarine: outside contact was almost non-existent once the submarine had sailed for patrol and the only person who could see what was going on was the officer at the periscope. Disasters, be they surface or submarine, were effectively the only events that a journalist could make interesting copy out of, *and* not necessarily be dependent on the Royal Navy for direct assistance.

Thus Britons, at least those outside the submarine service, were faced with a problem; how does someone get to experience submarines, short of actually becoming a submariner? Journalism was limited by operational circumstances while opportunities to see submarines have always been restricted to Naval Reviews (see Chapter One), a lucky glimpse of one on the surface entering or leaving harbour, or a tour around a submarine during Navy Days. Factual articles in magazines, newspapers or books could only expose the submarine so far, and could fall foul of censorship.

On the other hand, the fictional use of the submarine presents an opportunity for mass engagement with submarines, realistic or otherwise, through the imagination of the audience or reader. Popular literature, and more recently film, have been the major means of such engagement.[4] Therefore, the way submarines are used in fiction can have a powerful pull on how the meaning of submarines is constructed and understood by those with no direct experience of such a weapon. George Orwell famously noted that 'people are influenced more than they would care to admit by novels…'[5] and it is certainly true that ahistorical representations of the submarine through film and fiction can have far greater impact than operational histories. Michael Paris has discussed at length the fascination for war in popular culture, and in particular the role played by fiction.[6] The fascination with war in popular culture, combined with the powerful sway exerted by film and works of fiction, can have a great impact on how submarines are understood by those who cannot have experienced personally submarine operations in war or peace. Just as importantly, the depiction of the submarine is essentially an expression of the values of the reader ashore, even if the author has professional knowledge of, or insight into, submarines, the Navy, or the sea.[7] Film and fiction presents an opportunity for mass participation in the experience of submarines, thus helping to both shape and reflect the way in which submarines are imagined and understood.

In many respects the submarine novel is merely a facet of a much wider and well established literary genre that stretches back to Daniel Defoe's *Robinson Crusoe* and beyond – the sea story. John Peck has argued that the sea story breaks into three elements competing for attention; an individual sailor who often plays a distinct masculine role; the sea and shore as places of danger – an 'other – where challenges have to be mastered; finally, there is a context – political, social, economic, technological – that the ship itself has a purpose, that there is a reason for the voyage.[8] The sea novel based around a submarine fits within this model, giving the story a context or reason for the voyage, yet the submarine also can form the challenge to be overcome. For the British the submarine is not just a type of ship, it is also an 'other', an enemy, supplanting the sea and hostile shores as a challenge to be mastered.

At the same time, submarine films and literature can fall into three different groups. First, and perhaps the easiest to categorize, are those where the submarine is merely a background to the story and is, in some cases, incidental to the plot. These films and books can cover a vast spectrum of subjects, from espionage, through adventure and resistance war stories, to romance. Two examples are Hammond Innes' *Wreckers Must Breathe* (1940),[9] and Alistair MacLean's *Night Without End* (1959).[10] *Wreckers Must Breathe* is an espionage and escape story set in the earliest days of the Second World War and centring on the discovery of a secret U-Boat base in a remote part of Cornwall.[11] *Night Without End* is also an espionage and escape story set high in the Greenland Ice cap that suggests a submarine as the final escape route for the villains.[12] This group also encompasses such novels and films that might include the submarine in a minor role as part of the plot or character development. A good example of the submarine as background to an espionage novel is Alistair MacLean's *Ice Station Zebra* (1963), where the under-ice capabilities of an American nuclear-powered hunter-killer submarine are used to transport a British Intelligence Officer to a weather station deep in the Arctic ice pack to deal with a case of espionage and murder.[13] On the other hand, Geoffrey Jenkin's *A Twist Of Sand* (1959) uses the hunt of a Nazi atomic-powered submarine in the latter part of the Second World War by a British submarine as background for an adventure story set in the skeleton coast of Namibia. *A Twist Of Sand* then goes on to produce a post-war story involving a hunt for a rare insect, murder, and the discovery of oil, all made possible by the now cashiered British submarine commander's knowledge of piloting a ship through the skeleton coast, gained by hunting the German submarine.

While such background use of a submarine may add little to the understanding of submarines generally, it does keep submarines in open view, but conversely does little to establish the submarine as an 'other' or challenge to be overcome or to provide anything but the most limited of context.. What is interesting is that the 1959 *Twist of Sand* and the 1963 *Ice Station Zebra* both make use of nuclear powered submarines either as a historical fiction (*Twist of Sand*) or portrayed as contemporary fact (*Ice Station Zebra*) at a time when nuclear propulsion was an exciting development, suggesting that submarines were seen as appropriate contexts for adventure narratives because they reflected images of modernity. In *Ice Station Zebra*, the American submarine is described by a British doctor as one that,

> made any British submarine I'd ever seen look like a relic from the Ice Age.... The size, combined with clever use of pastel paints for all the accommodation spaces, working spaces and passageways, gave an overwhelming impression of lightness, airiness and above all, spaciousness.[14]

The second group of novels and films use the submarine as an invisible threat – an 'other' – within part of the main story, providing it with a sense of tension and drama as well as being a challenge that the sailor or sailors must defeat. These works are almost all concerned in some way with unrestricted submarine warfare. The most well-known of this genre has to be *The Cruel Sea*, both the novel (1951) and the film (1953), where the submarine is an invisible threat lurking in the background and waiting for a time to strike without warning. Indeed, most novels relating to the experiences of the British merchant marine in the First and the Second World Wars, such as Brian Callison's *A Flock of Ships* (1970)[15] and James Pattinson's *Last in Convoy* (1957),[16] fall into this group.[17]

The third group is made up of those British films and novels that directly focus on submarines and the experiences of their crews. This third group has the submarine providing context, challenge, and the principle characters are submariners. As such, this group not only includes the activities of fictional British submarines, but also that of all other submarines, whether friendly or hostile, in war or peace. Included in this group are the films such as *We Dive At Dawn* (1943), *Above Us The Waves* (1955) and *Morning Departure* (1950), as well as the novels like *Submarine* (1982), *Go In And Sink* (1973) and *Fighting Submarine* (1978). *We Dive At Dawn* looked at the activities of a submarine sent to sink Germany's latest battleship, while *Above Us The Waves* was a fictionalised post-war account of the midget submarine attacks on the *Tirpitz*; only *Morning Departure* was set in peacetime and followed the handful of survivors from a sunken British submarine attempting to escape and the efforts made to rescue them. In *Submarine*, the action is set in during an imagined confrontation between NATO and the Warsaw Pact as the Cold War turns hot, while both *Go In And Sink* and *Fighting Submarine* are set in the Second World War. In *Go In And Sink* the Royal Navy uses a captured U-Boat to attack supply U-boats supporting Wolf Packs in the Atlantic; *Fighting Submarine* uses a British submarine to rescue captured Merchant seamen in a nod to the *Altmark* incident.[18]

Each of these three groups may emphasize a different element of the sea story, but these elements may in many cases be too simplistic for effective analysis of such a narrow section of the sea story genre as found in submarine stories. In order to effectively analyse the large number of novels and films involving submarines, it is necessary to look at how submarines and their crews are portrayed. What do the submarines do? What missions do the authors have their fictional submarines undertake and what do they sink and how? What are the reactions of the submariners and their victims? Who are the victims, the heroes and the villains? What was the relative popularity of these books and films? Additionally, when analysing films, the cinematography as well as the casting have to be considered. What non-verbal communication goes on between the cast as well as between the camera and the audience? Are film stars cast against type for shock value?

This chapter will look at how the British portrayed the submarine in film and fiction and the reaction to it in three main ways. First, it will consider what types of ships were sunk by fictional submarines and how, as well as what, messages such depictions conveyed. Second, it will analyse the behaviour of submarines and submariners; do they follow the generally considered rules of war; are submariners portrayed as chivalrous? Third, it will look at the depiction of heroism through the medium of submarines; not just the behaviour of the crews, but also whether the idea of submarines is used to depict generic heroism or villainy. Additionally, as well as looking at pertinent sections of films in these ways, the chapter will also examine the degree of popularity and critical acclaim that greeted novels and films featuring submarines.

Fictional Submarines and Their Targets

The targets sunk by submarines form, perhaps, the most important aspect of the submarine's fictional existence. They shed light on the values that a writer wishes to pass on to the reader and also on how the author wishes the submarine to be perceived in relation to preconceptions about maritime non-combatants. The type of target and the method of sinking will have an effect on the reader or audience as the author will be using deliberately image-laden language to provoke sympathy, hostility or approval in the reader. Consider Percy Westerman's comparison between British and German submariners in his *A Sub And A Submarine* (1919) as 'the Hon. Derek was a member of a time-honoured and unsullied profession, and not a pirate...'[19] The use of the word 'pirate' with the inference of killing survivors inherent within the term, is clearly designed to cast certain images before the reader and provoke feelings of approval for the actions of the British and hostility to that of the Germans.

The writers seeking a fictional portrayal of British submarines during the First World War had by far the easiest task; after all, Britain did not carry out unrestricted submarine warfare, thus allowing authors to emphasize the superior characteristics of British crews over their adversaries. Despite a lack of any use of British submarines in unrestricted warfare, authors often stressed the military use of the submarine by allowing their fictional crews a crack at a major German warship. In Westerman's *A Sub And A Submarine*, the British submarine *R19*'s first attack is on 'the towering outline of one of Germany's most recent battleships.'[20] Once the fictional submarines started operating against merchant vessels, authors such as Westerman went to considerable length not only to differentiate between the British and German submarine campaigns, but also to stress the superior character of British officers:

> Stockdale [the Captain of the R19] had them [German merchant vessels in an unescorted convoy] entirely at his mercy. Between the merchantmen and the shore he could have easily headed them off and destroyed them by gun-fire or torpedo. Had he been a German, and these vessels British ships, the latter would have been sent to the bottom, and their crews fired upon with machine – guns…[21]

Westerman's choice of Commanding Officer is important. His captain is the Honourable Derek Stockdale, a son of a peer and a gentleman by birth and upbringing, whose social class as well as naval training would promote ideals of chivalry. As discussed in Chapter Two, the cult of the gentleman and ideas centred on chivalrous behaviour were important in late Victorian and Edwardian Britain, but these were not concepts associated with submarine warfare, even before the First World War. The choice of a peer's son to be the commanding officer of a British submarine in a First World War story, written in the immediate aftermath of hostilities, shows a shift in attitudes to the submarine and the beginning of the end of the 'damned un-English' school of thought. At the same time by placing a gentleman in command, Westerman is underlining the idea that British submarines were morally upright weapons that fought according to the rules of civilized society and – just as importantly – that the men who crewed them were not to be confused with the 'pirates' on the German U-boats.

The defining characteristic of the fictional British submarine on film and in literature from the Second World War onwards is the absence of unrestricted submarine warfare. This is not perhaps that surprising in the period prior to the British adopting unrestricted submarine warfare in April 1940, but its absence from that date onwards is surprising, particularly given the successes of British submarines which would have provided ample examples for fictional exploits. This avoidance of unrestricted submarine warfare is not confined only to fictional accounts of past wars, but also extends to imaginary conflicts set in the near future. The fictional British submarines operate sink on sight rules solely against military targets such as warships, military transports (which are carefully identified as such), or targets like dry docks at sea or in harbour. Such a concentration on military targets demonstrates two themes. First, that despite the experience of two world wars, the British still were having problems with attacks on non-combatants at sea, especially with the idea that British submarines should be carrying out such activities. Second, it shows that submarines were an increasingly acceptable context for the display of British naval heroism and success.

Importantly, the passage of time did not seem to alter the way in which British submarines were employed. In 1943, two films, *We Dive At Dawn* and *Close Quarters*, and two novels, *Fathoms Deep* and *Proceed At Will*, did not have British submarines carrying out unrestricted submarine warfare, but between them they managed to sink a battleship, a battlecruiser, a U-boat and a floating dock. In the 1950s, films did not depict British unrestricted submarine warfare and Royal Navy submarines only managed to sink the *Tirpitz*. Novels published in the same period contrived to sink numerous Japanese junks with gunfire, and a Japanese cruiser, and like the films did not show British forces embarking on unrestricted submarine warfare. From the 1960s onwards, fictional British submariners were very active, with X craft[22] sinking a floating dock and a liner that was being used as a rocket laboratory (thus a legitimate military target), while normal submarines successfully attacked two U-boats, a destroyer, an armed trawler, a disguised merchant raider, a Japanese aircraft carrier and an anti-submarine trawler, to name but a few of the fictional incidents.[23] Again the selection of fictional targets emphasizes a deep-seated discomfort with the idea that unrestricted submarine warfare was something that should be used by British submarines. At the same time, the number and successful nature of these fictional attacks on military targets subverts the notion that British submarines were underhand, while the inclusion of disguised merchant raiders in the list of targets destroyed helps characterize the enemy as underhand and ungentlemanly.

Even the depiction of British submarines in juvenile literature fifty years after the British started using unrestricted submarine warfare, noted the difference between the treatment of enemy warships and merchant vessels. Comic magazines for children emphasized the fact that merchant ships were not sunk without warning, but warships and auxiliaries could be.[24] In one *Commando* comic story 'Into Danger', the submarine's captain clearly differentiates between how the enemy warships should be treated and the methods to be used in dispatching the merchantmen. By stating that merchant vessels were to be sunk by gunfire, it is implied that they will not be sunk without warning and hence the attack conforms to the spirit, if not perhaps the letter, of the prize rules. The war comics also emphasized the fact that the auxiliaries were legitimate targets even if they looked like merchantmen. Indeed, in the 'Battle' comic *One Way To Die* it was never even suggested that the targets could be anything other than a naval auxiliary vessel.[25] Thus, by inference, British submarines were not carrying out any form of unrestricted submarine warfare as part of their fictional battles with the enemy.

In the 1943 films *We Dive At Dawn* and *Close Quarters*, both produced when the Submarine Service was fighting a major unrestricted submarine warfare campaign in the Mediterranean, the fictional British submarines had military targets in the North Sea and Norwegian waters. In *We Dive At Dawn* the target was the German battleship *Brandenburg*, while in *Close Quarters* the submarine manages to sink a U–boat as well as a floating dock. Yet in one of the opening scenes where the viewer is still being introduced to the characters within *We Dive At Dawn* and the submarine *Sea Tiger*, there was a veiled allusion to unrestricted submarine warfare. As the *Sea Tiger* comes alongside the depot ship after an unsuccessful patrol, John Mills, playing the part of the submarine's Commanding Officer, is hailed by the Captain of another submarine:

> Medium shot of other CO: Hello Freddie, a nice quiet trip?
> Medium shot of Mills: Yes, worse luck (shot cuts to other submarine's Jolly Roger, Mills voice continues) (jokingly) I see you've sunk another couple of fishing smacks.
> Medium shot of other CO: (looking pleased) Yes, just a 10,000 tonner and a 4,000.
> Medium shot of Mills: (sounding exasperated) What the hell do you work with? Old Moore's Almanac?[26]

Although the exchange is very short, it does indicate that the submarine service was attacking non-combatants. Deliberately, no doubt, the exchange does not throw any light as to whether the 10,000 tonner and 4,000 tonner were warships (unlikely as the CO would have bragged about the type of warship), or merchant vessels (very likely). Importantly, the exchange does not give any indication as to how these vessels were sunk, either by stopping, boarding and dispatch by gunfire or demolition charges in accordance with the prize rules, or torpedoed without warning. In this way the viewer is allowed to impose their own preconception of the correct manner for a British submarine to behave onto the film. It does not seem that avoiding unrestricted warfare images was accidental. In the same year as *We Dive at Dawn* was released, M. Dawson's novel *Fathoms Deep* describes a British submarine stopping a German merchant vessel with a shot across its bows, putting the crew into lifeboats a short distance from the shore and then sinking the merchantman with gunfire.[27]

As John Ramsden has pointed out, the post-war war films were important in confirming that Britain did win the war as well as explaining why,[28] and this is also true of war novels. However with submarines, films and novels also had to explain that victory occurred by using acceptable methods to an extent unseen in fictional accounts of strategic bombing or Bomber Command activities. British submarines had to be seen as a morally acceptable as well as a militarily acceptable weapon.

In this way, both the depiction of unrestricted submarine warfare in *The Cruel Sea* was acceptable as it was carried out by the Germans, and the depiction of the British submarines in *We Dive At Dawn* and *Above Us The Waves* because it did not show attacks on merchantmen. The *Spectator*'s review of *We Dive At Dawn* did not discuss how British submarines were portrayed but acknowledged the propaganda value of the film, without drawing any attention to the far more important work that British submarines were doing through *unrestricted* submarine warfare in the Mediterranean.[29] The fact that the Crown Film Unit's 1943 film of British submarines at war, *Close Quarters*, did not show any images of unrestricted sinkings of merchantmen indicates a degree of official policy, even perhaps censorship, in ignoring this aspect of submarine warfare, and those reviewing the film did not see anything odd in such an omission.[30] Ignoring an aspect of submarine warfare that was at the time playing such a large part in the British submarine service's activities, reveals that Britain's submarines were still perceived as having a moral code to follow; this applied even at a time of total warfare when effectively indiscriminate attacks on non-combatants at sea and from the air were a regular part of life.

The omission of unrestricted warfare in two films about British submarines is of importance. The films were released within months of each other at the height of both the British and German unrestricted submarine campaigns in the Mediterranean and Atlantic respectively, reinforcing the idea that the British response to the problem of disparaging hostile submarines while at the same time praising their own, was to ignore many of the activities of the latter, as discussed in Chapter Four. Furthermore, the omission of any significant mention of unrestricted submarine warfare in either film or reviews indicates that still, after four years of total war including the Blitz, area bombing of Germany and defeat in almost every theatre of operations, a submarine victory still had to conform to pre-war ideals regarding attacks on non-combatants. That such a morally acceptable depiction of submarines was carried over into visions of future war and peacetime operations is an indication of how crucial the treatment of maritime non-combatants was to British national identity. Interestingly, there also seems to have been a similar reticence to publicize, at least in the early years of the war, the bombing of population centres by the RAF. *Target For Tonight* (1941) showed a Wellington bomber making a precision attack on an oil refinery avoiding any suggestion that real attacks were nowhere near as accurate as the film depiction.[31] As a result, a realistic portrayal of British submarine operations and capabilities would have made most uncomfortable reading and viewing for the public. Hence, the concentration on military targets and the perpetuation of the paradox the British encountered in the Second World War: how to castigate an enemy and applaud your own forces for doing essentially the same thing to each other.

In *Diving Stations* (1980), Edwyn Gray came up with a rather elegant solution to the problem of unrestricted submarine warfare not being compatible with perceptions of British submarines. Gray has his hero, Hamilton, an officer who had come up through the ranks, succeed at special operations while failing at run of the mill submarine operations having 'survived two years of war without sinking a single enemy ship in the course of normal patrol operations.'[32] In this way, Gray was able to produce a series of novels based around atypical behaviour for a British submarine in the Second World War, but still provided a great deal of action without the recourse to unrestricted warfare. Hamilton's longevity in the face of such 'inexplicable failure'[33] was, however, not necessarily based on historical fact. The real Submarine Service was ruthless in removing unsuccessful Commanding Officers; even the 'ace' Lieutenant Commander Wanklyn was nearly removed from *HMS Upholder* early in his command due to a series of unsuccessful attacks.[34]

The paradox of the depiction of British submarines in action continued in visionary accounts of what would happen if the Cold War turned hot. In John Wingate's *Submarine*, set in the early 1980s, the reader is told how, in the fight against Soviet aggression in Norway and elsewhere in Europe, a British *Oberon* class submarine, HMS *Orcus*, sank a 'Russian Fleet replenishment ship' escorted by a destroyer.[35] Wingate leaves the reader in no doubt that the ship is a legitimate target, and not a merchantman, thanks to his description of it and its sinking: 'she must have been carrying ammunition, for she literally disintegrated into the darkening twilight.'[36] The main thrust of the novel is, however, the hunt for a Soviet *Typhoon* class submarine by both HMS *Orcus* and an *S* class hunter-killer submarine HMS *Safari*, but again the target is naval not civilian.[37] Indeed, by hunting a *Typhoon* ballistic missile submarine, the British boats are actively protecting all civilians – British and others – from the dangers of a nuclear attack on the west and preventing the war from escalating by demonstrating to the Soviets that their ballistic missile submarines are vulnerable at sea.

The depiction of British submarines as a weapon system that is used only against naval targets does not stop with the end of the fictional accounts of war. Even in peacetime, the British submarine and its crew is shown as being concerned with attacks on warships rather than practising unrestricted submarine warfare. In John Winton's *Down The Hatch* (1961), a humorous look at life in submarines during the late 1950s, the Commanding Officer of the Royal Navy's latest submarine HMS *Seahorse* (clearly meant to be based on the *Porpoise* class SSK) is found 'lightly dreaming of fat aircraft carriers steaming towards him on steady courses'.[38] Furthermore, when *Seahorse* is sent on a NATO exercise, playing the part of a 'pink' (Soviet) submarine against the NATO, or blue force, the pink submarines are sent against a NATO carrier battlegroup rather than carrying out the unrestricted submarine warfare that in reality the Royal Navy was actually expecting.[39] *Seahorse*, however, manages to penetrate the anti-submarine screen and for exercise purposes sinks or disables the 'largest warship afloat', the American aircraft carrier USS *Little Richard*.[40]

In the light of how the British wrote about their own submarines, it is unsurprising that when writing about enemy submarines they did not find discussing unrestricted submarine warfare a sensitive issue. As authors who had built a series of novels around the careers of fictional U-boat men, both Gray and Kenneth Bulmer do not attempt to disguise the U-boat's mode of warfare. In *U-Boat: Action Atlantic* (1975) Gray calls an attack on a convoy 'a massacre of the innocents',[41] while Bulmer's U-Boat Captain Wolz made submerged attacks without warning throughout his fictional career.[42] Indeed, authors generally preferred to have their imaginary enemy submarines sink merchant vessels rather than British warships;[43] but in the unlikely event that they do take a shot at a major warship, the torpedo fails to explode[44] or, if successful, is against a minor vessel such as an escort or submarine.[45]

There is, however, an important qualification to the analysis of how British writers depicted German and enemy submarines. Fictional enemy submarines did carry out unrestricted submarine warfare, but the low level of detail in those passages detailing with sinking merchantmen might also show that British writers were still uncomfortable with such actions, even if carried out by a fictional enemy. Douglas Reeman illustrates this problem in *With Blood And Iron* (1964) when his U-boat attacks a convoy, but Reeman does not give any description of the targets.[46] Later in the same novel, the U-boat attacks a tanker, but again there is a very limited description of the sinking.[47] This was not necessarily a British trait: J. Lehnhoff's *The Homeward Run*, a German novel published in English in 1957, surpasses all with the brevity of its description of an attack on a convoy.[48]

It is easy to conclude that the omission of British warships from the merry massacre of the world's shipping by hostile submarines was also a function of the role of the Navy in British national identity. As the British constructed the meaning of sea power around first the battleship and then the balanced fleet, it was easier to conceive of merchant ships being sunk (with admittedly some level of criticism, unspoken or otherwise, of the Royal Navy for allowing such affairs to take place), rather than admit a direct challenge to British seapower by allowing successful attacks on a key component of national identity – the supremacy of the Navy.

Despite the successes of the British fictional submarines and perhaps because of the successes of fictional Axis U-boats, there was an undercurrent of dislike for the submarine. Gray, in a scene set just before 7 December 1941, has the Executive Officer of a Hong Kong-based patrol boat comment that:

> I don't see anything brave in sneaking along under the sea and torpedoing some poor bloody ship that doesn't event know you're there. They ought to try standing on the surface in broad daylight and fighting the enemy face to face.[49]

The selection of fictional targets – merchant vessels and the like – reinforced the negative aspects of being a victim of submarine warfare, while the targets attacked by British submarines were depicted as being warships or auxiliaries. The choice of targets not only emphasized the role of the submarine in gaining command of the sea, but reinforced British perceptions of the importance of avoiding attacks on non-combatants. It is clear, therefore, that submarines might be successful in their attacks, but, depending on the target in question, they were not always considered as conducting themselves in a civilized or chivalrous manner.

Chivalry and the Fictional Submarine

Given the general British perception of the submarine as a less than chivalrous weapon system and definitely not a desirable way to wage war at sea, the rendition of the activities of fictional submarines is worth consideration. There are two important indicators of the degree to which submarines were considered to be chivalrous: first, how submarines treated survivors, and second, how the use of the 'pirate' accolade changed over time.

In *A Sub and a Submarine*, Westerman makes it quite clear that even operating in accordance with the prize rules and sinking a merchant vessel by means of a boarding party opening the sea cocks, was still something that a British officer would not enjoy:

> It was not a pleasant sight nor a congenial duty, but stern necessity demanded the sacrifice of those seven ships to the exigencies of war; and Fordyce [the Sub of the title], remembering the fate of many a hapless British merchantman, torpedoed without mercy in the midst of an angry sea and far from land, steeled his heart.[50]

The fact that scuttling ships was not enjoyable meant that by inference it was also not chivalrous. However, Westerman did stress the protection granted to survivors by ensuring the crew had time to take to the lifeboats and that the survivors were close to shore.[51] Despite scuttling merchant vessels being regarded as not particularly chivalrous, such actions throw up another cultural perception of gentlemanly behaviour: that of duty. In the above excerpt, Fordyce follows the requirements of his duty, which is stressed as not a happy one, but one forced by the needs of war, even if it means that a non-combatant is deprived of his property or livelihood. Such attack on property – even within the prize rules – was something that had been abhorrent to many British radicals and free trade liberals since the mid-Victorian period – men who believed in the ideas of national war but commercial peace.[52]

On the other hand, British depictions of German submarine activity stressed attacks on non-combatants. In *The Keepers Of The Narrow Seas*, Westerman alludes to the German torpedoing of a hospital ship in the Mediterranean as the motivation for the fitting out of a disguised armed merchantman for operations against U-boats: 'Outwardly the felucca looked like a peaceful trader but had a stern and retributive duty to perform – to avenge a certain hospital ship that had been wantonly torpedoed in broad daylight.'[53] Westerman's use of language is also important as it adds emphasis to the dislike of German submarine operations. The hospital ship is not just torpedoed; it is torpedoed 'wantonly' and in 'broad daylight' suggesting that this could not be an accident caused by mistaken identity. Moreover, the enthusiastic use of a disguised armed merchantman, which is a somewhat underhand and secretive counter to the submarine threat, suggests that attitudes to what was gentlemanly were changing at a fundamental level.

Nor was Westerman the only author to have German submarines carrying out the war crime of sinking hospital ships. In M. Catto's *Murphy's War* (1969), set in the Second World War off the African coast, the German submarine at the centre of the story sinks a hospital ship and machine guns many of the survivors.⁵⁴ As a result of this murderous action, the sole survivor, Murphy, wages a solitary war of revenge against the U-boat that ultimately leads to the destruction of the submarine, himself and the German officer who ordered the massacre.

The machine gunning of survivors has, since the First World War, been a favourite trope of authors to illustrate the evil and uncivilized nature of submarine warfare. As well as Westerman making use of it as a comparison to the civilized behaviour of British submarines, and Catto's use of it as a catalyst for revenge, many other writers have made their fictitious German submarines machine-gun survivors. In A. Chatham's *Sea Sting* (1982), a converted German type XXI submarine shot up a Norwegian fishing vessel, leaving no survivors.⁵⁵ The idea that Germans routinely machine gunned survivors was given added weight by its inclusion in wartime films such as *Western Approaches* (1945), where the atrocity is not actually seen, but is referred to by survivors once they are in the lifeboat,⁵⁶ while in A. Trew's *Yashimoto's Last Dive* (1986), a Japanese submarine sinks a Liberty ship and then machine guns the survivors.⁵⁷

Juvenile fiction was not exempt from depicting submarines as the vehicle for war crimes such as the machine gunning of survivors. Indeed, most of the major war comics, such as *Commando*, *Battle* and *War Picture Library* all used images of survivors being shot by victorious U-boat crews.⁵⁸ The dialogue of the characters often linked the submariners with references to Nazi Germany: 'That's how we treat enemies of the Reich – without mercy!'⁵⁹ Such depictions of certain aspects of submarine warfare cannot help but form a mental image for the juvenile reader of submarines as something quite immoral.

The treatment handed out to survivors by British submarines could not have been more different. Percy Westerman had his First World War submariners pick up the survivors of a German destroyer that had been trying to avenge the submarine's earlier successes.⁶⁰ Nor did the Second World War change the behaviour of Britain's fictional submarine heroes, with the Commanding Officer of *HMS Seahound* in *Surface* (1953) worried about how to look after Japanese survivors if he came across some enemy vessels.⁶¹ When the *Seahound* gets in amongst a Japanese convoy, its Commander decides to sink the two escorting motor launches with gunfire, allowing a leisurely round up of the junks, which are sunk by demolition charges with all the crews transferred to the smallest junk, which had been left alone specifically for that purpose.⁶² Even if there was no suitable vessel on to which the crews of sunken vessels could be transferred, a point was made of picking up the survivors and looking after them until they could be transferred to a small ship such as a fishing boat. ⁶³

This chivalrous behaviour by British submarines was repeated in film. In *We Dive At Dawn*, the British submarine *HMS Sea Tiger* came across a German rescue buoy with three Luftwaffe airmen onboard. The *Sea Tiger* picked up the Germans and continued on her mission. The way in which the British go about the rescue is of interest as they are not passive observers, doing as little as possible to help the Germans, but instead actively try to reach them as quickly as possible by throwing lines to the Germans so that they can be pulled to the submarine. Admittedly, the British had shot away the buoy's radio mast, causing the Germans to abandon the float, but as the *Sea Tiger*'s commanding officer pointed out to the Germans, trying to use their radio to inform the Germans of the *Sea Tiger*'s position was not on either. The fact that the British submarine's Commanding Officer understates the importance of the German activity is also of interest. By attempting to use a radio to pass on the *Sea Tiger*'s position they were actually making themselves active combatants, so justifying the British response. Indeed, according to the rules of war, the British would have been entitled to have taken more vigorous action if they had wished. The act of picking up the Germans then takes on greater significance as the British are rescuing those who a moment earlier had been actively trying to have them destroyed.

Yet for all the depictions of British submarines being more civilized than their Axis counterparts, there was no way that British writers were able to square the circle of British submarines carrying out unrestricted submarine warfare. Indeed, they usually followed the tactic of ignoring the problem. The fact that the unrestricted aspects of the British Second World War submarine campaign were ignored in wartime was referred to in William Gage's *The Cruel Coast* (1967), where a damaged U-boat seeks to make repairs in an isolated harbour in Ireland. One of the U-boat officers defends the actions of German submarines in the Battle of the Atlantic in a discussion with a local woman by drawing parallels between the actions of the Germans and those of the Allies:

> It's our job, Nora. English submarines sink merchantmen. So do the Yankees.[64]

In an 'Authors Note' in *With Blood And Iron*, Reeman quoted Nicolas Monsarrat to make essentially the same point that 'There is a current Anglo-American illusion, skilfully fostered during the war, that whereas the Germans used *U-boats*, which were beastly, we only used submarines which were different and rather wonderful.'[65] There was a hint of desperation in Reeman's question 'Can anyone fight with such weapons and not be tainted?'[66] Reeman clearly thinks that the answer to his question is no; submarines and the manner in which they have to be used to be effective preclude any civilized warfare at sea. Such sentiments were echoed in G. Griffin's *An Operational Necessity* (1968) where survivors of a German U-boat are captured and indicted for war crimes. Mr Shellybeare, the Tanganyikan District Commissioner, points out to his sceptical wife that:

> We have submarines too, my dear. They are presumably very much like U-boats and do the same work. The only difference is that ours are manned by heroes and theirs by villains – or so one is asked to believe.[67]

By likening the activities of British and German submarines, subtle allusions are made to unrestricted warfare. This suggests that by the late 1960s, the British were more willing to face up to the unpalatable realities of submarine warfare (although it was, at times, still avoided) and that the experiences of both the Second World War and the Cold War had emphasized the total war aspects of modern combat.

Heroes and Villains

The portrayal of submariners in the pre-Second World War period tallies with the wider image of the soldier or sailor hero as identified in Paris's *Warrior Nation*; that of an individual characterized by manliness, duty and an enjoyment of battle.[68] Paris has also noted that in general terms the juvenile comics from the 1950s onwards venerated both heroism and patriotism, but also that, unlike the films of the 1950s and 1960s, they rejected the middle-class officer ideal and instead produced working-class heroes.[69] However, any attempt to introduce working-class heroes in preference to the middle-class officer ideal could not easily be replicated due to the nature of submarine warfare. In the pre-nuclear submarine age the submarine's success was dependent on the ability of the Commanding Officer to conduct an attack based on what he alone could see through the periscope; thus action tended to centre on the Captain at the expense of other characters. In *We Dive At Dawn*, the main story centres on the Captain, with a sub-plot involving his working-class (and northern) sonar operator, who, through his ability to speak German, comes to the fore in dealing with German prisoners and later when sneaking ashore to reconnoitre a German-held Danish fishing village. Uniquely, Grey gets round this problem of action needing to be based on the Commanding Officer's actions by having his submarine Captain in the *Fighting Submarine* series come from the ranks,[70] an unlikely event for the interwar Royal Navy, but one that does address class issues in a way acceptable to the trends identified by Paris.[71]

More important than the depiction of class was the depiction of the horrors experienced by the survivors of ships torpedoed without warning, which provided authors with rich material to exploit to the detriment of the submarine. Perhaps the most memorable, both as literature and in film is the depiction of the sinking of HMS *Compass Rose* in *The Cruel Sea*. When the U-boat's torpedo strikes the *Compass Rose* it traps a large number of the crew in their mess deck and the screams of the trapped men, 'an agonised animal howling, like a hundred dogs going mad in a pit'[72] reached the Captain via a voice pipe. Monsarrat gives the reader an idea how little time it took the 37 trapped men to die; four minutes after the torpedo hit, silence had already descended on the riven fo'c'sle:

> The shambles that followed was mercifully brief; but until the water quenched the last screams and uncurled the last clawing hands, it was as Ericson [the Captain] had heard it through the voice pipe – a paroxysm of despair, terror, and convulsive violence, all in full and dreadful flood, an extreme corner of the human zoo for which there should be no witnesses.[73]

Once the survivors of the initial explosion entered the water, there then started a new phase with men not embracing a noble death in the idealistic manner favoured in Edwardian melodramas. There was no hero hurling defiance and brandishing the White Ensign at the enemy as his ship sank beneath him, in the manner of the frontispiece of Westerman's *Keepers Of The Narrow Seas*. Instead, some of the men fought each other, begged for help, gave up and even murdered each other in their futile efforts to avoid death from drowning or exposure.[74] The matter-of-fact narrative reinforces the sense of shock for the reader; the emotion of losing a ship and the struggle against the sea made more forceful by the writer's cool prose. Men dying at the hand of a hostile submarine is such a normal occurrence that it can be simply put as 'Presently, men began to die.'[75] The film, however, does not do justice to the image, presenting instead a rather sanitized image in preference to the daylight creeping over the dead and living:

> …it showed the rafts, horrible in themselves to be the only single items in a whole waste of cruel water, on which countless bodies rolled and laboured amid countless bits of

wreckage, adrift under the bleak sky. All around them, on the oily, fouled surface, the wretched flotsam, all that was left of *Compass Rose*, hurt and shamed the eye.

The picture of the year thought Lockhart [*Compass Rose*'s First Lieutenant]: 'Morning with the corpses.'[76]

The experiences of the *Compass Roses'* crew are repeated in J. MacGregor's *When The Ship Sank* (1960) which gives a torrid description of the deaths of many passengers from a liner torpedoed without warning in September 1939 in the south-western approaches.[77] The novel then follows the struggles of those passengers that make it off the liner to survive until rescued, but with a final twist, one of the rescue ships is herself torpedoed on her way back to a British port, and very few of the original survivors survived their second bout in the water. Yet MacGregor makes some telling observations about the reactions of his characters, which do not fall into line with the traditional image of Britons abandoning ship in the footsteps of the *Birkenhead*[78] or *Titanic*:

> Along the line, helped by stewards and seamen, men, women and children filled the boats. There was no question of women and children first.[79]

The fact that there was no question of women and children first is an important difference as to how the British saw themselves when victims of aggression. If it is accepted that the tradition of the *Birkenhead* and *Titanic* were realistic portrayals of the way the British faced shipwreck, then the failure to observe this tradition in wartime can be attributed to two very different causes. First, that there were sufficient lifeboats for all negating the need for the displays of heroic self sacrifice that characterized the loss of the *Birkenhead* and later the *Titanic*. The second possible cause is that the scene described in *When the Ship Sank* was not an accident, it was a deliberate act of war that in effect made all the passengers unwilling combatants and thus equal in the face of such life-threatening danger.

At the same time, MacGregor describes how some passengers behaved badly, stealing life belts from women and panicking.[80] No doubt this was a realistic portrayal of people fighting for their lives but not one that would have been in tune with the ideals of stoic self-sacrifice inherited from the Victorian and Edwardian eras. Importantly, the book was written in 1960, 21 years after the events it is supposed to be relating and long enough for the passage of time to allow the addressing of unpalatable images, such as panic. Yet it is the Germans, and not those passengers who behaved badly, who are treated with the least sympathy by the author: 'Against the German submarine or submarines which had been responsible for the sinkings there was no open, flaring anger, rather a cold, slow hate.'[81]

In the hands of post-Second World War authors, submarines had made dying for your country a terrible vision of humanity in its most repellant and primitive form. The authors, through the deaths of their characters, had reinforced how un-English submarine warfare could be. Submarine warfare did not produce 'good' or heroic deaths. Sailors, men, women and children died from drowning, burns, fuel oil poisoning and exposure; they were often alone in the darkness or shrieking like injured animals.[82] No longer were people brandishing the British flag at German submarines as their ship sank beneath them; instead there was a frantic struggle to get boats and life rafts away.[83] Anyone thinking that a war at sea was the last refuge of Wilfred Owen's 'The old Lie: Dulce et decorum est Pro patria mori'[84] was rudely disabused.

One interesting development in the way the British have written about their fictional submarines is the change in the way the villains have been described. In some novels, such as those by Gray and Bulmer, the traditional villains, the U-boats and their crews, are the heroes of the piece.[85] Such a change in status forced some interesting manoeuvring and character development in order to diffuse the problem of unrestricted submarine warfare and maritime atrocities. In Bulmer's *Sea Wolf: Shark America* (1981), the Captain of the U-boat shows some discomfiture at the techniques of unrestricted submarine warfare following the sinking of a merchant ship without warning off the American coast: 'there was a regret that he was not able to challenge the ship on the surface and sink her by gunfire; but the time would come he felt sure.'[86] Later in the novel, the U-boat's skipper, Balder Wolz, mused that:

> Sinking merchantmen was not, when he thought about it, really his kind of war from choice either. But to win this hideous war, the job had to be done. It was being cruel to be kind.[87]

Such a need to be 'cruel to be kind' and the need to win or end a 'hideous war' suggests that the morality of killing non-combatants was of lesser importance than the risks of defeat when fighting a war of national survival. Such a view avoided discussions of who should normally be considered as non-combatants and instead portrayed merchant ships as legitimate military targets, but only in order to end the fighting. This view of the combatant/non-combatant issue avoided the paradox that had shaped British responses to their own unrestricted submarine campaign: how was it possible to reconcile activities by non-combatants that support combat operations with their civilian status? By bringing up such an issue, Bulmer (writing in the late 1970s and early 1980s) was in fact reflecting fears about nuclear weapons and strategic bombing that made everyone part of the front-line. Furthermore, he was also demonstrating that in an age of total war everything contributes in some way to a combat operation; an issue that had already been aired in Griffin's 1968 novel *An Operational Necessity*.[88]

In another adventure it was again pointed out that Wolz, operating as part of a U-boat pack in the North Atlantic, did not like unrestricted submarine warfare – 'much as a seamen like Balder Wolz might regret the necessity, the harsh realities of war made this unholy cross the only one possible for U-boats.'[89] Yet later on in the series Wolz had 'got over his repugnance' but 'he would never overcome his feelings of horror at sinking great vessels and in the process possibly killing other men.'[90] Indeed, in the first novel of the series, Wolz's first attack on a merchant vessel was with gunfire, not a torpedo, with the comment that 'this was how submarine warfare should be carried out.'[91] Such a desire to operate within the Prize rules of stopping and sinking by gunfire enemy merchant vessels is a very British pre-Second World War view of submarine warfare and one that seems out of place in a German context, except to humanize images of German submarines at a time when the German Federal Republic was an important naval and land component of the NATO forces in Europe.

The other method used to diffuse the problem of submarines being involved in unsavoury incidents, was to have the instigator as someone other than the hero. To this end Bulmer has the 2nd Watch Officer (rather than the Captain) say that he would like to machine gun the survivors.[92] Gray's creation, Bergman, had to deal not with one of his officer's thinking about shooting survivors, but one who actually did:

> The Exec Officer is on the bridge with a machine-gun, Sir. He's apparently found a boatload of enemy survivors.[93]

Gray recounts in graphic detail the scene that met Bergman when he reached the bridge of his submarine and his feelings:

> A rust-streaked lifeboat bobbed forlornly in the mid-Atlantic swell a few yards away on *UB–44*'s starboard beam. Its metal skin was ripped and torn by bullet scars and dying men hung limply over the gunwales like tattered rag dolls. Other bodies, supported by canvas-covered life-jackets, floated face down in the water and the cold grey sea was tinted red with blood.
> Bergman stood petrified with horror as he stared at the carnage. Even in a nightmare, it was a scene that defied belief.[94]

These books by Bulmer and Gray, all written during the 1970s and 1980s suggest a change in agenda away from the submarine being a vehicle for action and adventure, as seen in the way that authors such as Alistair MacLean or Hammond Innes used submarines to support and develop a plot,[95] or indeed the wartime adventures written in the 1950s and 1960s,[96] to one showing the horror of war, as demonstrated by the lead characters' dismay at what modern warfare demanded.

Another technique was to disassociate the memories of Nazism with the actions of the novel's heroes. Gray's Bergman 'had become an avowed enemy of the mad clique of men who were riding his beloved Germany to destruction.'[97] Bulmer's hero too 'could do without dedicated Nazis in his boat.'[98] Other authors, who were using U-boats as a vehicle for even more horrific atrocities than machine gunning survivors (such as using submarines as a base for a rocket attack on London using anthrax spores), made it clear that is was the work of the SS and not ordinary U-boat men.[99] Such attempts to disassociate the U-boat arm and its fictional heroes from the Nazis, had a parallel in real life with the concerted attempts by captured German officers to disassociate the Wehrmacht from the Nazi party in postwar analysis of military operations.[100] This would also have had the effect of making the rearmament of post war Germany, its membership of NATO and above all the reacquisition of submarines, palatable to her former enemies and new-found allies.

Depictions of British submariners also sought to differentiate between certain types of behaviour, which although not set apart by ideology in the manner that characterizes novels about German submariners, contributed to ideas of British national identity – among them, the concept of personal courage. The submarine, through the film *Morning Departure* (1950), rams home the long-standing virtue of the true Briton being prepared to make the ultimate sacrifice and lay down his life to save his comrades.[101] In *Morning Departure* Richard Attenborough's character, Stoker Snipe, breaks under the strain of being trapped in a sunken submarine; however, he gains a more heroic and sympathetic image when he gives up one of the last remaining escape sets and instead remains behind with three others to await rescue or death. Reviews of the film thought that it was a sombre, yet tremendously inspiring and thrilling peacetime melodrama, dealing with the suffering and fortitude of the crew of a sunken submarine.[102] One reviewer likened *Morning Departure* to 'a "Journey's End" of the Navy…'[103] The importance of *Morning Departure* is not in its disaster content, nor the timing of the release of the film hard on the heels of the loss of *HMS Truculent* with heavy loss of life, but in the fact that the submarine had now become an acceptable vehicle for showing a facet of British national identity; that of facing an unpleasant end without complaint or shameful act – clearly strong popular feelings could still be stirred by perceived individual heroic sacrifice.[104]

Despite being an inanimate object, the submarine can, and has been, portrayed as either a hero (or perhaps heroine) or a villain; as Nicolas Monsarrat says, made famous by Jack Hawkins' gravelly voice at the start of the film *Cruel Sea*:

> But the men are the stars of this story. The only heroines are the ships: and the only villain the cruel sea itself.[105]

Understandably, however, Monsarrat also saw the submarine as the villain of *The Cruel Sea*. When the *Compass Rose* blew a submarine to the surface with a depth charge attack,

> She [the U-boat] had now fallen back on a level keel, and for the moment she rode at her proper trim: it was odd, and infinitely disgusting, suddenly to see this wicked object, the loathsome cause of a hundred nights of fear and disaster, so close to them, so innocently exposed. It was like seeing some criminal, who had outraged honour and society, and had been long shunned, taking his ease at one's own fireside.[106]

In such a short passage Monsarrat manages to do much; in the previous sections of the scene he describes the vessel as a U-boat and not a submarine, reinforcing the idea, mentioned in the previous section of this chapter, that there was a difference in moral status between British and German submarines. At the same time, the references to the U-boat as 'some criminal' emphasizes the lack of chivalry and the absolute villainy of the submarine, as does 'this wicked object' and the other pejorative language in the passage. Most importantly, Monsarrat does something very odd given the hostile language he employs – he personalises the submarine: it is not 'it', but is referred to as 'she'.[107] This has the effect of making the submarine less of a machine obeying the whims of men and instead an independent creature that is responsible for its own actions and is, therefore, easier to destroy. Douglas Reeman echoed these sentiments in the 'Author's Note' to his novel *With Blood And Iron*:

> We who took part in that battle hardly thought of the enemy as something human, as flesh and blood. We feared him because he was invisible yet ever-present, and out of that fear grew hatred and the power to hit back with ruthless determination.[108]

Furthermore, Catto's *Murphy's War* used the lack of names for submarines and the suggestion of personification, as well as some rather emotive language, as a way of suggesting submarines were very definitely the villain of the novel:

> U-boats are rarely named. Perhaps there is a natural anonymity about things that lurk like pillagers beneath the sea.[109]

The description of fictional submarines as 'pillagers' strikes a chord with the description of real, unrestricted submarine warfare as piracy.

Although the real-life castigation of submarine operations as piracy and submariners as pirates has been discussed in Chapter Three, there was an understandable crossover of the stigmatization of submarines into the fictional arena. Naturally, it was the depiction of German submarine operations that came in for the greatest opprobrium by British authors. Paralleling the interwar period language of hatred of the submarine, the prolific children's author Percy Westerman informed his juvenile readers that U-boat men were 'bounders', a 'piratical crew' and that the U-boat was a 'submerged pirate'.[110] Furthermore, these 'modern pirates lack even the faint spark of chivalry that was to be occasionally met with in the German Navy during the earlier stage of the Great War.'[111] When a U-boat was finally sunk it brought 'her career of black and ignominious piracy to a close…'[112]

Westerman, however, made use of the pirate trope more aggressively, and somewhat surprisingly made the villains British in *The Pirate Submarine* (1923). In this book, a cashiered naval officer uses his partnership in a Cornish breaker's yard to purchase a scrapped submarine and use it for robbery on the high seas; an activity that, unlike unrestricted submarine warfare, was actually piracy.[113] The use of a cashiered and disgraced British submariner as the lead villain adds weight to the image that not only were such activities wrong, but they were so unchivalrous that they could only be carried out by the most morally corrupt people. Fictional submarine warfare and its piracy imagery was an activity that emphasized a perversion of society.

The experience of the Second World War and the paradox that the similarity between Allied and Axis submarine operations posed for the British in particular, forced a revision of the pirate label for the fictional submariners as well as the flesh-and-blood variety. Whereas Westerman could draw attention in the interwar period to the use of the Jolly Roger by his pirate submarine and tell his readers that not only was there 'an ominous silence'[114] but on seeing the Jolly Roger flying from their submarine for the first time that 'the sinister significance of the term had struck home'[115] to his pirate submarine's crew, this was not an option after the Second World War, thanks to the enthusiastic use of this flag by British submarines. Such was the impact of the adoption of the Jolly Roger by British submarines that it made its way into fictional accounts as 'something to be proud of, that black flag with its central skull and cross bones: a record of achievement.'[116]

The revision of attitudes to the use of the Jolly Roger by British submarines was so rapid that by the time *We Dive At Dawn* was shot, it was acceptable to show the Jolly Roger with its various symbols denoting what had been sunk and how. Right at the very start of the film, as the *Sea Tiger* returned from an unsuccessful patrol, the film cuts to another submarine's Jolly Roger emblazoned with many symbols of successful actions during the conversation between the two commanding officers. When the *Sea Tiger* finally reaches her base after sinking the German battleship *Brandenburg* and her adventures in the Danish port seizing fuel and supplies from enthusiastic Danes and a rather angry German garrison, her Jolly Roger was much in evidence as she moved up harbour accompanied by cheers from the surrounding ships. The black and white film did, however, cover up any unrestricted sinkings on the flags; the white bars that denoted a merchantman torpedoed were almost indistinguishable from the red bars of a warship destroyed by torpedoes.

The dissociation of negative images of piracy and submarines continued with post-war authors writing about the German U-boat crews. As Gray's U-boat skipper, Bergman, commented to his Executive Officer, 'Whatever the enemy propaganda may say about me, Number One, I am not a pirate.'[117] Just as was the case with the disassociation of war crimes from ordinary U-boatmen, one can see this dissociation of piracy from U-boats as part of an unconscious process of adjustment to the realities of the Cold War and German membership of NATO.

The Submarine in Film and Fiction: a Popular Genre?

The fictional submarine has been depicted as both the curse of Britain and its saviour, quite a feat for a weapon system that only entered the British consciousness at the very end of the Victorian era. This does not mean, however, that novels and films with submarines as the subject have achieved critical acclaim. Given the lack of critical response to submarine novels, it is hard not to agree with Ramsden's comments regarding the literary critics' treatment of war stories, that the critics have ignored the middlebrow and popular writers and concentrated on high literature by Evelyn Waugh and Anthony Powell.[118] In particular, any analysis of the submarine in fiction is hampered in the same way that all war fiction is, by the fact that it has been 'passed over in complete silence.'[119] Indeed, so low is the critical interest that of all the novels about submarines cited in this chapter, only four books have any reviews listed in the *Periodicals Contents Index* (nine reviews in total).[120] Moreover, all the reviews tend to address the literary worth of the novel rather than how submarines are portrayed and thus tell us little about how the images the books presented were received. One exception to this is the review of Griffin's *An Operational Necessity* in the *RUSI Journal*, which discussed the import of the book's message about attacks on non-combatants.[121] Not only did the *RUSI Journal* feel that *An Operational Necessity* was one of the few works of fiction worth bringing their members attention to,[122] but that:

> ...after two world wars, it is still necessary to argue that the killing of shipwrecked persons who have taken to their lifeboats is forbidden. Even after Nuremburg it still may be held by some that a combatant must decide whether operational necessity will require their destruction. Such a decision, its justification, and its consequences on both the crews involved, is the theme of this book. It is one that should be considered by all thinking Servicemen and, in these days of total national involvement, of the nation in arms, by all thinking citizens.[123]

What sets the *RUSI Journal* review apart from others, is its concentration on the message rather than the literary skill of the writer, which was rated quite highly. The fact that a professional journal such as the *RUSI Journal* thought the topic was of sufficient importance to review a work of fiction is significant. It shows quite clearly that issues regarding the treatment of non-combatants were still active ones, and that it could be assumed that the deliberate murder of survivors in order to preserve operational security would not happen again.

Given the lack of reviews, it is necessary to consider other methods of assessing the impact of these novels. By looking at the number of printings or editions of each novel, a rough assessment of the popularity of each can be made, particularly when combined with the date range of the printings. However, as figure 6.1 shows, there is no obvious pattern. What can be seen from figure 6.1, however, is that irrespective of whether the novels concerned anti-submarine warfare, convoys, or British or German submarines, over half (26 out of 45) that have been cited in this chapter have had at least two print runs, which indicates some degree of popularity. There is not, however, any pattern to the distribution of the multiple print runs. Nor is there any consistency in the number of print runs for each type of novel; for example, it is not surprising, thanks to the quality of the writing, that Monsarrat's *The Cruel Sea* has the most issues at ten (not counting foreign editions), yet the novel with the next highest number of printings (six) is the otherwise unremarkable *A Twist Of Sand*, where the involvement of submarines is very small.

Figure 6.1: Cited Novels: Number of Printings or Editions and Date Range. (Data compiled from publisher's information and the British Library Integrated Catalogue)

Author	Title	Number of printings	Date range
Bulmer	Sea Wolf: Shark America	1	1982
Bulmer	Sea Wolf: Shark Pack	1	1980
Bulmer	Sea Wolf: Shark Trap	1	1982
Bulmer	Sea Wolf: Shark Africa	1	1981
Bulmer	Sea Wolf: Shark Raid	1	1982
Bulmer	Sea Wolf: Steel Shark	1	1979
Burland	A Fall from Aloft	3	1968–1987
Callison	Trapp's War	2	1976–1978
Callison	The Bone Collectors	2	1984–1985

Callison	A Flock of Ships	4	1970–1980
Catto	Murphy's War	1	1969
Chatham	Sea Sting	2	1982
Collenette	Ninety Feet To The Sun	1	1984
Dawson	Fathoms Deep	1	1943
Follett	U–700	2	1979–1989
Fullerton	The Waiting Game	4	1961–1974
Fullerton	Surface	4	1953–1974
Gage	The Cruel Coast	1	1967
Gray	U-Boat: Action Atlantic	2	1975
Gray	Tokyo Torpedo	2	1976–1977
Gray	Fighting Submarine	1	1979
Gray	Diving Stations	1	1980
Gray	Crash Dive 500	1	1981
Griffin	An Operational Necessity	4	1968–1999
Hackforth-Jones	Danger Below	1	1963
Jenkins	A Twist Of Sand	6	1959–1977
Lehnhoff	The Homeward Run	1	1957
MacGregor	When The Ship Sank	1	1960
MacHardy	Send Down A Dove	1	1968
Monsarrat	The Cruel Sea	10	1951–2002
Pattinson	Last In Convoy	3	1957–1972
Reeman	Dive In The Sun	2	1961–1972
Reeman	Strike From The Sea	2	1978–1989
Reeman	Surface With Daring	2	1976–1978
Reeman	With Blood And Iron	3	1964–1987
Trew	Kleber's Convoy	4	1972–2002
Trew	Yashimoto's Last Dive	1	1986
Westerman	The Flying Submarine	1	1912
Westerman	A Sub and a Submarine	2	1919–1940
Westerman	The Keepers Of The Narrow Seas	2	1918–1931
Westerman	The Pirate Submarine	2	1923–1940
Wingate	Frigate	4	1980–1990

Wingate	Carrier	4	1980–1990
Wingate	Submarine	4	1980–1990
Winton	Down The Hatch	3	1961–2004

As the graph at figure 6.2 shows, the majority of books listed in figure 6.1 were published in two main periods, both after the Second World War. The first major period of publishing activity is during the 1950s and 1960s, before falling off in the early 1970s. The second major period of publishing activity was in the late 1970s and early 1980s. The dip in submarine fiction in the early 1970s seems to correlate with the period of greatest anti-war sentiment following American involvement in Vietnam and détente with the Warsaw Pact. The second period of major activity seems to coincide with worsening relations with the Warsaw Pact and a resurgence in the possibility of major confrontation involving NATO, even though the subject for the novels

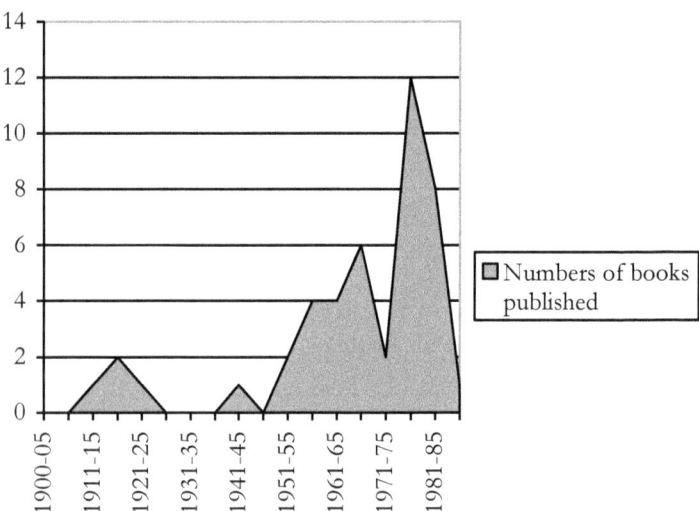

Figure 6.2: Graph showing the publication dates of the novels in figure 6.1.

was often Second World War submarine activities. What is also noticeable is the lack of new books being published on submarine warfare in the 1930s, coinciding with the upsurge in fears regarding aerial attack and the resulting wave of novels reflecting such public fears. Such a falling off of submarine novels in the 1930s supports the contention that the bomber supplanted the submarine as the most fearful weapon in British civil culture.

Fortunately, British war films that feature submarines in some shape or form did attract critical notice. The critics' comments were, however, often less than favourable, despite *The Times* calling *Above Us The Waves* 'an admirable film.'[124] The *Spectator* said that when considering *Above Us The Waves* 'most of us are weary of a 'Periscope up,' 'Periscope up, sir' dialogue, and shamefacedly salute the heroes, if not their achievement, with a stifled yawn.'[125] The *New Statesman* merely thought that *Above Us The Waves* lacked 'the sense of conviction, of insight'.[126] This did not mean that the critics disparaged the actual achievement of the wartime midget submarine crews, but that they did not consider the films to be especially distinguished.[127]

Unsurprisingly, the wartime *We Dive At Dawn* had a far more favourable response from E. Ansty in the *Spectator* with the reviewer feeling that 'no more convincing picture of the behaviour of men under fire has come from the studios' and he commended the director and John Mills.[128] Ansty finished his review with the simple accolade that 'This is film-making at its very best.'[129] *Kinematograph Weekly*, the trade magazine for cinema managers, thought that *We Dive At Dawn* was very good, calling it 'a thrilling and thoroughly convincing account of action at sea.'[130] The Times felt that *We Dive At Dawn* showed 'how normally we react to the abnormal strains and stresses of war.'[131] Yet neither Ansty, *The Times*, nor the *Kinematograph Weekly*'s reviewer made any reference to the lack of unrestricted submarine warfare. On the other hand, Dilys Powell in 1947 thought that *We Dive At Dawn* was 'efficient…in a cold war' but it 'lacked the warmth of life.'[132]

The wartime films featuring submarines were popular with audiences as well as the critics. *We Dive At Dawn* was felt to be 'excellent war fare' and 'good for youngsters'[133] and in order to support showings and maximize the propaganda value of the film managers used publicity stunts. One wartime (1943) 'tie-in' that was singled out by *Kinematograph Weekly* was that of the Grange Cinema, Dagenham (hardly a hotbed of naval enthusiasm), included Sea Cadet divisions marching to the theatre, bands, speeches by naval dignitaries and a performance of the 'Sunset' ceremony to raise the profile of the film.[134] The Crown Film Unit's *Close Quarters* also proved to be popular with the trade and audiences; *Kinematograph Weekly* called it an 'exciting tribute to the Submarine Service, it comes in the "must be seen" category' and that 'it is the duty of every landlubber, irrespective of age and sex, to see it.'[135] The *Times* thought that the film was 'a healthy reminder that our own submarine crews have, day and night since the moment war was declared, carried out their own difficult and dangerous offensive work.'[136]

The inference that it was the patriotic duty of people to see *Close Quarters* and that it was a healthy reminder of the work done by the submarine service, smacks of propaganda and to a certain degree this must be true. After all, *Close Quarters* was made by a government film unit. Even a nominally independently produced film such as *We Dive At Dawn* relied on government assistance; the Royal Navy lent the producers a submarine and took John Mills to sea to experience life on patrol.[137] Furthermore, it was considered that both *Close Quarters* and *We Dive At Dawn* would show British submarines hitting back at the Germans at a time (1943) when the public were anxious about U-boat activities in the Atlantic.[138] This does not mean, however, that either of these films should be regarded as pure propaganda. Certainly, they were used as vehicles to reinforce feeling of national unity, but they were also seen at the time as being more than just low grade propaganda. *Close Quarters*, made as it was in a documentary style, was greeted with critical and popular approval[139] and was regarded as being more objective than fictional representations.[140] *We Dive At Dawn* was not as openly propagandistic in tone when compared to *The Lion Has Wings* or *The Way Ahead*; there was no discussion about why

Britain was fighting, or emphasis on the building of national unity through the melding of a disparate platoon of recruits into a disciplined fighting force in the way that *The Way Ahead* did. Nor does *We Dive At Dawn* emphasize British successes; the viewer remains unsure of the success of their special mission to sink the *Brandenburg* until the very end of the film.

We Dive At Dawn is propagandist in its depiction of national character and in this way supports Richards' ideas of national identity in British war films in that they each exhibit three qualities that provide cultural strands in the national character.[141] Richards identified these three qualities as a sense of humour, which he regarded as vital, tolerance, the mixing of different groups or classes who are successfully welded together while retaining their individuality, and finally, the display of stoicism or emotional restraint.[142] It has been noted that *We Dive At Dawn* was written 'with an eye to class and regional variation as well as authenticity',[143] but as well as addressing the national characteristics identified by Richards, the film helps blur class distinctions through the cramped and dirty conditions onboard: when the *Sea Tiger* gets back from her patrol all the crew, from the Commanding Officer downwards are dirty and unshaven.[144] *We Dive At Dawn*, through its inclusion of a Canadian seaman in a talking part, also raises issues of Empire and Imperial cohesion in the fight against Germany.

The post-war films, *Above Us The Waves*, *Morning Departure* and *The Cruel Sea*, all attracted large audiences.[145] However, this does not explain why there was no move to deal with the unrestricted aspects of submarine warfare despite the obvious popular appeal of films about British submarines. Films such as *Above Us The Waves*, dealing as it did with midget submarine attacks, was seen as showing Britain winning the war 'through small-scale, imaginatively conceived and boldly carried out actions by small groups'[146] – which has been suggested is a more attractive image for the British than 'Britannia out in the middle of the ring beating the daylights out of a reeling opponent with the help of several larger allies.'[147] The use of small groups would also allow the part played by allies in the victory to be played down without creating ill-feeling. The use of small unit actions where personal courage played at important part in the success of the operation, also shaped the sort of battle that could be shown if accidental tension between physical and moral courage were to be avoid. In this way, even after victory, given the odium that had been previously attached to the submarine as being the tool of the morally weaker power when used for unrestricted submarine warfare, it was emotionally unacceptable to feature British submarines carrying out sink on sight engagements. Conversely, by avoiding unrestricted submarine warfare and concentrating on midget submarines and accidents, British film-makers were able to depict the submarine in an acceptable manner that reinforced British national identity regarding the moral superiority of its armed forces.

Conclusion

Fictional descriptions of submarines have provided the British with their best chance of experiencing submarine warfare that, due to the inaccessibility of real submarines to the bulk of the population, would otherwise be impossible. At the same time, the fictional fortunes of submarines at the hands of British writers and film-makers have mirrored their factual counterpart's progression along a road to perdition and then towards redemption.

Just like those considering factual British submarines, novelists and film-makers faced a problem over how to portray the unrestricted warfare activities without condoning similar activities by German and other enemy submarines. Again like their factual counterparts, the easiest solution to this otherwise insoluble paradox was to ignore it. What did not occur, unlike in the Royal Navy, was the post-Second World War acceptance of unrestricted warfare as a legitimate activity for British submarines. As a result, fictional descriptions of British submarines did not tally with reality and concentrated on reinforcing a myth about British submarine morality that those within the Submarine Service, who had used unrestricted submarine warfare themselves, would have recognized.

At times, the obsessional depiction of British submarines as either torpedoing legitimate targets such as warships or using Prize rules against merchantmen, says much about the way in which non-combatants at sea were viewed, even after being on the receiving end of not one but two unrestricted campaigns that were perceived as only having narrowly failed. By concentrating on using British submarines in such a manner, the writers projected an air of respectability onto British activities. Even those authors, such as Nicolas Monsarrat and Douglas Reeman, who recognized the fallacy of such an image of British submarine activity compared with that of the Germans, still could not help describing German activities in a more negative way than those of the British. Despite the less than factual depiction of British submarines, the mythology that this generated did help shape an image of British submarines being morally acceptable to the British public. This helped degrade the normal reaction to all submarines as being not only the weapon of the weaker power but also that of the morally weaker nation; the submarine had just started towards redemption, before falling back once more to perdition, thanks to the fear of nuclear weapons.

On the other hand it was very easy for British writers of all periods to emphasize the uncivilized nature of hostile submarine operations and play up the immoral actions of enemy submarines, especially through attacks on survivors once they were in the water waiting for rescue. The image of dastardly U-boatmen machine gunning survivors provided excellent links to the image of submarines as pirates, and of morally weaker actions that had flashed almost instantaneously into existence when Germany launched its first unrestricted submarine warfare campaign in 1915.

Unlike the depiction of British submarines, the image presented of German submarine activities did undergo a revision as some British authors sought to exploit the fictional possibilities of the U-boat arm. As a result of this, the use of atrocities, either the murder of survivors or the use of unrestricted submarine warfare, underwent a subtle change. With writers such as Bulmer and Gray, the emphasis shifted to the fact that although the individuals in command of the submarines might dislike what they were doing in the form of unrestricted warfare, it was necessary to carry out the task: a very British idea of doing one's duty. At the same time the instigators of atrocities became subsidiary characters, and a concerted effort, conscious or unconscious, was made to separate Nazism from the U-boat arm, probably as a result of the rehabilitation of West Germany and her increasingly important part in NATO.

What is remarkable given the amount of pejorative language about factual and fictional submarine in the interwar period, was the speed with which the Jolly Roger was accepted as the Royal Navy's Submarine Service's own insignia for a successful patrol. That film makers were comfortable in drawing attention to the symbol in propaganda films such as *We Dive At Dawn* in 1943, at the height of the Battle of the Atlantic; this is hard to believe in given the strength of pre–Second World War feeling, yet it is clear that this was indeed the case. On the other hand, the use of black and white film did avoid drawing attention to the fact that the Submarine Service itself denoted merchant ships sunk with a different colour from warships, thus helping to preserve the morally superior image of British submarines.

Overall, the films and books produced in Britain showed submarines in an acceptable, if not necessarily accurate, light. British submarines were shown as operating in a morally superior manner to those of the enemy, be it through avoiding the use of unrestricted submarine warfare or not being used to destroy enemy cities in imaginary accounts of the Cold War turning hot. That there was no revision of the way British submarines were depicted is due to the strength of preconceptions regarding non-combatants at sea. The lack of revision in the way the British wrote about submarines, contributed to the slow and faltering steps that the submarine took towards respectability during the Cold War by emphasizing their moral superiority, aided by the increased visibility of British submarines, fictional and factual, in the Second World War.

On the other hand, although hostile submarines were depicted as engaged in morally weaker activities, the depiction of hostile submarines did undergo some revision, if only to rehabilitate the German Navy; yet some of the more propaganda worthy episodes such as the machine-gunning of survivors remained in use for a considerable time in the post-Second World War period. With the increasing distance placed between the fictional lead characters of the U-boat arm and Nazism or atrocities, even the preferred weapon of the morally weaker powers also set foot of a path to respectability after over forty years of perdition.

Fictional submarines, friendly or hostile, had a hard and long journey in the hundred years after 1900, from indifference through hostility, to a sometimes grudging acceptance. This move from perdition to partial redemption was a combination of the way fictional submarines were depicted, and, as discussed in other chapters, also a consequence of existing cultural preconceptions and the reality of hot war and cold peace.

Conclusion

A hundred year journey from perdition to redemption

This book has charted the remarkable changes that have taken place in the way the submarine has been understood by the British. The submarine has physically changed too: larger, faster, quieter and better armed than the Royal Navy's submarine *Number 1*, it has been transformed from being a weapon that threatens British security and seapower to one that defends it. For much of the twentieth century, the submarine was not well regarded by the British as it threatened their navy, their global position, their economy, their freedom from starvation and indirectly their ability to resist invasion; that the submarine could also be an opportunity was not seriously considered. The submarine was regarded from the outset not as a means of opening up a new unexplored environment, but instead as a physical attack on the defenceless and on the very thing that kept the nation free – its Navy. Only with Britain's changing economic and global situation after 1945 was the submarine seen as a way of supporting rather than destroying Britain's global status. Even when re-imagined to become the sword and shield of Britain from the 1960s onwards, the submarine was feared by a minority for what might be unleashed by its use.

The relationship between practice and symbolism is important. In much of the British interaction with submarines, practice followed the symbolism attached to the submarine by British cultural preconceptions. The submarine was seen as a threat to the battlefleet, so it was used in practice in a way to support the battlefleet. Unrestricted submarine warfare was seen as immoral, so in the early interwar period the cruiser submarine was developed to allow a morally acceptable form of economic warfare by British submarines. Only with the British unrestricted submarine campaigns of the Second World War did practice cease to follow symbolism, this being associated with a clear divergence between corporate and civil attitudes to the submarine. Later, following the introduction of nuclear-powered submarines into British service after 1960, the roles were reversed, with the symbolism of the submarine building on the development of the SSN as one of the most powerful conventionally armed weapon systems available to Britain. The symbolism of the submarine can be seen through the analysis of the naval reviews at Spithead, with the submarine as a symbol increasing in importance throughout the twentieth century, just as it increased in importance in operational practice.

The importance of symbolism and practice lead on to the next significant argument in this book – the importance of existing cultural preconceptions in the shaping of British understanding of the submarine throughout the last century. With each permutation of signification and reception of the submarine following a new mode of use or technological advance, the basic method of understanding any new development remained through the impact it had on command of the sea or its effect on non-combatants. Perhaps because of their maritime predominance and the perceived envy of British supremacy by other powers, the British could only see the submarine as a weapon to be used against them, rather than simply a method of proceeding underwater, which could be used both for peaceful purposes like exploration, as well as for naval activities. At the same time, the longevity of the fleet submarine in the face of repeated technological failures demonstrates most clearly the power of cultural constructs in the assimilation, reception and signification of new technology.

The differences between corporate and civil culture may have been of short duration, or muted by the exigencies of war, but they are important nonetheless. The first clear difference between corporate and civil culture emerged in the aftermath of the First World War, where there was a desire to make the submarine acceptable to British civil culture through the pursuit of an ultimately unsuccessful concept, the cruiser submarine. The Royal Navy's enthusiasm for, and investment in, such an experimental concept shows that corporate culture was seeking to use the submarine to its maximum effect within the confines set by civil condemnation of unrestricted submarine warfare. That the Royal Navy should try to appease civil culture in this way indicates its awareness of differences between corporate (i.e. service) perceptions of the submarine and the perception of the wider civil culture, hence the steps taken to produce a submarine that did not threaten civil cultural preconceptions in the way that unrestricted submarine warfare had.

The most obvious difference between corporate and civil cultures occurred in the interwar period when, most significantly, the Royal Navy not only allowed Nazi Germany to build submarines but also considered the use of unrestricted submarine warfare and carried out successful unrestricted campaigns against all the Axis powers during the Second World War. In particular, the Anglo–German Naval Agreement in 1935 must be seen as a watershed in the British relationship with the submarine. The AGNA represented a change that was led by corporate culture using the submarine as part of a wider strategy to trap Nazi Germany into building the type of fleet the Royal Navy felt it would be best able to defeat in time of war, against a background chorus of disapproval from the civil sphere who still viewed the submarine as a threat rather than an opportunity. What is even more significant is the civil reaction to the corporate decision to carry out unrestricted warfare in 1940: they ignored it, not only during the war, but in peacetime as well. The British remained loath to discuss the possibility that British submarines were involved in unrestricted submarine warfare, even in fiction, yet writers were quite happy to use German submarines as vehicles for discussing unrestricted submarine warfare and the extent of Nazi penetration of the Kriegsmarine.

Moreover, the enthusiastic adoption of the Jolly Roger flag by the Submarine Service not only shows that there was a divergence between corporate and civil culture when the, at times, hysterical condemnation of submarines as pirates during the First World War and interwar period is considered, but also that British submariners were embarking on a process that was to set them apart from their general service colleagues. Post-Second World War, the difference between the submarine service and the general corporate culture became more pronounced with the submarine service being recognised as a distinct entity separate from the rest of the corporate (and indeed civil culture) through naval pageantry. The submarine service was set apart during this period by the decision to grant a branch badge and Queen's Colour; eventually even the names of the submarines venerated the submarines services' own history rather than the corporate history as a whole. At the same time, corporate and civil cultures remained at odds over the importance of the submarine: in corporate circles it was recognized as one of the most promising anti-submarine weapon systems, while except as a means of demonstrating British successes, it was largely undervalued by the civil sphere. Only with the 1977 Silver Jubilee review was the submarine – in the shape of the SSN – given the same level of civil recognition that had been prevalent in corporate circles since the 1960s and indeed earlier in some quarters, but this was in part a reflection of long-lasting cultural preconceptions.

The most significant interaction between cultural assumptions and operational or strategic issues has to be in the dominance of the battleship in naval thinking, a dominance that set the submarine along the road towards the fleet submarine, which was a concept that took until the 1990s to be perfected. The importance of the battleship and battlefleet in British cultural preconceptions was such that the submarine was seen as a threat to the dominance of the fleet. This in turn had an impact on perceptions of national identity as the idea that their navy was the foundation on which their security and freedom was based, was important to the British. This book shows that the Royal Navy had to integrate the submarine in a manner that was acceptable to the prevailing civil and corporate cultures, hence the emphasis on a fleet submarine that supported the battlefleet rather than threatened its position. Such a need to assimilate the submarine within an existing cultural framework also explains the development of a prototype cruiser submarine which presented the Royal Navy with a culturally acceptable means of using the submarine as an economic weapon in the light of the reaction to the German unrestricted submarine campaigns of the First World War, despite the fact that the nation that had the most to lose from a successful development of a cruiser submarine was Great Britain.

The other major impact that cultural preconceptions had was through the pre-1914 inability to see the submarine as an economic weapon and, indeed, the failure – despite the warnings of Admiral Fisher and Conan Doyle – to believe that unrestricted submarine warfare would actually take place. This cognitive dissonance was due to two preconceptions: first, the importance of the battlefleet and command of the sea being gained in a Mahanian fashion rather than a guerre de course; second, the importance of non-combatants and the sanctity of private property within British culture. The view of non-combatants and private property was of particular importance thanks to a combination of economic, political and philosophical ideas inherited from the Victorian period. These ideas defined war as conflict between states, not individuals, and insisted that in wartime, trade had to continue without disruption. Thus, when unrestricted warfare was experienced by the British it was viewed as morally repugnant. Such, indeed, was the vehemence of the civil response that the submarine was stigmatized by its involvement in unrestricted warfare until well into the interwar period. Thus it was the desire to produce a submarine that would avoid the stigmatization of the early interwar period by playing according to Britain's rules of maritime warfare, not technological advancements, which provided the impetus for the British development of the cruiser submarine concept.

The submarine also provides a very good example against the mono-causal arguments of 'hard' technological determinism.

The development of practical submarine technology throughout the latter half of the nineteenth century was effectively neutral in that it merely allowed the exploitation of the undersea environment. That those who chose to develop the technology as a weapon system, such as John Holland attracted more interest than those like Simon Lake who wanted to exploit civil uses was not determined by technology but by ideas and cultural attitudes. The persistence of the fleet submarine concept also demonstrates the importance of ideas rather than technological determinism. The fleet submarine started off as an idea that would promote the physical integration of the submarine with the British battlefleet, a concept that required a high speed. The fact that immature propulsion technologies were forced into submarines was not a function of technological determinism, but rather a desire to force through ideas that moulded technology within an existing framework of understanding and cultural preconceptions. When nuclear propulsion gave the submarine virtually unlimited power and endurance, as well as the ability to become independent of the surface, it was not determined by advances in the new field of nuclear sciences, but was the culmination of an ongoing quest for speed and greater submerged endurance.

Technological determinism did not play a part in the development of unrestricted submarine warfare. Indeed, those that prophesied unrestricted submarine warfare such as Fisher and Conan Doyle, either predicated their assumptions on existing technology (as in the case of Conan Doyle), or on the inability of the submarine to comply with the accepted rules of war (as in the case of Fisher). At the same time, there were no major changes in practical submarine technology between the start of the first German unrestricted submarine warfare campaign in 1915 and the start of the final German unrestricted campaign in 1939. The very negative response to the submarine in the interwar period by British civil culture was not caused by the technology with which merchant shipping was attacked; it was caused, rather, by the manner in which perceived non-combatants were attacked. In this way the British were able to carry out a successful campaign against Turkish shipping by remaining within their own assumptions of maritime warfare, while the Germans, who moved outside the British assumptions of civilized warfare, were castigated for it. Technology played no part in such an emotionally conditioned response to the different ways in which submarines could be used in maritime warfare. On the other hand, national identity has had a profound effect on the British understanding of the submarine.

The first interaction between submarines and British culture was over the threat they posed to the battleship and battlefleet on which was built much of Britain's global status as the world's first superpower. British concepts of national identity, as well as domestic and imperial security, were all bound up within images of the strength and security of the battlefleet and its constituent parts. Thus, any feeling of security that Britain's predominance in battleships generated would have been undermined by any reported successes in submarine navigation. Just as importantly, the immature concepts of deterrence in Edwardian Britain were based on seapower and the dominance of the battlefleet. Submarines attacked, literally, the basis of pre-nuclear deterrence. It is therefore no accident that the Royal Navy took to dismissing the submarine in the years before 1901 as the 'weapon of the weaker power'.

The submarine was not just the weapon of the materially weaker power, but also the morally weaker power. Unrestricted submarine warfare and the submarine had not only rendered the Royal Navy impotent during the First World War; it had introduced the concept of starvation despite the Royal Navy's undefeated strength in surface ships. The national identity issues raised by unrestricted submarine warfare all centre on ideas of being an island race. Britain's island status had protected it from invasion for centuries and the insularity conferred by being an island was a key concept in national identity; submarines were originally used by the Royal Navy as part of harbour and coast defences in order to prevent a seaborne attack and subsequent invasion, with the navy being seen as the first and last line of defence. The submarine, for civil culture, also threatened the security provided by island-hood, exposing the nation to starvation and economic turmoil, real and imagined, by attacking the non-combatant ships that Britain depended on for food and trade while the battlefleet sailed helplessly above. Island status was no longer a guarantor of security, especially for non-combatants.

From the Second World War onwards, the British slowly began to see the submarine not as a threat to their national identity, but as a means of shoring it up in the face of huge changes to Britain's position in the world. After the Second World War the submarine came to be seen as the Royal Navy's prime anti-submarine weapon, the weapon that would allow them to keep control of the seas when modern warfare made operations by surface ships increasingly difficult. At the same time the submarine was now seen as an acceptable vehicle for displaying British successes. The speed of the experimental submarines *Explorer* and *Excalibur* was emphasized in the press: the submarines were unofficially claimed to be the fastest submarines in the world with the obvious suggestion that Britain was leading the way in submarine technology despite the massive changes in British global status and economic power post-1945. Even the lack of nuclear power did not prevent the superiority of British submarines being trumpeted in the press. Submarines were being transformed from a threat to the civil populace to a part of the means of defending it from starvation in the event of a hostile cold-war unrestricted submarine warfare campaign.

The advent of nuclear power and submarine-based nuclear weapons hastened the changes in the relationship between the submarine and British culture. The nuclear submarine was by far the most complex piece of military hardware and the possession of one represented a massive national technological superiority that was only surpassed by the ability to put a man in space. With the 1966 decision to scrap the CVA–01 programme, the nuclear Fleet submarine was the only weapon that was capable of achieving that still-cherished ambition of the Royal Navy – command of the sea – but without having to rely on airpower. That the SSN was now the Royal Navy's primary strike weapon for the post-1966 Fleet can be seen as a watershed in the way corporate meaning of the submarine was constructed. In previous years, navies had seen the battleship and then the aircraft carrier as the culmination and embodiment of naval might; now this place had been taken by the submarine, the nuclear-powered and conventionally armed SSN. The nuclear submarine was now seen as vital in order for Britain to be regarded as a first-class naval power, and the nuclear deterrent based on the Polaris submarines supported the traditional patriotic constructions of Britain as a great power. Moreover, changes in the way the submarine was perceived as a part of national identity can be seen in the position of the submarines at the Spithead Reviews; as the submarine becomes more important to national identity it moves closer to the head of the capital ships' lines, until in 1977 it is equal in symbolic importance at the Review to the aircraft carrier. The submarine had reached its zenith in the way it was conceptualized by both corporate and civil cultures.

In the early stages of this project, an eminent naval historian jokingly told me that cultural methodologies represented 'history without facts'; this book, however, clearly demonstrating that cultural approaches to naval history produce a wide variety of 'facts' to be analysed and interpreted. This book has explored the workings of imagination and imagery on decisions that are supposed to be based on logic and reason. Furthermore, this book has highlighted some of the unspoken assumptions of both British civil culture and the Royal Navy's corporate culture. There is a rich seam that can be exploited by cultural historians within Britain's maritime past.

NOTES

Introduction

1. T. A. Brassey, 'The Progress of the British Navy', in T. A. Brassey (ed.), *The Naval Annual 1898* (Portsmouth, 1898), p. 12; W. Laird Clowes, 'The Great Naval Review', *Illustrated London News*, 3 July 1897, p. 10; A. J. Marder, *The Anatomy of British Sea Power* (New York, 1940), 281; R. K. Massie, *Dreadnought* (London, 1993), p. vii.
2. *Saturday Review*, 19 June 1897, p. 379.
3. The remarks of M. Maurice Loir, quoted by T. A. Brassey, 'The Position of the British Navy in 1898' in T. A. Brassey (ed.), *The Naval Annual 1898*, p. 241.
4. P. Kennedy, *The Rise and Fall of British Naval Mastery* (London, 1991), p. 243; Marder, *British Sea Power*, p. 281; Massie, *Dreadnought*, p. vii.
5. E. Weyl, 'The Progress of Foreign Navies', in T. A. Brassey (ed.), *The Naval Annual 1898*, 19.
6. *Saturday Review*, 3 July 1897, p. 5.
7. Laird Clowes, 'The Great Naval Review', p. 10.
8. Brassey, 'Progress of the British Navy', p. 16.
9. *Saturday Review*, 3 July 1897, p. 5.
10. H. W. Wilson, 'The Forthcoming Naval Review And Its Predecessors', *Nineteenth Century*, vol. XLI, p. 883.
11. Brassey, 'Progress of the British Navy', p. 12; Marder, *British Sea Power*, p. 281; Massie, *Dreadnought*, p. vii.
12. Weyl, 'Progress of Foreign Navies', p. 19.
13. Ibid.
14. Wilson, 'Forthcoming Naval Review', 883.
15. T. W. Corbin, *The Romance of Submarine Engineering* (London, 1913), 109; C. Field, *The Story of the Submarine* (London, 1908), 223.
16. S. Lake, *The Submarine in War and Peace* (London, 1918).
17. J. Winton, 'The Spithead Review', *Illustrated London News*, August 1977, p. 37.
18. Ibid.
19. L. Marx & M. R. Smith, 'Introduction', *Does Technology Drive History?* (Cambridge, MA, 1994), p. ix.
20. Ibid. pp. xi–xii.

21 Marx & Smith, 'Introduction', xiii; see also R. Williams & D. Edge, 'The Social Shaping of Technology', *Research Policy*, vol. 25 (1996), pp. 865–869.
22 R. Kline & T. Pinch, 'The Social Construction of Technology', in D. MacKenzie & J. Wajcman (eds), *The Social Shaping of Technology*, 2nd edn. (Maidenhead, 1999), p. 113.
23 H. Kearney, *The British Isles. A History of Four Nations* (Cambridge: Cambridge University Press, 1989), p. 4.
24 M. Hadley, *Count Not the Dead. The Popular Image of the German Submarine* (Montreal, 1995).
25 P. Wright, *Tank* (London, 2000).
26 E. Russell, *War and Nature: Fighting Humans and Insects with Chemicals from World War I to Silent Spring* (Cambridge, 2001)
27 J. Ellis, *The Social History of the Machine Gun* (London, 1975)
28 See J. Terraine, *The Smoke and the Fire: Myth and Anti-Myths of War 1861–1945* (London, 1980), pp. 36, 40, 130–133, 233; P. Griffith, *Battle Tactics of the Western Front: The British Army's Art of Attack 1916–18* (London 1994); P. H. Liddle (ed.), *Passchendaele in Perspective: The Third Battle of Ypres* (London, 1997).
29 Hadley, *Count Not the Dead*, pp. 3–5.
30 Ellis, *Machine Gun*, pp. 17–18, 70; Hadley, *Count Not the Dead*, pp. x–xi, 23–26, 179–182; Wright, *Tank*, pp. 124, 186, 382–384, 393–395, 403–404.
31 A. King, *Memorials of the Great War in Britain: The Symbolism and Politics of Remembrance* (Oxford, 1998); J. Winter, 'Catastrophe and Culture: Recent trends in the Historiography of the First World War', *Journal of Modern History*, 64 (1992), pp. 524–532; J. Winter, *Sites of Memory, Sites of Mourning: The Great War in European Cultural History* (Cambridge, 1998).
32 M. Paris, *Winged Warfare: The literature and theory of aerial warfare in Britain 1859–1917* (Manchester, 1992); M. Paris, *From the Wright brothers to Top Gun: aviation, nationalism and popular cinema* (Manchester, 1995); M. Paris, *Warrior Nation: Images of War in British Popular Culture* (London, 2000); M. Paris, *Over the Top: the Great War and Juvenile Literature in Britain* (Westport: CT, 2004).
33 J. Keegan, *The Face of Battle. A Study of Agincourt, Waterloo and the Somme* (London, 1978) pp. 25–35; J. Lynn, *Battle. A History of Combat and Culture* (Boulder: CL, 2003), pp. xvi.
34 Lynn, *Battle*, pp. xviv–xv, xix–xxii.
35 Keegan, *Face of Battle*, pp. 26–27.
36 Lynn, *Battle*, p. xvii.
37 works include: R. Compton-Hall, *Submarine Warfare – Monster and Midgets* (Poole, 1985); *The Submarine Pioneers* (Stroud, 1999); D. Van Der Vat, *Stealth at Sea* (London, 1999).
38 M. Dash, *British Submarine Policy 1853–1918* (Unpublished PhD: University of London , 1990); D. Henry, *British Submarine Development and Policy 1918–1939* (unpublished PhD: University of London, 1976)
39 works include: N. Lambert, *The Influence of the Submarine Upon Naval Strategic Thinking 1898–1914* (unpublished PhD thesis, University of Oxford, 1992); N. Lambert, *Sir John Fisher's Naval Revolution* (Columbia: SC, 2002); Marder, *British Sea Power*; S. W. Roskill, *Naval Policy Between the Wars* 2 vols (London, 1968 and 1976).

40 works include: M. Edmonds (ed), *100 Years of the Trade. Royal Navy Submarine Past, Present & Future* (Lancaster, 2001); A. Preston, *The Royal Navy Submarine Service: A Centennial History* (London, 2001)
41 N. Lambert (ed), *The Submarine Service 1900–1918* (Aldershot, 2001).
42 D. Kertzer, *Ritual, Power & Politics* (London, 1988), p. 1.
43 R. Bacon, *From 1900 Onward* (London, 1940), p. 50.
44 L. Colley, 'The Significance of the Frontier in British History', in W. R. Lewis (ed), *More Adventures with Britannia* (Austin: TX, 1998), pp. 16–17; H. Kearney, *The British Isles. A History of Four Nations* (Cambridge, 1989), p. 2; K. Kumar, '"Englishness" and English National Identity', in D. Morley, K. Robins (eds) *British Cultural Studies* (Oxford, 2001), p. 41; R. Langlands, 'Britishness or Englishness? The historical problem of national identity in Britain', *Nations and Nationalism* vol. 5 (1999), pp. 53–69; P. Mandler, *The English National Character* (London, 2006), p. 134; D. McCrone, 'Unmasking Britannia: the rise and fall of British national identity', *Nations and Nationalism*, vol. 3 (1997), p. 586; A. D. Smith, 'Set in the silver sea': English national identity and European Integration', *Nations and Nationalism*, vol. 12 (2006),p. 433.
45 C. Hall, 'British Cultural Identities and the legacy of Empire', in D. Morley, K. Robins (eds) *British Cultural Studies* (Oxford, 2001), p. 29.
46 *Navy League Journal* No 1 (1895).
47 R Samuel, *Island Stories* (London, 1999), p. 36.
48 Kumar, '"Englishness" and English National Identity', p. 43, see also D. McCrone, 'Scotland and the Union: Changing Identities in the British State', in D. Morley, K. Robins (eds) *British Cultural Studies* (Oxford, 2001), p. 99
49 McCrone, 'Unmasking Britannia', p. 584.
50 C. Matthew, 'Introduction', in C. Matthew (ed.), *Short Oxford History of the British Isles: The Nineteenth Century* (Oxford, 2000), p. 22.
51 J. Rüger, 'Nations , Empire and Navy: Identity Politics in the United Kingdom 1887–1914', *Past and Present*, No 185 (2004), p. 160.
52 J. Clark, 'Protestantism, Nationalism, and National Identity, 1660–1832', *History Journal*, vol. XLIII (2000); L. Colley, *Britons. Forging the Nation 1707–1837*, 2nd edn. (London, 2005); L. Colley, 'Britishness and Otherness: An Argument', *Journal of British Studies*, vol. XXXI (1992); Samuel, *Island Stories*; K. Robbins, *Great Britain: Identities, Institutions and the Idea of Britishness* (London, 1998); A. Smith, *Chosen Peoples. Sacred Sources of National Identity* (Oxford, 2003).
53 Rüger, 'Nations, Empire and Navy'; J. Rüger, *The Great Naval Game: Britain and Germany in the Age of Empire* (Cambridge, 2007) pp. 3–6; see also R Harrington, '"The Mighty Hood": Navy, Empire, War at Sea and the British National Imagination 1920–60', *Journal of Contemporary History*, vol. 38 (2003), pp. 172–3; K. Lunn and A. Day, 'Britain as Island: National Identity and the Sea', in H. Brocklehurst and R. Phillips (eds), *History, nationhood and the question of Britain* (Basingstoke, 2004), pp. 124–136.
54 Colley, *Britons*, pp. 5–6.
55 Matthew, 'Introduction', p. 22.
56 Colley, 'The Frontier in British History', p. 17.
57 Kearney, *The British Isles*, p. 1.
58 Ibid. p. 4.

59 Matthew, 'Introduction', p. 22.
60 N. Rodgers, *The Wooden World* (London, 1988), p. 15; R. Glass, 'The Image of the Sea Officer in English Literature 1660–1710', *Albion*, vol. 26 (1994), p. 583; Quintin Colville has noted naval fashion has moved closer to that of civil dress especially during the early and mid twentieth century, see Q. Colville, 'Jack tar and the Gentleman Officer: The Role of Uniform in shaping the class and gender-related identities of British Naval personnel, 1930–1939', *Transactions of the Royal Historical Society*, vol. 13 (2003), pp. 105–29.
61 When as an officer in the Royal Navy the author used to show guests round the various ships and submarines on which he served the most common comment was to the effect that 'it wasn't like we expected' closely followed by 'I don't know how you can cope with living here.'
62 See Colley, 'Britishness and Otherness: An Argument', pp. 309–329.
63 Colley, 'The Frontier in British History' p. 17.
64 K. Moll, 'Politics, Power and Panic: Britain's 1909 Dreadnought "Gap"', *Military Affairs*, vol. 29 (1965), p. 136.
65 G. H. S Jordan, 'Pensions not Dreadnoughts: The Radicals and Naval Retrenchment', in A. J. Morris (ed) *Edwardian Radicalism 1900–1914* (London, 1974), p. 163.
66 T. R. Threlfall, 'Labour and the Navy', *The Nineteenth century and After*, vol. LXXV (1914), p. 688.
67 C. Behrman, *Victorian Myths of the Sea* (Athens, OH, 1977), pp. 38–55, 111–135; K. Robbins, *Great Britain: Identities, Institutions and the Idea of Britishness* (London, 1998), pp. 4–5, 122–123, 228.
68 Colley, 'The Frontier in British History', p. 17.
69 R. H. Bacon, 'The Future Needs of the Navy', *Nineteenth Century and After*, vol. CXI (1922), p. 15.
70 Churchill, *World Crisis*, vol. II (London, 1938) pp. 1111; see also Behrman, *Victorian Myths*, pp. 57–76; L. Delap, '"Thus Does Man Prove His Fitness to Be the Master of Things": Shipwrecks, Chivalry and Masculinities in Nineteenth- and Twentieth-Century Britain', *Cultural and Social History* (2006).
71 *Daily Mail*, 17 Mar 1909, p. 6.
72 *The Morning Post*, 17 Mar 1909, p. 6.
73 Sir F. C. D. Sturdee, 'Naval Aspects of the Washington Conference', in Sir A. Richardson & A. Hurd (eds), *Brassey's Naval and Shipping Annual 1923* (London, 1923), p. 69.

Chapter One

1 A. T. Mahan, *The Influence of Seapower Upon the French Revolution and Empire 1793–1812*, vol. II, 4th edn. (London, 1892), p. 118.
2 C. Geertz, *The Interpretation of Cultures*, 2nd edn. (New York, 2000), p. 6.
3 Ibid. p. 15.
4 E. Hobsbawm, 'Inventing Traditions', in E. Hobsbawm & T. Ranger (eds.), *Inventing Traditions* (Cambridge, 1983), p. 1.
5 See also J. Rüger, *The Celebration of the Fleet in Britain and Germany, 1897–1914* (unpublished PhD: Cambridge University, 2003), pp. 51–52; J Rüger, *The*

NOTES 257

Great Naval Game. Britain and Germany in the Age of Empire (Cambridge, 2007), p. 19.

6 J. Leyland, 'The Navy and the Coronation', *Mariner's Mirror*, vol. I (1911), 164; *Army and Navy Gazette* (1911), p. 587.

7 *Daily Telegraph*, 16 August 1902, p. 7; *Birmingham Daily Mail*, 24 June 1911, p. 4; *Hampshire Telegraph & Naval Chronicle*, 'Coronation Naval Review Number' (1911), p. 15; *Hampshire Telegraph & Naval Chronicle*, 23 June 1911, p. 7; *Times*, 16 July 1935, p. 17; *Daily Telegraph*, 17 May 1937, p. 8; *Daily Mail*, 20 May 1937, p. 12; *Times*, 'Royal Navy Supplement', 15 June 1953, p. v; *Daily Mail*, 29 June 1977, p. 2; F. D. Arnold-Forster, 'Royal Naval Reviews at Spithead', *RUSI*, XCVIII (1953), pp. 177–183; R. E. Saw (ed.), *Coronation Review of the Fleet by Her Majesty the Queen at Spithead on Monday 15th June 1953* (Portsmouth, 1953), pp. 51–52; H. H. Wilson, 'The Forthcoming Naval Review and its Predecessors', *Nineteenth Century*, vol. XLI (1897), pp. 883–892; H. H. Wilson (ed.) *The Navy League Guide to the Naval Review* (London, 1897), p. 5; H. H. Wilson (ed.) *The Navy League Guide to the Coronation Review* (London, 1902), pp. 16–24; J. Winton, *Silver Jubilee Fleet Review Official Souvenir Programme* (Portsmouth, 1977), pp. 12–13; see also Rüger, *Celebration of the Fleet*, pp. 51–52.

8 Wilson (ed.), *Navy League Guide to the Coronation Review*; Cdr G. A. B. Hills (ret) (ed.), *Official Programme of the Silver Jubilee Review of the Fleet* (Portsmouth, 1935); Saw (ed.), *Coronation Review of the Fleet 1953*; Winton, *Silver Jubilee Fleet Review*. Separate maps of the review were also offered for sale to the public by the Admiralty; see ADM 116//3555, minute by the Hydrographer, 19 April 1937.

9 For examples see *Times*, 21 July 1935, p. 8; PRO RAIL 253/47, GWR Coronation notices 1911; RAIL 311/436, LSWR Special Notice 850. 1902 Coronation of King Edward VII, 83, 107, 111, 113, 126, 127, 155; RAIL 411/436, LSWR Special Notice 1100, 1911 Coronation Workings, 114, 147, 155, 156, 160.

10 See *Times*, 11 August 1902, p. 1 for representative examples; NMM, N4065, Coronation of HM King George V. Programme of facilities for witnessing the Royal Naval Review, Thos Cook & Son; NMM, Royal Mail Lines: Silver Jubilee Royal Naval Review Spithead 1935; NMM, A4299, Naval Review at Spithead 1937. Programme of Special Rail and Steamer Arrangements from London.

11 PRO, ADM 116/3551, Coronation Review of The Royal Navy by His Majesty the King.

12 M. Critchley, *The Silver Jubilee Review 24–29 June 1977* (n.p., 1977), pp. 5–9, 14.

13 J. Winton, 'The Spithead Review', *Illustrated London News* (August 1977), p. 44.

14 PRO, ADM 116/132, letter from LSWR to Admiralty, 3 July 1902; ADM 116/3555, loose minute 1 May 1937; letter from Lord Strabolgi to Admiralty, 15 April 1937; minute M2510/37, 26 April 1937; minute M2680/37, 8 May 1937; ADM 116/3918, CNI's Report on the Coronation Naval Review at Spithead, 15 June 1953.

15 Sir Robert Ensor, *England 1870–1914* (London, 1936), p. 304.

16 A. Marwick, *Britain in the Century of Total War* (London, 1968), p. 241; K. Rose, *King George V* (London, 1984), p. 395.

17 M. Lewis *Spithead an Informal History* (London, 1972), p. 167; see also G. Bennett, 'Royal Reviews at Spithead', *History Today*, vol. 27 (1977), p. 360.
18 *Daily Telegraph*, 26 June 1911, p. 12; see also *Manchester Guardian*, 18 August 1902, p. 4.
19 M. Daunton, *Trusting Leviathan. The Politics of Taxation in Britain, 1799–1914* (Cambridge, 2001), pp. 303–305, 307, 314–321; H. V. Emy, 'The Impact of Financial Policy on English Party Politics before 1914', *History*, vol. XV (1972), p. 115.
20 P. Cain, 'Political Economy in Edwardian England: The Tariff Reform Controversy', in A. O'Day (ed.), *The Edwardian Age: Conflict and Stability 1900–1914* (London, 1979), p. 55; D. Read, *Edwardian England 1901–15 Society and Politics* (London, 1972), p. 179; H. Weinroth, 'Left-wing opposition to Naval Armaments in Britain before 1914', *Journal of Contemporary History*, vol. VI (1971), p. 94.
21 Emy, 'The Impact of Financial Policy on English Party Politics', p. 112; Read, *Edwardian England*, p. 180; P. Thane, 'Social History 1860–1914', in R. Floud & D. McCloskey (eds.), *The Economic History of Britain since 1700*, vol. II (Cambridge, 1981), pp. 225–226.
22 Lewis, *Spithead*, p. 167.
23 *Army and Navy Gazette* (1902), p. 784.
24 Rüger, 'Nation, Empire and Navy', pp. 162, 164–167; see also Rüger, *Great Naval Game*.
25 Behrman, *Victorian Myths*, chapters 2 and 4; R. Colls, *Identity of England* (Oxford, 2004), pp. 238–242; K. Kumar, *The Making of English National Identity* (Cambridge, 2003), p. 8; see also M. Billig, *Banal Nationalism* (London, 1995), p. 72.
26 Behrman, *Victorian Myths*, pp. 116, 156
27 *Book of Common Prayer*, p. 538.
28 Sir Edward Reed, 'On Armaments' in H. H. Wilson (ed.), *The Navy League Guide to the Naval Review* (London, 1897), p. 11.
29 Behrman, *Victorian Myths*, p. 111.
30 Quoted in Kumar, *English National Identity*, p. 5.
31 Behrman, *Victorian Myths*, p. 111.
32 'Royal Navy Presentation with commentary', *Royal Navy Presentations & Films* (Grosvenor TV Production/Royal Navy, 2005)
33 Behrman, *Victorian Myths*, pp. 38–40, 46–53, 77; Kumar, *English National Identity*, p. 8.
34 *Hansard*, 4th series, 91, 18 March 1901, col. 332.
35 *Manchester Guardian*, 18 August 1902, p. 4.
36 PRO, ADM 116/131, Telegram from Capt Bacon to Admiralty, 10 August 1902.
37 Ibid. Hand written comment by 1SL.
38 PRO, ADM 1/7462, memo, 3 August 1900; PRO, ADM 1/7515, memo, 17 September 1900.
39 Winton, 'The Spithead Review', p. 37.
40 PRO, ADM 1/7462, Letter from Bacon to May, 13 May 1901.

NOTES 259

41 Dash, *British Submarine Policy*, pp. 72–73; N. Lambert, *Sir John Fisher's Naval Revolution* (Columbia: SC, 1999), pp. 39–43.
42 PRO, ADM 179/32, No 1785/490/09 From C-in-C Portsmouth to Admiralty, 30 June 1909.
43 PRO, ADM 179/32, No 3273/490/09, 18 November 1909; PRO, ADM 179/32, Letter from Admiralty to C-in-C Portsmouth, 20 November 1909.
44 R. Bacon, *From 1900 Onward* (London, 1940), pp. 64, 65.
45 PRO, ADM 116/131, Telegram from Capt Bacon to Admiralty, 10 August 1902 and attached minute.
46 A. N. Harrison, *BR3043 The Development of HM Submarines From Holland No. 1 (1901) to Porpoise (1930)* (MOD Ships Dept, 1976), p. 30.1.
47 Harrison, *BR3043*, p. 30.1.
48 Admiralty, *The Navy List for July 1902 corrected to the 18th June 1902* (London, 1902), p. 75
49 Col. Repington, 'New Wars for Old. 1. The Submarine Menace', *Blackwood's Magazine*, vol. 187 (1910), p. 900.
50 J. Grigg, *Lloyd George. The People's Champion 1902–1911* (London 2002), pp. 174–176; Offer, *First World War*, p. 206; H. P. Wilmott, 'The Liberals at Sea', *RUSI*, vol. 117 (1972), pp. 61–63.
51 O. D. Skelton, *Life and Letters of Sir Wilfred Laurier*, vol. II (Toronto, 1921; abridged edn. 1965), p. 114; quoted in Offer, *First World War*, pp. 205–206.
52 Coetzee, *For Party or Country*, p. 109; Daunton, *Trusting Leviathan*, p. 358; Grigg, *Lloyd George 1902–1911*, pp. 171, 175–176; 192–193; Lambert, *Fisher's Naval Revolution*, p. 185.
53 F. T. Jane (ed.), *Fighting Ships* (London, 1911), p. 119.
54 *Illustrated London News*, 1 July 1911, pp. 42–43.
55 Ibid.
56 PRO, ADM 179/60, Letter from C-in-C Portsmouth to Admiralty No 900/B, 25 April 1911.
57 RNML, V310, Review of the Fleet by HM King.
58 L. Willett, 'Royal Navy Submarines in World War I', in M. Edmonds (ed.), *100 Years of The Trade* (Lancaster, 2001), p. 16.
59 D. K. Brown, *The Grand Fleet. Warship Design and Development 1906–1922* (London, 1999), p. 81; N. Lambert, *The Influence of the Submarine on Naval Strategic Thinking 1898–1914* (unpublished PhD thesis, 1992), p. 179; Lambert *Fisher's Naval Revolution*, p. 10; Willett, 'Royal Navy Submarines in World War I', p. 16.
60 R. Bacon, *The Life of Lord Fisher of Kilverstone*, vol. II (London, 1929), pp. 30, 32, 36, 58; Lambert, *Fisher's Naval Revolution*, pp. 175, 180, 184–185; R. F. MacKay, *Fisher of Kilverstone* (Oxford, 1973), pp. 359, 362, 392–95, 400–403; A. J. Marder, *From the Dreadnought to Scapa Flow. The Royal Navy in the Fisher Era, 1904–1919*, vol. I (London, 1961), pp. 86, 89–90, 91–104, 186–204; J. Morris, *Fisher's Face* (London, 1996), pp. 106, 155, 160, 161, 163–165.
61 Lambert, *Fisher's Naval Revolution*, pp. 186,187–193; N. A. Lambert, 'Strategic Command and Control for Manoeuvre Warfare: Creation of the Royal Navy's "War Room" System, 1905–1915', *Journal of Military History*, vol. 69 (2005), p. 387.

62 *Hampshire Telegraph and Naval Chronicle*, 23 June 1911, p. 7.
63 Charts of the 1909 reviews show the dreadnoughts picked out in different colours from the other battleships, presumably to allow an observer to spot them easily. See also press enthusiasm for dreadnoughts at the 1911 Coronation Review: *Birmingham Daily Mail*, 24 June 1911, p. 4; *Daily Mail*, 24 June 1911, p. 5; *Hampshire Advertiser County Newspaper*, 24 June 1911, p. 7.
64 PRO, ADM 179/60, M3526 letter from Admiralty to C-in-C Portsmouth, 14 March 1911.
65 Ibid.
66 *Army and Navy Gazette* (1911), p. 434.
67 PRO, ADM 179/60, letter from Admiralty to C-in-C Portsmouth, 5 May 1911.
68 PRO, ADM 179/60, item 264
69 Bacon, *Life of Lord Fisher*, vol. II, pp. 30, 32, 58; Marder, *From the Dreadnought to Scapa*, vol. I, pp. 89–90.
70 MacKay, *Fisher*, pp. 370, 400–403; Morris *Fisher's Face*, pp. 153–165. Both note Beresford's opposition to the fleet redistribution that was part of Flotilla Defence, but only MacKay makes an indirect allusion to Flotilla Defence.
71 PRO, ADM 179/60, chart 'The position of the Fleet at Spithead on the 24th June 1911.'
72 Lambert, *Fisher's Naval Revolution*, pp. 215–217.
73 'Navy Notes', *RUSI*, vol. LXXX (1935), p. 644; P. Ransome-Wallis, *The Royal Naval Reviews 1935–1977* (London, 1982), p. 10.
74 'Navy Notes', *RUSI*, vol. LXXX (1935), p. 644; F. E. M. McMurtie (ed.), *Jane's Fighting Ships 1935* (London, 1935), p. 10.
75 PRO, ADM 116/3015, minute by DNI (G. C. Dickens), 4 December 1934.
76 *Army and Navy Gazette* (1935), p. 572.
77 *Times*, 16 July 1935, p. 10.
78 PRO, ADM 116/3551, Letter from C-in-C Mediterranean Fleet to First Sea Lord, 9 January 1937.
79 Ibid. minute sheet with letter from C-in-C Mediterranean.
80 Ibid. minute by DOD, 14 January 1937.
81 Ibid. anonymous minute, possibly by Second Sea Lord or Deputy Chief of the Naval Staff, 19 January 1937.
82 PRO, ADM 116/3551, M01193/37, 20 January 1937; ADM 116/3551, signal from Admiralty to C-in-C Mediterranean Fleet, 23 January 1937.
83 *Times*, 21 July 1937, p. 8.
84 D. O'Reilly, 'Explorer & Excalibur: The Walther Boat, High Test Peroxide & British Submarine Policy 1945–1962. A Study in Technological Failure?', in M. Edmonds (ed.), *100 Year Of The Trade* (Lancaster, 2001), p. 71.
85 P. Akermann, *Encyclopaedia of British Submarines 1901–1955* (Penzance, 2002), pp. 383, 425–427; N. Friedman, *Submarine Design and Development* (London, 1984), pp. 59–60, 65–66.
86 *Times*, 'Royal Navy Supplement', 15 June 1953, p. iv.
87 *Daily Telegraph*, 15 June 1953, p. 6; *Daily Telegraph*, 16 June 1953, p. 11; *Manchester Guardian*, 15 June 1953, p. 4.
88 *Times*, 15 June 1953, p. 7.

89 *Hampshire Telegraph & Post and Naval Chronicle*, 19 June 1953, p. 4.
90 *Manchester Guardian*, 16 June 1953, p. 6.
91 *Manchester Guardian*, 15 June 1953, p. 4.
92 *Times*, 15 June 1953, p. 7.
93 Winton, *Silver Jubilee Fleet Review*, p. 6.
94 Ibid.
95 Ibid. p. 14–16.
96 Critchley, *Silver Jubilee Review*, pp. 31–33; see also *The News – Fleet Review Souvenir*, 28 June 1977, p. 14.
97 Critchley, *Silver Jubilee Review*, pp. 31–33.
98 Winton, 'The Spithead Review', pp. 36–40.
99 *The News*, 10 June 1977, p. 3; *The News*, 27 June 1977, p. 1; *Daily Telegraph*, 29 June 1977, p. 7.
100 *The News*, 27 June 1977, p. 1.
101 *The News – Fleet Review Souvenir*, 28 June 1977, p. 14.
102 *Daily Mail*, 29 June .1977, p. 2; *Times*, 29 June 1977, p. 3.
103 *Daily Express*, 27 June 1977, p. 14, photo caption; *Guardian*, 28 June 1977, p. 13; *Sunday Telegraph Magazine*, 26 June 1977, p. 17.
104 *Daily Express*, 27 June 1977, p. 14; *Guardian*, 29 June 1977, p. 24.
105 *Guardian*, 28 June 1977, p. 13.
106 Ibid.
107 Ibid.
108 *Daily Express*, 28 June 1977, p. 10.
109 *Guardian*, 28 June 1977, p. 13.
110 *Daily Express*, 27 June 1977, p. 14.
111 'R.G.H.', 'The Nuclear Attack Submarine', *Naval Review*, vol. LV (1967), p. 23.

Chapter Two

1 Bacon, *From 1900 Onward*, p. 50.
2 Behrman, *Victorian Myths*, pp. 11, 25–28, 32, 38, 39–45, 57–65.
3 Ibid. p. 155.
4 J. Leyland (ed.), *The Naval Annual 1900* (Portsmouth, 1900), pp. 196–311; Viscount Hythe & J. Leyland (eds.), *The Naval Annual 1914* (London, 1914), pp. 192–286; C. N. Robinson & H. M. Ross (eds.), *Brassey's Naval and Shipping Annual 1934* (London, 1934), pp. 231–310.
5 F. T. Jane (ed.), *All the World's Fighting Ships 1902* (London, 1902), pp. 77–87; F. T. Jane (ed.), *Fighting Ships 1908* (London, 1908), pp. 52–66; F. T. Jane (ed.), *Fighting Ships 1913* (London, 1913), pp. 37–57.
6 Marder, *British Sea Power*, pp. 105–107, 121,126–133, 143, 161, 162.
7 IHR, Admiralty NID No 676 'Submarines and the Naval Policy of England Translated from the Revue Maritime October 1902', *Papers on Naval Subjects 1903*, vol. I, pp. 39, 48.
8 Behrman, *Victorian Myths*, pp. 111–112; J. Walvin 'Symbols of moral superiority', in J. A. Mangan and J. Walvin (eds.), *Manliness and Morality* (Manchester, 1987), pp. 244–245, 248.
9 A. S. Hurd 'The Coming Of The Submarine – The New British Boats', *Nineteenth Century* (1902), p. 222.

10 Capt S. Eardley-Wilmot RN 'Our Navy – Its Decline and Restoration', *National Review*, vol. XXXVI (1900–1901), p. 655.
11 W. Mark Hamilton *The Nation and the Navy* (London, 1986), pp. 9–10.
12 Marder in *British Sea Power* points out that the battleship fixation started in about 1884 with W. T. Stead's 'The Truth About The Navy' and that the subsequent 'two power standard' effectively only referred to the battleship strength (pp. 106–107, 126–133); for the influence of the Navy League and naval jingoism see Coetzee, *For Party or Country*, pp. 18, 21, 22–26, 33–37, 121; W. Mark Hamilton, 'The "New Navalisim" and the British Navy League 1895–1914', *Mariners Mirror*, vol. 64 (1978).
13 Repington 'New Wars For Old', p. 900.
14 Keegan, *Face of Battle*, p. 295.
15 Perhaps the most famous example of an individual ship to ship action is Nelson's capture, while commanding the 74 gun HMS *Captain*, of the Spanish 74 gun battleship *San Nicolas* and the 112 gun *San Josef* at the Battle of Cape St Vincent in 1797; while the victories of The Glorious First of June (1794), Cape St Vincent (1797), Nile (1799), Copenhagen (1801) and Trafalgar (1805) were all gained by numerically inferior British forces.
16 R. Bacon, 'The Battleship of the Future', *Transactions of the Institute of Naval Architects*, vol. 52 (1910), pp. 1–21; C. Bridge, *The Art of Naval Warfare* (London, 1907), p. 38; Lambert, *Fisher's Naval Revolution*, pp. 215–221; J. P. Holland, 'The Submarine Boat and its Future', *North American Review*, vol. CLXXI (1900), p. 894.
17 Lambert, *Fisher's Naval Revolution*, p. 216.
18 'Democracy and Naval Policy', *The Nation*, vol. XIII (1913), p. 802
19 See M. Girouard, *The Return to Camelot. Chivalry and the English Gentleman* (London, 1981).
20 J. Harris, *Private Lives, Public Spirit: Britain 1870–1914* (London, 1994), p. 9.
21 M. Wiener, *English Culture and the Decline of the Industrial Spirit 1850–1980* (London, 1992), pp. 10–24.
22 J. R. Gillis (ed.), *The Militarization of the Western World* (London, 1989), p. 2–5.
23 The Reverend Garrett developed a method of storing heat from a boiler to allow steam propulsion submerged during the mid-1880s. His submarine, 'Resurgam' sank on trials. Having failed to interest the UK in his development he went to work for the Nordenfelt arms company and continued attempts to develop a practical submarine.
24 M. Stewart, *Monturiol's Dream* (London, 2003), pp. 201–203
25 J. Verne, trans W. Butcher, *Twenty Thousand Leagues Under the Sea* (Oxford, 1998), pp. 253–262, 291–312.
26 Ibid. pp. 368–373
27 J. Jules-Verne, trans R. Greaves, *Jules Verne A Biography* (London, 1976), p. 87.
28 First published in English in 1873
29 'Obituary for Jules Verne', *Spectator*, vol. VIC (1905), pp. 470–471.
30 Holland, 'The Submarine Boat and its Future', pp. 897–901.
31 'Leading Articles in the Reviews', *Review of Reviews*, vol. XXIII (1901), p. 45.
32 C. Field, *The Story of the Submarine* (London, 1908) p. 296.
33 'Leading Articles', *Review of Reviews*, vol. XXIII (1901), p. 45.

34 Field, *Story of the Submarine*, p. 286.
35 PmthRO, 34/1964/A, The A1 Disaster funeral at Haslar (Lt Mansergh's coffin); PmthRO, 34/1964/C, The A1 disaster crews of the submarines following their mess-mates coffins; *Daily Mail*, 19 March 1904, p. 5; *Daily Telegraph*, 19 March 1904, p. 9; *The Times*, 19 March 1904, p. 11; *Daily Mail*, 20 March 1904, p. 4; *Daily Mail*, 20 March 1904, p. 5; *Daily Telegraph*, 21 March 1904, p. 9; *The Times*, 21 March 1904, p. 9; *Hampshire Telegraph and Naval Chronicle*, 26 March 1904, p. 8.
36 PmthRO, 34/1964/A, The A1 Disaster funeral at Haslar (Lt Mansergh's coffin); 34/1964/C, The A1 disaster crews of the submarines following their mess-mates coffins; 1001/1974, B2 memorial service; H51/74, B2 memorial service; 187a/14, The ill-fated submarine A1; 494/a/121ph, The sad procession making its way past the Warner Light ship to Spithead; 494a/122ph, Submarine B2 lost off Dover; 494a/124ph, The French Submarine Disaster; 494a/36ph, Submarine B2 memorial service; 494a/37ph, Memorial service for B2; 494a/38ph, Memorial service for B2; 494a/39ph, Funeral of A3 victims.
37 *Spectator*, 94 (1905), pp. 275, 843.
38 E. Weyl, 'Progress of Foreign Navies', in T. A. Brassey (ed.), *Naval Annual* (Portsmouth, 1897), p. 47
39 Marder, *British Sea Power*, p. 357; Weyl, 'Progress of Foreign Navies', p. 47.
40 Dr David Livingston's explorations of South and Central Africa from 1852 until his death were financed by the London Missionary Society; the 1901 British National Antarctic Expedition was funded by private donations, grants from the Royal Geographical Society and a matching grant by the government; Shackleton's 1907–1909 expedition was funded by publishing deals, private subscriptions and a small grants from the New Zealand and Australian governments; Shackleton's 1914 Imperial Trans-Antarctic Expedition was financed by private individuals, selling of commercial rights, a token grant from the Royal Geographical Society and a moderate grant by Asquith's government that was less than half the size of the largest individual contributor.
41 R. A. S. Stafford, 'Scientific Exploration and Empire', in A. Porter & A. Low (eds.), *The Oxford History of the British Empire*, vol. III (Oxford, 1999), pp. 295, 297.
42 Burgoyne, *Submarine Navigation*, p. 232; Field, *The Story of the Submarine*, pp. 223, 285
43 See generally Stafford, 'Scientific Exploration and Empire'.
44 Examples are: Active List, 'Recent Naval Progress', *Blackwood's Edinburgh Magazine*, vol. CLXX (1901), pp. 443–457; 'The influence of the submarine on Naval Policy', *Naval Review*, vol. II (1914), pp. 47–52; A. H. Burgoyne 'The Future of the Submarine Boat', *RUSI*, vol. XLVIII (1904), pp. 1288–1311; A. S. Hurd 'The Coming of the Submarine', *Nineteenth Century*, vol. LI (1902), pp. 220–232; A. S. Hurd 'The Success of the Submarine', *Nineteenth Century*, vol. LIV (1903), pp. 711–721; E. Robertson 'The Question of Submarine Boats', *Nineteenth Century*, vol. XLVII (1900), pp. 713–722; E. Robertson 'The Admiralty and Submarine Boats', *Nineteenth Century*, vol. XLIX (1901), pp. 30–38.

45 Marder, *British Sea Power*, p. 358.
46 Behrman, *Victorian Myths*, pp. 11, 36, 57.
47 Ibid. p. 57; consider also John Masefield's poem *Sea Fever* or the allusions by William Shakespeare in *Richard II*: 'this sceptred isle', 'England, bound in with the triumphant sea'. Ideas on a special relationship with the sea can be traced back to 1588 and the defeat of the Spanish Armada.
48 Hurd, 'Coming Of The Submarine', pp. 222–223, 230–231.
49 Behrman, *Victorian Myths*, p. 116.
50 Ibid.
51 *Book of Common Prayer*, p. 538.
52 Hurd, 'Coming Of The Submarine', p. 222.
53 For coverage of the dreadnought type see: *Birmingham Daily Mail*, 24 June 1911, p. 7; *Daily Mail*, 24 June 1911, p. 5; *Hampshire Advertiser County Newspaper*, 24 June 1911, p. 7; see also Marder, *British Sea Power*, pp. 46–48.
54 *Hampshire Telegraph and Naval Chronicle*, Coronation Review Number', 1911, p. 30.
55 D. Hanney, 'The Fire Ship', *Blackwood's Magazine*, vol. CXCV (1914), p. 791.
56 Hurd, 'Coming Of The Submarine', p. 222.
57 Hanney, 'The Fire Ship', p. 791.
58 Examples are: 'Capital Ships of the Future', *RUSI*, vol. LIX (1914), pp. 240–241; W. E. Cairnes, 'The Duties of the Army and Navy' *The National Review*, vol. XXXVI (1900–1), p. 800; A. Conan Doyle, 'Danger', *Strand Magazine*, vol. XLVIII (1914), pp. 3–22; N. Lambert, *The Submarine Service* (Aldershot, 2001), pp. 225–229; Repington, 'New Wars For Old', pp. 898–899.
59 W. S. Churchill, *The World Crisis*, vol. II (London, 1938), p. 721.
60 Royal Navy officers of the late Victorian and early Edwardian period were educated in hulks on the River Dart at Dartmouth (later replaced by Britannia Royal Naval College). The education mirrored that of the public schools.
61 H. Newbolt, 'Vitaï Lampada', *Collected Poems 1897–1907* (London, 1907), p. 131.
62 A. F. Leach, *History of Warwick School with notices of the Collegiate Church, Guilds and Borough of Warwick* (London, 1906), p. 213.
63 N. Dixon, *On the Psychology of Military Incompetence* (London, 1976), p. 292.
64 J. Walvin, 'Symbols of Moral Superiority', p. 243; see also D. Leinster-Mackay, 'The nineteenth-century English preparatory school' in J. A. Mangan (ed.), *Benefits Bestowed* (Manchester, 1988), pp. 69–72
65 Girouard, *Return to Camelot*, pp. 260–263.
66 P. Gay, 'The Manliness of Christ' in R. W. Davies & R. J. Helmstadler (eds.), *Religion and Irreligion in Victorian Society* (London, 1992), pp. 109–110.
67 Gay, ' Manliness of Christ', p. 110.
68 Girouard, *Return to Camelot*, p. 260.
69 Wiener, *English Culture*, pp. 132, 139, 145.
70 P. A. Dunae, 'Education, emigration and empire', in Mangan (ed.), *Benefits Bestowed*, p. 196.
71 Dixon, *Military Incompetence*, p. 289
72 R. Kipling, *The Complete Verse* (London, 2002), p. 529.

NOTES 265

73 H. Collingwood, *With Airship and Submarine* (London, 1908), pp. 3, 4; G. Thorne, *Sweetheart Submarine* (London, 1911), pp. 11, 13, 45, 188–190, 190–91; P. F. Westerman, *The Flying Submarine* (London, 1912), pp. 3, 4, 71–72; P. F. Westerman, *The Rival Submarines* (London, 1913), pp. 18, 19, 64, 132–133.
74 Thorne, *Sweetheart Submarine*, pp. 11, 13, 45, 188–190.
75 Westerman, *The Flying Submarine*, pp. 3, 4.
76 Westerman, *Rival Submarines*, p. 101.
77 Verne, *Twenty Thousand Leagues*, pp. 70, 73–75, 76–82, 87.
78 Hurd, 'Coming Of The Submarine', p. 221.
79 A. H. Burgoyne, 'Editorial', *Submarine Navigation Past and Present: A Scientific Quarterly*, vol. I (1901), p. 69.
80 Bacon, *1900 Onward*, pp. 50–51; see also Lambert, *Fisher's Naval Revolution*, pp. 48–49.
81 Hobsbawm & Ranger (eds.), 'Inventing Tradition', p. 1
82 Gordon, *Rules of the Game*, pp. 183–191.
83 Ibid. pp. 59, 183.
84 Ibid. pp. 185–189.
85 cf. S. J. Cohen (ed.), *International Encyclopaedia of Dance* (Oxford, 1998), p. 620; A. J. Latimer, *A Bouquet of Old Time Dances* (London, 1948), pp. 13, 15.
86 R. Kipling, *A Fleet In Being. Notes of Two Trips With The Channel Squadron* (Leipzig, 1899), p. 21.
87 R. Dyer, '"I seem to find the happiness I seek" Heterosexuality and Dance in the Musical', in H. Thomas (ed.), *Dance, Gender and Culture* (London, 1993), p. 63; D. Leonard, *Sex and Generation: A Study of Courtship and Weddings* (London, 1980), pp. 90–92; J. Mackenzie, *A Victorian Courtship* (London, 1979), p. 10; M. Parson (ed.), *A Miles, Every Girls Duty. The Diary of a Victorian Debutante* (London, 1992), pp. 24–25, 30, 35.
88 Bacon, *1900 Onward*, p. 74; NHB, Eb06, Admiralty, Intelligence Division. No 817. 'Great Britain Naval Manoeuvres 1906', May 1907 in *British Naval Manoeuvres*, vol. IV, pp. 16, 43, 68, 79; NHB, Eb181, Admiralty Mobilisation Department, *Great Britain Naval Manoeuvres 1910*, p. 12; PRO, ADM 116/3381, Notes on the [1912] manoeuvres prepared for the Prime Minister by the First Lord, 7 October 1912, p. 10.
89 PRO, ADM 116/3381, Notes on the [1912] manoeuvres, p. 9.
90 Repington, 'New Wars For Old', p. 900.
91 Hanney, 'The Fire Ship', p. 791.
92 PRO, ADM 1/8128, Submarine Committee report No 4.
93 PRO, ADM 1/8128, Submarine Committee report No 4.
94 Willett, 'Royal Navy Submarines in World War I', p. 16.
95 Brown, *The Grand Fleet*, p. 81; Lambert, *Influence of the Submarine*, p. 179; Lambert *Fisher's Naval Revolution*, p. 10; Willett, 'Royal Navy Submarines in World War I', p. 16.
96 Lambert, *Fisher's Naval Revolution*, pp. 186, 187–193.
97 PRO, ADM 116/3381, Vice-Admiral Sir J. R. Jellicoe, Naval Manoeuvres 1913.
98 NMM, A Harrison, *BR 3043*, p. 4.3; PRO, ADM 1/8128, Submarine Committee report No 4.

99   PRO, ADM 116/3093, 'Submarine boats', April 1905 in Fisher's Naval Necessities II.
100 Lambert, *Fisher's Naval Revolution*, pp. 288–289.
101 PRO, ADM 116/3381, Jellicoe, Naval Manoeuvres 1913.
102 During the peacetime manoeuvres, in order to compensate for a lack of willing enemies, the British fleet was divided into friendly (usually described as the Blue Fleet) and hostile (or Red) fleets. The exercises sought to answer specific strategic, operational or tactical questions, which varied from year to year such as the neutralization of hostile submarines and assimilation of friendly ones.
103 PRO, ADM 116/3381, Admiral W. May, Report on the 1913 Naval Manoeuvres, 18 August 1913.
104 Ibid. Notes by Admiral R. Custance on the 1913 Naval Manoeuvres.
105 Mahan, *The Influence of Sea Power*, vol. II, 4th edn (London, 1892), p. 118.
106 PRO, ADM 116/3381, Jellicoe, Naval Manoeuvres 1913.
107 Even today it is hard to build a submarine that performs well on the surface and submerged. The Royal Navy's *T* class SSN has a very high silent underwater speed, and handles like an aircraft when dived. On the surface the *T* class is rather slow and at low speeds is hard to manoeuvre.
108 PRO, ADM 116/3381, Jellicoe, Naval Manoeuvres 1913.
109 C.W. Domville-Fife, *Submarines, Mines and Torpedoes in the War* (London, 1914), p. 125.
110 BL, Keyes MSS 4/22, Draft Keyes to Hall, 19 October 1912; Lambert, *The Influence of the Submarine*, p. 217.
111 W. Hackmann, *Seek and Strike* (London, 1984), pp. 74, 75, 115.
112 Gordon, *Rules of the Game*, pp. 354–355.
113 Even modern underwater telephones are susceptible to distortions which can make the message difficult or impossible to understand.
114 PRO, ADM 116/3381 Admiral W. May, Report on the 1913 Naval Manoeuvres, 18 August 1913.
115 'The Submarine Menace', *Naval Review*, vol. II (1914), p. 277.
116 'The Influence of the Submarine on Naval Policy', *Naval Review*, vol. I (1913), p. 258
117 D. K. Brown, *Warrior to Dreadnought. Warship development 1860–1905* (London, 1997), pp. 116–117, 137–138; L. Sondhaus, *Naval Warfare 1815–1914* (London, 2001), pp. 168–169.
118 The tendency to dive out of control was particularly unfortunate in a submarine that would implode after passing a depth of 150 feet. Many of these diving incidents were prevented from becoming serious because the North Sea, the submarine's operating area, was generally shallower than 150 feet, thus allowing the seabed to arrest the uncontrollable descent. When the *K* class submarines were deployed post-war with the Atlantic Fleet, the low technology solution of hitting the seabed was not available as the seabed was greater than 150 feet. *K5* is believed to have been lost due to an uncontrollable dive in between 600 and 12000 feet of water in the south-western approaches in 1921.

119 D. Everitt, *K Boats Steam-powered Submarines in World War I* (Shrewsbury, 1999), p. 105.
120 Adm. Sir Roger Keyes, *Naval Memoirs 1910–1915* (London, 1943), pp. 23–24.
121 R. Compton-Hall, *Submarines and the War at Sea 1914–1918* (London, 1991), p. 7.
122 Dash, *British Submarine Policy*, p. 164.
123 Ibid. p. 160.
124 Lambert, *The Influence of the Submarine,* pp. 213–214.
125 BL, Keyes MSS 4/22, Draft Keyes to Hall, 19 October 1912; Lambert, *The Influence of the Submarine*, p. 217.
126 PRO, ADM 137/2067, Memo, 6 June 1914; PRO, ADM 1/8331, Memo by DOD, 14 July 1913.
127 Gordon, *Rules of the Game*, p. 67; Lambert, *Fisher's Naval Revolution*, p. 268.
128 F. T. Jane *The British Battle-Fleet* (London, 1912), p. 358.
129 B. Ranft (ed.), *The Beatty Papers 1902–1918*, vol. I (Aldershot, 1989), pp. 479–481.

Chapter Three

1 A. S. Hurd, *Ordeal By Sea* (London, 1919), p. 95.
2 C. Barnett, *Engage The Enemy More Closely* (London, 1991), pp. 4–5; Gordon, *Rules of the Game*, pp. 2, 571, 574–5; R. Hough, *The Great War at Sea* (Edinburgh, 2000), p. 291; J. Moretz, *The Royal Navy and the Capital Ship in the Interwar Period* (London, 2002), pp. 8–10, 24; S. W. Roskill, *Naval Policy Between the Wars*, vol. I (London, 1968), p. 533.
3 CCRO, R85/7, *C.P. Alix Papers*, Scrapbook 1908–1918; Scrapbook 1918–1921.
4 In the original guide written by C.P. Alix it is just described as a British submarine.
5 CCRO, P150/6/19, C.P. Alix, *Explanation of the War Memorial Windows in St Mary's Church Swaffham Prior* (1920) p. 5; see also the current locally produced typescript guide to the church windows, no details on author or date of production.
6 CCRO, P150/6/19, pp. 5–6.
7 P. Dutton, 'Geschaeft uber Alles: Notes on some medallions inspired by the sinking of the Lusitania', *Imperial War Museum Review*, No. 1 (1986), pp. 30–37; G. S. Messinger, *British Propaganda and the State in the First World War* (Manchester, 1992), p. 66.
8 D. Messimer, *Find and Destroy. Antisubmarine Warfare in World War I* (Annapolis, 2001), p. 3.
9 J. Terraine, *Business in Great Waters* (London, 1989), p. 58.
10 A. Ross, 'Losing the Initiative in Mercantile Warfare: Great Britain's Surprising Failure to Anticipate Maritime Challenges to Her Global Trading Network in the First World War', *International Journal of Naval History*, vol. 1 (2002).
11 *Hansard*, 4th series, vol. 91, col. 332–333; *Hansard*, 4th series, vol. 91, col. 1048.

12 A. Offer, 'Morality and the Admiralty: 'Jacky' Fisher, Economic Warfare and the Laws of War', *Journal of Contemporary History*, vol. 23 (1988), p. 106.
13 PRO, ADM 116/3130; ADM 137/1926 Callaghan to de Roebeck, 6 August 1913.
14 BL Add Mss 49712, Fisher to Balfour, 15 May 1913; BL Add Mss 49712, f105 memo by Fisher entitled 'Submarines and Commerce', 28 May 1913; BL Add Mss 49712, f120 memo by Fisher 'The Oil Engine and the Submarine. Some Reflections on the impending vast change in Sea Fighting.'
15 Conan Doyle, 'Danger!', pp. 1–22.
16 Churchill *World Crisis*, vol. II, pp. 720–721; Conan Doyle, 'Danger!', pp. 20–22.
17 A. Gat, *A History of Military Thought: From the Enlightenment to the Cold War* (Oxford, 2001), p. 476; P. Colomb, *Essays on Naval Defence* (London, 1893), pp. 31–128, 154–159, 194–257.
18 B. Ranft, 'The protection of British seaborne trade and the development of systematic planning for war, 1860–1906', in B Ranft (ed.), *Technical Change and British Naval Policy 1860–1939* (London, 1977), pp. 1–22.
19 J. S. Corbett, *Some Principles of Maritime Strategy* (London, 1911), p. 99.
20 Ibid. pp. 263–284.
21 Dixon, *Military Incompetence*, pp. 164–166.
22 Darnton, *Great Cat Massacre*, p. 5
23 Lynn, *Battle*, pp. 121.
24 Ibid. pp. xx.
25 Conan Doyle, 'Danger!', pp. 4, 5.
26 W. E. Cairnes, 'The Duties and the Army and Navy', *National Review*, vol. 36 (1900–1901).
27 Conan Doyle, 'Danger!', pp. 1–20.
28 Ibid. pp. 4, 5.
29 Ibid. pp. 18–19.
30 Repington, 'New Wars for Old', p. 898.
31 Ibid.
32 Offer, *First World War*, pp. 81, 218–219.
33 Ibid. pp. 221–222.
34 Ibid. pp. 223–225, 231.
35 Conan Doyle, 'Danger!', pp. 20, 22.
36 C. D. Domville-Fife, *Submarines of the World's Navies* (London, 1910), p. 92; Repington, 'New Wars for Old', p. 898.
37 Conan Doyle, 'Danger!', p. 7.
38 Ibid. p. 8.
39 Ibid. p. 12.
40 Ibid. pp. 12, 16, 17, 18.
41 Ibid. p. 17.
42 Ibid. p. 18.
43 Ibid. pp. 20–22.
44 Ibid. p. 20.
45 Ibid. p. 21.
46 Ibid. pp. 20, 22.

47 Conan Doyle, 'Danger!', p. 20.
48 Ibid.
49 Ibid. pp. 20–22.
50 BL, Add Mss 49712, Fisher to Balfour, 15 May 1913, memo entitled 'Submarines and Commerce', 28 May 1913.
51 Churchill, *World Crisis,* vol. II, p. 720.
52 Ibid.
53 Repington, 'New Wars For Old ', p. 898.
54 T. Ropp, *The Development of a Modern Navy* (Annapolis, 1987), pp. 162–165, 168–170.
55 *Hansard*, 5th series, vol. 176, col. 2370; cf. Ropp *The Development of a Modern Navy*, p. 170 and A. Røksund, *The Jeune École: The Strategy of the Weak* (unpublished Dr. Art thesis, University of Oslo, 2004), pp. 204–224.
56 *Times*, 10 August 1901.
57 Churchill, *World Crisis,* vol. II, pp. 720–721; Conan Doyle, 'Danger!', pp. 20–22; D. Stashower, *Teller of Tales. The Life of Arthur Conan Doyle* (London, 2000), p. 301.
58 Stashower, *Teller of Tales*, pp. 299, 301.
59 *Illustrated London News*, 10 April 1915, p. 477.
60 A. S. Hurd, *The British Fleet in the Great War* (London, 1918), pp. 209–215.
61 Churchill, *World Crisis*, vol. II, p. 1111.
62 Ibid. p. 1230.
63 D. Stevenson, *1914–1918 The History of the First World War* (London, 2004), p. 186; see also T. Cook, '"Against God-Inspired Conscience": The Perception of Gas Warfare as a Weapon of Mass Destruction, 1915–1939', *War and Society*, vol. 18 (2000).
64 M. Brown, *The Imperial War Museum Book of the Western Front* (London, 1993), p. 77; Cook, 'Against God-Inspired Conscience', p. 55.
65 G. Corrigan, *Mud, Blood and Poppycock* (London, 2004), p. 161; Stevenson, *1914–1918*, p. 188.
66 P. Griffith, *Battle Tactics of the Western Front* (London, 1994), pp. 53, 62–63, 116–119.
67 S. W. Roskill, *Naval Policy Between the Wars*, vol. II (London, 1976), pp. 383, 384, 388.
68 C. E. Fayle *Seaborne Trade*, vol. II (London, 1923), pp. 4–5.
69 Hurd, *Ordeal By Sea*, pp. 95–108.
70 *Times*, 3 January 1918, p. 7; *Times*, 30 March 1918, p. 6; *Times*, 3 August 1918, p. 7; *Times*, 14 August 1918, p. 5; *Times*, 27 August 1918, p. 6; *Times*, 14 November 1918, p. 4; *Times*, 4 September 1919, p. 11; *Times*, 3 December 1919, p. 10; *Times*, 29 November 1920, p. 7; *Times*, 11 November 1920, p. 15; *Times*, 6 December 1920, p. 13; *Times*, 1 January 1921, p. 11; *Times*, 1 April 1921, p. 7; *Times*, 11 February 1930, p. 14; *Times*, 13 September 1937, pp. 12, 13.
71 Roskill, *Naval Policy*, vol. I, pp. 327–328.
72 PRO, ADM 1/8622/54, Objections to the term 'Pirates' being applied to submarine personnel as suggested in Mr Root's resolution III including Senator Pearce's amendment.

73 PRO, ADM 1/8622/54, Objections to the term 'Pirates' being applied to submarine personnel as suggested in Mr Root's resolution III including Senator Pearce's amendment.
74 PRO, ADM 1/8700/132, letter from the Superintendent, Secretaries Course to C-in-C Portsmouth, 27 September 1926.
75 Fayle, *Seaborne Trade*, vol. II, pp. 106, 160; PRO, ADM 1/8747/88 'Submarines and Their Illegitimate Use', 31 January 1930, p. 4.
76 Semmel, *Liberalism & Naval Strategy*, p. 56
77 *Illustrated London News*, 20 February 1915, p. 254.
78 In the *Illustrated London News* during 1915, Players ran 16 adverts. One had an image of a British destroyer, one had the image of E9, one had image of a Players tobacco tin that stopped a shrapnel bullet, eight had no images at all, two had images of a Berel Hydroplane, two contained images of a Bleriot Seaplane and one had an image of a Henry Farman Seaplane.
79 *Hansard*, 4th series, vol. 149, col. 944, 1186.
80 PRO, ADM 1/9728, 'Submarine Requirements' memo by Director of Plans, 26 February 1934.
81 PRO, ADM 1/8622/54, 'Extracted From The Conference On The Limitations of Armaments Washington'
82 *Evening Standard*, 10 December 1928, p. 6.
83 Ibid.
84 Lynn, *Battle*, p. xxi.
85 M. Howard, *War and the Liberal Conscience* (London, 1981), p. 53.
86 Howard, *Liberal Conscience*, pp. 36–39, 41–43; see also E. E. H. Green, *The Crisis of Conservatism*, (London, 1996), p. 2; J. Grigg, *Lloyd George. The People's Champion 1902–1911* (London, 2002), p. 61; A. Howe, *Free Trade and Liberal England 1846–1946* (Oxford, 1997), pp. 1, 90, 105, 153, 295–308; and M. Ceadel, *Semi-Detached Realists. The British Peace Movement and International Relations, 1854–1945* (Oxford, 2000), chapters 5 and 6 for links between the Liberal Party and the British peace movement.
87 P. Padfield, *Maritime Power and the Struggle for Freedom* (London, 2003), p. 247.
88 N. Rodger, *Command of the Ocean* (London, 2004), p. 418.
89 Ibid. p. 482.
90 Padfield, *Maritime Power*, pp. 241–244.
91 Semmel, *Liberalism & Naval Strategy*, pp. 57, 71; Rodger, *Command of the Ocean*, pp. 522–525.
92 see NHB Eb06, *British Naval Manoeuvres*, vols. III and IV.
93 J. Black, *The British Seaborne Empire* (London, 2004), p. 192; Howe, *Free Trade*, pp. 295–296.
94 Howe, *Free Trade*, p. 195.
95 Green, *Crisis of Conservatism*, p. 1.
96 R. Cobden to W. Lindsay, 29 August 1856, quoted in W. Lindsay, *Manning the Royal Navy and Merchant Marine; also Belligerent and Neutral Rights in the Event of War* (London, 1877), p. 116.
97 Semmel, *Liberalism & Naval Strategy*, p. 71.
98 Ibid. pp. 84–86.

99 R. Cobden, *The Political Writings of Richard Cobden*, vol. II (London, 1903), pp. 388–90, 392.
100 Offer, *The First World War*, pp. 270–273.
101 Cobden to Lindsay, 29 August 1856, quoted in Lindsay, *Manning the Royal Navy and Merchant Marine*, p. 116; Semmel, *Liberalism & Naval Strategy*, p. 71.
102 Offer, 'Morality and Admiralty', p. 102; see also G. Best, *Humanity in Warfare* (London, 1980), chapters III and IV.
103 Churchill, *The World Crisis*, vol. II, pp. 720–721.
104 Ropp, *The Development of a Modern Navy*, pp. 162–163.
105 Henry, 'British Submarine Policy', pp. 80, 81.
106 Lt W. S. King-Hall RN, 'The Influence of the Submarine In Naval Warfare in the Future', *RUSI*, vol. LXIV (1919), p. 381.
107 Lt C. M. Faure RN, 'The Influence of the Submarine in Naval Warfare in the Future', *RUSI*, vol. LXIV (1919), p. 575.
108 Ibid.
109 Hurd, *Ordeal by Sea*, pp. 1–58, 93, 123, 135, 183.
110 Viscount Jellicoe of Scapa, *The Crisis of the Naval War* (London, 1920), pp. 32, 38.
111 PRO, ADM 1/8658/61, minute, 15 August 1924.
112 PRO, ADM 1/8672/230, Remarks by RA (S) in PD02004/24.
113 PRO, ADM 1/8672/230, Tactical Section No. 3911.
114 Ibid.
115 PRO, ADM 116/2522, Future Submarines, 9 July 1927.
116 Ibid.
117 PRO, ADM 1/9373, Sketch designs of Submarines of about 1000 tons and about 400 tons standard displacement.
118 P. Akermann, *Encyclopaedia of British Submarines 1901–1955* (Penzance, 2002), p. 305; Henry, 'British Submarine Policy', p. 91.
119 PRO, ADM 116/2522, M02512/28 letter from Admiralty to CinC Atlantic Fleet and Mediterranean Fleet.
120 PRO, ADM 197/42, Review of Submarine Questions, 29August 1925.
121 Faure, 'The Influence of the Submarine in Naval Warfare in the Future', p. 575.
122 C. B. Barry, 'The Development of the Submarine', *RUSI*, vol. LXXX (1935), p. 138. J. S. Corbett, *England in the Seven Years' War*, vol. II (London, 1907, facsimile edn. 1992), pp. 375–376; Corbett, *Maritime Strategy*, pp. 99, 264; J. V. Creagh, 'The Fleet of the Future', *RUSI*, vol. LXXIV (1929), pp. 679–680; Faure, 'The Influence of the Submarine', p. 575; W. S. King-Hall, 'The Submarine and Future Naval Warfare', *RUSI*, vol. LXV (1920), pp. 369–370
123 PRO, ADM 1/8703/158, No. 955/S.100 Letter from RA (S) to Admiralty, 3 December 1926.
124 PRO, ADM 1/8703/158.
125 Ibid. Minute by Director of the Tactical Division, Naval Staff, 8 April 1925.
126 Stevenson, *1914–1918*, p. 312.
127 Henry, 'British Submarine Policy', pp. 84, 85.
128 PRO, ADM 1/8658/61, Proposals for 2 Man Midget Submarines.
129 Ibid.

130 PRO, ADM 1/8658/61, minute, 15 August 1924.
131 Ibid.
132 PRO, ADM 1/8694/2, Admiralty Board Minute 2142, 21 December 1925.
133 PRO, ADM 167/72, Memoranda 2138, 3 December 1925.
134 Ackermann, *Encyclopaedia*, pp. 286, 294.
135 Ibid. p. 199.
136 Ibid. p. 200.
137 Ibid. p. 208.
138 J. J. Colledge, *Ships of the Royal Navy* (London, 2003), pp. 223, 232, 236; T. D. Manning & C. F. Walker, *British Warship Names* (London, 1959), pp. 322, 327.
139 Ackermann, *Encyclopaedia*, p. 298, Colledge, *Ships*, pp. 242, 247, 266; Manning & Walker, *British Warship*, pp. 332, 339–340, 342, 363–364.

Chapter Four

1 Vice-Admiral Sir Arthur Hezlet, *British and Allied Submarine Operations in World War II*, vol. I (Gosport, 2001), p. 27.
2 NHB, CB 3006 (1), *Naval Staff History of the Second World War: Submarines*, vol. I, p. 32; W. S. Chalmers, *Max Horton and the Western Approaches* (London, 1954), pp. 76–77.
3 J. Maiolo, *The Royal Navy and Nazi Germany 1933–39* (Basingstoke, 1998), pp. 1–3.
4 Ibid. p. 11.
5 Sir Bolton Eyres Monsell, 'The Anglo–German Naval Agreement', *The Listener*, vol. VIII (1935), p. 1082.
6 Ibid.
7 *Times*, 19 June 1935, p. 15.
8 *Morning Post*, 19 June 1935, p. 10.
9 *Manchester Guardian*, 16 June 1935, p. 11; *Morning Post*, 20 June 1935, p. 15; 'Comment', *The New Statesman and Nation*, vol. IX (1935), p. 913.
10 P. Kennedy, *The Rise and Fall of the Great Powers* (London, 1989), p. 434; Maiolo, *Royal Navy*, pp. 1, 32; R. Overy, *The Road to War*, 2nd edn., (London, 1999), p. 139; Roskill, *Naval Policy*, vol. II, p. 307; B. Sullivan, 'More than meets the eye: The Ethiopian War and the origins of the Second World War', in G. Martel, (ed.) *The Origins of the Second World War Reconsidered*, 2nd edn., (New York, 1999), p. 180; A.J.P. Taylor, *The Origins of the Second World War* (London, 1991), p. 118.
11 for example *Daily Express*, 19 June 1935, p. 1; *Daily Mirror*, 19 June 1935, pp. 28, 35; *Manchester Guardian*, 19 June 1935, p. 10.
12 Admiral Sir Herbert Richmond, 'The Naval Conference', *Fortnightly Review*, vol. 138 (1935), p. 663.
13 Ibid.
14 *Spectator*, vol. 154 (1935), p. 1049.
15 H. Bywater, 'The German Naval Renaissance', *Nineteenth Century*, vol. CVXIII (1935), p. 51.
16 *Manchester Guardian*, 16 June 1935, p. 11; *Morning Post*, 20 June .1935, p. 15; *Daily Express*, 19 June 1935, p. 1; *Daily Mirror*, 19 June 1935, pp. 28, 35. *Manchester Guardian*, 19 June .1935, p. 10; 'Comment', *The New Statesman and*

Nation, vol. IX (1935), p. 913; Kennedy, *Rise and Fall of the Great Powers*, p. 434; Maiolo, *Royal Navy*, pp. 1, 32; Overy, *The Road to War*, p. 139; Sullivan, 'More than meets the eye: The Ethiopian War and the origins of the Second World War', p. 180; Taylor, *Origins of the Second World War*, p. 118.
17 Maiolo, *Royal Navy*, pp. 11, 66–73.
18 J. Cable, *Britain's Naval Future* (London, 1983), pp. 125–128, 186; P.M. Kennedy, 'The Relevance of the pre-war British and American Strategies to the First World War and its aftermath, 1898–1920', in J. B. Hattendorf & R. S. Jordan (eds.), *Maritime Strategy and the Balance of Power* (London, 1989), p. 167; MoD, *The Fundamentals of British Maritime Doctrine* (London, 1995), pp. 161–162.
19 Maiolo, *Royal Navy*, pp. 67–70; see also W. Rahn, 'German Naval Strategy and Armament 1919–1939', in P. Payson O'Brien (ed.), *Technology and Naval Combat in the Twentieth Century and Beyond* (London, 2001), pp. 119, 121–123.
20 Maiolo, *Royal Navy*, pp. 66–67, 68–70.
21 *Times*, 19 June 1935, p. 15.
22 G. Franklin, *Britain's Anti-Submarine Capability 1919–1939* (London, 2003), pp. 186–190; Hackmann, *Seek and Strike*, chapters 5, 6 & 8.
23 PRO, ADM 186/476, CB 3002/29; PRO, ADM 186/40, Mercantile Convoys: General Instructions for Port Convoy Officers, Ocean and Destroyer Escorts and Commodores of Convoy; PRO, ADM 239/126, Mercantile Convoy Instructions, (1934); PRO, CAB 4/26, Defence Against Submarine Attack, (1937), p. 4; see also Franklin, *Britain's Anti-Submarine Capability*, pp. 112–115, 142–147; A. Hague, *The Allied Convoy System* (St Catherines: Ontario, 2000), pp. 20–21; for a more negative view of the interwar period see J. Terraine, *Business in Great Waters* (London, 1989), pp. 179–182.
24 Hackmann, *Seek and Strike*, p. 212.
25 P. Elliott, *Allied Escort Ships of World War II: A Complete Survey* (Annapolis: MD, 1980), pp. 14–16, 136–137; Roskill, *Naval Policy*, vol. II, p. 228; J. T. Sumida, 'British Naval Procurement and Technological Change' in P. O'Brien (ed.), *Technology and Naval Combat in the Twentieth Century and Beyond* (London, 2001), pp. 140, 142–3.
26 Hackmann, *Seek and Strike*, pp. 187–188.
27 Franklin, *Britain's Anti-Submarine Capability*, pp. 113–114, 118–119, 123–129, 143–147, 147–152.
28 CB 3002, cited in Franklin, *Britain's Anti Submarine Capability*, figure 12, pp. 157–158.
29 Roskill, *Naval Policy*, vol. II, p. 332; Sumida, 'British Naval Procurement', pp. 139–140, 142–43.
30 See P. R. C. Groves, *Our Future in the Air: A Survey of the Vital Questions of British Air Power* (London, 1922), and *Behind the Smoke Screen* (London 1934); J. Griffin, *Glass Houses and Modern War* (London, 1938); L. E. O. Charlton, *War From the Air* (London, 1935), and *War Over England* (London, 1937), and *War From the Air* (London, 1938); the fear of aerial warfare must also be considered in the light of the WWI experience of chemical weapons, see Cook, 'Against God-Inspired Conscience'.

31 W. Murray, 'Strategic Bombing. The British, American, and German experiences', in W. Murray and A. R. Millett (eds.), *Military Innovation in the Interwar Period* (Cambridge, 1996), p. 102; see also I. F. Clarke, *Voices Prophesying War 1763–1984* (London, 1966), p. 170.
32 Conan Doyle, 'Danger!', XLVIII (1914), pp. 12, 16, 17, 18.
33 K. Middlemas & J. Barnes, *Baldwin: A Biography* (London, 1969), p. 736; P. Williamson, *Stanley Baldwin* (Cambridge, 1999), pp. 47, 305–306.
34 U. Bialer, *The Shadow of the Bomber. The Fear of Air Attack and British Politics 1932–1939* (London, 1980), pp. 20, 21; Middlemas & Barnes, *Baldwin*, p. 732; cf Williamson, *Baldwin*, pp. 305–306.
35 PRO, ADM 116/2827, PD 04/058/32 1SL minute, dated 13 April 1932.
36 T. D. Biddle, *Rhetoric and Reality* (Princeton: NY, 2002), pp. 102, 103.
37 In conversation with Mr W. Hetherington, archivist for the Peace Pledge Union; all of the surviving material from the Peace Pledge Union for the interwar period relates to air warfare only. The author is indebted to Mr Hetherington for the advice and assistance he provided.
38 PPU pamphlet, no reference number.
39 Churchill, *World Crisis*, vol. II, p. 720.
40 Behrman, *Victorian Myths*, pp. 38–40, 4344, 47–49; Colls, *Identity*, pp. 239–241; Kumar, *English National Identity*, p. 8.
41 See introduction as well as chapters 1 and 2.
42 Colls, *Identity*, p. 239.
43 D. Reynolds, *Britannia Overruled. British Policy and World Power in the 20th century*, 2nd edn., (Harlow, 2002), p. 50; Rodger, *Command of the Ocean*, pp. 578–579.
44 Murray, 'Strategic Bombing. The British, American, and German experiences', pp. 102–103.
45 PRO, ADM 1/8715/194, minute by Director of Plans Division, dated 3 March 1927, minute by Director of Torpedo Division, dated 13 March 1927, minute by Director Naval Intelligence, dated 21 March 1927.
46 J. Maiolo, 'Deception and Intelligence Failure: Anglo–German Preparations for the U-boat Warfare in the 1930s', *Journal of Strategic Studies*, vol. 22 (1999), p. 59
47 Maiolo, 'Deception and Intelligence Failure', p. 62.
48 *Hansard*, 5th series, vol. 299, cols. 674–7
49 Roskill, *Naval Policy*, vol. II, p. 228.
50 Ibid. p. 229.
51 *Daily Express*, 1 September 1937, p. 1.
52 Ibid. p. 2.
53 *Daily Express*, 3 September 1937, pp. 1, 2.
54 *Daily Express*, 3 September .1937, p. 2; *Daily Express*, 4 September 1937, p. 2.
55 A. Gordon, 'The Admiralty and Imperial Overstretch 1900–1941', in G. Till (ed.) *Seapower. Theory and Practice* (Ilford, 1994), pp. 63–85.
56 M. Simpson, 'Superhighway to the World Wide Web: The Mediterranean in British Imperial Strategy, 1900–1945', in J. Hattendorf (ed.), *Naval Strategy and Policy in the Mediterranean. Past Present and Future* (London, 2000), p. 57
57 Overy, *The Road To War*, p. 90; Taylor, *Origins of the Second World War*, p. 161.

NOTES 275

58 Fayle *Seaborne Trade*, vol. II, pp. 106, 160; PRO, ADM 1/8747/88, 'Submarines and Their Illegitimate Use', 31 January 1930, p. 4.
59 NHB, CB 3306(1), p. 9.
60 PRO, ADM 1/, RA (S)'s letter dated 3 August makes mention of a previous letter and resulting correspondence from June 1939, however, only the letter of 3 August and resulting minutes seem to have survived.
61 NHB, CB 3306(1), p. 9.
62 NHB, T6594–T6616 London Naval Conference 1930, part IV, article 22 (2).
63 Hezlet, *Submarine Operations*, vol. I, p. 51.
64 PRO, ADM 1/8622/54, Objections to the term "Pirates" being applied to submarine personnel as suggested in Mr Root's resolution III including Senator Pearce's amendment.
65 NHB, CB 3306(1), pp. 2, 53, 61, 62, 65, 66, 67; see also page 32 'sunk without warning', p. 34 'extended the freedom of action for submarines', p. 64 'attack at sight'.
66 Fayle *Seaborne Trade*, vol. II, pp. 106, 160; ADM 1/8747/88 'Submarines and Their Illegitimate Use', 31 January 1930, p. 4.
67 *Hansard*, 5th series, vol. 295, col. 316; *Hansard*, 5th series, vol. 310, col. 316; Biddle, *Rhetoric and Reality*, pp. 102–103, 106, 109–110; H. M Hyde, *British Air Policy Between the Wars 1918–1939* (London, 1976), pp. 308, 309, 447, 449, 450; T. H. O'Brien, *Civil Defence* (London, 1955), pp. 143, 144, 172, 215.
68 NHB, CB 3306(1), p. 31.
69 G. Hessler, *The U-boat War in the Atlantic* (London, 1989), pp. 5, 40–42.
70 Hessler, *U-boat War*, p. 42; S. W. Roskill, *The War At Sea*, vol. I (London, 1954), p. 103.
71 PRO, ADM 1/8622/54, Objections to the term "Pirates" being applied to submarine personnel as suggested in Mr Root's resolution III including Senator Pearce's amendment.
72 Roskill, *War at Sea*, vol. I, p. 103.
73 Roskill, *War at Sea*, vol. I, p. 104. See also Hessler, *U-boat War*, pp. 41–46 where Hessler occasionally refers to unrestricted areas during his analysis of German operations, but the directives he quotes from studiously avoid mentioning unrestricted submarine warfare.
74 PRO, CAB 65/6, War Cabinet Minutes 86/40.
75 Ibid.
76 Ibid.
77 Ibid.
78 Barnett, *Engage the Enemy*, pp. 114, 122, 125, 128, 130; Roskill, *War at Sea*, vol. I, pp. 171, 179, 191, 199.
79 NHB, CB 3306(1), p. 31.
80 Hezlet, *Submarine Operations*, vol. I, p. 27; Roskill, *War at Sea*, vol. I, p. 171.
81 Hezlet, *Submarine Operations*, vol. I, p. 27.
82 Roskill, *War at Sea*, vol. I, pp. 171–172.
83 *Karlsruhe*, damaged so badly that she was sunk by her escorts; *Lutzow* and *Gneisenau* damaged so badly that they were out of action for many months. Aircraft of the Fleet Air Arm sank the cruiser *Konigsberg* and a torpedo from a British destroyer had damaged the *Scharnhorst*.

84 D. Masters, *Up Periscope* (London, 1942), p. 7.
85 *Daily Mirror*, 14 December 1939, p. 9.
86 *Daily Express*, 13 December 1939, p. 1; *Daily Mirror*, 13 December 1939, p. 1.
87 *Daily Express*, 13 December 1939, p. 1; *Daily Express*, 13 December 1939, p. 5; *Daily Mirror*, 13 December 1939, p. 1; see also *Daily Mail*, 16 December 1939, p. 6.
88 *Daily Mail*, 13 December 1939, p. 6.
89 *Manchester Guardian*, 13 December 1939, p. 6.
90 *Times*, 13 December 1939, p. 8; *Times*, 14 December 1939, p. 8; *Times*, 19 December 1939, p. 8.
91 *Daily Mail*, 13 December 1939, p. 2; *Daily Mail*, 16 December 1939, p. 2; *Manchester Guardian*, 14 December 1939, p. 7; *Manchester Guardian*, 15 December .1939, p. 7.
92 *Times*, 7 January 1943, p. 4; see also *Times*, 21 January 1943, p. 4; *Times*, 8 February 1943, p. 3.
93 PRO, INF 1/292, Weekly Home Intelligence Report No 148, 5 August 1943.
94 Quoted by J. Tall, 'The Submariner: Who or what is he?' in M. Edmonds (ed), *100 Years of the Trade* (Lancaster, 2001), p. 111.
95 MoI, *His Majesty's Submarines* (London, 1945), p. 20.
96 N. Monsarrat, *Three Corvettes* (London, 2000), p. 341.
97 Monsarrat, 'H M Corvette' in *Three Corvettes*, pp. 57, 62–63, 65–66.
98 The use of a Jolly Roger continued after the Second World War. In 1982 *HMS Conqueror* flew a Jolly Roger on her return from the Falklands conflict having sunk the Argentine cruiser *General Belgrano*.
99 PRO, CAB 131/2, DO (46) 20, 14 February 1946.
100 E. Grove, *Vanguard to Trident* (London, 1987), p. 21.
101 Ibid. p. 219.
102 Hezlet, *Submarine Operations*, vol. I, p. 27.
103 PRO, ADM 205/23, A Balanced Post War Fleet.
104 PRO, ADM 1/23729, FOSM's 705/sm.068.M, 8.9.1952; PRO, ADM 1/25252, M/TASW 289/47 quoted in C-in-C Home Fleet to Admiralty 'Submarine War Plans', 4 January 1951.
105 *Times*, 7 April 1900, p. 8; *Times*, 19 June 1935, p. 15.
106 The 8 units of the *Porpoise* class were laid down between 1954 and 1958, with the last boat of the class being delivered in 1961. By the end of October 1962 5 *Oberon*s had been delivered and another 6 were under construction.
107 Grove, *Vanguard*, p. 228;
108 PRO, ADM 1/25252, Submarine V Submarine Trials; Grove, *Vanguard*, pp. 223–224; Hackmann, *Seek and Strike*, p. 352
109 The relative failure of the High Test Peroxide powered submarine *Excalibur* and *Explorer*, and the failure of the of the Mark 12 and Mark 23 torpedoes, the partial success of the *T* class modernisations as although having better performance they were too noisy for anti-submarine warfare, unlike the modernized *A* class.
110 *Times*, 20 March 1957, p. 3; *Times*, 11 April 1957, p. 10; *Times*, 1 December 1961, p. 6; for the importance of anti-submarine warfare see *Daily Telegraph*, 15 June 1953, p. 6; *Manchester Guardian*, 15 June 1953, p. 4; *Times*, 9 March

NOTES 277

1959, p. 11; *Times*, 2 May 1960, p. 7; *Times*, 1 November 1960, p. 4; see also chapter 1 for a discussion of the 1953 Coronation Naval Review.
111 *Times*, 20 March 1957, p. 3.
112 *Times*, 11 April 1957, p. 10.
113 *Birmingham Post*, 16 June 1953, p. 1; *Daily Mail*, 16 June 1953, pp. 1, 2; *Daily Mail*, 17 June 1953, p. 1; *Daily Telegraph*, 16 June 1953, pp. 1, 12; *Manchester Guardian*, 16 June 1953, p. 1.
114 *Daily Mail*, 16 June 1953, p. 1.
115 *Times*, 1 November 1960, p. 4.
116 *Manchester Guardian*, 15 June 1953, p. 4.
117 *Times*, 5 June 1954, p. 6; see also *Times*, 22 January 1952, p. 4; *Times*, 28 March 1952, p. 4; *Times*, 16 May 1952, p. 6; *Times*, 16 June 1952, p. 6; *Times*, 21 July 1952, p. 3; *Times*, 1 August 1952, p. 6; *Times*, 14 May 1953, p. 5.
118 M. Llewellyn-Jones, 'A Flawed Contender: The "Fighter" Submarine, 1946–1950' in M. Edmonds (ed.), *100 Years of the Trade* (Lancaster, 2001), pp. 58–67.
119 The Royal Navy had not felt the need to run recruiting campaigns prior to 1945.
120 PRO, INF 2/160, E4887, advert for the July 1957 *Sea Cadet*
121 *Manchester Guardian*, 15 June 1953, p. 4; *Times*, 15 June 1953, p. 7.
122 PRO, INF 2/160.
123 Ibid.
124 PRO, INF 2/89; INF 2/90; INF 2/91.
125 Grove, *Vanguard*, p. 219.
126 Chalmers, *Max Horton*, p. 71.

Chapter Five
1 J. Winton, *Down the Hatch*, (London, 1961), p. 102.
2 *Times*, 29 June 2005, p. 6.
3 *Guardian*, 29 June 2005, p. 1; *Guardian*, 29 June 2005, p. 4; *Daily Telegraph*, 29 June 2005, p. 1; *Times*, 29 June 2005, p. 6.
4 *Daily Telegraph*, 28 June 2005, p. 7; *Daily Telegraph*, 30 June 2005, pp. 11, 27.
5 *Daily Mail*, 29 June 2005, p. 1; see also *Guardian*, 29 June 2005, p. 1.
6 *Illustrated London News*, 1 July 1911, pp. 42–43.
7 PRO, ADM 116/3551, minute by DOD, 14 January 1937.
8 *Guardian*, 28 June 2005, p. 3; *Daily Telegraph*, 28 June 2005, p. 7; *Guardian*, 29 June 2005, p. 1; *Guardian*, 29 June 2005, pp. 4, 5; *Daily Mail*, 29 June 2005, p. 1; *Daily Mail*, 29 June 2005, pp. 8, 9; *Daily Telegraph*, 29 June 2005, p. 1; *Daily Telegraph*, 29 June 2005, p. 4; *Daily Telegraph*, 29 June 2005, p. 5; *Times*, 29 June 2005, p. 1; *Times*, 29 June 2005, p. 6.
9 *Army and Navy Gazette*, 1935, p. 572; *Times*, 16 July 1935, p. 10.
10 *Daily Mail*, 29 June 2005, p. 16.
11 *Daily Mail*, 29 June 2005, p. 8; *Daily Mail*, 29 June 2005, p. 16; *Daily Telegraph*, 29 June 2005, p. 1; *Daily Telegraph*, 29 June 2005, p. 4; *Guardian*, 29 June 2005, p. 1; *Guardian*, 29 June 2005, p. 5; *Times*, 29 June 2005, p. 6; *Times*, 29 June 2005, p. 16; *Times*, 29 June 2005, p. 17.

12 *Guardian, G2 supplement*, 28 June 2005, p. 5.
13 PRO, ADM 1/26756, *Analysis of Operation Rum Tub*; J. Coote, *Submariner* (London, 1991), p. 212; Hackmann, *Seek & Strike*, p. 355.
14 Coote, *Submariner*, p. 213.
15 N. Freidman 'Where Do We Go From Here?', in M. Edmonds (ed.), *100 Years Of The Trade* (Lancaster, 2001), p. 128.
16 N. Freidman 'Where Do We Go From Here?', p. 128. Friedman points out in his notes that the original specification for the computer system for HMS *Dreadnought*'s type 2001 sonar emphasized underwater escort missions and that contemporary US documents show that the Royal Navy led the way in submarine direct support operations. Contemporary documents in The National Archives support Friedman's contention about the emphasis the Royal Navy placed on the direct support or escort of surface surfaces; see DEFE 24/194, *Future Fleet Working Party action on further studies*, 'Submarines – The State of the Art' by DUSW(N).
17 For a general view on the RN thinking on tactical submarine communications see PRO, ADM 219/642, The Communication Problems for The Nuclear Submarine In the Escort Role; see also PRO DEFE 24/194, FFWP action on further studies, 'Submarine – The State of the Art' by DUSW(N); DEFE 24/238, Future Fleet Working Party Report, II, annex U3; Cdr N. Harrap, 'The Role of the SSN in Modern UK Defence Policy', in M. Edmonds (ed.), *100 Years of the Trade* (Lancaster, 2001), p. 86; N. Friedman, 'Where do we go from here?', pp. 128–129; Friedman, *Submarine Design*, pp. 72–74.
18 Friedman, 'Where do we go from here?', pp. 128–129
19 PRO, DEFE 48/285, The Nuclear Submarine in Defence of Surface Forces and Interdiction of Enemy Surface Movement, November 1974.
20 J. Wingate, *Carrier* (London, 1982), pp. 89, 105, 127.
21 PRO, DEFE 48/285, para. 109.
22 PRO, DEFE 48/285, para. 110, 111, 112; *Broadsheet 81* (London, 1981), p. 33.
23 Rear Admiral J. Perowne OBE, 'The Submarine Service', *Broadsheet 96/7* (London, 1997), p. 24.
24 'The Submarine Service – A Bright Future', *Broadsheet 97/8* (London, 1998), p. 22.
25 Grove, *Vanguard to Trident*, pp. 209, 255–256.
26 *Hansard*, 5th series, vol. 725, col. 239, 241.
27 CVA–01 was an ambitious and expensive aircraft carrier replacement programme implemented during the early 1960s. It was viewed as by the RAF as a direct threat to their existence following the decision to place the strategic nuclear deterrent in the Royal Navy's hands rather than it remaining under RAF control. After bitter inter-service disputes in private and public CVA–01 was cancelled in 1966 by Denis Healey who also announced the end of traditional fixed-wing carrier aviation in the Royal Navy by the mid to late 1970s on the grounds of cost and the allegedly greater efficiency of land based aircraft; see D. Healey, *The Time of My Life* (London, 1989), pp. 275-276.
28 PRO, DEFE 24/149, minute DS4/41/4A, August 1967 by A.R.M. Jeffray.
29 *Hansard*, 5th series, vol. 725, col. 239, 241.

NOTES 279

30 PRO, DEFE 24/149, minute DS4/41/4A, August 67; see also DEFE 24/149, Enclosure to AUS (NS)/53/3, 6 April 1967; DEFE 24/149, The Future Fleet note on Minister (RN)'s submission of 28 October 1966; DEFE 24/149, Options For meeting The Concept of Operations: The Fleet in 1975; T. T. Lewin, 'The Royal Navy In The Next decade', *RUSI*, vol. CXIII (1968), p. 205.
31 PRO, DEFE 24/149, Annex II to Minister (RN)'s letter to Secretary of State for Defence, 28 October 1966; DEFE 24/150, Future Concept of Naval Operations West of Suez, Annex III.
32 PRO, DEFE 24/149, Options For meeting The Concept of Operations: The Fleet in 1975.
33 R. Blackman, *Jane's Fighting Ships 1966–67*, (London, 1966); see also *Times*, 14 December 1966, p. 9.
34 'R.G.H.', 'The Nuclear Attack Submarine', p. 24.
35 Ibid.
36 A. J. Pierre, *Nuclear Politics. The British experience with an independent strategic force 1939–1970*, (London, 1972), p. 193.
37 'Moryak', 'Manning the Polaris Submarine Force', pp. 108, 109.
38 Pierre, *Nuclear Politics*, pp. 293–294.
39 'Moryak', 'Manning the Polaris Submarine Force', p. 108.
40 PRO, AIR 20/10057, minute by Vice-Chief of the Air Staff, 28 November 1960.
41 Command of the sea can be defined as the ability to use the sea in its entirety for ones own purposes at any time and to deny the use of ships to the enemy; BR 1806 *The Fundamentals of British Maritime Doctrine*, p. 207.
42 'R.G.H.', 'The Nuclear Attack Submarine', p. 23; Walters, 'The Submersible Fleet of the Future', p. 322.
43 PRO, DEFE 24/238, Future Fleet Working Party Report, vol. I, para 15, 167; vol. II, Annex U3 para 7; DEFE 24/149, 'Options for meeting the Concept of Operations – the Fleet in 1975', 22 July 1966.
44 'R.G.H.', 'The Nuclear Attack Submarine', p. 23.
45 R. Coopey, 'Industrial policy in the white heat of the scientific revolution', in R. Coopey, S. Fielding, N. Tiratsoo (eds.), *The Wilson Government 1964–1970* (London, 1993), p. 112; S. Fielding, '"White heat" and white collars: the evolution of "Wilsonism"', in Coopey, Fielding, Tiratsoo (eds.), *The Wilson Government*, pp. 29, 37; D. Horner, 'The Road to Scarborough: Wilson, Labour and the scientific revolution', in Coopey, Fielding, Tiratsoo (eds.), *The Wilson Government*, p. 48; A. Morgan, *Harold Wilson* (London, 1992), p. 246; B. Pimlott, *Harold Wilson* (London, 1993), pp. 310–305; P. Ziegler, *Wilson. The Authorised Life of Lord Wilson of Rievaulx* (London, 1993), pp. 143–146.
46 Ziegler, *Wilson*, p. 208.
47 Lyndon Johnson Library, PM Wilson Briefing Book, 32, Sec of State to Johnson, 27 July 1966, quoted in Ziegler, *Wilson*, p. 210.
48 Reynolds, *Britannia*, pp. 199, 201, 202, 208, 211–212.
49 Lyndon Johnson Library, PM Wilson Briefing Book, 32, Sec of State to Johnson, 27 July 1966, quoted in Ziegler, *Wilson*, p. 210; Ziegler, *Wilson*, p. 208.

50 PRO, DEFE 24/238, Future Fleet Working Party Report, vol. I, para 15, 167; vol. II, Annex U3 para 7.
51 I. McGeoch, 'Submarine Matters', *The Naval Review*, vol. LVI (1968), p. 6.
52 Ibid.
53 McGeoch, 'Submarine Matters', p. 6.
54 J. R. Hill, 'British Naval Planning post 1945', in N. A. M. Rodger (ed.), *Naval power in the Twentieth Century* (London, 1996), p. 223; Admiral Sir Benjamin Bathurst, 'View from the First Sea Lord', *Broadsheet 93*, p. 2.
55 *Times*, 23 August 1961, p. 5; see also PRO, INF 2/91.
56 *Times*, 23 August 1961, p. 5.
57 Ibid.
58 B. Callison *A Frenzy of Merchantmen* (London, 1977), p. 20.
59 *Times*, 14 March 1966, p. 7; see also PRO, INF 2/69; INF 2/89; INF 2/90; INF 2/91; INF 2/92; INF 2/160; INF 2/161; INF 2/162.
60 *Times*, 12 June 1968, p. 2; see also PRO, INF 2/166; INF 2/167; INF 2/168.
61 *Manchester Guardian*, 9 June 1959, p. 2; *Times*, 9 June 1959, p. 6.
62 *Manchester Guardian*, 9 June 1959, p. 2; *Times*, 9 June 1959, p. 6.
63 *Times*, 16 July 1971, p. 3.
64 Ibid.
65 *Times*, 16 July 1971, p. 3.
66 W. M. Thornton, *Submarine Insignia & Submarine Services of the World* (London, 1997), p. 133.
67 Ibid.
68 Wiener, *English Culture*, pp. 159–166.
69 Ibid. p. 164.
70 Ibid. p. 163.
71 Ibid. p. 165.
72 Friedman, *British Carrier Aviation*, pp. 344, 346, 347; Grove, *Vanguard*, pp. 252, 278, 292–293, 307, 310–311, 312, 338, 341
73 *Times*, 16 July 1971, p. 3.
74 PRO, ADM 1/12520, 'Wearing of Pilot's or Observer's "wings" by Naval Officers.' minute, 25 November 1942.
75 Ibid.
76 A ship or submarine's sponsor is the woman who breaks the champagne bottle over the bows and says 'I name this ship…'; 'A submarine launched', *Times*, 16 May 1961, p. 26.
77 *Times*, 16 May 1961, p. 26.
78 P. Boniface, *Dreadnought. Britain's First Nuclear Powered Submarine* (Penzance, 2003), p. 18; *Times*, 13 June 1959, p. 8.
79 'Symbolic "Keel-Laying" of Dreadnought', *Manchester Guardian*, 13 June 1959, p. 12.
80 See C. Barnett, *The Verdict of Peace* (London, 2002), chapter 2.
81 Rüger, *The Celebration of the Fleet*, p. 24.
82 *Times*, 22 October 1960, p. 6.
83 *Guardian*, 21 October 1960, p. 8.
84 Ibid.
85 Boniface, *Dreadnought*, p. 23.

86 PRO, DEFE 24/103, letter from MoD to C-in-C Home Fleet/Flag Officer Submarines/ Flag Officer Scotland and Northern Ireland, 11 February 1965; DEFE 24/103, letter from Lt Col Sir Michael Adeane to Rear Admiral W.D. O'Brien, 18 January 1965; DEFE 24/103, note from Naval Secretary to VCNS, 12 November 1964.
87 *Times*, 22 October 1960, p. 6.
88 *Times*, 12 October 1960, p. 8.
89 *Times*, 3 June 1959, p. 9.
90 *Times*, 16 September 1966, p. 10; *Times*, 16 September 1966, p. 22.
91 *Times*, 27 February 1967, p. 2, and picture on p. 7.
92 *Guardian*, 3 December 1963, p. 16; *Guardian*, 4 December 1963, p. 3; *Times*, 4 December 1963, p. 7.
93 *Peace News*, 2 October 1964, p. 3; *Peace News*, 29 July 1966, p. 3; *Peace News*, p. 9 September 1966, p. 10; *Times*, 16 September 1966, p. 10; *Peace News*, 7 October 1966, p. 12; *Peace News*, 10 February 1967, p. 10; *Times*, 27 February 1967, p. 2; *Peace News*, 3 March 1967, pp. 1, 10; *Peace News*, 13 October 1967, p. 12; *Evening Mail*, 4 November 1967, p. 3; *Peace News*, 10 November 1967, pp. 1, 12; *Times*, 16 March 1968, p. 2.
94 *Daily Mirror*, 16 September 1966, p. 4.
95 *Guardian*, 16 September 1966, p. 18
96 *Daily Telegraph*, 16 September 1966, p. 21.
97 *Guardian*, 27 February 1967, p. 1.
98 *Times*, 19 September 1969, p. 5.
99 Ibid.
100 P. Byrne, *The Campaign For Nuclear Disarmament* (London, 1988), pp. 46–47.
101 LSE, CND 3/17, Annual Conference 1968.
102 Byrne, *CND*, p. 45; P. Byrne, 'Nuclear Weapons and CND', in F. R. Ridley & G. Jordan (eds.), *Protest Politics: Cause Groups and Campaigns* (Oxford, 1998), p. 117.
103 *Peace News*, 3 March 1967, p. 1.
104 PRO, HO 325/149, Aldermaston Protest March 1958; PRO, PREM 13/2371, Aldermaston Protest March 1968, minute from Home Secretary to Prime Minister, 10 April 1968.
105 As the Navigator of the SSN *HMS Tireless* in 1998–2000 I was treated to the welcome the peace camp activists gave to SSBNs when the latest *V* class SSBN was diverted to Coulport and the protestors had to vent their spleen on the conventionally armed *Tireless*. It was a good protest, lots of noise, banners and slogans, although why a group kept screaming 'murderers' and 'baby killers' as we sailed past was rather lost on me. You'd think the Navy had the recruiting slogan 'Join Submarines and learn to pitchfork babies.'
106 LSE, CND 1/17, Barrow in Furness Protest.
107 LSE, CND add mss 5/12, Scottish Campaign Against Trident.
108 J. Hinton, *Protests & Visions. Peace Politics in 20th Century Britain* (London, 1989), p. 184.
109 M. Ceadel, 'Britain's Nuclear Disarmers', in W. Laqueur and R. Hunter (eds.), *European Peace Movements and the future of the Western Alliance* (Oxford, 1988), p. 218; see also R. Bandon, *The Burning Question* (London, 1987), p. 60; Hinton,

Protests & Visions, p. 165; R. Taylor, 'The Labour Party and CND 1957 to 1984', in R. Taylor and N. Young (eds.), *Campaigns for Peace: British peace movements in the Twentieth Century* (Manchester, 1987), p. 120; R. Taylor, *Against the Bomb: The British Peace Movement 1958–1965* (Oxford, 1988), pp. 91, 105, 112.
110 Byrne, *CND*, pp. 45–47.
111 Byrne, *CND*, p. 51; Ceadel, 'Britain's Nuclear Disarmers', p. 225; Taylor, *Against the Bomb*, p. 91.
112 LSE, CND 1/71, CND Conference Pamphlets; CND 3/12, Annual Conference 1967; CND 3/17, Annual Conference 1968; CND 3/18, Annual Conference 1969.
113 LSE, CND 3/12, Annual Conference 1967.
114 LSE, CND 3/12, Annual Conference 1967; CND 3/17, Annual Conference 1968; CND 3/18, Annual Conference 1969; see also Taylor, *Against the Bomb*, p. 105.
115 Hinton, *Protests & Visions*, pp. 164–165.
116 Ziegler, *Wilson*, p. 208.
117 PRO, DEFE 69/325, letter from PS Sec State for Defence to PS Minister (RN), 22 April 1965.
118 LSE, CND add mss 5/12, Scottish Campaign Against Trident.
119 LSE, CND add mss 5/12.
120 'Drake', 'The Challenge of Polaris', *Naval Review*, vol. LIII (1965), p. 340.
121 Ibid. p. 341.
122 RNSubM, A1950/5 letter from Capt SM1 (at Malta) to FOSM, 15 May 1958.
123 Boniface, *Dreadnought*, p. 17.
124 PRO, ADM 1/26779, MAT 5954/57, 2 February 1957.
125 Manning & Walker, *British Warship*, pp. 13–14. When Queen Elizabeth II succeeded to the throne, there were no battleships planned and all the aircraft carriers completed in the late 1950's had been laid down during the Second World War, although a large aircraft carrier replacement was envisaged but not ordered. Thus the first major warship to be laid down and launched in her reign was a submarine.
126 PRO, DEFE 69/325, loose minute, 8 February 1965.
127 PRO, ADM 1/26779, loose minute, 26 September 1958.
128 Ibid., loose minute, 7 January 1960.
129 Ibid., loose minute, 16 November 1960.
130 Ibid.
131 Ibid.
132 PRO, ADM 1/28583, loose minute, 21 November 1963.
133 'Drake', 'The Challenge of Polaris', p. 343.
134 'R.G.H.', 'The Nuclear Attack Submarine', p. 23; PRO, DEFE 69/354, loose minute N/5.50218/68, 8 April 1968; J. Winton, 'Have Polaris, Will Travel', *Naval Review*, vol. LX (1972), p. 236.
135 *HMS Courageous* was rebuilt into an aircraft carrier in the 1920s.
136 RNSubM, A1950/5, letter from Capt SM1 (at Malta) to FOSM, 15 May 1958.
137 Both battleships had been hard fighting members of the Mediterranean Fleet and at different times Admiral 'ABC' Cunningham's flagship.

NOTES   283

138 Colledge, *Ships*, p. 341; Manning, & Walker, *British Warship*, pp. 463–464.
139 Colledge, *Ships*, p. 353; Manning & Walker, *British Warship*, pp. 480–481.
140 PRO, DEFE 69/325, loose minute, 8 February 1965.
141 Ibid. letter from PS Minister (RN) to Sec State for Defence, 14 April 1965.
142 PRO, DEFE 69/325, loose minute, 8 February 1965; loose minute 25 February 1965; letter from PS Minister (RN) to Sec State for Defence, 14 April 1965; letter from PS Sec State for Defence to PS Minister (RN), 22 April 1965.
143 Ibid. letter from PS Sec State for Defence to PS Minister (RN), 22 April 1965.
144 Ibid. letter from PS Minister (RN) to PS to Sec of State Defence, 7 May 1965; letter from PS Minister (RN) to Head of Mat.1 (N), 19 May 1965.
145 PRO, ADM 1/26779, loose minute, 26 September 1958.
146 PRO, DEFE 69/354, loose minute N/5 50218/68, 9 April 1968.
147 Colledge, *Ships*, pp. 304, 312, 317.
148 Ibid. pp. 290, 306.
149 Ibid. pp. 318, 327, 328, 332, 334, 336.
150 Ibid. p. 334.
151 Lt Cdr Wanklyn, *HMS Upholder*; Cdr Miers, *HMS Torbay*; Lt Cdr Linton, *HMS Turbulent*; W Jameson, *Submariners VC*, (Penzance, 2002), chapters 7, 9 and 10.
152 *Navy News*, May 1997, p. 6.
153 Ibid.

Chapter Six

1   G. Orwell, *Collected Journalism and Letters* (London, 1970), p. 528.
2   House of Commons session 1990–91, Defence Committee Sixth Report: Royal Navy Submarines, 12 June 1991 (London, 1991), p. vi.
3   IWM, ADM 76/8/1, papers of W. G. Roberts.
4   Paris, *Warrior Nation*.
5   Orwell, *Collected Journalism and Letters*, p. 528.
6   Paris, *Warrior Nation*.
7   B. Klein, 'Britain and the Sea', in B. Klein (ed), *Fictions of the Sea. Critical perspectives on the ocean in British literature and culture* (Aldershot, 2002), p. 9; J. Peck, *Maritime Fiction. Sailors and the sea in British and American Novels, 1719–1917* (London, 2001), p. 14.
8   Peck, *Maritime Fiction*, p. 14.
9   H. Innes, *Wreckers Must Breathe* (London, 1940).
10 A. MacLean, *Night Without End* (London, 1959).
11 H. Innes, *Great Sea Novels* (London, 1978), p. 9.
12 MacLean, *Night Without End*, p. 197.
13 A. MacLean, *Ice Station Zebra* (London, 1973), pp. 9–23.
14 MacLean, *Ice Station Zebra*, p. 32.
15 B. Callison, *A Flock Of Ships* (London, 1970).
16 J. Pattinson, *Last In Convoy* (London, 1957).
17 Other examples include B. Burland, *A Fall from Aloft* (London, 1987); B. Callison, *The Bone Collectors. A novel of the Atlantic Convoys* (London, 1984); A. Trew, *Kleber's Convoy* (Long Preston, 1981).

18 E. Gray, *Fighting Submarine* (London, 1978); D. Reeman, *Go In And Sink* (London, 1973), pp. 74–80; J. Wingate, *Submarine* (London, 1982), pp. 2, 12, 40, 41.
19 P. Westerman, *A Sub And A Submarine* (London, 1919), p. 219.
20 Ibid.
21 Ibid.
22 X craft were midget submarines that were armed with limpet mines that were attached to the side of a warship while in harbour or large explosive charges that were laid on the bottom of the harbour underneath a target, but they were not armed with torpedoes.
23 A. Fullerton, *The Waiting Game* (London, 1961); G. Jenkins, *A Twist Of Sand* (London, 1961); D. Reeman, *Dive In The Sun* (London, 1961); G. Hackforth-Jones, *Danger Below* (London, 1963); C. MacHardy, *Send Down A Dove* (London, 1968); Gray, *Fighting Submarine*; D. Reeman, *Strike From The Sea* (London, 1978); E. Gray, *Diving Stations* (London, 1980); E. Gray, *Crash Dive 500* (London, 1981); E. Collenette *Ninety Feet To The Sun*, (London, 1984); D. Reeman, *Surface With Daring* (London, 1976).
24 Commando No 1409, *Into Danger* (London, 1980), p. 19.
25 Battle No 99 *One Way To Die* (London, undated).
26 *We Dive at Dawn*, dir. A. Asquith, 1943.
27 M. Dawson, *Fathoms Deep* (London, 1943), pp. 27–31
28 J. Ramsden 'Refocusing "The People's War": British War Films if the 1950s', *Journal of Contemporary History*, vol. 33 (1998), p. 59.
29 E. Ansty, 'The Cinema', *The Spectator*, 170 (1943), p. 499.
30 *Kinematograph Weekly*, 1 July 1943, p. 20.
31 J. Chapman, *The British At War* (London, 1998), p. 129; R. Murphy, *British Cinema and the Second World War* (London, 2000), pp. 129–130.
32 Gray, *Diving Stations*, pp. 7–8.
33 Ibid.
34 I. McGeoch, *An Affair Of Chances* (London, 1991), p. 52.
35 Wingate, *Submarine*, p. 3.
36 Ibid.
37 Ibid., pp. 38–41.
38 J. Winton *Down The Hatch*, (Liskeard, 2004), p. 67.
39 PRO, ADM 1/20414, Submarines: Possibilities as Fighters, TAWS 289/47(2), dated November 47; ADM 1/23729, FOSM's 705/sm.068.M, dated 8 September 1952; ADM 1/25252, M/TASW 289/47 quoted in C-in-C Home Fleet of Admiralty 'Submarine War Plans', dated 4 January 1951; ADM 1/25252 Submarine V Submarine Trials; E. Grove, *Vanguard to Trident*, (London, 1987), pp. 219, 223–224; Hackmann, *Seek and Strike*, p. 354; Llewellyn-Jones, 'A Flawed Contender', pp. 58–67; Winton, *Down The Hatch*, pp. 62, 73–85.
40 Winton, *Down The Hatch*, pp. 80–85.
41 E. Gray, *U-Boat. Action Atlantic* (London, 1975), p. 117.
42 K. Bulmer, *Sea Wolf: Shark America* (London, 1981), pp. 2–5; K. Bulmer, *Sea Wolf: Shark Raid* (London, 1982), pp. 14–17;

NOTES 285

43 M. Catto, *Murphy's War* (London, 1969), pp. 70–77; J. Follett, *U-700* (London, 1979), pp. 7–9; G. Griffin, *An Operational Necessity* (London, 1968), p. 21; J. MacGregor, *When The Ship Sank* (London, 1960), pp. 52–61; D. Reeman, *With Blood And Iron* (London, 1964), pp. 51–53, 182–184; A. Trew, *Yashimoto's Last Dive* (London, 1986), pp. 39–40.
44 K. Bulmer, *Sea Wolf: Steel Shark* (London, 1979), pp. 5–11.
45 B. Callison, *Trapp's War* (Bolton-By-Bowland, 1978), p. 184–185; J. Wingate, *Frigate* (London, 1982), pp. 212–214; Wingate, *Carrier*, pp. 74, 81, 87, 119–123.
46 Reeman, *With Blood*, pp. 51–53.
47 Ibid. pp. 182–4.
48 J. Lehnhoff, trans. L. Wilson, *The Homeward Run* (London, 1957), p. 84.
49 Gray, *Diving Stations*, p. 141.
50 Westerman, *A Sub*, p. 220.
51 Ibid.
52 Semmel, *Liberalism & Naval Strategy*, pp. 53–56, 63, 68–83, 110, 157.
53 P. Westerman, *The Keepers Of The Narrow Seas. A Story of the Great War* (London, 1931).
54 Catto, *Murphy's War*, pp. 77–82.
55 A. Chatham, *Sea Sting* (London, 1982), p. 113.
56 PRO, INF 1/213 Western Approaches, File F/256/453 Western Approaches Shooting Script, p. 5.
57 A. Trew, *Yashimoto's Last Dive* (London, 1986), pp. 44–45.
58 Commando No 2458 *U-boat Curse* (London, undated), p. 8; Commando No 3019 *Killer Sub* (London, 1997), p. 9; War Picture Library No 137, *Up Periscope* (London, undated), p. 18.
59 Commando No 3019 *Killer Sub* (London, undated), p. 9.
60 Westerman, *A Sub*, pp. 222–228
61 A. Fullerton, *Surface* (London, 1953), pp. 74–75.
62 Ibid. p. 79.
63 Ibid. 26–27, 44.
64 W. Gage, *The Cruel Coast* (London, 1967), p. 137.
65 Reeman, *With Blood*, p. i; similar sentiments were expressed by Monsarrat in *Three Corvettes*, pp. 278–279: 'The convention that whereas we had submarines (noble and skilful), the hated Hun actually used U-boats (wicked and treacherous) was still a persistent gloss on history, continued from 1914.'
66 Reeman, *With Blood*, p. i.
67 Griffin, *Operational Necessity*, p. 215.
68 Paris, *Warrior Nation*, p. 68.
69 Ibid. 232–235.
70 See Gray, *Fighting Submarine*; *Devil Flotilla* (London, 1979); *Diving Stations*; *Crash Dive 500*.
71 Paris, *Warrior Nation*, pp. 232–235.
72 N. Monsarrat, *The Cruel Sea* (London, 2002), p. 279.
73 Ibid. p. 282.
74 Ibid. pp. 287–292.
75 Ibid. p. 286.
76 Ibid. p. 298.

77 MacGregor, *When The Ship Sank*, pp. 52–61
78 L. Delap, '"Thus Does Man Prove His Fitness to Be the Master of Things": Shipwrecks, Chivalry and Masculinities in Nineteenth- and Twentieth-Century Britain', *Cultural and Social History*, vol. 3 (2006), pp. 49–52, 57–58; Paris, *Warrior Nation*, p. 29.
79 MacGregor, *When The Ship Sank*, p. 76.
80 Ibid. p. 65.
81 Ibid. p. 218.
82 Callison, *The Bone Collectors*, pp. 219–227; MacGregor, *When The Ship Sank*, pp. 52–61, 65; Monsarrat, *The Cruel Sea*, pp. 282, 287–292.
83 Monsarrat, *The Cruel Sea*, pp. 280–1.
84 C. Day Lewis (ed.), *The Collected Poems of Wilfred Owen* (London, 1963), p. 55.
85 Bulmer, *Steel Shark*; K. Bulmer, *Sea Wolf: Shark Pack* (London, 1980); Bulmer, *Shark America*; K. Bulmer, *Sea Wolf: Shark Africa* (London, 1981); K. Bulmer, *Sea Wolf: Shark Trap* (London, 1983); Gray, *Action Atlantic*; E. Gray, *Tokyo Torpedo* (London, 1977).
86 Bulmer, *Shark America*, p. 3.
87 Ibid. p. 54.
88 Griffin, *Operational Necessity*, p. 284.
89 Bulmer, *Shark Pack*, p. 65.
90 Bulmer, *Shark Trap*, p. 19.
91 Bulmer, *Steel Shark*, p. 26.
92 Bulmer, *Shark America*, p. 6.
93 Gray, *Action Atlantic*, p. 213.
94 Ibid. p. 123.
95 See Jenkins, *Twist of Sand*, MacLean, *Ice Station Zebra* or Innes, *Wreckers Must Breathe*.
96 Fullerton, *Surface*; Fullerton, *Waiting Game*; Hackforth-Jones, *Danger Below*; K. Poolman, *Wolf-Pack* (London, 1959); D. Reeman, *Dive in the Sun* (London, 1961); B. Wilkinson, *Proceed at Will* (London, 1957)
97 Gray, *Tokyo Torpedo*, p. 100.
98 Bulmer, *Shark Africa*, p. 26.
99 Chatham, *Sea Sting*, pp. 38–40, 110.
100 J. Wood, 'Captive Historians, Captivated Audience: The German Military History Program, 1945–1961', *The Journal Of Military History*, vol. 69 (2005), pp. 127.
101 Paris, *Warrior Nation*, p. 69.
102 *Kinematograph Weekly*, 23 February 1950, p. 17.
103 Ibid. p. 18.
104 J. Wolffe, *Great Deaths: Grieving, Religion, and Nationhood in Victorian and Edwardian Britain* (Oxford, 2000), p. 261.
105 Monsarrat, *The Cruel Sea*, p. 10.
106 Ibid. p. 235.
107 'She' rather than 'it' is the manner in which a sailor, as Monsarrat was, would refer to a ship. It is possible that the use of 'she' is merely an author's slip.
108 Reeman, *With Blood*, p. i.
109 Catto, *Murphy's War*, p. 31.

110 Westerman, *Keepers*, pp. 127, 97, 115.
111 Ibid. p. 127.
112 Ibid. p. 131.
113 P. Westerman, *The Pirate Submarine* (London, 1923).
114 Ibid. p. 45.
115 Ibid.
116 Fullerton, *The Waiting Game*, p. 67.
117 Gray, *Tokyo Torpedo*, p. 189.
118 Ramsden, 'British War Films', pp. 38–39.
119 K. Worpole, *Dockers and Detectives* (London, 1983), p. 49.
120 *The Cruel Sea* was reviewed in *Books on Trial*, Oct 1951, *Punch*, Jan 1971, Jul 1981 (and indeed other editions have been extensively reviewed although not noted as such in the PCI); *Send Down a Dove*, was reviewed in *The RUSI Journal*, Nov 1968; *An Operational Necessity* was reviewed in *The New Statesman*, May 1968, *Punch*, May 1968, *The RUSI Journal*, May 1968; *A Fall From Aloft*, was reviewed by the *New Statesman* and *Punch* magazines in 1968.
121 *RUSI*, vol. 113 (1968), p. 171
122 Ibid.
123 Ibid.
124 *Times*, 4 April 1955, p. 6.
125 V. Graham, 'Cinema', *The Spectator*, vol. 194 (1955), p. 339.
126 W. Whitebait, 'Nature Concerto', *The New Statesman*, vol. 49 (1955), p. 535.
127 Graham, *The Spectator*, vol. 194 (1955), p. 392; Whitebait, *The New Statesman*, vol. 49 (1955), p. 534.
128 E. Ansty, 'The Cinema', *The Spectator*, vol. 170 (1943), p. 499.
129 Ibid.
130 *Kinematograph Weekly*, 22 April 1943, p. 29.
131 *Times*, 20 May 1943, p. 6.
132 D. Powell, *Films Since 1939* (London, 1947), p. 30.
133 *Kinematograph Weekly*, 22 April 1943, p. 24.
134 *Kinematograph Weekly*, 5 August 1943, p. 35.
135 *Kinematograph Weekly*, 1 July 1943, p. 20.
136 *Times*, 23 June 1943, p. 6.
137 P. MacKenzie, *British War Films 1939–1945. The Cinema and the Services* (London, 2001), p. 84; J. Mills, *Up in the Clouds Gentlemen Please* (London, 2001), p. 215.
138 MacKenzie, *British War Films*, p. 83; see also PRO, INF 1/292, Home Intelligence Unit Reports.
139 Chapman, *British At War*, p. 133.
140 *Times*, 23 June 1943, p. 6.
141 J. Richards, 'National Identity in British War Films', in P. M. Taylor (ed.), *Britain and the Cinema in the Second World War* (Basingstoke, 1988), p. 58
142 Ibid.
143 MacKenzie, *British War Films*, p. 85.
144 Chapman, *The British At War*, p. 187.
145 *Kinematograph Weekly*, 17 December 1953, p. 10; *Kinematograph Weekly*, 15 December 1955.

146 N. Rattigan, 'The Last Gasp of the Middle Class: British War Films of the 1950s', in W. W. Dixon, (ed.) *Re-viewing British Cinema 1900–1992* (New York, 1994), p. 148.
147 Ibid. p. 149.

BIBLIOGRAPHY

MANUSCRIPT COLLECTIONS

The British Library, London
Add MSS [Balfour Papers]
Keyes papers

Cambridgeshire Country Records Office
C. P. Alix Papers
Parish Records, Swaffham Prior

Churchill College, Cambridge
Churchill Papers
Fisher Papers

The Hampshire Naval Collection, Hampshire County Council, Gosport Library, Gosport, Hampshire
Anon, *Silver Jubilee Fleet Review Official Souvenir Programme*
Critchely, M. *Silver Jubilee Review 24–29 June 1977 for HM Queen Elizabeth II*

The Imperial War Museum
Papers of W. G. Roberts

The Institute of Historical Research
Admiralty NID No 676 'Submarines and the Naval Policy of England Translated from the Revue Maritime October 1902', *Papers on Naval Subjects 1903*, vol. I

The London School of Economics
Campaign For Nuclear Disarmament papers [CND 1, CND 3, CND 7, CND 10, CND 11, CND add 5, CND add 9]

The National Maritime Museum, London
Papers of Sir Terrance Eustace d'Enycourt
A4299 Naval Review at Spithead 1937. Programme of Special Rail and Steamer arrangements from London
N4065 Coronation of HM King George V. Programme of facilities for witnessing the Royal Naval Review 1911 by Thos Cook & Son
Ships Covers
Harrison, A. N. *BR3043 The Development of HM Submarines From Holland No. 1 (1901) to Porpoise (1930)* (Ministry of Defence (Ships Dept), 1976)

The Naval Historical Branch, Ministry of Defence
Anon, *A List of His Majesty's Ships in Commission. January 1911*, (London, HMSO, 1910)
Ea03, *Grand Fleet Battle Orders* vols. I–III
Eb06, Admiralty, Intelligence Division. No 817. 'Great Britain Naval Manoeuvres 1906', dated May 1907 in *British Naval Manoeuvres*, vol. IV
Eb181, Admiralty Mobilisation Department, *Great Britain Naval Manoeuvres 1910*
BR 1806(47) *Naval War Manual 1947*
CB 3306(1) *Naval Staff History, Second World War, Submarines* (London: Admiralty, 1953)
CB 3306(2) *Naval Staff History, Second World War, British Submarines in the Mediterranean* (London: Admiralty, 1955)
CB 3306(3) *Naval Staff History, Second World War, British Submarines in the Far East* (London: Admiralty, 1956)
OU 5316 *Naval Prize Manual,* dated September 1923
P340, CB 01360 *Ruthless Submarine Warfare. German Orders For*, dated October 1917
T6594-T6616 London Naval Conference 1930

The Peace Pledge Union, London
PPU Pamphlets 1936–1940

The Public Record Office, London

Atomic Energy Authority papers [AB 16, AB 45]
Admiralty papers [ADM 1, ADM 116, ADM 137, ADM 167, ADM 178, ADM 179, ADM 186, ADM 204, ADM 205, ADM 219, ADM 239, ADM 256, ADM 279, ADM 280, ADM 281]
Air Ministry and Air Staff papers [AIR 20]
Cabinet Office papers [CAB 4, CAB 21, CAB 62, CAB 65, CAB 131]
Prints and negatives [CN 11]
Ministry of Defence papers [DEFE 2, DEFE 7, DEFE 13, DEFE 24, DEFE 25, DEFE 48, DEFE 67, DEFE 69]
Papers extracted from other series [EXT 1, EXT 3]
Foreign and Commonwealth Office papers [FCO 41, FO 93, FO 177, FO 371]
Home Office papers [HO 325]
Ministry of Information papers [INF 1, INF 2, INF 3]
Prime Minsters' papers [PREM 1, PREM 3, PREM 11, PREM 13]
British Railway Board (and predecessors) papers [RAIL 253, RAIL 311, RAIL 411]
HM Treasury papers [T 225]
War Office papers [WO 32]

Portsmouth Record Office

Postcards

The Royal Naval Museum Library, Portsmouth

V310, Review of the Fleet by HM King 31 July 1909
V310, 20th Anniversary Review of NATO Navies by HM Queen Elizabeth II Operations Order
V310, Silver Jubilee Review Orders dated 2 May 1977

The Royal Navy Submarine Museum, Gosport

Rear Admiral Submarines registry files
'Devastator' comments by M. Horton in 'Progress in the Atlantic Fleet' No 21/74, 3 Jan 1923 [A1923/11]
Submarines and their employment, Royal Navy Staff College Greenwich, by Capt C. B. Barry DSO RN [A1930/21/004]
Papers of the late Chief Engine Room Artificer J. G. Harris [A1983/072]
Draft 1939 RUSI Journal article by (then) Lt I. McGeoch RN [A1991/409]

Papers of the late Cdr C. B. Mills DSC RN [A1997/107]

Unpublished Theses

Dash, M. *British Submarine Policy 1853–1918* (PhD thesis, University of London, 1990)

Grenwood, I. R. *After Munich: Strategic Priorities in British Rearmament, October 1938–August 1939* (MPhil thesis, University of London, 1995)

Henry, D. *British Submarine Development and Policy 1918–1939* (PhD thesis, University of London, 1976)

Lambert, N. *The Influence of the Submarine Upon Naval Strategic Thinking 1898–1914* (PhD thesis, University of Oxford, 1992)

Llewellyn-Jones, M. *The Royal Navy on the Threshold of Modern Anti-Submarine Warfare 1944–1949* (PhD thesis, University of London, 2004)

Røksund, A. *The Jeune École: The Strategy of the Weak* (Dr. Art thesis, University of Oslo)

Ruger, J. *The Celebration of the Fleet in Britain and Germany 1897–1914* (PhD thesis, University of Cambridge)

PUBLISHED MATERIAL

Periodicals and Newspapers consulted

Army and Navy Gazette
Birmingham Daily Mail
Birmingham Post
Blackwood's Magazine
Broadsheet
Bystander Magazine
Daily Express
Daily Mail
Daily Mirror
Daily Telegraph
Evening Standard
Evening News
Fortnightly Review
Guardian
Hampshire Advertiser County Newspaper
Hampshire Telegraph and Naval Chronicle

Illustrated London News
Kinematograph Weekly
Manchester Guardian
Monthly Review
Morning Post
Naval Review
Navy List
New Statesman and Nation
Nineteenth Century
Parliamentary Debates
Peace News
Punch
Saturday Review
Spectator
Sun
Sunday Telegraph
The Listener
The Nation
The Times
Times Literary Supplement

Books

Ackermann, P. *Encyclopaedia of British Submarines 1901–1955* (Penzance, 1989)
Anon, *The Navy List for July 1902, corrected to the 18th June 1902* (London, 1902)
Anscomb, C. *Submariner* (London, 1957)
Ashplant, T. G. & Smyth, G. *Explorations in Cultural History* (London, 2001)
Austin, R. *Images of the Dance* (London, 1975)
Bacon, R. *The Life of Lord Fisher of Kilverstone* (London, 1929)
———, *From 1900 Onwards* (London, 1940)
Bagnasco, E. *Submarines of World War Two* (London, 1977)
Barnett, C. *The Audit Of War. The Illusion and Reality of Britain as a Great Nation* (Basingstoke, 1987)
———, *The Lost Victory: British Dreams, British Realities 1945–1950* (London, 1995)
———, *Engage The Enemy More Closely* (London, 1991)
———, *The Verdict of Peace. Britain Between Her Yesterday and the Future* (London, 2002)

Bartlett, C. J. *The Long Retreat* (London, 1972)
Basinger, J. *The World War II Combat Film: Anatomy of a Genre* (New York, 1986)
Bassett, R. *The Tinfish Run* (London, 1978)
Bateman, C. T. *U-Boat Devilry. Illustrating the Heroism and Endurance of Merchant Seamen* (London, 1918)
Battle No 99, *One Way To Die* (London, undated).
Behrman, C. F. *Victorian Myths of the Sea* (Athens: OH, 1977)
Bell, C. M. *The Royal Navy Seapower and Strategy between the Wars* (London, 2000)
Bennett, G. *Charlie B* (London, 1968)
Beresford, Lord C. *The Memoirs of Admiral Lord Charles Beresford* (London, 1914)
Best, G. *Humanity in Warfare* (London, 1980)
Bialer, U. *The Shadow of the Bomber. The Fear of Air Attack and British Politics 1932–1939* (London, 1980)
Biddle, T. D. *Rhetoric and Reality* (Princeton: NY, 2002)
Billig, M. *Banal Nationalism* (London, 1995)
Blackman, R. V. B. (ed) *Janes Fighting Ships 1953–54* (London, 1953).
———, *Janes Fighting Ships 1966–67* (London, 1966)
Blanning, T. C. W. *The Culture of Power and the Power of Culture, Old Regime Europe 1660–1789* (Oxford, 2002)
Bond, B. & Roy, I. (eds) *War and Society* (London, 1975).
Boniface, P. *Dreadnought. Britain's First Nuclear Powered Submarine* (Penzance, 2003)
Bonnell, V. E. & Hunt, L. (eds) *Beyond the Cultural Turn* (London, 1999)
Brassey, T. A. (ed) *The Naval Annual 1898* (Portsmouth, 1898).
Breisach, E. *Historiography: Ancient, Medieval and Modern* 2nd edn (London, 1994)
Bridge, Adm Sir C. *The Art of Naval Warfare: Introductory Observations* (London, 1907)
———, *Sea Power and Other Studies* (London, 1910)
Brown, D. K. *The Future British Surface Fleet. Options for medium-sized navies* (London, 1991)
———, *Warrior to Dreadnought* (London, 1997)
———, *The Grand Fleet. Warship Design and Development 1906–1922* (London, 1999)
Brown, M. B. *The Imperial War Museum Book of The Western Front* (London, 2003)
Bulmer, K. *Sea Wolf: Steel Shark* (London, 1979)

———, *Sea Wolf: Shark North* (London, 1979
———, *Sea Wolf: Shark Hunt* (London, 1980)
———, *Sea Wolf: Shark Pack* (London, 1980)
———, *Sea Wolf: Shark Africa* (London, 1981)
———, *Sea Wolf: Shark America* (London, 1981)
———, *Sea Wolf: Shark Raid* (London, 1982)
———, *Sea Wolf: Shark Trap* (London, 1983)
Burgoyne, A. H. *Submarine Navigation Past and Present* 2 vols. (London, 1903)
Burke, P. *The French Historical Revolution: The Annales School 1929–89* (Cambridge, 1990)
———, *History and Social Theory* (Cambridge, 1992)
———, *Varieties of Cultural History* (Oxford, 1997)
———, *New Perspectives on Historical Writing* 2nd edn (Cambridge, 2001)
———, *What is Cultural History* (Cambridge, 2004)
Burland, B. *A Fall From Aloft* (London, 1987)
Byrne, P. *The Campaign for Nuclear Disarmament* (London, 1988)
Cable, J. *Britain's Naval Future* (London, 1983)
Cain, P. & Hopkins, A. G. *British Imperialism: Innovation and Expansion 1688–1914* (London, 1993)
Callison, B. *A Flock of Ships* (London, 1970)
———, *A Frenzy of Merchantmen* (London, 1977)
———, *Trapp's War* (Bolton-by-Bowland, 1978)
———, *The Judas Ship* (Long Preston, 1981)
———, *The Bone Collectors. A novel of the Atlantic Convoys* (London, 1984)
Calvocoressi, P. *The British Experience 1945–75* (London, 1978)
Carew, A. *The Lower Deck of the Royal Navy 1900–39* (Manchester, 1981).
Carter, A. (ed) *The Routledge Dance Studies Reader* (London, 1998).
Catto, M. *Murphy's War* (London, 1969)
Ceadel, M. *Semi-Detached Realists. The British Peace Movement and International Relations, 1854–1945* (Oxford, 2000)
Cecil, H. *The Flower of Battle. How Britain Wrote the Great War* (South Royalton: VT, 1996)
Chapman, J. *The British At War* (London, 1998)
Charlton, L. E. O. *War From the Air* (London, 1935)
———, *War Over England* (London, 1937)
Chatham, A. *Sea Sting* (London, 1982)
Chew, S. C. & Knottnerous, J. D. *Structure, Culture and History* (Lanham: MA, 2002)

Churchill, W. S. *The World Crisis* vol. II (London, 1938)
Clancy, T. *The Hunt for Red October* (London, 1986)
Clarke, I. F. *The Tale of the Future* (London, 1961)
——, *Voices Prophesising War 1763–1984* (London, 1966)
Cobden, R. *The Political Writings of Richard Cobden* vol. II (London, 1903)
Coetzee, F. *For Party or Country. Nationalism and the Dilemmas of Popular Conservatism in Edwardian England* (Oxford, 1990)
Cohen, S. J. *International Encyclopaedia of Dance* (Oxford, 1998).
Colledge, J. J. rev Warlow, Lt Cdr B. *Ships of the Royal Navy. The Complete Record of all Fighting Ships of the Royal Navy From the Fifteenth Century To The Present* (London, 2003)
Collenette, E. J. *Ninety Feet To The Sun* (London, 1984)
Collingwood, H. *The Log of the Flying Fish* (London, 1894)
——, *With Airship and Submarine* (London, 1908)
Collini, S. Whatmore, R. & Young, B. (eds) *History, Religion and Culture, British intellectual History 1750–1950* (Cambridge, 2000)
Colls, R. *Identity of England* (Oxford, 2002)
Colomb, P. *Essays on Naval Defence* (London, 1893)
Commando No 1409, *Into Danger* (London, 1980)
Compton-Hall, R. *Submarine Warfare – Monsters and Midgets* (Poole, 1985)
——, *Submarines and the War at Sea 1914–1918* (London, 1991)
——, *The Submarine Pioneers* (Stroud, 1999)
Connelly, M. *Reaching For The Stars. A New History of Bomber Command* (London, 2001)
Coopey, R., Fielding, S., Tiratsoo, N. (eds) *The Wilson Government 1964–1970* (London, 1993)
Coote, J. *Submariner* (London, 1991)
Copeland, R. & Cohen, M. (eds) *What is Dance?* (Oxford, 1983)
Corbett, J. S. *Some Principles of Maritime Strategy* (London, 1911)
——, *England in the Seven Years' War* vol. II (London, 1907, facsimile edn. 1992)
Corbin, T. W. *The Romance of Submarine Engineering* (London, 1913)
Corrigan, G. *Mud, Blood and Poppycock* (London, 2004)
Cubitt, G. & Warren, A. *Heroic Reputations and Exemplary Lives* (Manchester, 2000)
Darnton, R. *The Great Cat Massacre And Other Episodes in French Cultural History* (London, 2001)
Daunton, M. & Rieger, B. *Meanings of Modernity. Britain from the late-Victorian Era to World War II* (Oxford, 2001)

Daunton, M. *Trusting Leviathan. The Politics of Taxation in Britain 1799–1914* (Cambridge, 2001)
——, *Just Taxes. The Politics of Taxation in Britain 1914–1979* (Cambridge, 2002
Davies, R. W. & Helmstadter, J. R. *Religion and Irreligion in Victorian Society* (London, 1992)
Davis, R. *Nautilus: The Story of Man Under the Sea* (London, 1995)
Dawson, M. *Fathoms Deep* (London, 1943)
Day Lewis, C. (ed) *The Collected Poems of Wilfred Owen* (London, 1963)
Defence Committee Sixth Report, *Royal Navy Submarines* (London, 1991)
Devereux, G. R. M. *The Lover's Guide to Courtship and Marriage* (London, 1903)
Dixon, Professor N. *On the Psychology of Military Incompetence* (London, 1976).
Dixon, W. W. (ed) *Re-viewing British Cinema 1900–1992* (Albany: NY, 1994)
Domville-Fife, C. *Submarines of the World's Navies* (London, 1910)
——, *Submarines, Mines and Torpedoes in the War* (London, 1914)
Edmonds, M. (ed.) *100 Years of the Trade: Royal Navy Submarines, Past Present and Future* (Lancaster, 2001)
Eksteins, M. *The Rites of Spring: The Great War and the Birth of the Modern Age* (London, 1989).
Elliott, P. *Allied Escort Ships of World War II: A Complete Survey* (Annapolis: MD, 1980),
Ellis, J. *The Social History of the Machine Gun* (London, 1975)
Ensor, Sir R. *England 1870–1914* (London, 1936)
Everitt, D. *K Boats Steam-powered submarines in World War I* (Shrewsbury, 1999)
Fayle, C. E. *Seaborne Trade* vol. II (London, 1923)
Feuchtwanger, E. J. *Democracy and Empire, Britain 1865–1914* (London, 1985)
Field, Lt Col C. *The Story of the Submarine* (London, 1908)
Field, F. *British and French Writers of the First World War: Comparative Studies in Cultural History* (Cambridge, 1991)
Flack, J. *100 Years of Royal Navy Submarines* (Shrewsbury, 2002)
Floud, R. & McCloskey, D. *The Economic History of Britain Since 1700* vol. II (London, 1981)
Follett, J. *U-700* (London, 1979)

Franklin, G. *Britain's Anti-Submarine Capability 1919–1939* (London, 2003)
Friedman, N. *Submarine Design And Development* (London, 1974)
——, *British Carrier Aviation: The Evolution of the Ships and Their Aircraft* (London, 1988)
Frost, W. *German Submarine Warfare* (London, 1918)
Fullerton, A. *Surface* (London, 1953)
——, *The Waiting Game* (London, 1961)
Fussell, P. *The Great War and Modern Memory* (London, 1977)
——, *Wartime: Understanding Behaviour in the Second World War* (Oxford, 1989)
Fyfe, H. C. *Submarine Warfare Past, Present and Future* (London, 1902)
Gage, W. *The Cruel Coast* (London, 1967)
Gardiner, L. *The British Admiralty* (London, 1968)
Garrett, S. A. *Ethics and Airpower In World War II: The British Bombing of German Cities* (London, 1997)
Gat, A. *A History of Military Thought: From the Enlightenment to the Cold War* (Oxford, 2001)
Geertz, C. *The Interpretation of Cultures* (New York, 2000)
Gillis, J. R. *The Militarization of the Western World* (New Brunswick, 1989)
——, *Commemorations: The Politics of National Identity* (Princeton: NJ, 1994)
Ginsbury, B. W. (ed) *The Visit of the Fleet to the Thames July 17th to 24th* (London, 1909)
Girouard, M. *The Return to Camelot. Chivalry and the English Gentleman* (London, 1981)
Gordon, A. *The Rules of the Game* (London, 2000)
Grant, W. *Pressure Groups and British Politics* (London, 2000)
Gray, C. S. & Barnett, R. W. (eds) *Seapower and Strategy* (London, 1989)
Gray, E. *U-Boat: Action Atlantic* (London, 1975)
——, *Tokyo Torpedo* (London, 1977)
——, *Fighting Submarine* (London, 1978)
——, *The Last Command* (London, 1978)
——, *Devil Flotilla* (London, 1979)
——, *Diving Stations* (London, 1980)
——, *Crash Dive 500* (London, 1981)
Gray, E. *British Submarines In The Great War. A damned un-English weapon* (London, 2001)

Green, E. H. H. *The Crisis of Conservatism. The Politics, economics and ideology of the British Conservative Party, 1880–1914* (London, 1996)
Grenfell, Cdr R, *Sea Power in the Next War* (London, 1938)
Griffin, J. *Glass Houses and Modern War* (London, 1938)
Griffin, G. *An Operational Necessity* (London, 1968)
Griffith, G. *The Stolen Submarine: A Tale of the Russo-Japanese War* (London, 1904)
Griffith, P. *Battle Tactics of the Western Front: The British Army's Art of Attack 1916–18* (London, 1994).
Grigg, J. *Lloyd George. The People's Champion 1902–1911* (London, 2002)
Grove, E. *Vanguard to Trident* (Annapolis: MA, 1987)
——, *The Future of Sea Power* (London, 1990)
Groves, P. R. C. *Our Future in the Air: A Survey of the Vital Questions of British Air Power* (London, 1922)
——, *Behind the Smoke Screen* (London, 1934)
Hackforth-Jones, G. *Danger Below* (London, 1963)
Hackmann, W. *Seek and Strike* (London, 1984).
Hadley M. L. *Count Not the Dead. The Popular Image of the German Submarine* (Montreal, 1995)
Hague, A. *The Allied Convoy System 1939–1945* (St Catherines: Ontario, 2000)
Hampshire, A. C. *The Royal Navy Since 1945: Its Transition to the Nuclear Age* (London, 1975)
Hardy, R. *Longbow: A Social and Military History* (Sparkford, 1992)
Harootunian, H. *History's Disquiet: Modernity, Cultural Practice and the Question of Everyday Life* (New York, 2000)
Harris, J. *Private Lives, Public Spirit* (London, 1994)
Harvey, D. *The Condition of Postmodernity. An Enquiry into the Origins of Cultural Change* (Oxford, 1990)
Hattendorf, J. B. & Jordan, R. S. (eds) *Maritime Strategy and the Balance of Power* (London, 1989)
Healey, D. *The Time of My Life* (London, 1989)
Henry, J. *Submarines* (London, 1994)
Hessler, G. *The U-boat War in the Atlantic* (London, 1989)
Hezlet, Vice Admiral Sir A. *British and Allied Submarine Operations in World War II* 2 vols. (Gosport, 2001)
Hill, Rear Admiral J. R. *Maritime Strategy For Medium Powers* (London, 1986)
Hill-Norton, Lord & Dekker, J. *Sea Power* (London, 1982)

Hills, G. A. B. *Official Programme of the Silver Jubilee Review of the Fleet* (Portsmouth, 1935)
Hobsbawm, E. & Ranger, T. (eds) *The Invention of Tradition* (Cambridge, 1983)
Hodges, P. *Airfix Magazine Guide 7: Warship Modelling* (Cambridge, 1975)
Horst, K. *Caribbean Pirate* (London, 1982)
Hough, R. *The Great War at Sea* (Edinburgh, 2000)
Howard, M. *War and the Liberal Conscience* (London, 1986)
Howe, A. *Free Trade and Liberal England 1846–1946* (Oxford, 1997)
Hughes, T. P. *Human-Built World. How to think about technology and culture* (Chicago: IL, 2004)
Humble, R. *Undersea Warfare* (London, 1981)
——, *The Rise and fall of the British Navy* (London, 1986)
Hunt, B. D. *Sailor – Scholar: Admiral Sir Herbert Richmond 1871–1946* (Waterloo: Ontario, 1982)
Hunt, L. (ed) *The New Cultural History* (London, 1989)
Hurd, A. S. *Naval Efficiency: The War-Readiness of the Fleet* (London, 1902)
——, *The British Fleet in The Great War* (London, 1918)
——, *Ordeal By Sea. The Story of the British Seaman's Fight for Freedom* (London, 1919)
Hyam, R. *Britain's Imperial Century, 1815–1914. A Study of Empire and Expansion* 3rd edn (Basingstoke, 2002)
Hynes, S. *A War Imagined* (London, 1990)
Innes, H. *Great Sea Novels* (London, 1978)
James, Admiral Sir W. M. *The Influence of Sea Power on the History of the British People* (Cambridge, 1948
Jameson, W. *The Most Formidable Thing* (London, 1965)
——, *Submariners VC* (Penzance, 2002)
Jane, F. T. (ed) *Fighting Ships* (London, 1902)
——, *Heresies of Sea Power* (London, 1906)
——, (ed) *Fighting Ships* (London, 1911)
——, *The British Battle-Fleet* (London, 1912)
——, (ed) *Fighting Ships 1905/6* (Newton Abbott, 1970)
Jellicoe of Scapa, *The Crisis of the Naval War* (London, 1920)
Jenkins, G. *A Twist Of Sand* (London, 1961)
Jones, G. S. *Languages of Class. Studies in English working class history 1832–1982* (Cambridge, 1983)

Jules-Verne, J. trans Greaves, R. *Jules Verne. A Biography by Jean Jules-Verne* (London, 1976)
Karsten, P. & Modell, J. (eds) *Theory, Method and Practice in Social and Cultural History* (New York, 1992)
Kearney, H. *The British Isles. A History of Four Nations* (Cambridge, 1989)
Keegan, J. *The Face of Battle, A Study of Agincourt, Waterloo and the Somme* (London, 1978)
——, *A History of Warfare* (London, 1993)
Kemp, P. K. *HM Submarines* (London, 1952)
——, *British Submarines in World War Two* (Poole, 1987)
Kennedy, P. *The Rise and Fall of the Great Powers: Economic Change and Military Conflict From 1500 to 2000* (London, 1989)
——, *The Rise and Fall of British Naval Mastery* 3rd edn (London, 1991)
Kern, S. *The Culture of Time and Space 1880–1918* (Cambridge: MA, 1983)
Kertzer, D. I. *Ritual, Politics & Power* (London, 1988)
Keyes, Admiral of the Fleet Sir Roger *The Naval Memoirs of Admiral of the Fleet Sir Roger Keyes: The Narrow Seas to The Dardanelles 1910-1915* (London, 1934)
King, A. *Memorials of the Great War in Britain: The Symbolism and Politics of Remembrance* (Oxford, 1998)
Kingham, D. & Hargreaves B. *Destroyers of the Royal Navy from 1926* part 1, (London, Privately published no date)
King, Cdr W. DSO, DSC RN *Dive and Attack* (London, 1983)
Kinney, T. *The Dance* (New York, 1935)
Kipling, R. *Fringes of the Fleet* (London, 1915)
——, *The Complete Verse* (London, 2002)
'Klaxon', *The Story of Our Submarines* (London, 1919)
Klein, H (ed) *The Second World War in Fiction* (London, 1984)
Klein, B. (ed) *Fictions of the Sea. Critical perspectives on the ocean in British literature and culture* (Aldershot, 2002)
Krell, A. *The Devil's Rope: A Cultural History of Barbed Wire* (London, 2002)
Kuhn, W. M. *Democratic Royalism. The Transformation of the British Monarchy, 1861–1914* (Basingstoke, 1996)
Kumar, K. *The Making of English National Identity* (Cambridge, 2003)
LaCapra, D. & Kaplan, S. L. (eds.) *Modern European Intellectual History: Reappraisals and New Perspectives* (London, 1982)
LaCapra, D. *History & Criticism* (London, 1985)

Lake, S. *The Submarine in War and Peace* (London, 1918)
Lambert, N. *Sir John Fisher's Naval Revolution* (Columbia: SC, 1999)
——, (ed) *The Submarine Service* (Aldershot, 2001)
Landy, M. *British Genres: Cinema and Society, 1930–1960* (Princeton: MA, 1991).
Latimer, A. J. *A Bouquet of Old Time Dances* (London, 1948).
Lawrence, P. *A Century of Submarines* (Stroud, 2001)
Leach, A. F. *History of Warwick School with notices of the Collegiate Church, Guilds and Borough of Warwick* (London, 1906)
Lehnhoff, J. trans. Wilson, W. *The Homeward Run* (London, 1957)
Leonard, D. *Sex and Generation. A Study of Courtship and Weddings* (London, 1980)
Lewis, M. *Spithead an Informal History* (London, 1972)
Liddle, P. H. (ed.), *Passchendaele in Perspective: The Third battle of Ypres* (London, 1997).
Liddle-Hart, B. H. *Deterrent or Defense. A Fresh Look at the West's Military Position* (New York, 1960)
Lindsay, W. *Manning the Royal Navy and Merchant Marine; also Belligerent and Neutral Rights in the Event of War* (London, 1877)
Lipscomb, Cdr F. W. *The British Submarine* (London, 1954)
Lloyd, C. *The Nation and the Navy* rev edn (London, 1961)
Longford, E. *Victoria R. I.* (London, 1964)
Low, Professor A. M. *The Submarine at War* (London, 1941?)
Lynn, J. A. *Battle. A History of Combat and Culture* (Oxford, 2003)
MacGregor, J. *When The Ship Sank* (London, 1960)
MacHardy, C. *Send Down A Dove* (London, 1968)
MacKay, R. F. *Fisher of Kilverstone* (Oxford, 1973)
MacKenzie, D. & Wajcman, J. (eds) *The Social Shaping of Technology* 2nd edn (Maidenhead, 1999)
MacKenzie, J. M. *A Victorian Courtship* (London, 1979)
——, *Propaganda and Empire: The Manipulation of British Public Opinion 1880–1960* (Manchester, 1986)
——, (ed) *Imperialism and Popular Culture* (Manchester, 1986)
MacKenzie, P. *British War Films 1939–1945. The Cinema and the Services* (London, 2001)
MacLean, A. *Night Without End* (London, 1973).
——, *Fear is the Key* (London, 1973)
——, *Ice Station Zebra* (London, 1973)
Mahan, A. T. *The Influence of Seapower Upon the French Revolution and Empire 1793–1812* vol. 2, 4th edn (London, 1892)

Maiolo, J. *The Royal Navy and Nazi Germany 1933–39* (London, 1998)
Mandler, P. *The Fall and Rise of the Stately Home* (London, 1997)
——, *History and National Life* (London, 2002)
Mangan, J. A. and Walvin, J. (eds) *Manliness and Morality* (Manchester, 1987)
Mangan, J. A. (ed) *Benefits Bestowed* (Manchester, 1988)
Manning, Capt RN, T. D. & Walker, Cdr RN, C. F. *British Warship Names* (London, 1959)
Manvell, R. *Films and the Second World War* (New York, 1974)
Marcus, G. *The Maiden Voyage. A Complete and documented Account of the 'Titanic' Disaster* (London, 1988)
Marder, A. J. *The Anatomy of British Sea Power* (London, 1940)
——, *From the Dreadnought to Scapa Flow* vol. I (London, 1961)
——, *From the Dreadnought to Scapa Flow* vol. V (London, 1970)
——, *From the Dardenelles to Oran* (London, 1974)
Mark Hamilton, W. *The Nation and the Navy* (London, 1986)
Mars, A. *British Submarines at War 1939–1945* (London, 1971)
Marsh, D. (ed) *Pressure Politics Interest Groups in Britain* (London, 1983)
Martel, G. (ed) *The Origins of the Second World War Reconsidered* 2nd edn (New York, 1999)
Marwick, A. *The Deluge. British Society and the First World War* (Boston: MA, 1965)
——, *Britain in the Century of Total War* (London, 1968)
——, *The Nature of History* 3rd edn (London, 1989)
Marx, L. & Smith, M. R. *Does Technology Drive History?* (Cambridge: MA, 1994)
Massie, R. K. *Dreadnought: Britain, Germany and the Coming of the Great War* (London, 1993)
Masters, D. *Up Periscope* (London, 1942)
McCartney, I. *Lost Patrols. Submarine Wrecks of the English Channel* (Penzance, 2003)
McFee, G. *Understanding Dance* (London, 1992)
McGeoch, Vice Admiral Sir Ian, *An Affair of Chances* (London, 1991)
McKibbin, R. *Classes and Cultures: England 1918–1951* (Oxford, 1998)
McMurtie, F. E. M. (ed) *Jane's Fighting Ships 1935* (London, 1935)
——, (ed) *Jane's Fighting Ships 1937* (London, 1937)
Messimer, D. *Find and Destroy. Antisubmarine Warfare in World War I* (Annapolis: MD, 2001)
Messinger, G. S. *British Propaganda and the State in the First World War* (Manchester, 1992)

Middlemas, K. *Diplomacy of Illusion. The British Government and Germany 1937–39* (Aldershot, 1991)
Mills, Sir J. *Up In The Clouds Gentlemen Please* (London, 2001)
Ministry of Information, *Bomber Command* (London, 1941)
Monsarrat, N. *The Cruel Sea* (London, 1956, reissued 2002)
——, *HMS Marlborough will enter harbour* (London, 1972
——, *Life Is A Four Letter Word* vol. II (London, 1970)
——, *Three Corvettes* (London, 1975)
Moore, Capt J. E. (ed) *Jane's Fighting Ships 1976–77* (London, 1976)
——, (ed) *The Impact of Polaris* (Huddersfield, 1999)
Moore, R. *The Royal Navy and Nuclear Weapons* (London, 2001)
Moretz, J. *The Royal Navy and the Capital Ship in the Interwar Period* (London, 2002)
Morgan, M. *Harold Wilson* (London, 1992)
Mori, K. *The Submarine in War. A Study of the Relevant Rules and Problems* (Tokyo, 1931)
Morris, A. J. *Edwardian Radicalism 1900–14* (London, 1974).
Morris, J. *Fisher's Face* (London, 1996)
Munton, A. *English Fiction of the Second World War* (London, 1989)
Murray, W. & Millett, A. R. (eds) *Military Innovation in the Interwar Period* (Cambridge, 1998)
Newbolt, H. *Collected Poems 1897–1907* (London, 1907)
——, *Submarine and Anti-Submarine* (London, 1919)
O'Brien, P. P. *Technology and Naval Combat in the Twentieth Century and Beyond* (London, 2001)
O'Day, A. (ed) *The Edwardian Age: Conflict and Stability* (London, 1979)
Offer, A. *The First World War: An Agrarian Interpretation* (Oxford, 1989)
Oliver, E. (ed) *Researcher's Guide to British Films & Television Collections*, new rev edn (London, 1989)
Orwell, S. Angus, I (eds) *The Collected Essays, Journalism and Letters of George Orwell* vols. 1–4 (Harmondsworth, 1970)
Overy, R. *The Road to War* 2nd edn (London, 1999)
Padfield, P. *Rule Britannia. The Victorian and Edwardian Navy* (London, 2002)
——, *Maritime Power and the Struggle for Freedom* (London, 2003)
Paris, M. *The Novels of World War Two* (London, 1990)
——, *Winged Warfare. The literature and theory of aerial warfare in Britain 1859–1917* (Manchester, 1992)
——, *From the Wright brothers to Top Gun: aviation, nationalism and popular cinema* (Manchester, 1995)

Paris, M. *Warrior Nation. Images of war in British Popular Culture* (London, 2000)
——, *Over the Top: the Great War and Juvenile Literature in Britain* (Westport: CT, 2004)
Parker, J. *The Silent Service* (London, 2002)
Parker, M. *Shadow of the Wolf* (London, 1984)
Parson, M. (ed) *A Miles, Every Girls Duty: The Diary of a Victorian Debutante* (London, 1992)
Pattinson, J. *Last In Convoy* (London, 1957)
Peck, J. *Maritime Fiction. Sailors and the Sea in British and American Novels, 1719–1917* (Basingstoke, 2001)
Pick, D. *War Machine: The Rationalisation of Slaughter in the Modern Age* (London, 1996)
Pierre, A. J. *Nuclear Politics. The British experience with an independent strategic force 1939–1970* (London, 1972)
Pimlott, B. *Harold Wilson* (London, 1993)
Poolman, K. *Wolf Pack* (London, 1959)
Porter, A. & Low, A. (eds) The *Oxford History of the British Empire* vol. III (Oxford, 1999)
Post, G. Jnr. *Dilemmas of Appeasement. British Deterrence and Defence 1934–37* (Icthia: NY, 1993)
Powell, D. *Films Since 1939* (London, 1947)
Preston, A. *The Royal Navy Submarine Service: A Centennial History* (London, 2001)
Prince, S (ed) *Sam Peckinpah's The Wild Bunch* (Cambridge, 1999)
Ranft, B. (ed.) *Technical change and British Naval Policy* (London, 1977)
——, (ed) *The Beatty Papers 1902–1918* vol. I (Aldershot, 1989)
Ransome-Wallis, P. *The Royal Naval Reviews 1935–1977* (London, 1982).
Rayner, D. A. *The Crippled Tanker* (London, 1960)
Read, D. *The Age of Urban Democracy. England 1869–1914* rev edn (London, 1994)
——, *Edwardian England 1901–1915 Society and Politics* (London, 1972)
Reeman, D. *Dive In The Sun* (London, 1961)
——, *With Blood and Iron* (London, 1964)
——, *Go In And Sink!* (London, 1973)
——, *Surface With Daring* (London, 1976).
——, *Strike From The Sea* (London, 1978)
——, *Killing Ground* (London, 1991)
Reynolds, D. *Britannia Overruled. British Policy and World Power in the 20th Century* 2nd edn (London, 2000)

Richmond, Adm. Sir H. W. *Imperial Defence and Capture at Sea* (London, 1932)
——, *Sea Power in the Modern World* (London, 1934)
Ridley, F. F. & Jordan, G. (eds) *Protest Politics Cause Groups and Campaigns* (Oxford, 1998)
Ring, J. *We Come Unseen: The Untold Story of Britain's Cold War Submariners* (London, 2001)
Robertson, S. *The Development of RAF Strategic Bombing Doctrine 1919– 1939* (London, 1995)
Robertson, T. *Full Speed To Heaven* (London, 1960)
Rodger, N. A. M. *The Admiralty* (Lavenham, 1979)
——, (ed) *Naval Power in the Twentieth Century* (Basingstoke, 1996)
——, *Command of the Ocean* (London, 2004)
Ropp, T. *The Development of a Modern Navy* (Annapolis: MD, 1987)
Rose, J. *The Intellectual Life of the British Working Classes* (New Haven: CT, 2002)
Rose, K. *King George V* (London, 1984)
Roskill, S. W. *The War at Sea* 4 vols. (London, 1954–1961)
——, *Naval Policy Between the Wars* 2 vols. (London, 1968 & 1976)
Ross, S *Admiral sir Francis Bridgeman: The Life and Times of an Officer and a Gentleman* (Cambridge, 1998)
Rousseau, J. *The Social Contract and Discourses* (London, 1946)
Rüger, J. *The Great Naval Game: Britain and Germany in the Age of Empire* (Cambridge, 2007)
Russell, A. K. *Liberal Landslide: The General Election of 1906* (Newton Abbott, 1973)
Russell, E. *War and Nature: Fighting Humans and Insects with Chemicals from World War I to Silent Spring* (Cambridge, 2001)
Rutherford, A. *The Literature of War. Five Studies in Heroic Virtue* (London, 1978)
Samuel, R. *Theatres of Memory* (London, 1996)
——, *Island Stories, Unravelling Britain* (London, 1999)
Saw, R. E. (ed) *Coronation Review of the Fleet by Her Majesty the Queen at Spithead on Monday 15th June 1953* (Portsmouth, 1953)
Scott, Admiral Sir P. *Fifty Years in the Royal Navy* (London, 1919)
Semmel, B. *Liberalism & Naval Strategy* (London, 1986)
Smith, M. R. & Marx, L. *Does Technology Drive History. The Dilemma of Technological Determinism* (Cambridge: MA, 1994)
Sondhaus, L. *Naval Warfare 1815–1914* (London, 2001)
St Aubyn, G. *Edward VII: Prince and King* (London, 1979)

Strang, H. *Lord of the Seas. A Story of a Submarine* (London, 1909)
Stashower, D. *Teller of Tales. The Life of Arthur Conan Doyle* (London, 2000)
Steele, V. *The Corset, A Cultural History* (London, 2001)
Steni, L. *Soldier Adrift* (London, 1954)
Stevenson, D. *1914–1918 The History of the First World War* (London, 2004)
Stewart, M *Monturiol's Dream* (London, 2003)
Sueter, Cdr M. F. *The Evolution of the Submarine Boat, Mine and Torpedo* (Portsmouth, 1907)
Taylor, A. J. P. *The Origins of the Second World War* (London, 1964)
Terraine, J. *The Life and Times and Lord Mountbatten* (London, 1968)
———, *Impacts of War 1914 & 1918* (London, 1970)
———, *The Smoke and the Fire: Myths and Anti-myths of War 1861–1945* (London, 1980)
———, *Business in Great Waters: The U-boat Wars 1916–1945* (London, 1989)
Thomas, H. *Dance, Gender and Culture* (London, 1993).
Thorne, G. *Sweetheart Submarine* (London, 1911)
———, *The Secret Service Submarine* (London, 1920)
Thornton, Lt Cdr W. M. *Submarine Insignia and Submarine Services of the World* (London, 1997)
Trew, A. *Kleber's Convoy* (Long Preston, 1981)
———, *Yashimoto's Last Dive* (London, 1986)
Turner, E. *The Submarine Girl* (London, 1909)
Van Der Vat, D. *Stealth at Sea* (London, 1999).
Verne, J. trans Butcher W. *Twenty Thousand Leagues Under the Sea* (Oxford, 1998)
Ward, A. *Airfix. Celebrating 50 Years Of The Greatest Plastic Kits In The World* (London, 2003)
Wells, Capt J. *The Royal Navy. An Illustrated Social History 1870–1982* (Stroud, 1994)
Westerman, P. F. *The Flying Submarine* (London, 1912)
———, *The Rival Submarine* (London, 1913)
———, *A Sub and A Submarine* (London, 1919)
———, *The Keepers Of The Narrow Seas. A Story Of The Great War* (London, 1931)
———, *The Phantom Submarine* (London, 1947)
———, *The Pirate Submarine* (London, 1940)
Wettern, D. *The Decline of British Seapower* (London, 1982)

Wiener, M. J. *English Culture and the Decline of the Industrial Spirit 1850–1980* (Cambridge, 1982)
Wilkinson, B. *Proceed At Will* (London, 1949)
Williams, H. *Britain's Naval Power* vol. II (London, 1908)
Williams, R. *Keywords: A Vocabulary of Culture and Society* rev edn (London, 1983)
Williamson, P. *Stanley Baldwin* (Cambridge, 1999)
Wilson, H. H. (ed) *The Navy League Guide to the Naval Review* (London, 1897)
——, (ed) *The Navy League Guide to the Coronation Review* (London, 1902)
Wilson, M. *Baltic Assignment: British Submarines in Russia 1914–19* (London, 1985)
Wingate, J. *Frigate* (London, 1982)
——, *Carrier* (London, 1982)
——, *Submarine* (London, 1982)
Winter, J, *The Great War and the British People* (London, 1985)
——, *Sites of Memory, Sites of Mourning: The Great War in European Cultural History* (Cambridge, 1998).
Winter, J. & Sivan, E. *War and Remembrance in the Twentieth Century* (Cambridge, 1999)
Winton, J. *Down the Hatch* (London, 1961)
——, *Hurrah For The Life of a Sailor* (London, 1977)
——, *Silver Jubilee Fleet Review Official Souvenir Programme* (Portsmouth, 1977)
——, *Captains and Kings: The Royal Family and the Royal Navy 1901–1981* (Llandrnog, 1981)
——, *Convoy* (London, 1983)
——, *The Submariners: Life in British Submarines 1901–1999* (London, 1999)
Wolffe, J. *Great Deaths. Grieving, Religion, and Nationhood in Victorian and Edwardian Britain* (Oxford, 2000)
Worpole, K. *Dockers and Detectives. Popular Readings: Popular Writing* (London, 1983)
Wright, P. *Tank* (London, 2000)
Yeazell, R. B. *Fictions of Modesty* (Chicago, 1991)
Young, E. *One Of Our Submarines* (St Albans, 1982)
Ziegler, P. *Mountbatten. The Official Biography* (London, 1986)
——, *Wilson. The Authorised Life of Lord Wilson of Rievaulx* (London, 1993)

Articles and Essays

Active List, 'Recent Naval Progress', *Blackwood's Edinburgh Magazine*, vol. CLXX (1901)
Anon, 'System of naming His Majesty's Ships', *United Services Journal* (1830)
———, 'Before the Naval Review', *Saturday Review* (1897)
———, 'The Submarine Has Arrived', *Review of Reviews*, vol. XXIII (1901).
———, 'Leading Articles in the Reviews', *Review of Reviews*, vol. XXIII (1901)
———, 'Obituary for Jules Verne', *Spectator*, vol. VIC (1905)
———, 'Germany's Worst Piracy. The Torpedoing Of The Liner "Falaba"', *Illustrated London News*, 10 April 1915
———, 'Democracy and Naval Policy', *The Nation*, vol. XIII (1913)
———, 'The Influence of the Submarine on Naval Policy', *Naval Review*, vol. I (1913)
———, 'The Submarine Menace', *Naval Review*, vol. II (1914)
———, 'Capital Ships of the Future', *Journal of the Royal United Services Institution*, vol. LIX (1914)
———, 'Navy Notes', *Journal of the Royal United Services Institution*, vol. LXXX (1935)
———, 'Navy Notes', *Journal of the Royal United Services Institution*, vol. LXXXII (1937)
———, 'The Submarine Service – A Bright Future', *Broadsheet 97/8* (London, 1998)
Arnold-Forster, Rear Admiral F. D. 'Royal Naval Reviews at Spithead', *Journal of the Royal United Services Institution*, vol. XCVIII (1953)
Ashplant, T. G. & Smyth, G. 'In Search of Cultural History' in Ashplant, T. G. & Smyth, G. (eds) *Explorations in Cultural History* (London, 2003)
Bacon, Admiral Sir Reginald. 'The Battleship of the Future', *Transactions of the Institute of Naval Architects*, vol. 52 (1910)
Barry, C. B. 'The Development of the Submarine', *Journal of the Royal United Services Institution*, vol. LXXX (1935)
Bathurst, Admiral Sir Benjamin, 'View from the First Sea Lord', *Broadsheet 93* (London, 1993)
Bennet, G. 'Royal Reviews at Spithead', *History Today*, vol. 277 (1977)
Biersack, A. 'Local Knowledge Local History' in Hunt, L. ed., *The New Cultural History* (London, 1989)

Biernacki, R. 'Method and Metaphor' in Bonnell, V. & Hunt, L. (eds.) *Beyond the Cultural Turn* (London, 1999)
——, 'Language and the Shift From Signs to Practices in Cultural History', *History and Theory*, vol. 39 (2000)
Brassey, Lord 'Our Naval Strength and Navy Estimates', *Nineteenth Century*, vol. LVI (1904)
Brassey, T. A. 'The Progress of the British Navy', in Brassey, T. A. (ed) *The Naval Annual 1898* (Portsmouth, 1898)
——, 'The Position of the British Navy in 1898' in Brassey, T. A. (ed) *The Naval Annual 1898* (Portsmouth, 1898)
Burgoyne, A. H. 'Editorial', *Submarine Navigation Past and Present: A Scientific Quarterly*, vol. I (1901)
——, 'The Future of the Submarine Boat', *Journal of the Royal United Services Institution*, vol. XLVIII (1904)
Byatt, A. S. 'The Half Fiction Novel', *The New Statesman*, vol. 75 (1968)
Byrne, P. 'Nuclear Weapons and CND', in Ridley, F. F. & Jordan, G. (eds) *Protest Politics Cause Groups and Campaigns* (Oxford, 1998)
Bywater, H. 'The German Naval Renaissance', *The Nineteenth Century*, vol. CXVIII (1935)
Cain, P. 'Political Economy in Edwardian England: the Tariff reform controversy', in O'Day, A. (ed) *The Edwardian Age: Conflict and Stability 1900–1914* (London, 1979)
Cannadine, D. 'The Context, Performance and Meaning of Ritual: The British Monarchy and the "Invention of Tradition", c. 1820–1977', in Hobsbawm, E. & Ranger, T. (eds) *The Invention of Tradition*, (Cambridge, 1983)
Cairnes, W. E. 'The Duties of the Army and Navy' *National Review*, vol. XXXVI (1900–1)
Chartier, R. 'Intellectual History or Sociocultural History? The French Trajectories', in LaCapra, D. & Kaplan, S. L. (eds) *Modern European Intellectual History: Reappraisals and New Perspectives* (London, 1982)
Collier, C. 'History, Culture and Communication', *History and Theory*, vol. 20 (1981)
Conan Doyle, Sir Arthur 'Danger! Being the Log of Captain John Sirius', *Strand Magazine*, vol. XLVIII (1914).
Cook, T. '"Against God-Inspired Conscience": The perception of Gas Warfare as a Weapon of Mass Destruction, 1915–1939', *War and Society*, vol. 18 (2000)

Coopey, R. 'Industrial policy in the white heat of the scientific revolution', in Coopey, R., Fielding, S., Tiratsoo, N. (eds) *The Wilson Government 1964–1970* (London, 1993)
Corfield, P. J. 'The State of History', *Journal of Contemporary History*, vol. 36 (2001)
Creagh, J. V. 'The Fleet of the Future', *Journal of the Royal United Services Institution*, vol. LXXIV (1929)
DeVries, W. A. 'Meaning and Interpretation in History', *History and Theory*, vol. 22 (1983)
'Drake', 'The Challenge of Polaris', *Naval Review*, vol. LIII (1965)
Dunae, P. A. 'Education, emigration and empire', in Mangan, J. A. (ed) *Benefits Bestowed* (Manchester, 1988)
Dutton, P. 'Geschaeft uber Alles: Notes on some medallions inspired by the sinking of the Lusitania', *Imperial War Museum Review*, No. 1 (1986)
Eardley-Wilmot, S. Capt RN, 'Our Navy – Its Decline and Restoration', *National Review*, vol. XXXVI (1900–1901)
Elliott, J. 'Ice Cold', *New Statesman*, vol. 76 (1968)
Emy, H. V. 'The Impact of Financial Policy on English Party Politics before 1914', *Historical Journal*, vol. XV (1972)
Excubitor, 'The British Navy.–II The Navy: Some Faults and Fallacies', *Fortnightly Review*, vol. LXX (1901)
Eyres Monsell, Sir B. 'The Anglo–German Naval Agreement', *The Listener*, vol. VIII (1935)
Faure, Lt RN C. M. 'The Influence of the Submarine in Naval Warfare in the Future', *Journal of the Royal United Services Institution*, vol. LXIV (1919)
Fielding, S. '"White heat" and white collars: the evolution of "Wilsonism"', in Coopey, R., Fielding, S., Tiratsoo, N. (eds) *The Wilson Government 1964–1970* (London, 1993)
Finley, M. 'Myth. Memory, and History', *History and Theory*, vol. 4 (1965)
Ford, C. 'Religion and Popular Culture in Modern Europe', *Journal of Modern History*, vol. 65 (1993)
Freidman, N. 'Where Do We Go From Here?', in Edmonds, M. (ed), *100 Years Of The Trade* (Lancaster, 2001)
Gay, P. 'The Manliness of Christ' in Davies, R. W. & Helmstadler, R. J. *Religion and Irreligion in Victorian Society* (London, 1992)

Geertz, C. 'Thick Description: Toward an Interpretative Theory of Culture', in his *The Interpretation of Cultures: Selected Essays* (New York, 1973)

Gooch, J. 'Attitudes to War in Late Victorian and Edwardian England', in Bond, B. & Roy, I. (eds) *War and Society* (London, 1975)

Gordon, G. 'The Admiralty and Imperial Overstretch 1900–1941', in Till, G. (ed) *Seapower. Theory and Practice* (Ilford, 1994)

Hall, J. R. 'Cultural meanings and Cultural Structures in Historical Explanations', *History and Theory*, vol. 39 (2000)

Hanney, D. 'The Fire Ship', *Blackwood's Magazine*, vol. CXCV (1914)

Harrap, Cdr N 'The Role of the SSN in Modern UK Defence Policy', in Edmonds, M. (ed) *100 Years of 'the Trade'* (Lancaster, 2001)

Harrington, R. 'The Mighty Hood': Navy, Empire, War at Sea and the British National Imagination, 1920–1960', *Journal of Contemporary History*, vol. 38 (2003)

Henry, D. 'British Submarine Policy, 1918–1939', in Ranft, B. (ed) *Technical change and British Naval Policy* (London, 1977)

Herwig, H. H. 'Innovation Ignored: The Submarine Problem – Germany, Britain and the United States', in Murray, W. & Millett, A. R. (eds) *Military Innovation in the Interwar Period* (Cambridge, Cambridge University Press, 1998)

Hill, J. R. 'British Naval Planning post 1945', in Rodger, N. A. M. (ed) *Naval Power in the Twentieth Century* (London, 1996)

Hillard A. A. 'The Tactics Of The Submarine', *Monthly Review*, vol. IV (1901)

Hobsbawm, E. 'Inventing Traditions', in Hobsbawm, E. & Ranger, T. (eds) *The Invention of Tradition* (Cambridge, 1983)

Holland, J. P. 'The Submarine Boat And Its Future', *North American Review*, vol. CLXXI (1900)

Horner, D. 'The Road to Scarborough: Wilson, Labour and the scientific revolution', in Coopey, R., Fielding, S., Tiratsoo, N. (eds) *The Wilson Government 1964–1970* (London, 1993)

Hurd, A. S. 'The Coming Of The Submarine – The New British Boats', *Nineteenth Century*, vol. LI (1902)

——, 'The Success Of The Submarine – The New British Boats', *Nineteenth Century*, vol. LIV (1903)

——, 'The Submarine In War: Its Menace And Achievement', *Fortnightly Review*, vol. XCVI (1914)

Hutton, P. H. 'The History of Mentalities: The New Map of Cultural History', *History and Theory*, vol. 20 (1981)

Kane, A. 'Reconstructing Culture in Historical Explanation: Narratives as Cultural Structure and Practice', *History and Theory*, vol. 39 (2000)
Kennedy, P. 'The Relevance of the pre war British and American Strategies to the First World War', in Hattendorf, J. B. & Jordan, R. S. (eds) *Maritime Strategy and the Balance of Power* (London, 1989)
King-Hall, Lt RN W. S. 'The Influence of the Submarine In Naval Warfare in the Future', *Journal of the Royal United Services Institution*, vol. LXIV (1919)
——, 'The Submarine and Future Naval Warfare', *Journal of the Royal United Services Institution*, vol. LXV (1920)
Kline, R. & Pinch, T. 'The Social Construction of Technology', in MacKenzie, D. & Wajcman, J. (eds) *The Social Shaping of Technology*, 2nd edn (Maidenhead, 1999)
LaCapra, D. 'Is Everyone a *Mentalite* Case? Transference and the "Culture" Concept', *History and Theory*, vol. 23 (1984)
Laird Clowes, W. 'The Great Naval Review', *Illustrated London News* (3 July 1897).
Lambert, N. A. 'Strategic Command and Control for Manoeuvre Warfare: Creation of the Royal Navy's "War Room" System, 1905–1915', *Journal of Military History*, vol. 69 (2005)
Leinster-Mackay, D. 'The nineteenth-century English preparatory school' in Mangan, J. A. (ed) *Benefits Bestowed* (Manchester, 1988)
Lewin, T. T. 'The Royal Navy In The Next Decade', *Journal of the Royal United Services Institution*, vol. CXIII (1968)
Leyland, J. 'The Navy and the Coronation', *Mariner's Mirror*, vol. I (1911)
Lindenfield, D. 'Categories for Intellectual and Social History' in Karsten, P. & Modell, J. (eds) *Theory, Method and Practice in Social and Cultural History* (New York, 1992)
Llewellyn-Jones, M. 'A Flawed Contender', in Edmonds, M. (ed) *100 Years of 'the Trade'* (Lancaster, 2001)
Lorenz, C. 'Some Afterthoughts on Culture and Explanation in Historical Inquiry', *History and Theory*, vol. 39 (2000)
Maiolo, J. 'Deception and Intelligence Failure: Anglo–German Preparations for the U-boat Warfare in the 1930s', *Journal of Strategic Studies*, vol. 22 (1999)
Mark Hamilton, W. 'The "New Navalisim" and the British Navy League 1895–1914', *Mariner's Mirror*, vol. 64 (1978)

Marwick, A. 'Two approaches to historical Study: The Metaphysical (Including 'Postmodernism') and the Historical', *Journal of Contemporary History*, vol. 30 (1995)
McGeoch, I. L. M. 'Submarine Developments', *Journal of the Royal United Services Institution*, vol. CXI (1966)
——, 'Submarine Matters', *Naval Review*, vol. LVI (1968)
McMillan, J. F. 'Social History, "New Cultural History," and the Rediscovery of Politics: Some Recent Work on Modern France', *Journal of Modern History*, vol. 66 (1994)
Mead Cdr RN, H. P. 'Great Naval Reviews', *Journal of the Royal United Services Institution*, vol. LXXX (1935)
'Moryak', 'Manning The Polaris Submarine Force', *Naval Review*, vol. LV (1967)
Murray, W. 'Strategic Bombing. The British, American, and German experiences', in Murray, W. and Millett, A. R. (eds) *Military Innovation in the Interwar Period* (Cambridge, 1996)
Offer, A 'Morality and Admiralty: 'Jacky' Fisher, Economic Warfare and the Laws of War', *Journal of Contemporary History*, vol. 23 (1988)
O'Reilly, D. 'Explorer & Excalibur: The Walther Boat, High Test Peroxide & British Submarine Policy 1945–1962. A Study in Technological Failure?' in Edmonds, M. (ed) *100 Year Of 'the Trade'* (Lancaster, 2001
Perowne, Rear Admiral J. OBE, 'The Submarine Service', *Broadsheet 96/7* (London, 1997)
Rahn, W. 'German Naval Strategy and Armament, 1919–1939', in O'Brien, P. P. (ed) *Technology and Naval Combat in the Twentieth Century and Beyond* (London, 2001)
Ramsden, J. 'Refocusing "The peoples War": British war Films of the 1950s, *Journal of Contemporary History*, vol. 33 (1998)
Ranft, B. 'The protection of British seaborne trade and the development of systematic planning for war, 1860–1906', in Ranft, B. (ed) *Technical Change and British Naval Policy 1860–1939* (London, 1977)
Rattigan, N. 'The last gasp of the Middle Class: British War Films of the 1950s' in Dixon, W. W. (ed) *Re-viewing British Cinema 1900–1992* (Albany: NY, 1994)
——, 'The Demi-Paradise and Images of Class in British Wartime Films', in Dixon, W. W. (ed) *Re-viewing British Cinema 1900–1992* (Albany: NY, 1994)

Reed, Sir Edward 'On Armaments' in Wilson, H. H. (ed) *The Navy League Guide to the Naval Review* (London, 1897)
Repington, Col. A Court 'New Wars For Old.- I. The Submarine Menace', *Blackwood's Edinburgh Magazine*, vol. 187 (1910)
'R. G. H.' 'The Nuclear Attack Submarine', *Naval Review*, vol. LV (1967)
Richards, J. 'National Identity in British War Films', in Taylor, P. M. (ed) *Britain and the Cinema in the Second World War* (Basingstoke, 1988)
Richmond, Admiral Sir Herbert 'The Naval Conference', *Fortnightly Review*, vol. 138 (1935)
Ringer, F. 'The Intellectual Field, Intellectual History, and the Sociology of Knowledge', in Karsten, P. & Modell, J. (eds) *Theory, Method, and Practice in Social and Cultural History* (New York, 1992)
Robinson Cdr RN C. N. 'Naval Reviews Milestones in Warship Development', *Journal of the Royal United Services Institution*, vol. LXXI (1926)
Robertson, E. 'The Question of Submarine Boats', *Nineteenth Century*, vol. XLVII (1900)
——, 'The Admiralty and Submarine Boats', *Nineteenth Century*, vol. XLIX (1901)
Ross, A. 'Losing the Initiative in Mercantile Warfare: Great Britain's Surprising Failure to Anticipate Maritime Challenges to Her Global Trading Network in the First World War', *International Journal of Naval History* (2002)
Rüger, J. 'Nation, Empire and Navy: Identity Politics in the United Kingdom 1887–1914', *Past and Present* (2004)
Schofield, B. B. 'The Employment Of Nuclear Weapons At Sea', *Journal of the Royal United Services Institution*, vol. CVIII (1963)
Sewell, W. H. 'The Concept(s) of Culture', in Bonnell, V. & Hunt, L. (eds) *Beyond the Cultural Turn* (London, 1999)
Simpson, M. 'Superhighway to the World Wide Web: The Mediterranean in British Imperial Strategy, 1900–1945', in Hattendorf, J. (ed) *Naval Strategy and Policy in the Mediterranean. Past Present and Future* (London, 2000)
Stafford, R. A. S. 'Scientific Exploration and Empire', in Porter, A. & Low, A. (eds) *The Oxford History of the British Empire*, vol. III (Oxford, 1999)
Stewart, P. 'This Is Not A Book Review: On Historical Uses of Literature', *Journal of Modern History*, vol. 66 (1994)

Sullivan, B. R. 'More than meets the eye: the Ethiopian War and the origins of the Second World War', in Martel, G. (ed) *The Origins of the Second World War Reconsidered*, 2nd edn (New York, 1999)

Sumida, J. T. 'British Naval Procurement and Technological Change' in O'Brien, P. (ed) *Technology and Naval Combat in the Twentieth Century and Beyond* (London, 2001)

Thane, P. 'Social History 1860–1914', in Floud, R. & McCloskey, D. (eds) *The Economic History of Britain since 1700* vol. II (Cambridge, 1981)

Thomas, B. 'Future Concepts In Military Submarine Systems', *RUSI Journal*, vol. 117 (1972)

Thomas, R. D. 'Empire, Naval Pageantry and Public Spectacles', *Mariner's Mirror*, vol. 88 (2002)

Travers, T. H. E. 'Future Warfare: H. G. Wells and British Military Theory, 1985–1916', in Bond, B. & Roy, I. (eds) *War and Society* (London, 1975)

Tunstead, J. 'Advances In Marine Science And Technology: Defence Aspects', *Journal of the Royal United Services Institution for Defence Studies*, vol. CXVI (1971)

Van Creveld, M. 'Thoughts on Military History', *Journal of Contemporary History*, vol. 18 (1983)

Wainwright, R. C. P. 'Changes In Naval Warfare Owing To New And Modified Weapons', *Journal of the Royal United Services Institution*, vol. XCIII (1948)

Walters, R. E. 'The Submersible Fleet Of The Future', *Journal of the Royal United Services Institution*, vol. CXI (1966)

Walvin, J. 'Symbols of moral superiority', in Mangan, J. A. and Walvin, J. (eds) *Manliness and Morality*, (Manchester, 1987)

Webber, E. 'From the Culture Wars Front', *Journal of Contemporary History*, vol. 35 (2000)

Weinroth, H. 'Left Wing Opposition to Naval Armaments in Britain before 1914', *Journal of Contemporary History*, vol. 6 (1971)

Wells, H. G. 'Anticipations VI – War', *Fortnightly Review*, vol. LXX (1901)

Weyl E. 'The Progress of Foreign Navies', in Brassey, T. A. (ed.), *The Naval Annual 1898* (Portsmouth, 1898)

White, H. 'Response to Arthur Marwick', *Journal of Contemporary History*, vol. 30 (1995)

Willett, L. 'Royal Navy Submarines in World War I', in Edmonds, M. (ed) *100 Years of 'the Trade'* (Lancaster, 2001)

Williams, R. & Edge, D. 'The Social Shaping of Technology', *Research Policy*, vol. 25 (1996)
Wilson, G. A. M. 'The Development Of Nuclear Power For Marine Purposes', *Journal of the United Services Institution*, vol. CIII (1958)
Wilson, H. W. 'The Forthcoming Naval Review and its Predecessors', *Nineteenth Century*, vol. XLI (1897).
Winter, J. M. 'Catastrophe and Culture: Recent Trends in the Historiography of the First World War', *Journal of Modern History*, vol. 64 (1992)
Winton, J. 'Have Polaris, Will Travel', *Naval Review*, vol. LX (1975)
——, 'The Spithead Review', *Illustrated London News*, (August 1977)
Wood, J. 'Captive Historians, Captivated Audience: The German Military History Program, 1945–1961', *Journal Of Military History*, vol. 69 (2005)

INDEX

Above Us The Waves 207, 213, 237, 239
Anglo-German Naval Agreement 16, 33, 73, 125, 129–30, 131–42, 162, 164, 221, 246
An Operational Necessity 221, 226, 233
A Flock of Ships 206
A Sub And A Submarine 208–9, 217–18
A Twist of Sand 205, 206, 234

Bacon, Admiral Sir Reginald 10, 13, 26–8, 76, 87
Balanced fleet 132, 134–5, 142, 154, 162, 164, 173, 175, 182, 199, 216
Baldwin, Stanley 100, 136
Battleship, attitude to and importance of 4, 24, 29–30, 33, 35, 36–7, 40–1, 57–9, 67, 69–71, 79, 81, 85–8, 90, 92, 122, 131, 156, 172, 174–5, 184, 194–5, 217, 247–8, 250, 252
Barnett, Corelli 148
Behrman, Cynthia 24, 57
Beresford, Admiral Lord Charles 33, 35, 81, 101
Bombers and national identity 139–40
Bombers and public opinion 136–40
Bulmer, Kenneth 215, 225, 227–8, 241–2

Callison, Brian 177, 206
Campaign for Nuclear Disarmament 45, 186–9
Catto, M. 218–19, 230, 238
Close Quarters 210, 211, 213

Chatham, A. 219
Chemical warfare 105–6
Churchill, Winston 13–14, 71, 101–4, 122, 148, 195–6
Colley, Linda 11–12
Collingwood, H. 75
Compton-Hall, Richard 8
Conan-Doyle, Sir Arthur 95–6, 98–103, 136, 248–9
Corbett, Julian 98
Critchley, Michael 46
Cruel Coast, The 221
Cruel Sea, The 152, 206, 213, 222–4, 229–30, 234, 239
Custance, Admiral 82

Defoe, Daniel, 204
Diving Stations 214
Down The Hatch 215

Ellis, John 6–7

Fathoms Deep 210, 212
Fictional ships, *Brandenburg* 232, 239; *Compass Rose* 222–4, 229
Fictional submarines, *Nautilus* 60–1, 63; *Orcus* 215; *R19* 208–9; *Safari* 216; *Seahound* 219–20; *Sea Tiger* 211–12, 220, 232, 239
Fighting Submarine 207
Fisher, Admiral Sir John 29, 32–5, 68, 81, 95–7, 101–3, 114, 184, 190–3, 248–9

Fisher–Beresford dispute 33, 35, 81
Flag Officer Submarines 169, 202
Fleet manoeuvres 78–80, 84–5, 103
Fleetwork 77–8
Flotilla defence 32–5, 81–2
Flying Submarine, The 75, 222
Franklin, George 135

Gage, William 221
Geertz, Clifford 19–20, 25
Geneva General Disarmament Conference 110
Go In And Sink 207
Gray, Edwyn 214, 215, 222, 227–8, 241–2
Griffin, G. 221, 226, 233
Griffith, G. 75

Hackmann, Willem 135
Hadley, Michael 6, 7
Henry, David 115
Hezlet, Admiral Sir Arthur 144, 148–9
HM Corvette 152
Holland, John 3, 61–2, 63, 64, 249
Homeward Run, The 216
Horton, Admiral Sir Max 122, 153, 161
Hurd, Archibald 58, 76, 103, 106–7, 116

Ice Station Zebra 205, 206
Innes, Hammond 205, 228
Inspecting Captain of Submarines 86–7
Inter-service rivalries 173–4

Jenkin, Geoffrey 205
Jeune École 102, 114

Kearney, Hugh 5–6
Keegan, John 7, 58
Keepers Of The Narrow Seas 218, 223
Kertzer, David 9
Keyes, Admiral Sir Roger 86–7

Lake, Simon 3, 60, 61, 63–5, 249
Lambert, Nicholas 8, 9
Last in Convoy 206

Lehnhoff, J. 216
Lion Has Wings, The 238
Log of the Flying Fish, The 75
London Naval Treaty, 109–10
Lord of the Seas 75
Lynn, John 7

MacGregor, J. 224–5
MacLean, Alistair 205, 228
Mahan, Alfred 19, 58, 70, 77, 79, 82, 134, 248
Maiolo, Joe 131, 134
Marder, Arthur 8
Mills, Sir John 212, 237, 238
Moll, Kenneth 13
Monsarrat, Nicolas 152, 229–30, 234
Morning Departure 207, 228–9, 239, 241
Murphy's War 218–19, 230

Naval Reviews, 1897 Diamond Jubilee 1–3, 57; 1902 Coronation 20, 25–9; 1909 review for King Edward VII, 32–3; 1911 Coronation 20, 22, 29–36; 1935 Silver Jubilee 20, 22, 36–7, 38; 1937 Coronation 20, 37–40; 1953 Coronation 20, 40–4; 1977 Silver Jubilee 3–4, 20, 44–8; 2005 'Trafalgar 200' 21, 165–7; and British power 22–4, 43, 47–8, 52; and national identity 23–5, 46–8, 53; and taxation 22, 39; and the media 21, 35–6, 37, 38–9, 43, 45–9, 52–3; and the electoral franchise 21–2; and the political process 22; and transport 21; as an invented tradition 20–2, 51–2; as pageantry 19–20, 51; position of submarines at 25–8, 31–2, 36, 38, 41–2, 44–5; statistics 29–30, 32, 35, 36–7, 39, 40–1, 44, 48–50
Navy League 10, 23
Nicolson, Rear Admiral 119
Night Without End 205
Non-combatants 6, 15–16, 94, 103, 104, 106, 109, 111, 111–15, 119–21, 125–6, 139–40, 142, 144, 145, 149–50, 152, 155, 162–3, 170, 208,

INDEX

210, 212–14, 217, 218, 226, 233, 241–2, 245, 248, 250–1

Paris, Michael 7, 204, 222
Pattinson, James 206
Peace Pledge Union 136–9
Peck, John 204
Perceptions of maritime combat 59, 66–77, 111–15
Pirate Submarine, The 231
Proceed At Will 210
Public schools 72–4

Ramsden, John 212–13, 232–3
Rear Admiral (Submarines) 36–8, 118, 119, 143–4,
Reeman, Douglas 216, 230, 241
Repington, Colonel 58, 79, 99, 102–3
Rival Submarines, The 75
Robinson Crusoe, 204
Root resolutions 107–8
Roskill, Captain Stephen 8, 106, 140, 147, 148
Royal Navy and national identity 22–3, 24–5, 35, 43, 46–8, 53, 57–8, 59, 67–70, 88, 173, 216, 248
Royal Navy and perceptions of security 13–14, 23, 43, 59, 89, 180, 247–8, 250
Rüger, Jan 11
Russell, Edmund 6

Sea and national identity 10–14, 53, 56, 57, 111–15, 250–1
Sea as an 'other' 11–12, 204
Sea Sting 219
Sea Wolf: Shark America 225–6
Ships, *Amasis* 128; *Athenia* 146–7; *Bremen* 149–50; *Bulwark* 168; CVA–01 171, 178, 196, 200, 251; *Dreadnought* 33; *Falaba* 103; *Fearless* 195; *Havoc* 141; *Hazard* 27–8; *Lusitania* 92–3, 103, 105; *Queen Elizabeth* 192; *Titania* 36; *Turbina* 2; *Tropic Sea* 144; *Vanguard* 40; *Victoria and Albert* 1
Strang, H. 75

Sturdee, Admiral Sir Doveton 14, 84
Submarine 207, 214
Submarine, abolishing of 109–10
Submarine, and national identity 46–8, 53, 64, 66, 67, 74–7, 88, 111–15, 139–40, 163, 213–14, 228–9, 239–40, 248, 250–1, 252
Submarine, and the surface fleet 77–88
Submarine, as a force multiplier 118, 126
Submarine, as an 'other' 88, 126, 205, 206
Submarine, attacks on battleships 3, 63, 67, 210–11, 232
Submarine bases, *Dolphin* 161; Faslane 187
Submarine, branch badge 153, 176, 179–83, 196, 247
Submarine classes *A* 29, 157–8, 197; *B* 29; *C* 29, 79–80; *D* 29, 81–3, 95; *E* 81–3, 92, 95; *Ex* 158; *H* 38; *K* 85–8, 90, 117–18, 124; *L* 38; *Holland* 26, 27–8, 29; *M* 166–7; *O* 122–5; *Oberon* 157; *Porpoise* 157, 159; *R* 117, 156, 193–4, 200; *River* 37–8, 118; *Resolution* 26; *S* 38, 42, 128, 157, 182 196–7; *Swiftsure* 200; *T* 42, 144, 157–8, 159–60, 182, 196–7; *Thames* 118; *Trafalgar* 200; *U* 42, 196–7; *V* 194, 196, 200; *Valiant* 200
Submarine, civil uses of 60–6
Submarine Girl, The 74
Submarine, integration with the fleet 56, 75, 77, 80–8, 89–90, 122–3, 135, 168–71, 180, 199, 248–9
Submarine, 'jolly roger' flag 152–3, 156, 212, 231–3, 242, 247
Submarine, militarisation of 60–6
Submarine, naming policy 123–5, 127, 190–9
Submarine, perceptions of maritime combat 66–77, 111–15
Submarine, perceptions of maritime security 59, 67–70, 76, 89, 127, 139, 244, 250
Submarine, physical and moral weakness of 16, 32, 70–2, 89, 90,

103–5, 114–17, 127, 155–6, 162, 209, 213–14, 219, 229–30, 231, 240, 241–3, 247, 248, 250–1
Submarine, pioneers 60
Submarine types, anti-submarine 117, 156–8; cruiser 118–21; fast battery 157–8; Fleet submarine 85–8, 90, 117–18, 123, 167–8, 248, 249–51; midget 122–3; mine-laying 117; monitor 116–17; nuclear powered 159, 167; patrol 117; polaris 173, 188, 195; SSBN 44–5, 172–3, 176, 180–1, 185–6, 188, 193–4, 198–9; SSK 44–5, 157, 196–7; SSN 44–5, 46–7, 167–72, 174–5, 176, 180–2, 188, 193, 195–200, 245, 247, 252; trident 189
Submarine, unrestricted warfare 36, 70, 88–9, 90, 92–104, 106–12, 114–17, 119–23, 125–7, 128–30, 136, 139–40, 142–55, 159, 162–3, 167, 206, 208–16, 220–1, 225–6, 230–2, 237, 239–42, 245–52
Submarine warfare and the prize rules 95, 99–101, 118–21, 140, 143–9, 151, 211–12, 217–18, 227, 241
Submarine warfare as piracy, 103–4, 106–9
Submarines, *Number 1* 244; *No 2* 27; *No 3* 27; *A1* 62; *A5* 62; *A8* 62; *AO1* 122; *AO2* 122; *Ambush* 197; *Andrew* 158–9, 160; *Argonaut* 3, 60, 63–4; *Artful* 197; *Astute* 197; *Churchill* 188, 194–6; *Clyde* 38; *Conqueror* 194; *Courageous* 194–5; *Dreadnought* 159, 167, 176, 182–5, 190–2, 194, 200; *E9* 122; *Excalibur* 158, 160, 251; *Explorer* 158, 160, 251; *Grampus* 38; *Gustave Zede* 3, 63; *Holland 1* 88; *Inflexible* 192–3, 198; *Invincible* 192–3; *K26* 124; *Nautilus* 168; *O1* 123; *Oberon* 123; *Olympus* 124; *Oswald* 124; *Otter* 182; *Otus* 124; *Otway* 124; *Oxley* 124; *Nautilus* 60–1, 63; *Renown* 187, 193–4; *Repulse* 193–4; *Resolution* 185–6, 193–4; *Revenge* 193–4; *Rorqual* 38; *Sceptre* 197; *Severn* 38;

Sovereign 196–7; *Spartan* 196–7; *Splendid* 197 *Sunfish* 128; *Superb* 196–7; *Swiftsure* 196–7; *Talent* 197; *Thames* 38; *Tireless* 197; *Torbay* 197; *Trenchant* 197; *Triumph* 197; *Truant* 144; *Turbulent* 197; *Valiant* 185, 194–5; *Vanguard* 194; *Victorious* 194; *Vengeance* 194; *Vigilant* 194; *Warspite* 194–5; *X1* 118–21
Surface 219–20
Sweetheart Submarine 74, 75

Target For Tonight 214
Thorne, G. 74, 75
Trew, A. 219
Turner, E. 74
Twenty Thousand Leagues Under the Sea 76

U-Boats 6, 104, 146, 205, 207, 209–10, 215–16, 218–19, 221, 223, 225–6, 228–32, 238, 241–3
U-Boat: Action Atlantic 215–16

Van Der Vat, Dan 8
Verne, Jules 60–1, 74, 75–6
Versailles treaty 109

Wanklyn, Lt Cdr 214
War memorial images 91–3
Washington Naval Treaty 107–8
Way Ahead, The 238–9
We Dive At Dawn 153, 207, 210, 211–12, 213, 220, 222, 232, 237–8, 239, 242
Westerman, Percy 75, 208–9, 217–18, 219, 223, 231
Western Approaches 219
When The Ship Sank 224–5
Wilson, Admiral Sir Arthur 103
Wingate, John 214–15
Winton, John 45–6, 215
With Airship and Submarine 75
With Blood And Iron 216, 230
Wreakers Must Breathe 205
Wright, Patrick 6

Yashimoto's Last Dive 219

www.ingramcontent.com/pod-product-compliance
Ingram Content Group UK Ltd.
Pitfield, Milton Keynes, MK11 3LW, UK
UKHW020819240326
469204UK00019B/79